Learning C# by Developing Games with Unity 6

Eighth Edition

Get to grips with coding in C# and build simple 3D
games in Unity from the ground up

Harrison Ferrone

‹packt›

Learning C# by Developing Games with Unity 6
Eighth Edition

Portfolio Director: Rohit Rajkumar
Relationship Lead: Kaustubh Manglurkar
Project Manager: Sandip Tadge
Content Engineer: Anuradha Vishwas Joglekar
Technical Editor: Tejas Mhasvekar
Copy Editor: Safis Editing
Indexer: Rekha Nair
Proofreader: Anuradha Vishwas Joglekar
Production Designer: Pranit Padwal
Growth Lead: Namita Velgekar
Marketing Owner: Nivedita Pandey

First edition: September 2013
Second edition: March 2016
Third edition: December 2017
Fourth edition: March 2019
Fifth edition: August 2020
Sixth edition: October 2021
Seventh edition: November 2022
Eighth edition: October 2025

Production reference: 1220925

Published by Packt Publishing Ltd.
Grosvenor House
11 St Paul's Square
Birmingham
B3 1RB, UK.

978-1-80580-871-8

www.packtpub.com

"If people reach perfection, they vanish, you know."

– T.H. White, The Once and Future King

Foreword

I was first introduced to Harrison about four years ago when I reviewed the sixth edition of this book. I quickly became a fan of his writing style, and specifically his approach to combining theory and practical application in a way that is so well-suited for beginners. In fact, at the time, I titled that review *The Best C#/Unity Beginner Resource I've Read*, and I'm excited for the release of the eighth edition; you should be too!

Harrison is a well-established educator, and it's clear he has a passion for making programming and game development accessible to everyone. His style introduces new concepts at just the right time and reinforces them throughout in a way that sticks. There's a reason this book has reached its eighth edition: his approach works.

Game development is challenging, but it's also incredibly rewarding. If you take the time to understand the theory and how to apply it, you'll be well on your way to crafting your own worlds. From there, continue building your knowledge by creating small games, and consider joining game jams! They're a great opportunity to continue learning and experiment with new game design ideas, whether on your own or as part of a small team.

Finally, I encourage you to join our awesome game dev community. It's a welcoming and supportive group where you can share your work, ask questions, and eventually give back by helping others.

I wish you the best of luck with your game development journey!

Justin Horner

Founder at Emberwell Games, ex-Meta Reality Labs

Contributors

About the author

Harrison Ferrone was born in Chicago, Illinois, and was raised all over. He's worked at Microsoft, PricewaterhouseCoopers, and a handful of small start-ups, but most days you can find him creating instructional content for LinkedIn Learning or working on new projects.

He holds various fancy-looking pieces of paper from the University of Colorado at Boulder and Columbia College, Chicago. Despite being a proud alumnus, these are stored in a basement somewhere.

After a few years as a full-time iOS and Unity developer, he fell into a teaching career and never looked back. Throughout all of this, he's bought many books, been owned by several cats, worked abroad, and continually wondered why Neuromancer isn't on more course syllabi.

Completing this book wouldn't have been possible without loving support from Kelsey, my wife and partner in crime on this journey.

About the reviewer

Simon Jackson is a long-time software engineer and architect with many years of game development experience, as well as an author of several game development titles. He loves to create game projects as well as lend a hand to help educate others, whether it's via a blog, vlog, user group, or major speaking event.

His primary focus at the moment is with the *Reality Toolkit* project, which is aimed at building a cross-platform mixed reality framework to enable both VR and AR developers to build efficient solutions in Unity and then build/distribute them to as many platforms as possible. He is also a board member of the MonoGame Foundation, aiming to secure and promote open source game development for all developers.

Join our community on Discord

Join our community's Discord space for discussions with the authors and other readers: `https://packt.link/gamedevelopment`

Table of Contents

Preface   **xxi**

Chapter 1: Getting to Know Your Environment   **1**

Getting the most out of this book – get to know your free benefits 2

Next-gen reader • 2

Interactive AI assistant (beta) • 3

DRM-free PDF or ePub version • 3

Technical requirements 4

Getting started with Unity 6 4

Using macOS • 9

Creating a new project • 10

Navigating the editor • 12

Using C# with Unity 13

Setting up Visual Studio Code in Unity 6 • 14

Working with C# scripts • 15

Introducing the Visual Studio Code editor • 17

Opening a C# file • 17

Beware of naming mismatches • 19

Syncing C# files • 20

Exploring the documentation 22

Accessing Unity's documentation • 22

Locating C# resources • 24

Summary 25

Pop quiz: Dealing with scripts 26

Chapter 2: The Building Blocks of Programming   29

Defining variables 30

   Names are important • 31

   Variables act as placeholders • 31

Understanding methods 36

   Methods drive actions • 37

   Methods are placeholders too • 37

Introducing classes 40

   A common Unity class • 41

   Classes are blueprints • 41

   Communication among classes • 42

Working with comments 43

   Single-line comments • 43

   Multi-line comments • 44

   Adding comments • 44

Putting the building blocks together 45

   Scripts become components • 45

   A helping hand from MonoBehaviour • 48

   Unity application lifecycle • 48

Summary 48

Pop quiz: C# building blocks 49

Chapter 3: Diving into Variables, Types, and Methods   51

Writing proper C# 52

Debugging your code 54

Understanding variables 56

   Declaring variables • 56

     Type and value declarations • 57

Type-only declarations • 57

Using access modifiers • 58

Working with variable types • 59

Common built-in types • 60

Type conversions • 63

Inferred declarations • 65

Custom types • 65

Naming variables • 66

Understanding variable scope • 67

Introducing operators **68**

Understanding methods **71**

Declaring methods • 72

Naming methods • 74

Methods as logic detours • 74

Specifying parameters • 76

Specifying return values • 78

Using return values • 79

Hero's trial: methods as arguments • 80

Dissecting common Unity methods • 81

The Start() method • 81

The Update() method • 81

Summary **82**

Pop quiz: Variables and methods **83**

Chapter 4: Control Flow and Collection Types   **85**

Selection statements **85**

The if-else statement **86**

Using the NOT operator • 91

Nesting statements • 93

Evaluating multiple conditions • 94

Putting it all together • 95

The switch statement **97**

Pattern matching • 98

Fall-through cases • 100

Pop quiz 1: if, and, or but **102**

Collections at a glance **103**

Arrays • 103

  Indexing and subscripts • 104

  Multidimensional arrays • 105

  Range exceptions • 106

Lists • 107

  Setting up a list • 108

  Accessing and modifying lists • 109

Dictionaries • 111

  Creating a dictionary • 112

  Working with dictionary pairs • 113

Pop quiz 2: all about collections **114**

Iteration statements **114**

for loops • 114

foreach loops • 118

Looping through key-value pairs • 120

  Hero's trial: finding affordable items • 121

while loops • 121

To infinity and beyond • 124

Summary **124**

Chapter 5: Working with Classes, Structs, and OOP   127

Introducing OOP **128**

Defining classes **128**

Creating a class • 128

Instantiating class objects • 129

Adding class fields • 130

Using constructors • 132

Declaring class methods • 134

Declaring structs **136**

Understanding reference and value types **139**

Reference types • 140

Value types • 141

Integrating the object-oriented mindset **143**

Encapsulation • 143

Inheritance • 144

Base constructors • 145

Composition • 147

Polymorphism • 148

Applying OOP in Unity **149**

Objects are a class act • 150

Accessing components • 151

Accessing components in code • 151

Drag and drop • 155

Summary **156**

Pop quiz: All things OOP **156**

Chapter 6: Getting Your Hands Dirty with Unity · 159

A game design primer **160**

Game design documents • 160

The Hero Born one-pager • 161

Building a level **162**

Creating primitives • 162

Thinking in 3D • 164

Applying materials • 166

White-boxing • 169

Editor tools • 170

Hero's trial: putting up drywall • 171

Keeping the hierarchy clean • 173

Working with Prefabs • 174

Hero's trial: creating a health pickup • 180

Lighting basics **181**

Creating lights • 181

Light component properties • 183

Animating in Unity **184**

Creating animations in code • 184

Creating animations in the Unity Animation window • 187

Recording keyframes • 190

Curves and tangents • 193

Summary **194**

Pop quiz: Basic Unity features 195

Chapter 7: Movement, Camera Controls, and Collisions   197

Managing player movement **198**

Moving the player with the Transform component **199**

Understanding vectors • 201

Getting player input • 203

Moving the player • 204

Scripting camera behavior **207**

Working with the Unity physics system **211**

Rigidbody components in motion • 213

Colliders and collisions • 217

Picking up an item • 218

Using Collider triggers • 221

Creating an enemy • 221

Hero's trial—all the prefabs! • 224

Physics roundup **225**

Summary **225**

Pop quiz: Player controls and physics **226**

Chapter 8: Scripting Game Mechanics   227

Making the player jump 227

    Introducing enumerations • 228

    Underlying types • 229

    Working with layer masks • 232

Shooting projectiles 239

    Instantiating objects • 239

      Adding the shooting mechanic • 240

    Managing object build-up • 243

Creating a game manager 245

    Tracking player properties • 245

    The get and set properties • 247

    Updating item collection • 250

Creating a GUI 251

    Displaying player stats • 251

    Win and loss conditions • 261

    Pausing and restarting the game with using directives and namespaces • 265

Summary 269

Pop quiz: Working with mechanics 270

Chapter 9: Basic AI and Enemy Behavior   273

Navigating 3D space in Unity 274

    Unity's navigation components • 274

    Adding a NavMeshSurface • 275

    Setting up enemy agents • 279

    Moving enemy agents • 281

Procedural programming 281

    Referencing the patrol locations • 281

    Moving the enemy • 284

Enemy game mechanics **289**

Seek and destroy: Changing the agent's destination • 289

Lowering player health • 291

Detecting bullet collisions • 293

Updating the game manager • 295

Refactoring and keeping it DRY **298**

Summary **300**

Pop quiz: AI and navigation **300**

Chapter 10: Revisiting Types, Methods, and Classes   303

Access modifiers **304**

Constant and read-only properties • 304

Using static classes • 305

Revisiting methods **307**

Overloading methods • 307

ref parameters • 309

out parameters **312**

Intermediate OOP **312**

Interfaces • 313

Abstract classes • 318

Class extensions • 320

Namespace conflicts and type aliasing • 323

Summary **324**

Pop quiz: Leveling up **324**

Chapter 11: Specialized Collection Types and LINQ   327

Introducing stacks **328**

Popping and peeking • 332

Common methods in a stack class • 333

Working with queues **334**

Adding, removing, and peeking • 335

Using HashSets 336

Performing set operations • 337

Querying data with LINQ 339

LINQ basics • 340

Lambda expressions • 343

Chaining queries • 344

Transforming data into new types • 345

Simplifying with optional syntax • 347

Summary 348

Pop quiz: Intermediate collections 349

Chapter 12: Saving, Loading, and Serializing Data   **351**

Introducing data formats 352

Breaking down XML • 352

Breaking down JSON • 354

Understanding the filesystem 356

Working with asset paths • 359

Creating and deleting directories • 361

Creating, updating, and deleting files • 364

Working with streams 369

Managing your stream resources • 370

Using StreamWriter and StreamReader • 371

Creating an XMLWriter • 375

Automatically closing streams • 378

Serializing data 379

Serializing and deserializing XML • 380

Serializing and deserializing JSON • 384

Data roundup 391

Summary 392

Pop quiz: Data management 392

Chapter 13: Connecting to the World Wide Web   393

The web request blueprint 394

Creating the request manager • 395

Formatting a URL • 397

Configuring the web request 398

Synchronous versus asynchronous code • 400

Using Unity coroutines • 402

Managing request responses • 404

Deserializing request data • 406

Adjusting the game lighting • 410

Additional web request formats 412

Summary 413

Pop quiz: Requesting data 414

Chapter 14: Exploring Generics, Delegates, and Beyond   415

Introducing generics 415

Generic classes • 416

Generic methods • 418

Constraint type parameters • 423

Adding generics to Unity objects • 426

Delegating actions 427

Creating a debug delegate • 428

Delegates as parameter types • 429

Firing events 431

Creating and invoking events • 432

Handling event subscriptions • 433

Cleaning up event subscriptions • 435

Handling exceptions **436**

Throwing exceptions • 437

Using try-catch • 439

Summary **442**

Pop quiz: Intermediate C# **443**

Chapter 15: The Journey Continues   445

Diving deeper 445

Remembering your object-oriented programming 446

Design patterns primer 447

Approaching Unity projects 448

Unity features we didn't cover 448

Next steps 449

C# resources • 449

Unity resources • 449

Unity certifications • 450

Hero's trial: Putting something out into the world 451

Summary 451

Chapter 16: Unlock Your Book'sExclusive Benefits   453

How to unlock these benefits in three easy steps 453

Pop Quiz Answers   457

Other Books You May Enjoy   465

Index   469

Preface

Unity is one of the most popular game engines in the world, catering to hobbyists, professional AAA studios, and cinematic production companies. While known for its use as a 3D tool, Unity has a host of dedicated features supporting everything from 2D games and virtual reality to post-production and cross-platform publishing.

Developers love its drag-and-drop interface and built-in features, but it's the ability to write custom C# scripts for behaviors and game mechanics that really takes Unity the extra mile. Learning how to write C# code might not be a huge obstacle to a seasoned programmer with other languages under their belt, but it can be daunting for those of you who have no programming experience. That's where this book comes in, as I'll be taking you through the building blocks of programming and the C# language from scratch while building a fun and playable game prototype in Unity.

Who this book is for

This book is written for those of you who don't have any experience with the basic tenets of programming or C#. However, if you're a competent novice or seasoned professional coming from another language, or even C#, but need to get hands-on with game development in Unity, this is still where you want to be.

What this book covers

Chapter 1, Getting to Know Your Environment, starts off with the Unity installation process, the main features of the editor, and finding documentation for C# and Unity-specific topics. We'll also go through creating C# scripts from inside Unity and look at Visual Studio, the application where all our code editing takes place.

Chapter 2, The Building Blocks of Programming, begins by laying out the atomic-level concepts of programming, giving you the chance to relate variables, methods, and classes to situations in everyday life. From there, we'll move on to simple debugging techniques, proper formatting and commenting, and how Unity turns C# scripts into components.

Chapter 3, Diving into Variables, Types, and Methods, takes a deeper look at the building blocks from *Chapter 2*. This includes C# data types, naming conventions, access modifiers, and everything else you'll need for the foundation of a program. We'll also go over how to write methods, add parameters, and use return types, ending with an overview of standard Unity methods belonging to the MonoBehaviour class.

Chapter 4, Control Flow and Collection Types, introduces the common approaches to making decisions in code, consisting of the if...else and switch statements. From there, we'll move on to working with arrays, lists, and dictionaries, and incorporating iteration statements for looping through collection types. We'll end the chapter with a look at conditional looping statements and a special C# data type called enumerations.

Chapter 5, Working with Classes, Structs, and OOP, details our first contact with constructing and instantiating classes and structs. We'll go through the basic steps of creating constructors, adding variables and methods, and the fundamentals of subclassing and inheritance. The chapter will end with a comprehensive explanation of **object-oriented programming (OOP)** and how it applies to C#.

Chapter 6, Getting Your Hands Dirty with Unity, marks our departure from C# syntax into the world of game design, level building, and Unity's featured tools. We'll start by going over the basics of a game design document and then move on to blocking out our level geometry and adding lighting and a simple particle system.

Chapter 7, Movement, Camera Controls, and Collisions, explains different approaches to moving a player object and setting up a third-person camera. We'll discuss incorporating Unity physics for more realistic locomotion effects, as well as how to work with collider components and capture interactions within a scene.

Chapter 8, Scripting Game Mechanics, introduces the concept of game mechanics and how to effectively implement them. We'll start by adding a simple jump action, creating a shooting mechanic, and building on the previous chapters' code by adding logic to handle item collection.

Chapter 9, Basic AI and Enemy Behavior, starts with a brief overview of **artificial intelligence (AI)** in games and the concepts we will be applying to *Hero Born*. Topics covered in this chapter will include navigation in Unity, using the level geometry and a navigation mesh, smart agents, and automated enemy movement.

Chapter 10, Revisiting Types, Methods, and Classes, takes a more in-depth look at data types, intermediate method features, and additional behaviors that can be used for more complex classes. This chapter will give you a deeper understanding of the versatility and breadth of the C# language.

Chapter 11, Specialized Collection Types and LINQ, dives into stacks, queues, hash sets, and the different development scenarios that each is uniquely suited for. This chapter also explores filtering, ordering, and transforming data collections using LINQ.

Chapter 12, Saving, Loading, and Serializing Data, gets you ready to handle your game's information. Topics covered in this chapter include working with the filesystem and creating, deleting, and updating files. We'll also cover different data types, including XML, JSON, and binary data, and end with a practical discussion on serializing C# objects directly into data formats.

Chapter 13, Connecting to the World Wide Web, introduces the basics of web requests, downloading data from web servers, and turning that information into actionable game mechanics. We'll also cover the differences between synchronous and asynchronous code and how Unity handles both.

Chapter 14, Exploring Generics, Delegates, and Beyond, details intermediate features of the C# language and how to apply them in practical, real-world scenarios. We'll start with an overview of generic programming and progress to concepts such as delegation, events, and exception handling.

Chapter 15, The Journey Continues, reviews the main topics you've learned throughout the book and leaves you with resources for further study in both C# and Unity. Included in these resources will be online reading material, certifications, and a host of my favorite video tutorial channels.

To get the most out of this book

The only thing you need to get the most from your upcoming C# and Unity adventure is a curious mind and a willingness to learn. Having said that, doing all the code exercises, *Hero's trials*, and *Quiz* sections is a must if you hope to cement the knowledge you're learning. Lastly, revisiting topics and entire chapters to refresh or solidify your understanding before moving on is always a good idea. There is no sense in building a house on an unstable foundation.

You'll also need a current version of Unity installed on your computer—version 6.0 or later is recommended. All code examples have been tested with Unity 6000.0.50f1 and should work with future versions without issues.

This is the software/hardware covered in the book:

- Unity 6.0 or later
- Visual Studio 2019 or later
- C# 9.0 or later

Before starting, check that your computer setup meets the Unity system requirements at `https://docs.unity3d.com/6000.0/Documentation/Manual/system-requirements.html`.

Download the example code files

The code bundle for the book is hosted on GitHub at `https://github.com/PacktPublishing/Learning-C-by-Developing-Games-with-Unity-6_8th-Edn`.

We also have other code bundles from our rich catalog of books and videos available at `https://github.com/PacktPublishing`. Check them out!

Download the color images

We also provide a PDF file that has color images of the screenshots/diagrams used in this book. You can download it here: `https://packt.link/gbp/9781805808718`.

This book contains long screenshots captured to provide you with an overview of the entire Unity window. As a result, the text on these images may appear small at 100% zoom. We recommend referring to the graphics bundle for ease of understanding.

Conventions used

There are a number of text conventions used throughout this book.

`CodeInText`: Indicates code words in text, database table names, folder names, filenames, file extensions, pathnames, dummy URLs, user input, and X/Twitter handles. For example: "For simple text or individual variables, use the standard `Debug.Log()` method."

A block of code is set as follows:

```
public int CurrentAge = 30;
```

Any command-line input or output is written as follows:

```
[12:58:12] Player detected - attack!
UnityEngine.Debug:Log (object)

[12:58:15] Player deaths: 0
UnityEngine.Debug:Log (object)

[12:58:18] Player deaths: 1
UnityEngine.Debug:Log (object)
```

```
[12:58:18] Next time you'll be at number 2
UnityEngine.Debug:Log (object)
```

Bold: Indicates a new term, an important word, or words that you see on the screen. For instance, words in menus or dialog boxes appear in the text like this. For example: "For reference, the name of each GameObject can be found at the top of the **Inspector** tab with the object selected."

> Warnings or important notes appear like this.

> Tips and tricks appear like this.

Get in touch

Feedback from our readers is always welcome.

General feedback: Email feedback@packtpub.com and mention the book's title in the subject of your message. If you have questions about any aspect of this book, please email us at questions@packtpub.com.

Errata: Although we have taken every care to ensure the accuracy of our content, mistakes do happen. If you have found a mistake in this book, we would be grateful if you reported this to us. Please visit http://www.packtpub.com/submit-errata, click **Submit Errata**, and fill in the form.

Piracy: If you come across any illegal copies of our works in any form on the internet, we would be grateful if you would provide us with the location address or website name. Please contact us at copyright@packtpub.com with a link to the material.

If you are interested in becoming an author: If there is a topic that you have expertise in and you are interested in either writing or contributing to a book, please visit http://authors.packtpub.com/.

Share your thoughts

Now you've finished *Learning C# by Developing Games with Unity 6, Eighth Edition*, we'd love to hear your thoughts! Scan the QR code below to go straight to the Amazon review page for this book and share your feedback or leave a review on the site that you purchased it from.

https://packt.link/r/1805808710

Your review is important to us and the tech community and will help us make sure we're delivering excellent quality content.

1

Getting to Know Your Environment

Pop culture loves to market computer programmers as outsiders, lone wolves, or geeky hackers – people who possess extraordinary mental gifts for algorithmic thought, little social IQ, and the odd anarchic bent. While this generalization is often incorrect (like all widescale generalizations), there is something to the idea that learning to code fundamentally changes the way you look at the world.

The good news is that your naturally curious mind already wants to see patterns in the world, and you may even come to enjoy this new way of thinking. From the moment your eyes snap open in the morning to the last glimpse of your ceiling fan before you go to sleep, you're unconsciously using analytical skills that directly translate to programming—you're just missing the right language and syntax to map those life skills into code.

You know your age, right? That's a variable. When you cross the street, I presume you look down the road in both directions before stepping off the curb like the rest of us. That's evaluating different conditions, better known as control flow in programming terminology. When you look at a can of soda, you instinctively identify that it has certain properties, such as shape, weight, and contents. That's a class object! You get the idea.

With all that real-world experience at your fingertips, you're more than ready to cross over into the realm of programming. To kick off your journey, you'll need to know how to set up your development environment, work with the applications involved, and know exactly where to go when you need help.

To that end, we're going to begin by delving into the following C# topics:

- Getting started with Unity 6
- Using C# with Unity
- Exploring the documentation

Let's get started!

Getting the most out of this book — get to know your free benefits

Unlock exclusive **free** benefits that come with your purchase, thoughtfully crafted to supercharge your learning journey and help you learn without limits.

Here's a quick overview of what you get with this book:

Next-gen reader

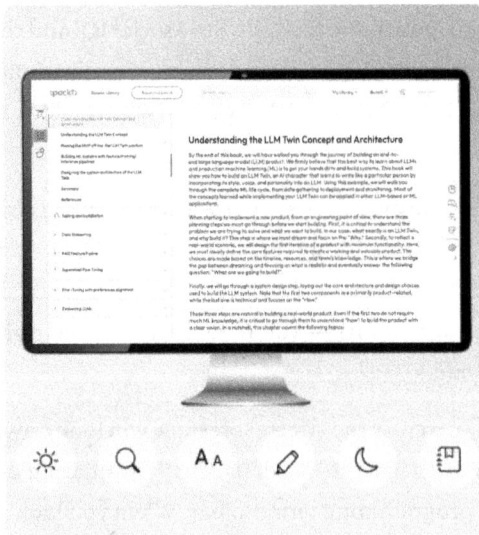

Our web-based reader, designed to help you learn effectively, comes with the following features:

⌁ Multi-device progress sync: Learn from any device with seamless progress sync.

🖺 Highlighting and notetaking: Turn your reading into lasting knowledge.

🔖 Bookmarking: Revisit your most important learnings anytime.

☀ Dark mode: Focus with minimal eye strain by switching to dark or sepia mode.

Figure 1.1: Illustration of the next-gen Packt Reader's features

Interactive AI assistant (beta)

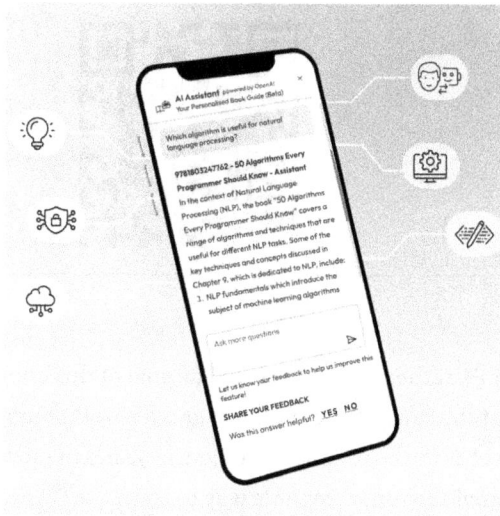

Our interactive AI assistant has been trained on the content of this book, to maximize your learning experience. It comes with the following features:

- ❖ Summarize it: Summarize key sections or an entire chapter.
- ❖ AI code explainers: In the next-gen Packt Reader, click the Explain button above each code block for AI-powered code explanations.

Note: The AI assistant is part of next-gen Packt Reader and is still in beta.

Figure 1.2: Illustration of Packt's
AI assistant

DRM-free PDF or ePub version

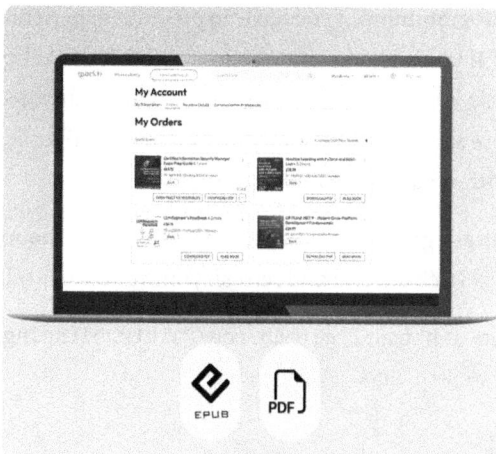

Learn without limits with the following perks included with your purchase:

- 📖 Learn from anywhere with a DRM-free PDF copy of this book.
- 📱 Use your favorite e-reader to learn using a DRM-free ePub version of this book.

Figure 1.3: Free PDF and ePub

Technical requirements

Sometimes it's easier to start with what a thing isn't, rather than what it is. The goal of this book *isn't* to teach you everything there is to know about the Unity game engine or game development. By necessity, we'll cover these topics at a basic level at the beginning of our journey, and in more detail in *Chapter 6*. These topics are included to provide a fun, accessible way to learn the C# programming language from the ground up, not an in-depth Unity tutorial. With programming as our main goal, there will be times when we opt for a code-based solution even though Unity may have a specific feature that does the same thing without any code. Don't worry, I'll point you in the right direction should you want to try them out later on in your game development journey!

Since this book is aimed at complete beginners to programming, if you have no previous experience with either C# or Unity, you're in the right place! If you've had some experience with the Unity Editor but not with programming, guess what? This is still the place to be. Even if you've dabbled in a bit of C# mixed with Unity, but want to explore some more intermediate or advanced topics, the later chapters of this book can provide you with what you're looking for.

If you're an experienced programmer in other languages, feel free to skip the beginner theory and dive right into the parts you're interested in, or stick around and refresh your fundamentals.

All code is available in the book's GitHub repository at `https://github.com/PacktPublishing/Learning-C-by-Developing-Games-with-Unity-6_8th-Edn`.

Getting started with Unity 6

If you don't have Unity installed (or are running an earlier version), follow these steps to set up your environment:

1. Head over to `https://www.unity.com/`.

2. Select **Download** (shown in *Figure 1.4*):

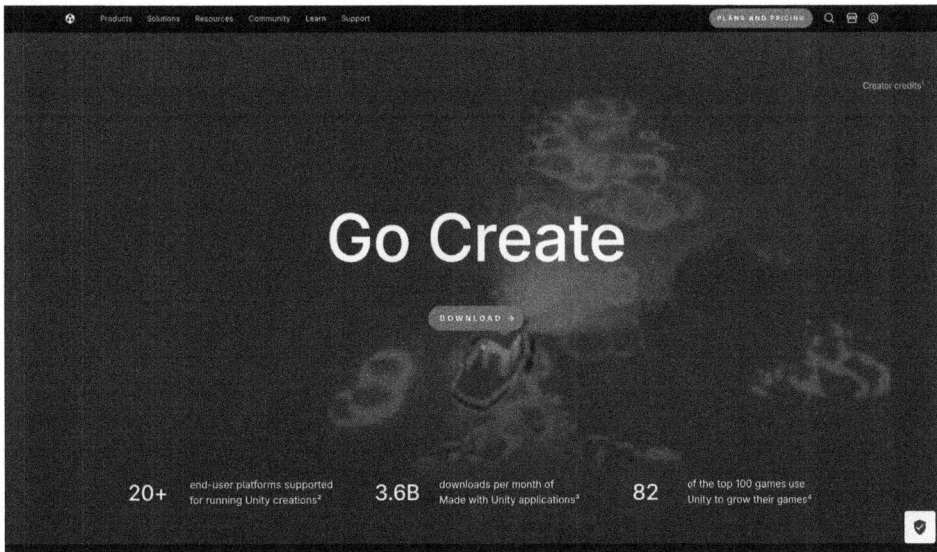

Figure 1.4: Unity homepage

> **Note**
>
> To provide a complete view of the Unity Editor, all our screenshots are taken in fullscreen mode. For color versions of all book images, use the following link: `https://packt.link/gbp/9781805808718`.

3. This will take you to the Unity store page. Don't feel overwhelmed by this—you can download Unity completely for free!

   If the Unity homepage looks different for you than what you can see in *Figure 1.4*, you can go directly to `https://store.unity.com`.

4. Scroll down to the **How to get started** section and download the **Unity Hub** application for either Windows or Mac, as shown in *Figure 1.5*. I'll be using a Mac, but everything works the same on a Windows machine:

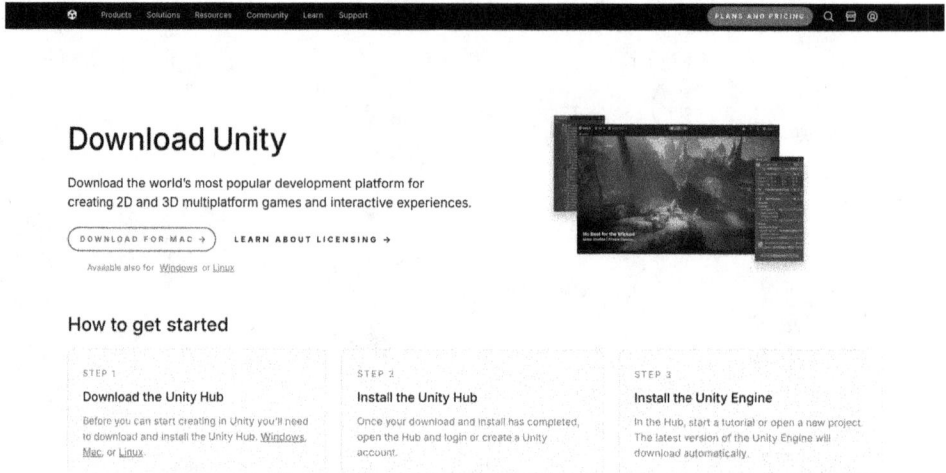

Figure 1.5: Start creating with the Unity portal

5. Once the download is complete, follow these steps:

    1. Open up the installer (by double-clicking it).

    2. Accept the user agreement.

    3. Follow the installation instructions.

6. When you get the green light, go ahead and fire up the **Unity Hub** application!

    If Unity asks you to choose a license option, select the **Personal** license option (which is completely free) and follow the instructions to set up your account.

7. The newest version of **Unity Hub** will prompt you to install the latest **LTS** (**Long Term Support**) version of Unity, as shown in *Figure 1.6*. If the default version is **Unity 6** or higher when you're reading these instructions, select **Install Unity Editor** and follow the instructions:

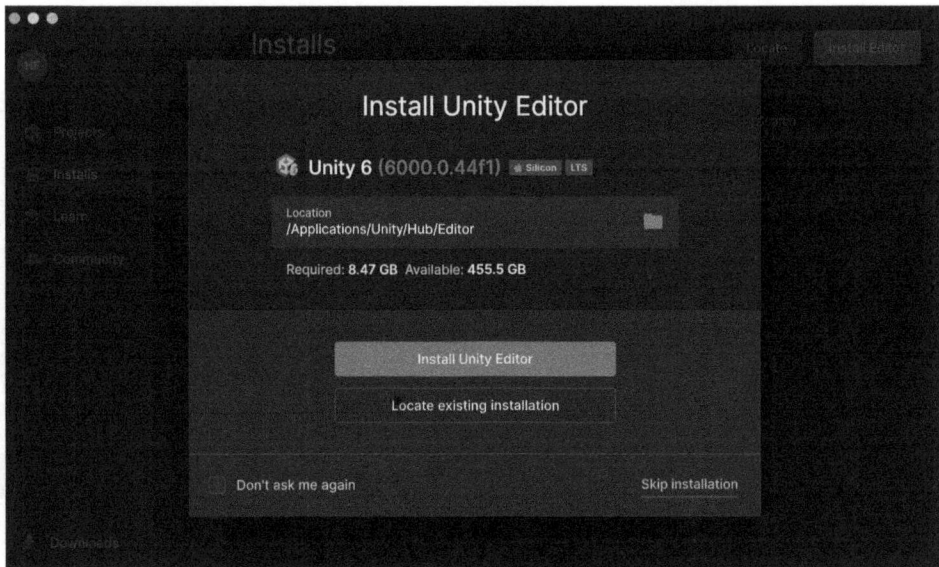

Figure 1.6: Install Unity Editor window

8. If **Unity 6** is not the default version when you're reading this, select **Skip installation** in the bottom-right corner of *Figure 1.6*.

9. Switch to the **Installs** tab from the left-hand menu and select **Install Editor**, as shown in *Figure 1.7*:

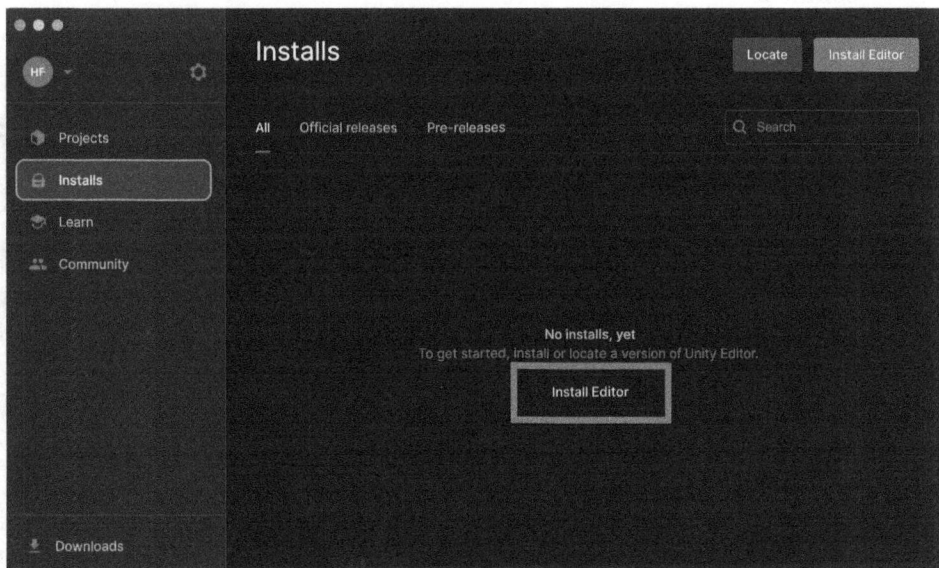

Figure 1.7: Unity Hub Installs panel

10. On the **Official releases** tab, select your desired version of **Unity 6** as shown in *Figure 1.8*, then click **Install** (*Silicon* for Macs, *Intel* for Windows).

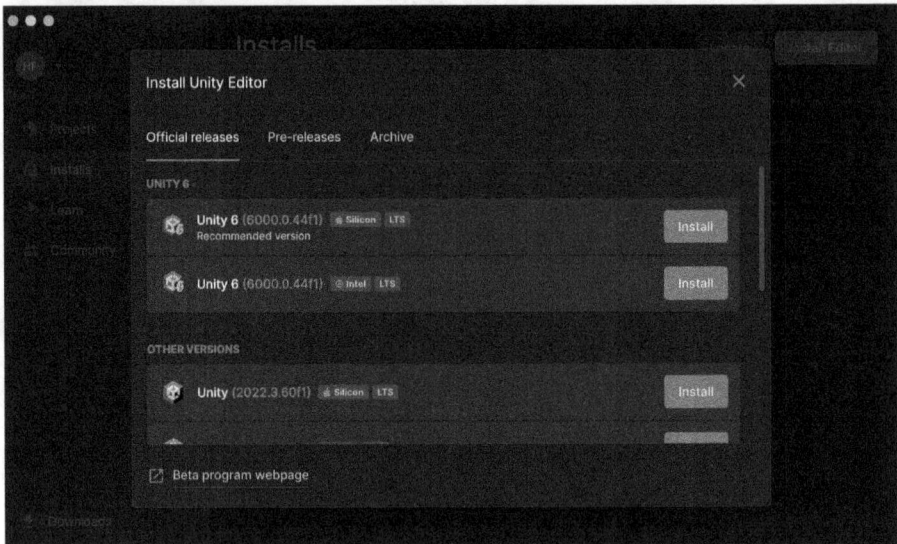

Figure 1.8: Add Unity version pop-up window

11. You'll then be given the option to add various modules to your installation. Make sure the **Visual Studio Code** (for Mac or Windows, accordingly) module is selected and click **Continue**:

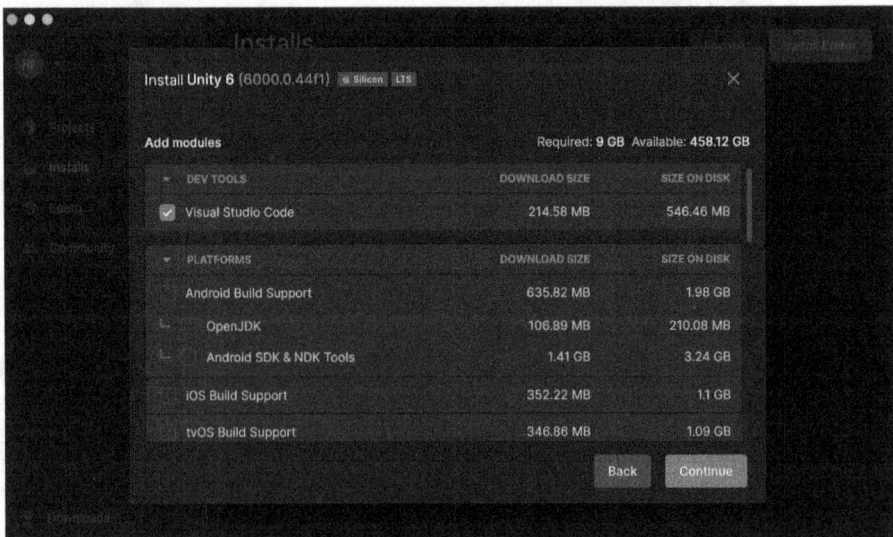

Figure 1.9: Adding install modules

12. If you want to add any modules later, you can click the gear icon to the right of any installed version in the **Installs** window, as shown in *Figure 1.7*.

Grab a coffee or a quick nap while Unity is downloading – when the installation is complete, you'll see a new version in your **Installs** panel, as shown in *Figure 1.10*:

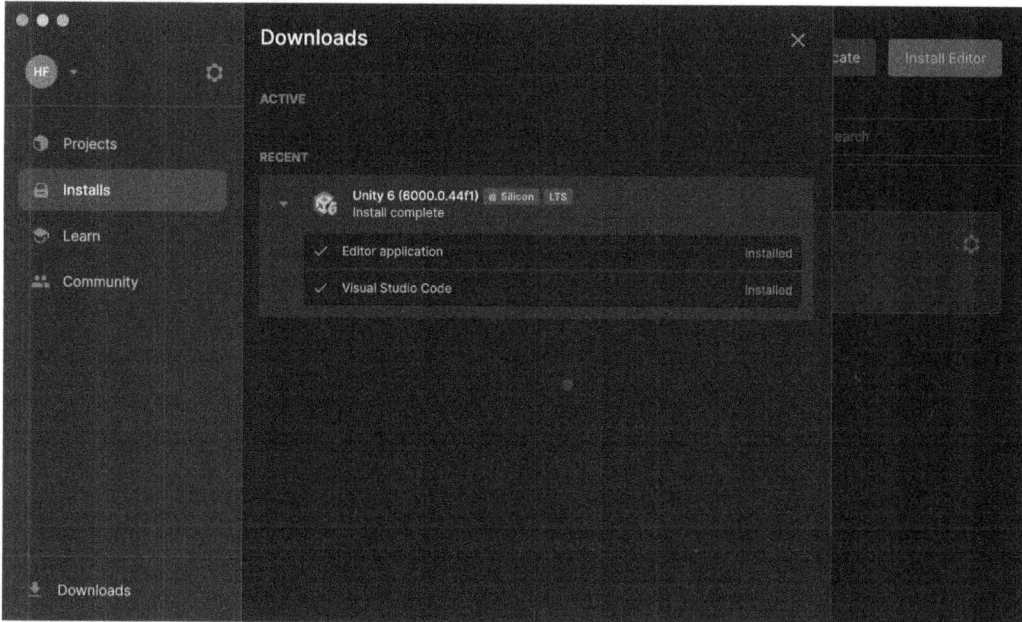

Figure 1.10: Installs tab with Unity versions

You can find additional information and resources about the **Unity Hub** application at `https://docs.unity3d.com/hub/manual/index.html`.

There's always a chance of something going wrong, so be sure to check the following section if you're using macOS Catalina or later, which has been known to throw up issues.

Using macOS

If you're working on a Mac with OS Catalina or later, there is a known issue when using some versions of **Unity Hub** to install **Unity**. If this is the case for you, take a deep breath, go to the **Unity download archive**, and grab any version you need (`https://unity3d.com/get-unity/download/archive`).

Remember to use the **Downloads (Mac)** or **Downloads (Win)** option instead of the **Unity Hub** download:

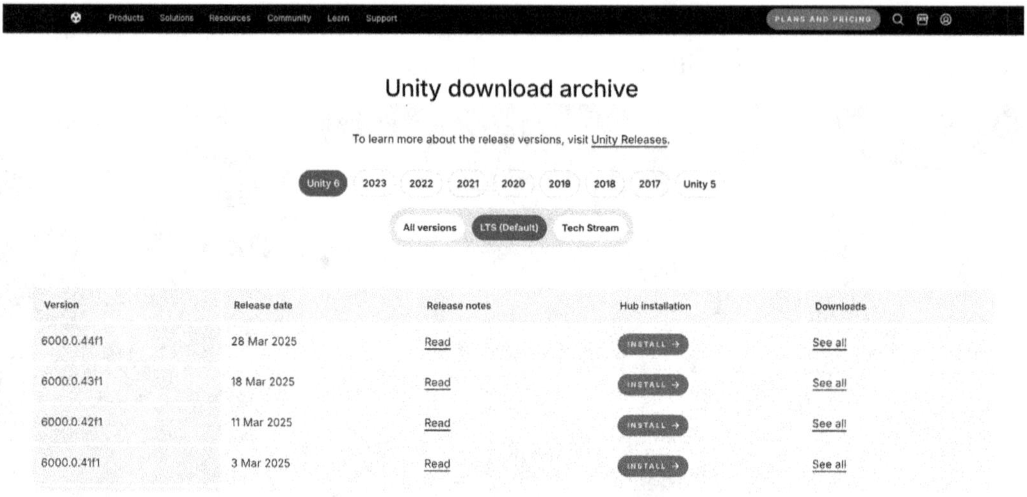

Figure 1.11: Unity download archive

Once the installer application downloads, open it up and follow the setup instructions!

All the examples and screenshots for this book were created and captured using **Unity 6.000.0.44f1**. If you're using a newer version, things might look slightly different in the Unity Editor, but this shouldn't affect your following along.

Now that **Unity Hub** and **Unity 6** are installed, it's time to create a new project!

Creating a new project

Launch the **Unity Hub** application, which is your staging area—you can see a list of all your projects and **Unity** versions and access learning resources and community features here. Then, take the following steps:

1. To get started, click on **New project** in the top-right corner:

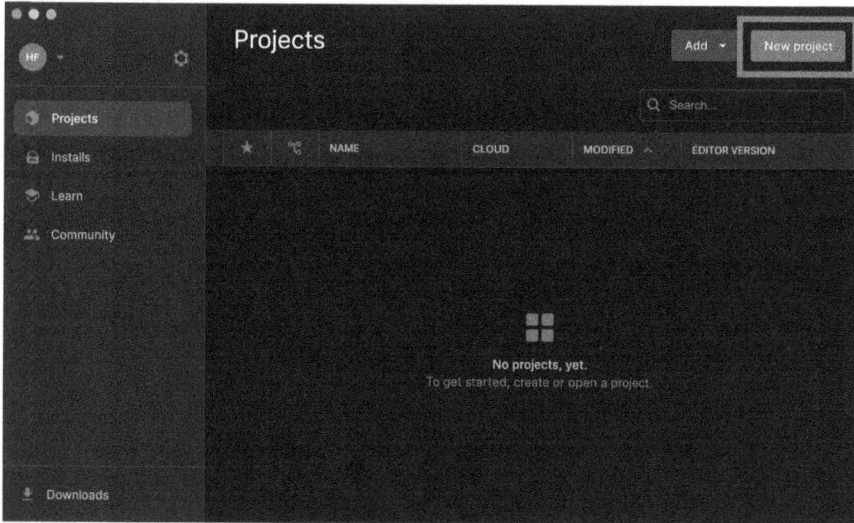

Figure 1.12: Unity Hub Projects panel

2. Make sure the editor version at the top is set to your Unity 6 version and set the following fields:

    - **Templates:** The project will default to **Universal 3D**.
    - **Project name:** I'll be calling mine Hero Born.
    - **Location:** Wherever you'd like the project to be saved.

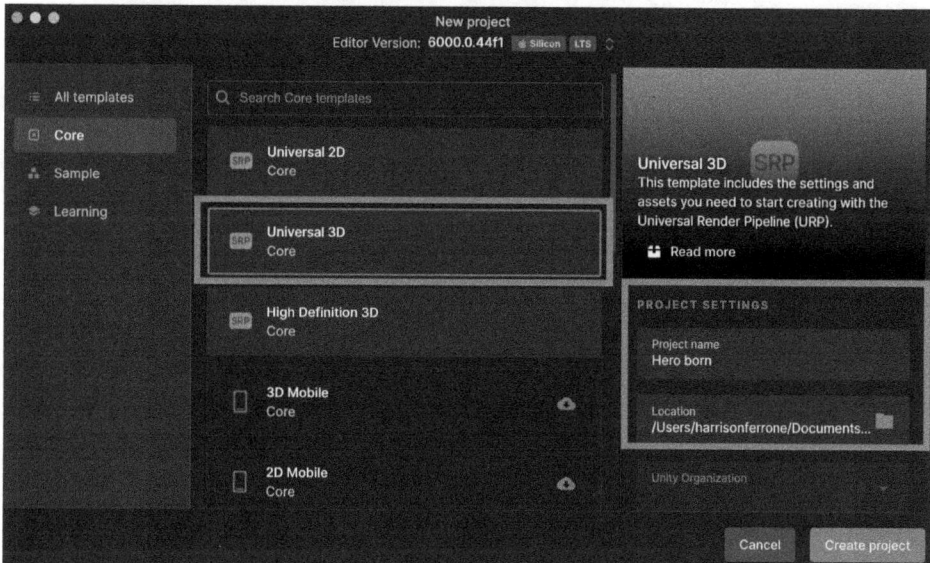

Figure 1.13: Unity Hub with the New project configuration popup

3. Once the settings have been configured, hit the **Create project** button in the bottom right of *Figure 1.13.*

With the project created, you're all set to explore the Unity interface! You can re-open your project anytime from the **Projects** panel in Unity Hub, but if your computer is running a little slow with both Unity and Unity Hub open, feel free to close Unity Hub.

Navigating the editor

When the new project finishes initializing, you'll see the glorious Unity Editor! I've marked the important tabs (or windows, if you prefer) in *Figure 1.14:*

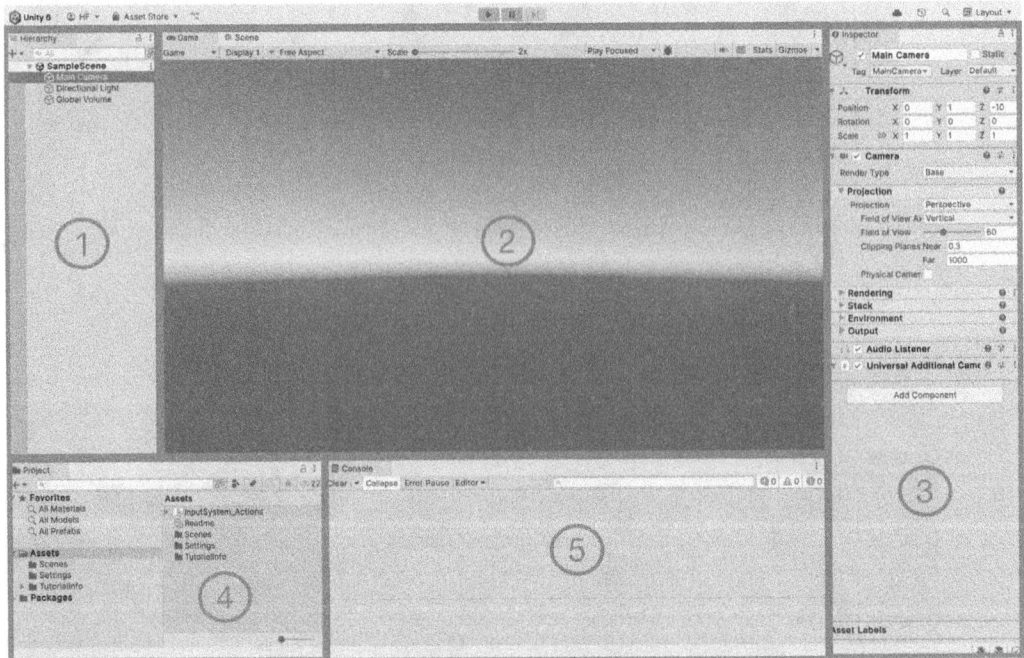

Figure 1.14: Unity interface

This is a lot to take in, so we'll look at each of these panels in more detail:

1. The **Hierarchy** window shows every item currently in the game scene. In the starter project, this is just the default camera and directional light, but when we create our prototype environment, this window will start to get filled in with the objects we create in the scene.

2. The **Game** and **Scene** windows are the most visual aspects of the editor. Think of the **Scene** window as your stage, where you can move and arrange 2D and 3D objects. When you hit the **Play** button, the **Game** window will take over, rendering the **Scene** view and any programmed interactions. You can also use the **Scene** view when you're in play mode.

3. The **Inspector** window is your one-stop shop for viewing and editing the properties of objects in the scene. If you select **Main Camera** in the **Hierarchy** (highlighted in blue in *Figure 1.14*), you'll see several parts displayed, which Unity calls components—all of which are accessible from the **Inspector**.

4. The **Project** window holds every asset that's currently in your project. Think of this as a representation of your project's folders and files.

5. The **Console** window is where any output we want our scripts to print will show up. From here on out, if we talk about the console or debug output, this panel is where it will be displayed.

If any of these windows get closed by accident, you can re-open them anytime from **Unity menu | Window | General**. You can find more in-depth breakdowns of each window's functionality in the Unity docs at `https://docs.unity3d.com/Manual/UsingTheEditor.html`.

I know that was a lot to process if you're new to Unity, but rest assured that any instructions going forward will always reference the necessary steps. I won't leave you wondering what button to push. With that out of the way, let's start creating some actual C# scripts.

Using C# with Unity

Going forward, it's important to think of Unity and C# as symbiotic entities. Unity is the engine where you'll create scripts and GameObjects, but the actual programming takes place in another program called **Visual Studio Code**.

Setting up Visual Studio Code in Unity 6

Before continuing, it's important that Visual Studio Code is set up as the script editor for your project. Go to the **Unity menu | Settings | External Tools** and check that **External Script Editor** is set to **Visual Studio Code** (or **Windows**):

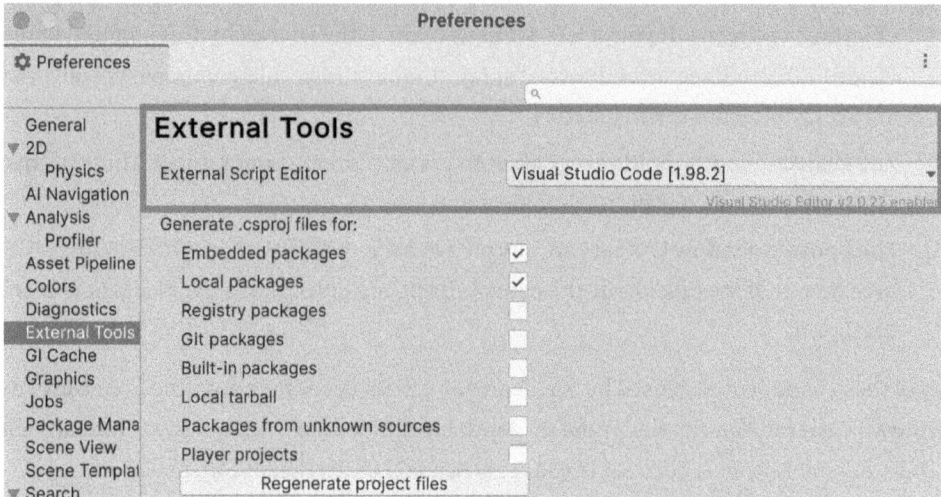

Figure 1.15: Changing External Script Editor to Visual Studio

As a final tip, if you want to switch between light and dark modes, go to the **Unity menu | Preferences | General** and change **Editor Theme**:

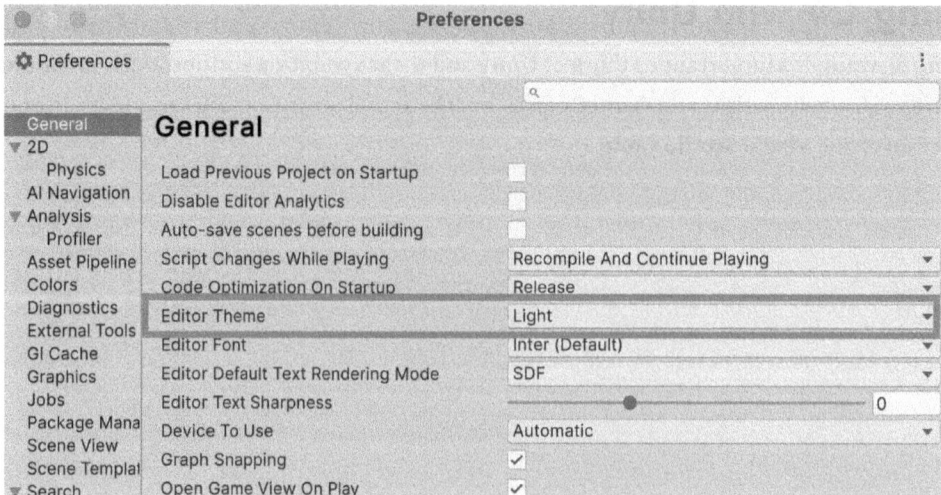

Figure 1.16: Unity general preferences panel

We haven't covered any basic programming concepts yet, but they won't have a home until we know how to create an actual C# script in Unity. Let's see how we can achieve this in the next section!

Working with C# scripts

A C# script is a special kind of C# file in which you'll write C# code. These scripts can be used in Unity to do virtually anything, from controlling an in-game character with your keyboard to animating objects in your level.

There are several ways to create C# scripts from the editor:

- Select **Assets | Create | Scripting | MonoBehaviour Script**
- Right under the **Project** tab, select the + icon | **Scripting | MonoBehaviour Script**
- Right-click on the **Assets** folder in the **Project** tab and select **Create | Scripting | MonoBehaviour Script** from the pop-up menu
- Select any **GameObject** in the **Hierarchy** window and click **Add Component | New Script**

A MonoBehaviour script is a type of C# script that's specific to Unity (don't get too bogged down with this right now; we'll get into more details as we go along). Whenever you're instructed to create a C# script, please use whichever method you prefer, and I'll call out any additional information you may need.

Resources and objects other than C# scripts can be created in the editor using the preceding methods. I'm not going to call out each of these variations every time we create something new, so just keep the options in the back of your mind.

For the sake of organization, we're going to store our various assets and scripts inside their own named folders. This isn't just a Unity-related task—it's something you should always do, and your co-workers will thank you (I promise):

1. Select **Assets** | **Create** | **Folder** and name it Scripts:

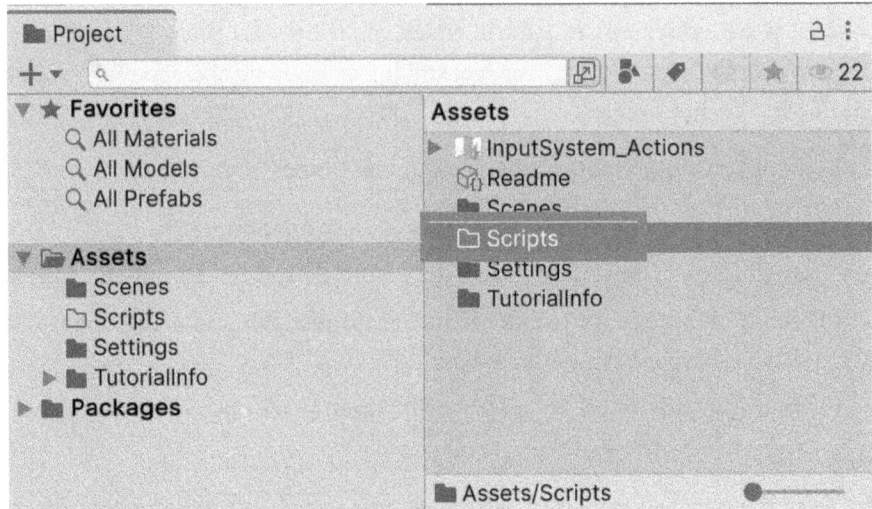

Figure 1.17: Creating a C# script

2. Double-click on the **Scripts** folder and create a new C# script. By default, the script will be named NewBehaviourScript, but you'll see the filename highlighted, so you have the option to immediately rename it. Type in LearningCurve and hit *Enter*:

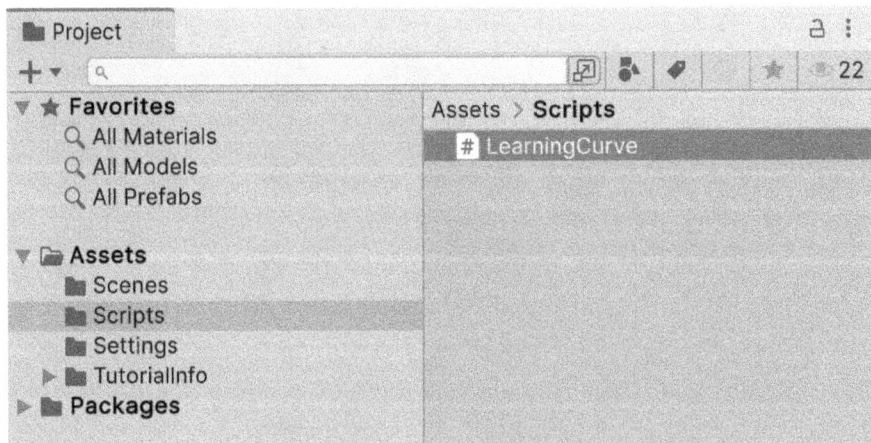

Figure 1.18: Project window with the Scripts folder selected

3. You can use the small slider in the bottom right of the **Project** tab to change how your files are displayed.

So, you've just created a subfolder named Scripts, as shown in the preceding screenshot. Inside that parent folder, you created a C# script named LearningCurve.cs (the .cs file type stands for **C-Sharp**, in case you were wondering), which is now saved as part of our Hero Born project assets. All that's left to do is open it up in our code editor program!

Introducing the Visual Studio Code editor

While Unity can create and store C# scripts, they need to be edited using **Visual Studio Code** (which we downloaded as a pre-packaged module) and will open automatically when you double-click any C# script from inside the editor.

Opening a C# file

Unity will synchronize with **Visual Studio Code** the first time you open a file. The simplest way to do this is by selecting the script from the **Project** tab. Take the following steps:

1. Double-click on LearningCurve.cs, which will open the C# file in **Visual Studio Code**:

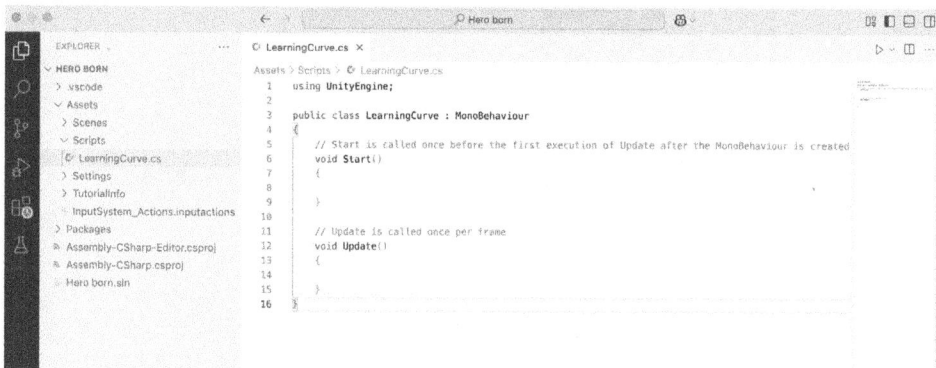

Figure 1.19: LearningCurve C# script in Visual Studio

2. You'll see a folder structure on the left-hand side of the interface that mirrors the one in Unity, which you can access like any other.

3. On the right-hand side is the actual code editor where the magic happens (all the code you write will live here). There are far more features to the **Visual Studio Code** application, but this is all we need to get started.

♡ **Quick tip**: Enhance your coding experience with the **AI Code Explainer** and **Quick Copy** features. Open this book in the next-gen Packt Reader. Click the **Copy** button

(**1**) to quickly copy code into your coding environment, or click the **Explain** button

(**2**) to get the AI assistant to explain a block of code to you.

```
                                                              Copy        Explain

function calculate(a, b) {                                      1           2
    return {sum: a + b};
};
```

🔒 **The next-gen Packt Reader** is included for free with the purchase of this book. Scan the QR code OR go to `https://packtpub.com/unlock`, then use the search bar to find this book by name. Double-check the edition shown to make sure you get the right one.

The **Visual Studio Code** interface is slightly different for Windows and Mac environments, but the code we'll be using throughout this book will work equally well with both. All the screenshots in this book have been taken in a Mac environment, so if things look different on your computer, there's no need to worry.

Beware of naming mismatches

One common pitfall that trips up new programmers is file naming—more specifically, naming mismatches—which we can illustrate using *line 5* from *Figure 1.19* of the C# file in **Visual Studio Code:**

```
public class LearningCurve : MonoBehaviour
```

The LearningCurve class name is the same as the LearningCurve.cs filename. This is an essential requirement. It's OK if you don't know what a class is quite yet. The important thing to remember is that, in Unity, the filename and the class name need to be the same. If you're using C# outside of Unity, the filename and class name don't have to match.

When you create a C# script file in Unity, the filename in the **Project** tab is already in **Edit** mode, ready to be renamed. It's a good habit to rename it then and there. If you rename the script later, the filename and the class name won't match.

If you were to rename the file at a later point, the filename would change, but line 5 would be as follows:

```
public class NewBehaviourScript : MonoBehaviour
```

If you accidentally do this, it's not the end of the world. All you need to do is right-click on the script in the **Project** tab and choose **Rename**:

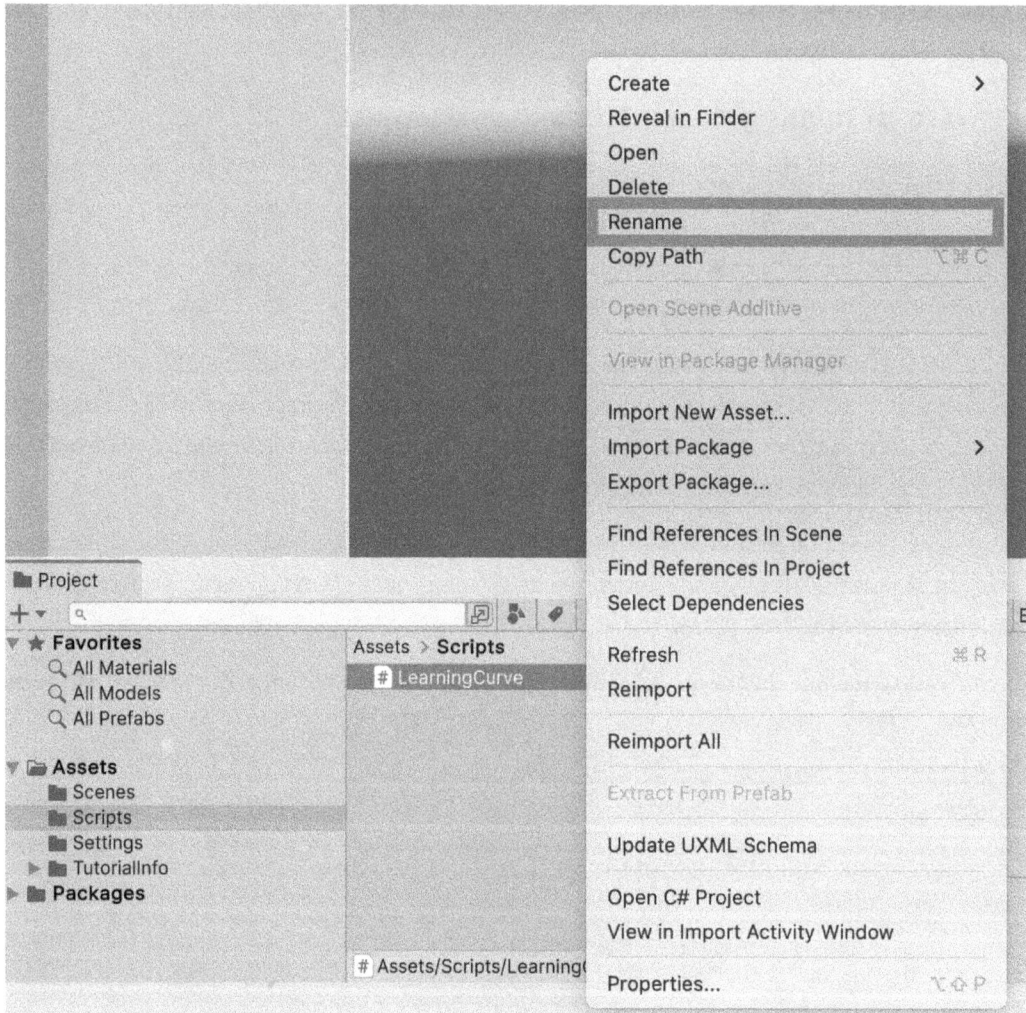

Figure 1.20: Renaming a C# script

Syncing C# files

As part of their symbiotic relationship, Unity and **Visual Studio Code** communicate with each other to synchronize their content. This means that if you add, delete, or change a script file in one application, the other application will see the changes automatically.

So, what happens when Murphy's Law, which states that *"anything that can go wrong will go wrong,"* strikes and syncing just doesn't seem to be working correctly? If you run into this situation, take a deep breath, select the troublesome script in Unity, right-click, and select **Refresh**.

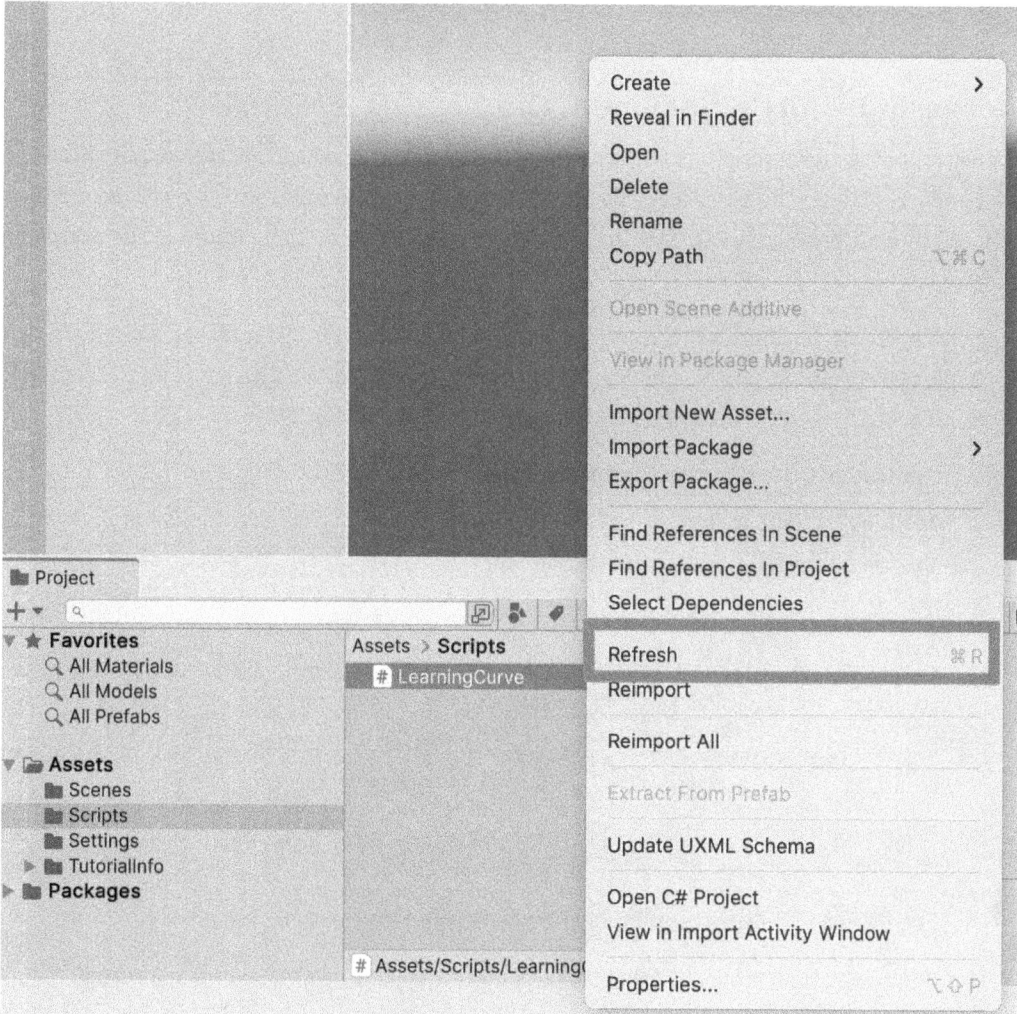

Figure 1.21: Refreshing a C# script

You now have the basics of script creation under your belt, so it's time we talk about finding and efficiently using helpful resources.

Exploring the documentation

The last topic we'll touch on in this first foray into Unity and C# scripts is documentation. Not sexy, I know, but it's important to form good habits early when dealing with new programming languages or development environments.

Accessing Unity's documentation

Once you start writing scripts in earnest, you'll be using Unity's documentation quite often, so it's beneficial to know how to access it early on. The **Reference Manual** will give you an overview of a component or topic, while specific programming examples can be found in the **Scripting Reference**.

Every GameObject (an item in the **Hierarchy** window) in a scene has a **Transform** component that controls its **Position, Rotation**, and **Scale**. To keep things simple, we'll just look up the camera's **Transform** component in the Reference Manual:

1. In the **Hierarchy** tab, select the **Main Camera** GameObject.
2. Move over to the **Inspector** tab and click on the information icon (question mark, **?**) at the top right of the **Transform** component:

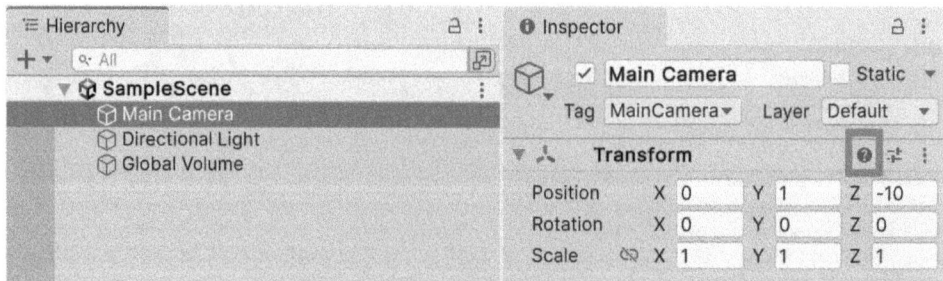

Figure 1.22: Main Camera GameObject selected in the Inspector

3. You'll see a web browser open on the **Transforms** page of the **Reference Manual**:

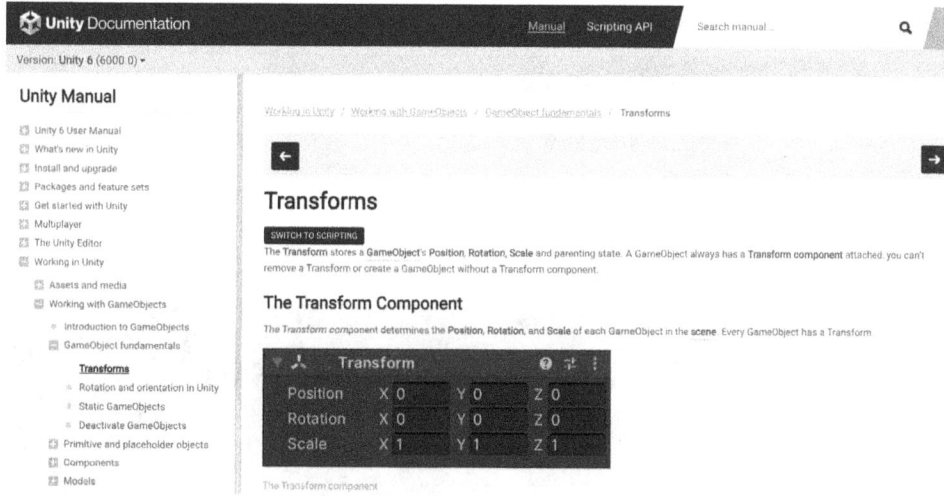

Figure 1.23: Unity Reference Manual

All the components in Unity have this feature, so if you ever want to know more about how something works, you know what to do.

So, we've got the **Reference Manual** open, but what if we wanted concrete coding examples related to the **Transform** component? It's simple—all we need to do is ask the **Scripting Reference**:

1. Click on the **SWITCH TO SCRIPTING** link underneath the component or class name (**Transforms**, in this case):

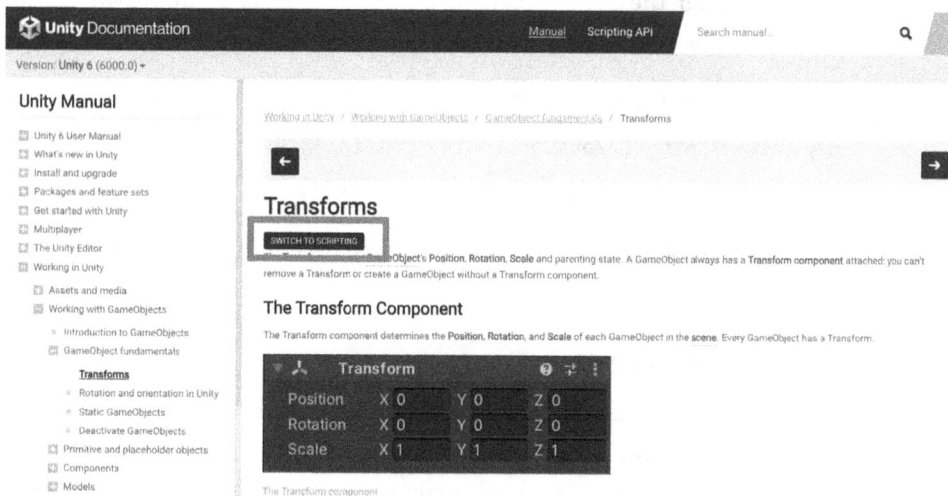

Figure 1.24: Unity Reference Manual with the SWITCH TO SCRIPTING button highlighted

2. By doing so, the **Reference Manual** automatically switches to the **Scripting Reference**:

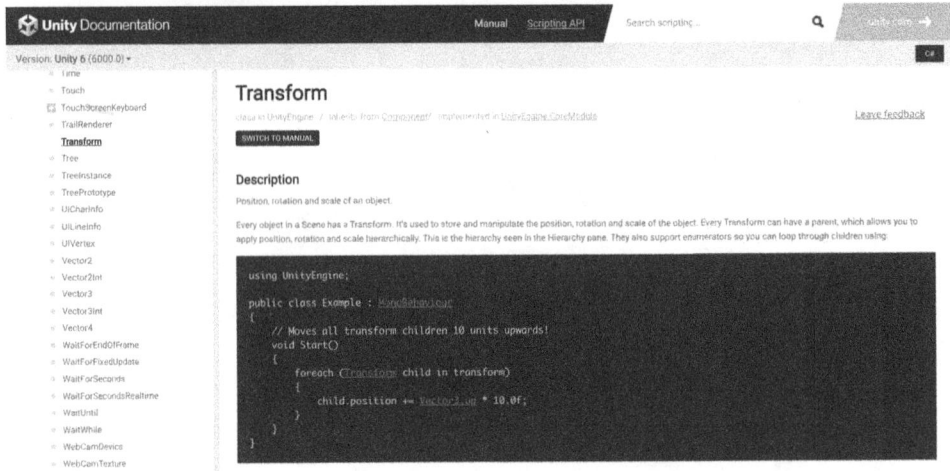

Figure 1.25: Unity scripting documentation with SWITCH TO MANUAL

3. As you can see, as well as coding help, there is also an option to switch back to the **Reference Manual** if necessary.

The **Scripting Reference** is a large document because it has to be. However, this doesn't mean you have to memorize it or even be familiar with all of its information to start writing scripts. As the name suggests, it's a reference, not a test.

If you find yourself lost in the documentation, or just out of ideas regarding where to look, you can also find solutions within the rich Unity development community in the following places:

- Unity Forum: `https://forum.unity.com/`
- Unity Answers: `https://answers.unity.com/index.html`
- Unity Discord: `https://discord.com/invite/unity`

On the other side of things, you'll need to know where to find resources on any C# question, which we'll cover next.

Locating C# resources

Now that we've got our Unity resources taken care of, let's take a look at some of Microsoft's C# resources. For starters, the Microsoft Learn documentation at `https://docs.microsoft.com/en-us/dotnet/csharp` has a ton of great tutorials, quick start guides, and how-to articles. You can also find great overviews of individual C# topics at `https://docs.microsoft.com/en-us/dotnet/csharp/programming-guide/index`.

For detailed information on a specific C# language feature, the reference guides are the place to go. These reference guides are an important resource for any C# programmer, but since they aren't always the easiest to navigate, let's take a few minutes to learn how to find what we're looking for.

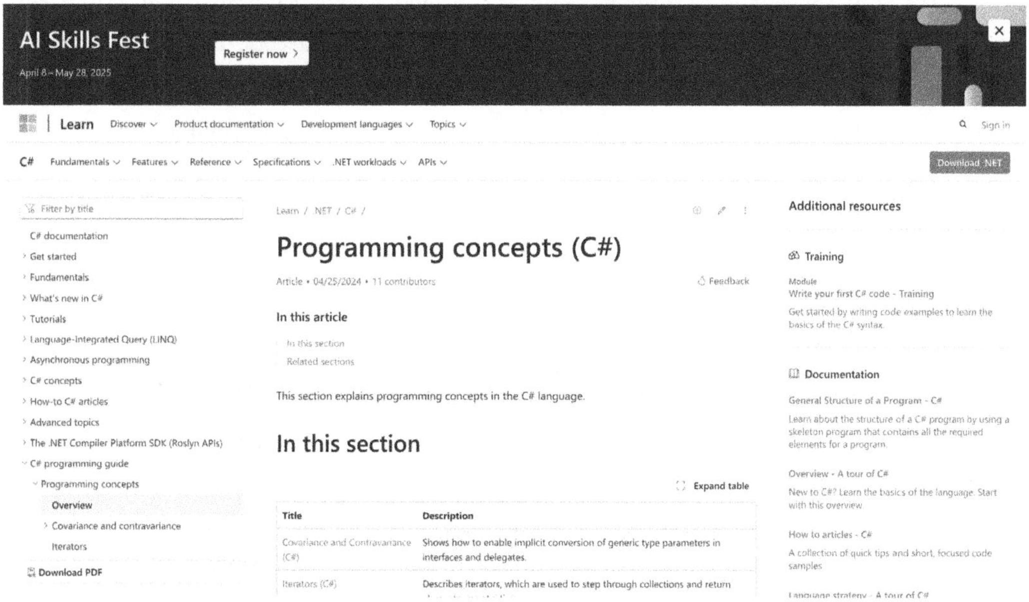

Figure 1.26: Microsoft .NET documentation

Unlike Unity's documentation, the C# reference and scripting information is all bundled up into one, but its saving grace is the subtopic list on the right-hand side. Use it well! It's extremely important to know where to find help when you're stuck or have a question, so be sure to circle back to this section whenever you hit a roadblock.

Summary

We covered quite a bit of logistical information in this chapter, so I can understand if you're itching to write some code. Starting new projects, creating folders and scripts, and accessing documentation are topics that are easily forgotten in the excitement of a new adventure. Just remember that this chapter has a lot of resources you might need in the coming pages, so don't be afraid to come back and visit. Thinking like a programmer is like strengthening a muscle: the more you work it, the stronger it gets.

In the next chapter, we'll start laying out the theory, vocabulary, and main concepts you'll need to prime your coding brain. Even though the material is conceptual, we'll still be writing our first lines of code in the LearningCurve script. Get ready!

Pop quiz: Dealing with scripts

a. What type of relationship do Unity and Visual Studio Code share?

b. The Scripting Reference supplies example code in regard to using a particular Unity component or feature. Where can you find more detailed (non-code-related) information about Unity components?

c. The Scripting Reference is a large document. How much of it do you have to memorize before attempting to write a script?

d. When is the best time to name a C# script?

Don't forget to check your answers against mine in the *Pop Quiz Answers* appendix to see how you did!

Subscribe to Game Dev Assembly Newsletter!

We are excited to introduce **Game Dev Assembly**, our brand-new newsletter dedicated to everything game development. Whether you're a programmer, designer, artist, animator, or studio lead, you'll get exclusive insights, industry trends, and expert tips to help you build better games and grow your skills. Sign up today and become part of a growing community of creators, innovators, and game changers: https://packt.link/gamedev-newsletter.

Scan the QR code to join instantly!

Join our community on Discord

Join our community's Discord space for discussions with the authors and other readers: `https://packt.link/gamedevelopment`

2

The Building Blocks of Programming

Any programming language starts off looking like ancient Greek to the unaccustomed eye, and C# is no exception. The good news is that beneath the initial mystery, all programming languages are made up of the same essential building blocks. Variables, methods, and classes (or objects) make up the DNA of conventional programming; understanding these simple concepts opens up an entire world of diverse and complex applications. After all, there are only four different DNA nucleobases in every person on Earth, yet each of us is a totally unique organism.

If you are new to programming, there's going to be a lot of information coming at you in this chapter, and this could mark the first lines of code that you've ever written. The point is not to overload your brain with facts and figures; it's to give you a holistic look at the building blocks of programming using examples from everyday life.

This chapter is all about the high-level view of the bits and pieces that make up a program. Getting the hang of how things work before getting into the code directly will not only help you new coders find your feet but it will also solidify the topics with easy-to-remember references. Ramblings aside, we'll focus on the following topics throughout this chapter:

- Defining variables
- Understanding methods
- Introducing classes
- Working with comments
- Putting the building blocks together

Let's dive in!

Defining variables

To start, we need to ask ourselves a simple question: what is a variable? Depending on your point of view, there are a few different ways of answering this question (all of which are valid):

- Conceptually, a variable is the most basic unit of programming, as an atom is to the physical world (except in string theory). Everything starts with variables, and programs can't exist without them.

- Technically, a variable is a tiny section of your computer's memory that holds an assigned value. Every variable keeps track of where its information is stored (this is called a **memory address**), its value, and its type (for instance, numbers, words, or lists).

- Practically, a variable is a container. You can create new ones whenever you want, fill them with stuff, move them around, change what they're holding, and reference them as needed. They can even be empty and still be useful!

You can find an in-depth explanation of variables in the Microsoft C# documentation at `https://docs.microsoft.com/en-us/dotnet/csharp/language-reference/language-specification/variables`.

A practical real-life example of a variable is a mailbox—remember those?

Figure 2.1: A row of colorful mailboxes

Note

To provide a complete view of the Unity editor, all our screenshots are taken in fullscreen mode. For color versions of all book images, use the following link: https://packt.link/gbp/9781805808718.

They can hold letters, bills, a picture from your aunt Mabel—anything. The point is that what's in a mailbox can vary: they can have a name and hold information (physical mail), and their contents can even be changed if you have the right security clearance.

Similarly, variables can hold different kinds of information. Variables in C# can hold strings (text), integers (numbers), and even Booleans (binary values that represent either true or false).

Names are important

Referring to *Figure 2.1*, if I asked you to go over and open the mailbox, the first thing you'd probably ask is: which one? If I said the Smith family mailbox, or the red mailbox, or even the droopy mailbox on the far right, then you'd have the necessary context to open the mailbox I'm referencing. Similarly, when you are creating variables, you have to give them unique names that you can reference later. We'll get into the specifics of proper formatting and descriptive naming in *Chapter 3*, but for now, let's keep things simple.

Variables act as placeholders

When you create and name a variable, you are creating a placeholder for the value that you want to store. Let's take the following simple math equation as an example:

```
2+9=11
```

Okay, no mystery here, but what if we wanted the number 9 to be its own variable? Consider the following code block:

```
MyVariable = 9
```

Now we can use the variable name, MyVariable, as a substitute for 9 anywhere we need it:

```
2 + MyVariable = 11
```

If you're wondering whether variables have other rules or regulations, they do. We'll get to those in *Chapter 3*, so sit tight.

Even though this example isn't real C# code, it illustrates the power of variables and their use as placeholder references.

Alright, enough theory—let's create a real variable in the LearningCurve script we created in *Chapter 1*:

1. Double-click on LearningCurve.cs from the **Project** window in Unity to open it in Visual Studio Code.

2. Add a space between *lines 4* and *5*, and add the following line of code to declare a new variable:

    ```
    public int CurrentAge = 30;
    ```

3. Inside the Start method brackets, add two debug logs to print out the following calculations:

    ```
    Debug.Log(30 + 1);
    Debug.Log(CurrentAge + 1);
    ```

Let's break down the code we just added. First, we created a new variable called CurrentAge and assigned it a value of 30. Then, we added two debug logs to print out the result of 30 + 1 and CurrentAge + 1 to show how variables are storage for values. They can be used in the exact same way as the values themselves.

It's also important to note that public variables appear in the Unity Inspector, while private ones don't. Don't worry about the syntax right now—just make sure your script is the same as the script that is shown in the following screenshot:

```
C# LearningCurve.cs ✕

Assets > Scripts > C# LearningCurve.cs > ⬡ LearningCurve
  1     using UnityEngine;
  2
       0 references
  3     public class LearningCurve : MonoBehaviour
  4     {
         1 reference
  5         public int CurrentAge = 30;
  6
  7         // Start is called once before the first execution of Update after the MonoBehaviour is created
           0 references
  8         void Start()
  9         {
 10             Debug.Log(30 + 1);
 11             Debug.Log(CurrentAge + 1);
 12         }
 13
 14         // Update is called once per frame
           0 references
 15         void Update()
 16         {
 17
 18     }
 19 }
```

Figure 2.2: LearningCurve script open in Visual Studio Code

To finish, save the file using **Editor | File | Save** or whichever hotkey combination your computer supports. Saving is a crucial step when editing scripts because Unity only recognizes saved changes back in the editor. If you add code to a script in Visual Studio Code but don't save it, Unity won't know about it.

For scripts to run in Unity, they have to be attached to GameObjects in the scene. Unity considers everything in your game as a GameObject—lights, player avatars, items, buildings, all of it.

By default, the sample scene in *Hero Born* has a camera for rendering the scene and a directional light to light the scene, so let's attach LearningCurve to the camera to keep things simple:

Drag and drop LearningCurve.cs onto **Main Camera**.

1. Select **Main Camera** so that it appears in the **Inspector** panel, and verify that the LearningCurve.cs (script) component is attached properly.

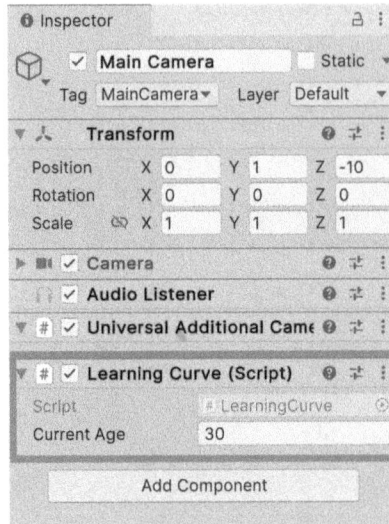

Figure 2.3: LearningCurve script attached to Main Camera in the Inspector

2. Click the **Play** button at the top-middle of the Unity editor and watch for the output in the **Console** panel:

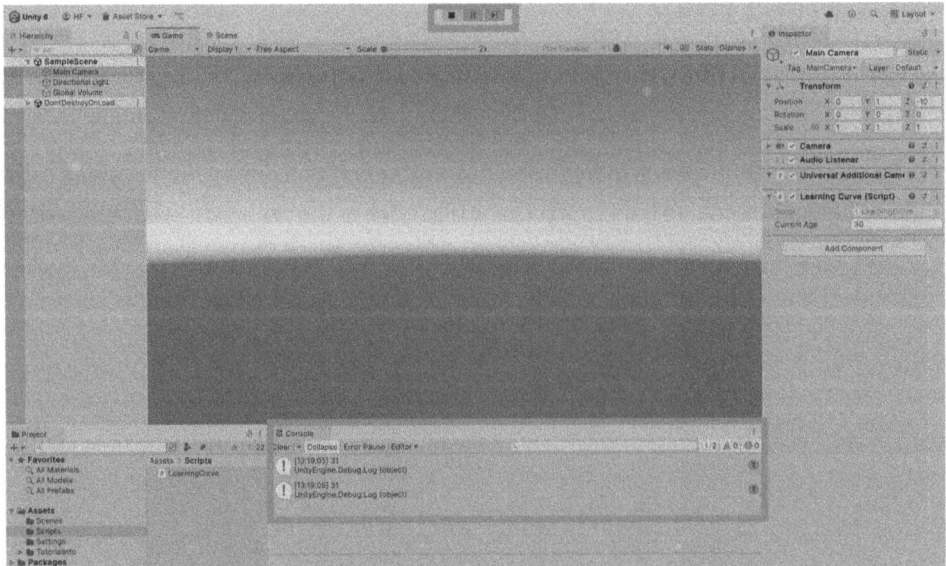

Figure 2.4: Unity Editor window with callouts for dragging and dropping scripts

You may have noticed the editor has a slightly darker tint and the **Play** button turned blue when you ran the game. This is because Unity has two states: editor and runtime. When you're working on scripts or adding objects to your scene, you're in the editor state.

Any changes will be saved to the project in this state. However, when you hit the **Play** button, Unity switches to the runtime state. Any changes you make while the game is running won't be saved, so pay special attention to *when* you're making updates.

The Debug.Log() statements printed out the result of the simple math equations we put in between the parentheses. As you can see in the following **Console** screenshot, the equation that used our variable, CurrentAge, worked the same as if it were a real number:

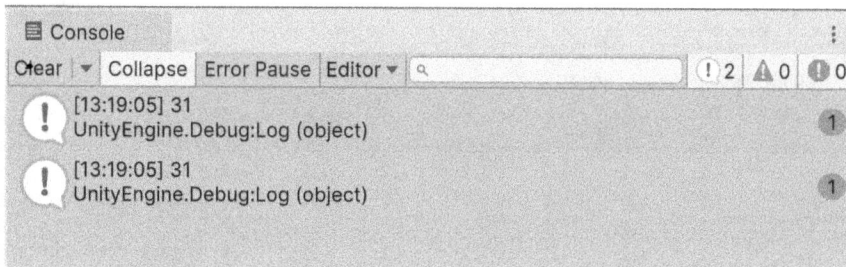

Figure 2.5: Unity console with debug output from the attached script

🔍**Quick tip:** Need to see a high-resolution version of this image? Open this book in the next-gen Packt Reader or view it in the PDF/ePub copy.

📖**The next-gen Packt Reader** and a **free PDF/ePub copy** of this book are included with your purchase. Scan the QR code OR visit https://packtpub.com/unlock, then use the search bar to find this book by name. Double-check the edition shown to make sure you get the right one.

We'll get into how Unity converts C# scripts into components in the *Scripts become components* section at the end of this chapter, but first, let's work on changing the value of one of our variables.

Since CurrentAge was declared as a variable on *line 5*, as shown in *Figure 2.2*, the value it stores can be changed in the script or in the Unity **Inspector** since it's **public**. The updated value will then trickle down to wherever the variable is used in code. Let's see this in action:

1. Stop the game by clicking the **Play** button if the scene is still running.

2. Change **Current Age** to 18 in the **Inspector** panel.

3. Play the scene again and look at the new output in the **Console** panel:

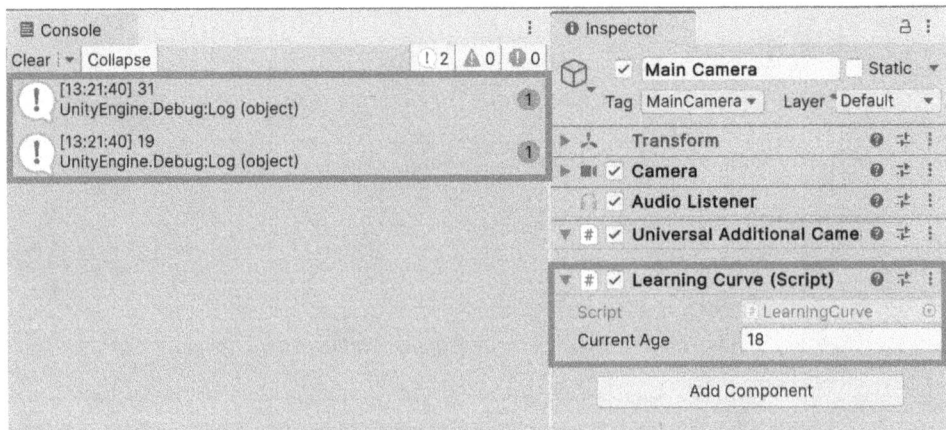

Figure 2.6: Unity console with debug logs and the LearningCurve script attached to Main Camera

The first output will still be 31 because we didn't change anything in the script, but the second output is now 19 because we changed the value of CurrentAge in the **Inspector**.

The goal here wasn't to go over variable syntax but to show how variables act as containers that can be created once and referenced elsewhere.

Now that we know how to create variables in C# and assign them values, we're ready to dive into the next important programming building block: methods!

Understanding methods

On their own, variables can't do much more than keep track of their assigned values. While this is vital, they are not very useful on their own in terms of creating meaningful applications. So, how do we go about creating actions and driving behavior in our code? The short answer is by using methods.

> **Important note**
>
> Before we get to what methods are and how to use them, we should clarify a small point of terminology. In the world of programming, you'll commonly see the terms *method* and *function* used interchangeably, especially in regard to Unity.
>
> Since C# is an object-oriented language (this is something that we'll cover in *Chapter 5*), we'll be using the term *method* for the rest of the book to conform to standard C# guidelines.
>
> When you come across the word *function* in the **Scripting Reference** or any other documentation, think *method*.

Methods drive actions

Like variables, defining programming methods can be tediously long-winded or dangerously brief; here's another three-pronged approach to consider:

- Conceptually, methods are how work gets done in an application.
- Technically, a method is a block of code containing executable statements that run when the method is called by name. Methods can take in arguments (also called parameters), which can be used inside the method's scope.
- Practically, a method is a container for a set of instructions that runs every time it's executed. These containers can also take in variables as inputs, which can only be referenced inside the method itself.

Taken all together, methods are the bones of any program—they connect everything and almost everything is built off of their structure.

You can find an in-depth guide to methods in the Microsoft C# documentation at https://docs. microsoft.com/en-us/dotnet/csharp/programming-guide/classes-and-structs/methods.

Methods are placeholders too

Let's take an oversimplified example of adding two numbers together to drive the concept home. When writing a script, you're essentially laying down lines of code for the computer to execute in sequential order. The first time you need to add two numbers together, you could just add them like in the following code block:

```
SomeNumber + AnotherNumber
```

But then you conclude that these numbers need to be added together somewhere else.

Instead of copying and pasting the same line of code, which results in sloppy or "spaghetti" code and should be avoided at all costs (every time you repeat code you multiply the places you need to update when making future changes), you can create a named method that will take care of this action:

```
AddNumbers()
{
    SomeNumber + AnotherNumber
}
```

Now AddNumbers holds a place in memory, just like a variable; however, instead of a value, it holds a block of instructions. Using the name of the method (or calling it) anywhere in a script puts the stored instructions at your fingertips without having to repeat any code:

```
AddNumbers()
```

If you find yourself writing the same lines of code over and over, you're likely missing a chance to simplify or condense repeated actions into common methods.

This produces what programmers jokingly call **spaghetti code** because it can get messy. You'll also hear programmers refer to a solution called the **Don't Repeat Yourself** (**DRY**) principle, which is a mantra you should keep in mind.

As before, once we've seen a new concept in pseudocode, it's best if we implement it ourselves, which is what we'll do in the *Introducing classes* section to drive it home.

Let's open up LearningCurve again and see how a method works in C#. Just like with the variables example, you'll want to copy the code into your script exactly as it appears in *Figure 2.7*. I've deleted the previous example code to make things neater, but you can, of course, keep it in your script for reference:

1. Open up LearningCurve in Visual Studio Code.

2. Add a new variable to *line 6*:

    ```
    public int YearsToAdd = 1;
    ```

3. Add a new method to *line 15* that adds `CurrentAge` and `YearsToAdd` together and prints out the result:

```
void ComputeAge()
{
    Debug.Log(CurrentAge + YearsToAdd);
}
```

4. Replace the code inside the `Start` method with the following line of code, which calls our new `ComputeAge` method:

```
void Start()
{
    ComputeAge();
}
```

5. Double-check that your code looks like the following screenshot before you run the script in Unity:

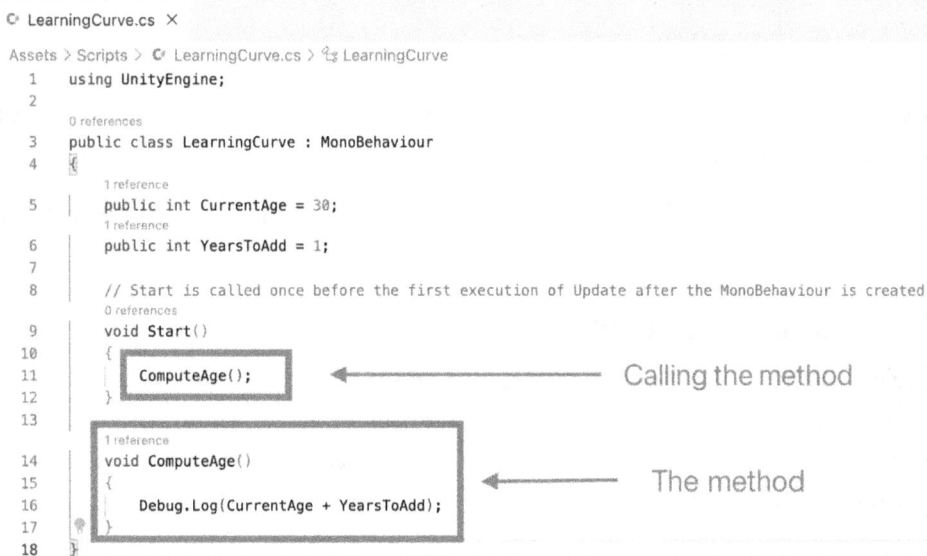

Figure 2.7: LearningCurve with the new ComputeAge method

6. Save the file, and then go back and hit **Play** in Unity to see the new **Console** output.

You defined your first method on *lines 14* to *17* and called it on *line 11*. Now, wherever ComputeAge() is called, the two variables will be added together and printed to the console, even if their values change. Remember, you set CurrentAge to 18 in the Unity **Inspector**, and the **Inspector** value will always override the value in a C# script:

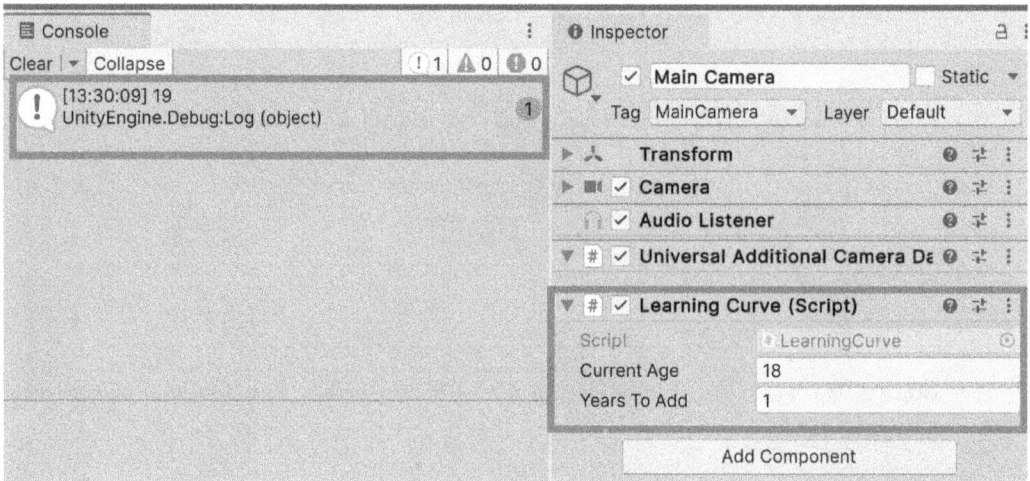

Figure 2.8: Console output from changing the variable value in the Inspector

Go ahead and try out different variable values in the **Inspector** panel to see this in action! More details on the actual code syntax of what you just wrote are coming up in the next chapter.

With a bird's-eye view of methods under our belts, we're ready to tackle the biggest topic in the programming landscape—classes!

Introducing classes

We've seen how variables store information and how methods perform actions, but our programming toolkit is still somewhat limited. We need a way of creating a sort of super container, containing variables and methods that can be referenced from within the container itself. Enter classes:

- Conceptually, a class holds related information, actions, and behaviors inside a single container. They can even communicate with each other.

- Technically, classes are data structures. They can contain variables, methods, and other programmatic information, all of which can be referenced when an object of the class is created.

- Practically, a class is a blueprint. It sets out the rules and regulations for any object (called an instance) created using the class blueprint.

You've probably realized that classes surround us not only in Unity but in the real world as well. Next, we'll take a look at the most common Unity class and how classes function in the wild.

You can find an in-depth guide to classes in the Microsoft C# documentation at https://docs. microsoft.com/en-us/dotnet/csharp/fundamentals/types/classes.

A common Unity class

Before you start wondering what a class looks like in C#, you should know that you've been working with a class this whole chapter. By default, every script created in Unity is a class, which you can see from the class keyword on *line 3*:

```
public class LearningCurve: MonoBehaviour
{
}
```

MonoBehaviour just means that this class can be attached to a GameObject in the Unity scene, and the two brackets mark the boundaries of the class—any code inside those brackets belongs to that class.

Classes can exist on their own, which we'll see when we create standalone classes in *Chapter 5*.

> **Important note**
>
> The terms *script* and *class* are sometimes used interchangeably in Unity resources. For consistency, I'll be referring to C# files as *scripts* if they're attached to GameObjects and as *classes* if they are standalone.

Classes are blueprints

For our last example, let's think about a local post office. It's a separate, self-contained environment that has properties, such as a physical address (a variable), and the ability to execute actions, such as sending out your mail (methods).

This makes a post office a great example of a potential class that we can outline in the following block of pseudocode:

```
public class PostOffice
{
    // Variables
    public string Address = "1234 Letter Opener Dr."

    // Methods
    DeliverMail() {}
    SendMail() {}
}
```

The main takeaway here is that when information and behaviors follow a predefined blueprint, complex actions and inter-class communication become possible. For instance, if we had another class that wanted to send a letter through our PostOffice class, it wouldn't have to wonder where to go to fire this action. We would create an instance of the PostOffice class and store it in its own unique variable so we can access it whenever we want (because there could be several post offices in your town and we need to tell them apart):

```
MyLocalPostOffice = new PostOffice()
```

Now we can call the SendMail function from the PostOffice instance, as follows:

```
MyLocalPostOffice().SendMail()
```

Alternatively, you could use it to look up the address of the post office, so you know where to post your letters:

```
MyLocalPostOffice().Address
```

If you're wondering about the use of periods (called **dot notation**) between words, we'll be diving into that in the next section—hold tight.

Communication among classes

Up until now, we've described classes and, by extension, Unity components as separate stand-alone entities; in reality, they are deeply intertwined. You'd be hard-pressed to create any kind of meaningful software application without invoking some kind of interaction or communication between classes.

In the preceding post office example, the example code made use of periods (or dots) to reference classes, variables, and methods. If you think of classes as directories of information, then **dot notation** is the indexing tool:

Any variables, methods, or other data types within a class can be accessed with dot notation. This applies to nested, or subclass, information as well, but we'll tackle all those subjects when we get to *Chapter 5*.

Dot notation is also what drives communication between classes. Whenever a class needs information about another class or wants to execute one of its methods, dot notation is used:

```
MyLocalPostOffice().DeliverMail()
```

Dot notation is sometimes referred to as the **. operator**, so don't be thrown off if you see it mentioned this way in the documentation.

If dot notation doesn't quite click with you yet, don't worry – it will. It's the bloodstream of the entire programming body, carrying information and context wherever it's needed.

Now that you know a little more about classes, let's talk about the tool you'll use the most in your programming career—comments!

Working with comments

You might have noticed that LearningCurve has an odd line of text (*line 8* in *Figure 2.6*) starting with two forward slashes, which were created by default with the script.

These are code comments! In C#, there are a few ways you can create comments, and Visual Studio Code (and other code editing applications) will often make it even easier with built-in shortcuts.

Some professionals wouldn't call commenting an essential building block of programming, but I'll have to respectfully disagree. Correctly commenting out your code with meaningful information is one of the most fundamental habits a new programmer can develop.

Single-line comments

The following single-line comment is like the one we included in LearningCurve:

```
// This is a single-line comment
```

Visual Studio Code doesn't compile lines starting with two forward slashes (without empty space) as code, so you can use them as much as needed to explain your code to others or your future self.

Multi-line comments

Since it's in the name, you'd be right to assume that single-line comments only apply to one line of code. If you want multi-line comments, you'll need to use a forward slash and an asterisk, (/* and */ as opening and closing characters respectively) around the comment text:

```
/* this is a
    multi-line comment */
```

You can also comment and uncomment blocks of code by highlighting them and using the *Cmd* + / shortcut on macOS and *Ctrl* + *K* + *C* on Windows.

Visual Studio Code also provides a handy auto-generated commenting feature; type in three forward slashes on the line preceding any line of code (variables, methods, classes, and more) and a summary comment block will appear, which you can see in *Figure 2.9*.

Seeing example comments is good, but putting them in your code is always better. It's never too early to start commenting!

Adding comments

Open up `LearningCurve` and add in three backslashes above the `ComputeAge()` method:

```
13
14  ∨      /// <summary>
15         /// Computes a modified age by adding two variables together
16         /// </summary>
           1 reference
17  ∨      void ComputeAge()
18         {
19             Debug.Log(CurrentAge + YearsToAdd);
20         }
21  
```

Figure 2.9: Triple-line comment automatically generated for a method

You should see a three-line comment with a space for a description of the method generated by Visual Studio Code, sandwiched between two <summary> tags. You can, of course, change the text, or add new lines by hitting *Enter* just as you would in a text document; just make sure not to touch the <summary> tags, or Visual Studio Code won't recognize the comments correctly.

The useful part about these detailed comments is clear when you want to know something about a method you've written. If you've used a triple-forward-slash comment, all you need to do is hover over the method name anywhere it's called within a class or script, and Visual Studio Code will pop up with your summary:

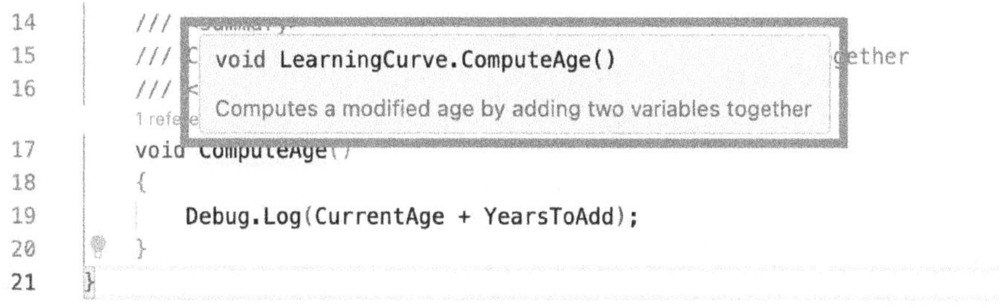

```
14      ///
15      ///  void LearningCurve.ComputeAge()                  gether
16      ///
        1 refe  Computes a modified age by adding two variables together
17      void ComputeAge()
18      {
19          Debug.Log(CurrentAge + YearsToAdd);
20      }
21  }
```

Figure 2.10: Visual Studio Code pop-up info box with the comment summary

Your basic programming toolkit is now complete (well, the theory drawer, at least). However, we still need to understand how everything we've learned in this chapter applies to the Unity game engine, which is what we'll be focusing on in the next section!

Putting the building blocks together

With the building blocks squared away, it's time to do a little Unity-specific housekeeping before wrapping up this chapter. Specifically, we need to know more about how Unity handles C# scripts attached to GameObjects.

For this example, we'll keep using our LearningCurve script and **Main Camera** GameObject.

Scripts become components

All GameObject components are scripts, whether they're written by you or the good people at Unity. The only difference is that Unity-specific components such as Transform and their respective scripts just aren't supposed to be edited by users.

The moment a script that you have created is dropped onto a GameObject, it becomes another component of that object, which is why it appears in the **Inspector** panel. To Unity, it walks, talks, and acts like any other component, complete with public variables underneath the component that can be changed at any time. Even though we aren't supposed to edit the components provided by Unity, we can still access their properties and methods, making them powerful development tools.

Unity also makes some automatic readability adjustments when a script becomes a component. You might have noticed in *Figures 2.4* and *2.6* that when we added `LearningCurve` to **Main Camera**, Unity displayed it as `Learning Curve`, with `CurrentAge` changing to `Current Age`.

We looked at how to update a variable in the **Inspector** panel in the *Variables act as placeholders* section, but it's important to reiterate how this works in more detail. There are three situations in which you can modify a property value:

- In **Play Mode** in the Unity Editor window (editor state)
- In **Development Mode** in the Unity Editor window (runtime state)
- In the Visual Studio Code editor

Changes made in **Play Mode** take effect in real time, which is great for testing and fine-tuning gameplay. However, it's important to note that any changes made while in **Play Mode** will be lost when you stop the game and return to **Development Mode**. It can be extremely frustrating to lose any changes you've made while in **Play Mode**, so please, please keep an eye on which mode you're in when playtesting.

Here's how to copy over any changes you made from **Play Mode**:

1. Select the three-vertical-dots icon at the top right of the component you changed and select **Copy Component**, as shown in *Figure 2.11*:

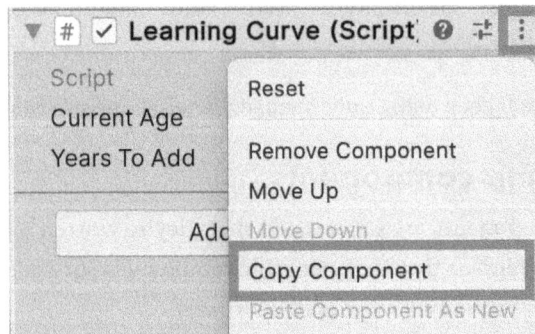

Figure 2.11: Copying component values from the Inspector

2. Exit **Play Mode** and right-click on the component again, this time selecting **Paste Component Values**, as shown in *Figure 2.12*:

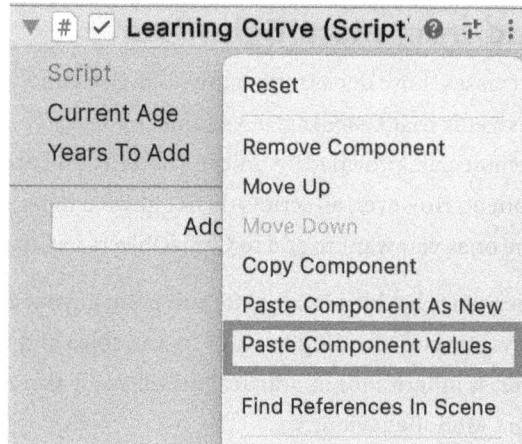

Figure 2.12: Pasting component values from the Inspector

When you're in **Development Mode**, any changes that you make to the variables will be saved by Unity. This means that if you were to quit Unity and then restart it, the changes would be retained.

The changes that you make to values in the **Inspector** panel while in **Play Mode** do not modify your script, but they will override any values you had assigned in your script when in **Development Mode**.

Any changes made in **Play Mode** will always reset automatically when you stop **Play Mode**. If you need to undo any changes made in the **Inspector** panel, you can reset the script to its default (sometimes called **initial**) values. Click on the three-vertical-dots icon to the right of any component, and then select **Reset**, as shown in the following screenshot:

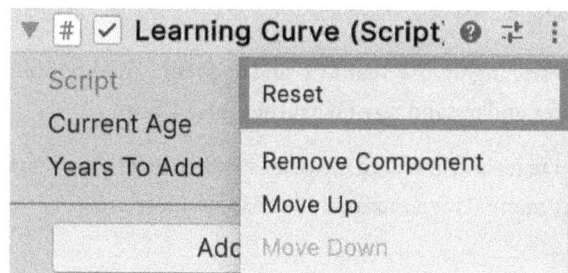

Figure 2.13: Script reset option in the Inspector

This should give you some peace of mind—if your variables get out of hand, there's always the hard reset.

A helping hand from MonoBehaviour

Since C# scripts are classes, how does Unity know to make some scripts components and not others? The short answer is that LearningCurve (and any script created in Unity) inherits from MonoBehaviour (a default class provided by Unity). This tells Unity that the C# class can be transformed into a component. However, all scripts do not have to inherit from MonoBehaviour—it's only necessary for the ones you want to add to GameObjects in your Unity scenes.

The topic of class inheritance is a bit advanced for this point of your programming journey; think of it as the MonoBehaviour class lending a few of its variables and methods to LearningCurve. *Chapter 5* will cover class inheritance in practical detail. We'll also go over how to write classes that don't inherit from MonoBehaviour.

Unity application lifecycle

The Start() and Update() methods that we've used belong to MonoBehaviour, which Unity runs automatically on any script attached to a GameObject. The Start() method runs once when the scene starts playing, while the Update() method runs once per frame (depending on the frame rate of your machine).

Now that your familiarity with Unity's documentation has gotten a nice bump, I've put together a short optional challenge for you to tackle!

> **Hero's trial—MonoBehaviour in the Scripting API**
>
> Now it's time for you to get comfortable using the Unity documentation on your own, and what better way than to look up some of the common MonoBehaviour methods?
>
> Try searching for the Start() and Update() methods in the Scripting API to gain a better understanding of what they do in Unity.
>
> If you're feeling brave, go the extra step and have a look at the MonoBehaviour class in the manual for a more detailed explanation.

Summary

We've come a long way in a few short pages, but understanding the overarching theory of fundamental concepts such as variables, methods, and classes will give you a strong foundation to build on.

Bear in mind that these building blocks have very real counterparts in the real world. Variables hold values like mailboxes hold letters; methods store instructions like recipes, to be followed for a predefined result; and classes are blueprints just like real blueprints. You can't build a house without a well-thought-out design to follow if you expect it to stay standing.

The rest of this book will take you on a deep dive into C# syntax from scratch, starting with more detail in the next chapter on how to create variables, manage value types, and work with simple and complex methods.

Pop quiz: C# building blocks

    a.   What is the main purpose of a variable?

    b.   What role do methods play in scripts?

    c.   How does a script become a component?

    d.   What is the purpose of dot notation?

Don't forget to check your answers against mine in the *Pop Quiz Answers* appendix to see how you did!

Subscribe to Game Dev Assembly Newsletter!

We are excited to introduce **Game Dev Assembly**, our brand-new newsletter dedicated to everything game development. Whether you're a programmer, designer, artist, animator, or studio lead, you'll get exclusive insights, industry trends, and expert tips to help you build better games and grow your skills. Sign up today and become part of a growing community of creators, innovators, and game changers: `https://packt.link/gamedev-newsletter`.

Scan the QR code to join instantly!

Unlock this book's exclusive benefits now

UNLOCK NOW

Scan this QR code or go to `https://packtpub.com/unlock`,
then search this book by name.

Note: Keep your purchase invoice ready before you start.

3

Diving into Variables, Types, and Methods

The initial steps into any programming language are plagued with a fundamental issue—you can understand the words being typed out, but not the meaning behind them. Normally, this would be cause for a paradox, but programming is a special case.

C# is not its own language; it's written in English. The discrepancy between the words you use every day and the code in Visual Studio comes from missing context, which is something that must be learned all over again. You know how to say and spell the words used in C#, but what you don't know is where, when, why, and, most importantly, how they make up the syntax of the language.

This chapter marks our departure from programming theory and the beginning of our journey into actual coding. We'll talk about accepted formatting, debugging techniques, and putting together more complex examples of variables and methods. There's a lot of ground to cover, but by the time you reach the last quiz, you'll be comfortable with the following high-level topics:

- Writing proper C#
- Debugging your code
- Understanding variables
- Introducing operators
- Defining methods

Let's get started!

Writing proper C#

Lines of code function like sentences, meaning they need to have some sort of separating or ending character. Every line of C# (called a **statement**) *must* end with a semicolon to separate them for the code compiler to process.

However, there's a catch that you need to be aware of. Unlike the written word we're all familiar with, a C# statement doesn't technically have to be on a single line; whitespace and new lines are ignored by the code compiler. For example, a simple variable could be written like this:

```
public string FirstName = "Harrison";
```

Alternatively, it could also be written as follows:

```
public
string
FirstName

=

"Harrison";
```

> 💡 **Quick tip**: Enhance your coding experience with the **AI Code Explainer** and **Quick Copy** features. Open this book in the next-gen Packt Reader. Click the **Copy** button (1) to quickly copy code into your coding environment, or click the **Explain** button (2) to get the AI assistant to explain a block of code to you.
>
> ```
>                                                              Copy        Explain
> function calculate(a, b) {                                    1            2
>   return {sum: a + b};
> };
> ```

> 📕 **The next-gen Packt Reader** is included for free with the purchase of this book. Scan the QR code OR go to `https://packtpub.com/unlock`, then use the search bar to find this book by name. Double-check the edition shown to make sure you get the right one.

These two code snippets are both perfectly acceptable to Visual Studio, but the second option is highly discouraged in the software community as it makes code extremely hard to read. The idea is to write your programs as efficiently and clearly as possible.

There will be times when a statement will be too long to reasonably fit on a single line, but those are few and far between. Just make sure that it's formatted in a way someone else can understand, and don't forget the semicolon:

```
Debug.Log("This is an extremely long statement and may not fit on a
          single line, but do your best to format these cases so
             everything is legible!");
```

The second formatting rule you need to drill into your coding muscle memory is the use of curly brackets or braces: {}. Methods, classes, and interfaces all need a set of curly brackets after their declaration.

The traditional practice in C# is to include each bracket on a new line, as shown in the following method:

```
public void MethodName()
{
}
```

However, you might see the first curly bracket located on the same line as the declaration out in the wild. It's all down to personal preference:

```
public void MethodName() {
}
```

While this isn't something to tear your hair out over, the important thing is to be consistent. In this book, we'll stick with "pure" C# code, which will always put each bracket on a new line, while C# examples that have to do with Unity and game development will often follow the second example.

A good, consistent formatting style is paramount when starting in programming, but so is being able to see the fruits of your work. In the next section, we'll talk about how to print out variables and information straight to the Unity console.

Debugging your code

While we're working through practical examples, we'll need a way to print out information and feedback to the **Console** window in the Unity editor. This information is just to help you mark where and when things are happening in your code and won't be visible in the game itself. The programmatic term for this is **debugging**, and both C# and Unity provide helper methods to make this process easier for developers. You already debugged your code from the last chapter, but we didn't go into much detail about how it actually works. Let's fix that.

Whenever I ask you to debug or print something out, use one of the following methods:

- For simple text or individual variables, use the standard Debug.Log() method. The text needs to be inside a set of parentheses and variables can be used directly with no added characters:

  ```
  Debug.Log("Text goes here!");
  Debug.Log(CurrentAge);
  ```

  Adding the above code to the Start() method inside LearningCurve.cs would produce the following in the **Console** panel:

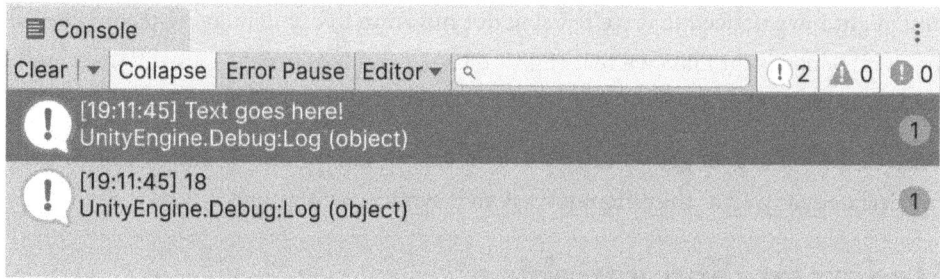

Figure 3.1: Observing the Debug.Log output

> **Note**
>
> To provide a complete view of the Unity editor, all our screenshots are taken in full-screen mode. For color versions of all book images, use the following link: `https://packt.link/gbp/9781805808718`.

- For more complex debugging, use `Debug.LogFormat()`. This will let you place variables inside the printed text by using placeholders. These are marked with a pair of curly brackets, each containing an index. An **index** is a regular number, starting at 0 and increasing sequentially by 1. In the following example, the `{0}` placeholder is replaced with the `CurrentAge` value, `{1}` with `FirstName`, and so on:

```
Debug.LogFormat("Text goes here -> {0} and {1} are variable
    placeholders", CurrentAge, YearsToAdd);
```

Adding the above code to the `Start()` method in `LearningCurve.cs` would produce the following in the **Console** panel:

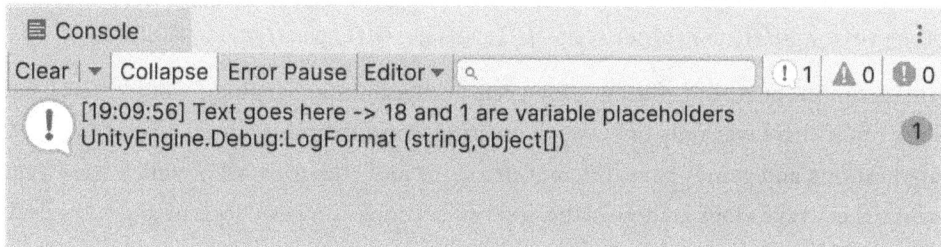

Figure 3.2: Observing Debug.LogFormat

You might have noticed that we're using **dot notation** in our debugging techniques, and you'd be right! Debug is the class we're using, and Log() and LogFormat() are different methods that we can use from that class.

With the power of debugging under our belts, we can safely move on and dive into how variables are declared, as well as the different ways that syntax can play out.

Understanding variables

In the previous chapter, we saw how variables are written and touched on the high-level functionality that they provide. However, we're still missing the syntax that makes all that possible, so let's start with the very basics: declaring variables.

Declaring variables

Variables don't just appear at the top of a C# script; they have to be declared according to certain rules and requirements. At its most basic level, a variable statement needs to satisfy the following requirements:

- The type of data the variable will store needs to be specified
- The variable has to have a unique name
- If there is an assigned value, it must match the specified type
- The variable declaration needs to end with a semicolon

The result of adhering to these rules is the following syntax:

```
dataType UniqueName = value;
```

Variables need unique names to avoid conflicts with words that have already been taken by C#, which are called **keywords**. You can find the full list of protected keywords at https://docs.microsoft.com/en-us/dotnet/csharp/language-reference/keywords/index.

This is simple, neat, and efficient. However, a programming language wouldn't be useful in the long run if there was only one way of creating something as pervasive as variables. Complex applications and games have different use cases and scenarios, all of which have a unique C# syntax. Let's take a look at these in the next two sections as we explore type and value declarations.

Type and value declarations

The most common scenario for creating variables is one that has all of the required information available when the declaration is made. For instance, if we knew a player's age, storing it would be as easy as doing the following:

```
int CurrentAge = 32;
```

Here, all of the basic requirements have been met:

- A data type is specified, which is int (short for *integer*, which is a fancy word for a whole number)
- A unique name is used, which is CurrentAge
- 32 is an integer, which matches the specified data type
- The statement ends with a semicolon

However, there will be scenarios where you'll want to declare a variable without knowing its value right away. We'll talk about this topic in the following section.

Type-only declarations

Consider another scenario—you know the type of data you want a variable to store and its name, but not its value. The value will be computed and assigned somewhere else, but you still need to declare the variable at the top of the script. This situation is perfect for a type-only declaration:

```
int CurrentAge;
```

Only the type (int) and unique name (CurrentAge) are defined, but the statement is still valid because we've followed the rules. With no assigned value, default values will be assigned according to the variable's type. In this case, CurrentAge will be set to 0, which matches the int type. As soon as the actual value of the variable becomes available, it can easily be set in a separate statement by referencing the variable name and assigning it a value:

```
CurrentAge = 32;
```

You can find a complete list of all C# types and their default values at https://docs.microsoft.com/en-us/dotnet/csharp/language-reference/builtin-types/default-values.

At this point, you might be asking why, so far, our variables haven't included the `public` keyword, called an *access modifier*, which we saw in earlier scripting examples. The answer is that we didn't have the necessary foundation to talk about them with any clarity. Now that we have that foundation, it's time to revisit them in detail.

Using access modifiers

Now that the basic syntax is no longer a mystery, let's get into the finer details of variable statements. Since we read code from left to right, it makes sense to begin our variable deep dive with the keyword that traditionally comes first—an **access modifier**.

Take a quick look back at the variables we used in the preceding chapter in `LearningCurve` and you'll see they had an extra keyword at the front of their statements: `public`. This is the variable's access modifier. Think of it as a security setting, determining who and what can access the variable's information.

Any variable that isn't marked `public` is defaulted to `private` and won't show up in the Unity **Inspector** panel. If you include a modifier, the updated syntax recipe we put together at the beginning of this chapter will look like this:

```
accessModifier dataType UniqueName = value;
```

While explicit access modifiers aren't necessary when declaring a variable, it's a good habit to get into as a new programmer. That extra word goes a long way toward readability and professionalism in your code.

There are four main access modifiers available in C#, but the two you'll be working with most often as a beginner are the following:

- `public`: This is available in any script without restriction.
- `private`: This is only available in the class they're created in (which is called the containing class). Any variable without an access modifier will default to `private`.

The two advanced modifiers have the following characteristics:

- **Protected**: Accessible from their containing class or types derived from it
- **Internal**: Only available in the current assembly (an automatically generated file that bundles your code, resources, and pretty much everything else together in a neat package)

There are specific use cases for each of these modifiers, but until we get to the advanced chapters, don't worry about **protected** and **internal**.

Two combined modifiers also exist, but we won't be using them in this book. You can find more information about them at https://docs.microsoft.com/en-us/dotnet/csharp/language-reference/keywords/access-modifiers.

Let's try out some access modifiers of our own! Just like information in real life, some data needs to be protected or shared with specific people. If there's no need for a variable to be changed in the **Inspector** window or accessed from other scripts, it's a good candidate for a private access modifier.

Perform the following steps to update LearningCurve:

1. Change the access modifier in front of CurrentAge from public to private and save the file.
2. Go back into Unity, select **Main Camera,** and take a look at what changed in the **Learning Curve** section:

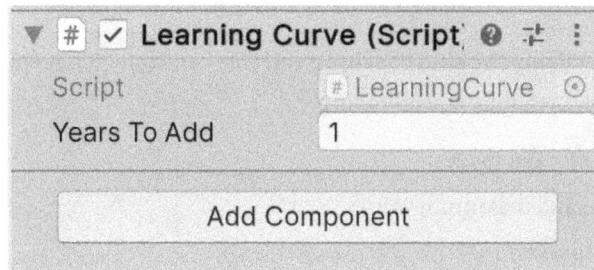

Figure 3.3: LearningCurve script component attached to Main Camera

Since CurrentAge is now private, it's no longer visible in the **Inspector** window and can only be accessed within the LearningCurve script in code. If we click **Play**, the script will still work exactly as it did before.

This is a good start on our journey into variables, but we still need to know more about what kinds of data they can store. This is where data types come in, which we'll look at in the next section.

Working with variable types

Assigning a specific type to a variable is an important choice, one that trickles down into every interaction a variable has over its entire lifespan. Since C# is what's called a *strongly typed* or *type-safe* language, every variable must have a data type without exception. In comparison, programming languages such as JavaScript, for example, are non-type-safe. This means that there are specific rules when it comes to performing operations with certain types, and regulations when converting a given variable type into another.

Common built-in types

All data types in C# trickle down (or **derive**, in programmatic terms) from a common ancestor: System.Object. This hierarchy, called the **Common Type System** (**CTS**), means that different types have a lot of shared functionality. The following figure lays out some of the most common data type options and the values they store:

Type	Contents of the variable
int	A simple integer, such as the number 3
float	A number with a decimal, such as the number 3.14
string	Characters in double quotes, such as,"Watch me go now"
bool	A Boolean, either **true** or **false**

Figure 3.4: Common data types for variables

In addition to specifying the kind of value a variable can store, types contain added information about themselves, including the following:

- Required storage space
- Minimum and maximum values
- Allowed operations
- Location in memory
- Accessible methods
- Base (derived) type

If this seems overwhelming, take a deep breath. Working with all of the types C# offers is a perfect example of using documentation over memorization. Pretty soon, using even the most complex custom types will feel like second nature.

You can find a complete list of all of the C# built-in types and their specifications at https://docs.microsoft.com/en-us/dotnet/csharp/programming-guide/types/index.

Before the list of types in *Figure 3.4* gets too overwhelming, it's best to experiment with them. After all, the best way to learn something new is to use it, break it, and then learn to fix it.

Go ahead and open up LearningCurve and add a new variable for each type in the preceding figure from the *Common built-in types* section. The names and values you use are up to you; just make sure they're marked as public so we can see them in the **Inspector** window. If you need inspiration, take a look at my code:

```
public class LearningCurve : MonoBehaviour
{
    private int CurrentAge = 30;
    public int YearsToAdd = 1;

    public float Pi = 3.14f;
    public string FirstName = "Harrison";
    public bool IsAuthor = true;

    // Start is called before the first frame update
    void Start()
    {
        ComputeAge();
    }

    /// <summary>
    /// Time for action - adding comments
    /// Computes a modified age integer
    /// </summary>
    void ComputeAge()
    {
        Debug.Log(CurrentAge + YearsToAdd);
    }
}
```

When dealing with string types, the actual text value needs to be inside a pair of double quotes, while float values need to end with a lowercase f, as you can see with FirstName and Pi.

All our different variable types are now visible. Take note of the bool variable that Unity displays as a checkbox (true is checked and false is unchecked).

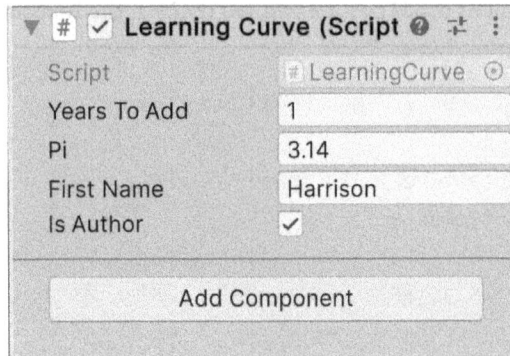

Figure 3.5: The LearningCurve script component with common variable types

Remember, any variables you declare as private won't show up in the **Inspector** window. Before we move on to conversions, we need to touch on a common and powerful application of the **string data type**—namely, the creation of strings that have variables interspersed at will.

While number types behave as you'd expect from grade school math, strings are a different story. It's possible to insert variables and literal values directly into text by starting with a $ character, which is called **string interpolation**. You've already used an interpolated string in your LogFormat() debugging; adding the $ character lets you use them anywhere!

Let's create a simple interpolated string of our own inside LearningCurve to see this in action. Print out the interpolated string inside the Start() method directly after ComputeAge() is called:

```
void Start()
{
    ComputeAge();
    Debug.Log($"A string can have variables like {FirstName}
        inserted directly!");
}
```

In the **Console** window, this string will output the following text:

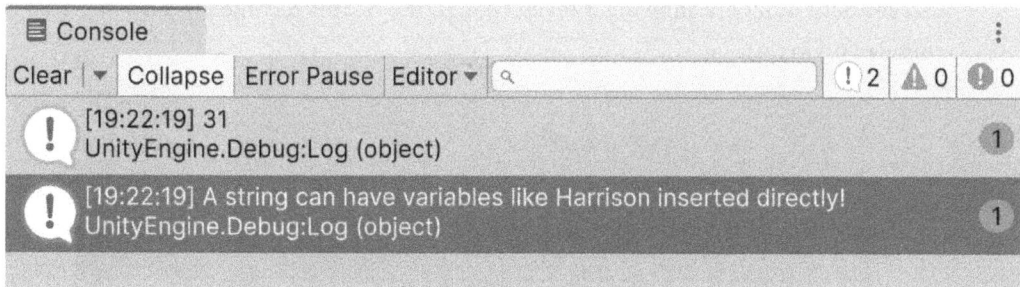

Figure 3.6: Console showing debug log output

Notice that because `CurrentAge` is now `private`, it defaults to using the value we set in code (30). It's also possible to create interpolated strings using the + operator, which we'll talk about in the *Introducing operators* section. For now, let's move on to type conversions.

Type conversions

We've already seen that variables can only hold values of their declared types, but there will be situations where you'll need to combine variables of different types. In programming terminology, these are called **conversions**, and they come in two main flavors:

- **Implicit**: Implicit conversions take place automatically, usually when a smaller value will fit into another variable type without any rounding. For example, any integer can be implicitly converted into a double or float value without additional code, so if we added the code below to the `Start()` method in `LearningCurve`:

```
int MyInteger = 3;
float MyFloat = MyInteger;

Debug.Log(MyInteger);
Debug.Log(MyFloat);
```

The output in the **Console** panel can be seen in the following screenshot, where you can see both numbers showing **3** (even though the float is technically 3.0—the zero is rounded off in C#):

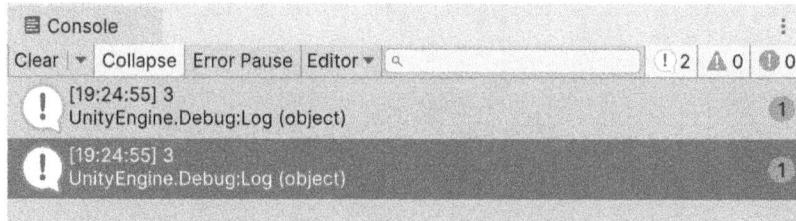

Figure 3.7: Implicit type conversion debug log output

- **Explicit**: Explicit conversions are needed when there is a risk of losing a variable's information during the conversion. For example, if we wanted to convert a double value into an int value, we would have to explicitly cast (convert) it by adding the destination type in parentheses before the value we want to convert.

  This tells the compiler that we are aware that data (or precision) might be lost:

  ```
  int ExplicitConversion = (int)3.14;
  Debug.Log(ExplicitConversion);
  ```

  In this explicit conversion, 3.14 would be rounded down to 3, losing the decimal values:

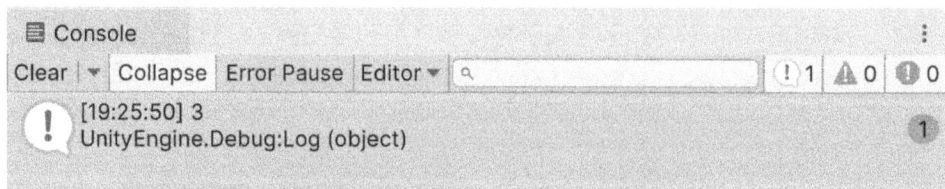

Figure 3.8: Explicit type conversion debug log output

C# provides built-in methods for explicitly converting values to common types. For example, any type can be converted into a string value with the ToString() method, while the Convert class can handle more complicated conversions. You can find more info about these features under the **Methods** section at: https://docs.microsoft.com/en-us/dotnet/api/system.convert?view=netframework-4.7.2.

So far, we've learned that types have rules regarding their interactions, operations, and conversion, but how do we handle a situation where we need to store a variable of an unknown type?

This might sound crazy, but think about a data-download scenario—you know the information is coming into your game, but you're not sure what form it will take. We'll discuss how to handle this in the following section.

Inferred declarations

Luckily, C# can *infer* a variable's type from its assigned value. For example, the var keyword can let the program know that the type of the data, CurrentAge, needs to be determined by its value of 32, which is an integer:

```
var CurrentAge = 32;
```

While this is handy in certain situations, don't be suckered into the lazy programming habit of using inferred variable declarations for everything. This adds a lot of guesswork to your code, where it should be crystal clear. Inferred variable declarations should really only be used when you're testing code and don't know the data type that's being stored. Once you do, changing the variable declaration to the specific type is recommended to avoid runtime errors later on. Before we wrap up our discussion on data types and conversion, we do need to briefly touch on the idea of creating custom types, which we'll do next.

Custom types

When we're talking about data types, it's important to understand early on that numbers and words (referred to as **literal values**) are not the only kinds of values a variable can store. For instance, a class, struct, or enumeration can be stored as variables. We will introduce these topics in *Chapter 5* and explore them in greater detail in *Chapter 10*.

Types are complicated, and the only way to get comfortable with them is by using them. However, here are some important things to keep in mind:

- All variables need to have a specified type (be it explicit or inferred).
- Variables can only hold values of their assigned type (a string value can't be assigned an int variable).
- If a variable needs to be assigned or combined with a variable of a different type, a conversion needs to take place (either implicit or explicit).

The C# compiler can infer a variable's type from its value using the var keyword, but this should only be used when the type isn't known when it's created.

That's a lot of nitty-gritty detail we've just jammed into a few sections, but we're not done yet. We still need to understand how naming conventions work in C#, as well as where the variables live in our scripts.

Naming variables

Picking names for your variables might seem like an afterthought in light of everything we've learned about access modifiers and types, but it shouldn't be a straightforward choice. Clear and consistent naming conventions in your code will not only make it more readable but will also ensure that other developers on your team understand your intentions without having to ask.

The first rule when it comes to naming a variable is that the name you give it should be meaningful; the second rule is that you use **Pascal case** (where the first letter of each compound word in a variable name is capitalized — i.e., HelloWorld).

C# does support **camel casing** (where the first letter of the variable name doesn't need to be capitalized — i.e., helloWorld), so if you're coming from another programming language such as Java or C and are more comfortable with that formatting, the compiler won't complain. Pascal case is the more generally accepted way of doing things in C#, so we'll use that going forward.

Let's take a common example from games and declare a variable to store a player's health:

```
public int Health = 100;
```

If you find yourself declaring a variable like this, alarm bells should be going off in your head. Whose health? Is it storing the maximum or minimum value? What other code will be affected when this value changes? These are all questions that should be easily answered by a meaningful variable name; you don't want to find yourself confused by your own code in a week or a month.

With that said, let's try to make this a bit better using a Pascal case name:

```
public int MaxPlayerHealth = 100;
```

Remember, Pascal case starts each word in the variable name with an uppercase letter.

That's much better. With a little thought, we've updated the variable name with meaning and context. Since there is no technical limit in terms of how long a variable name can be, you might find yourself going overboard and writing out ridiculously descriptive names, which will give you problems just as much as a short, non-descriptive name would.

As a general rule, make a variable name as descriptive as it needs to be—no more, no less. Find your style and stick to it.

Understanding variable scope

We're getting to the end of our dive into variables, but there's still one more important topic we need to cover: **scope**. Similar to access modifiers, which determine the outside classes that can grab a variable's information, the variable scope is the term used to describe where a given variable exists and its access point within its containing class.

There are three main levels of variable scope in C#:

- **Global scope** refers to a variable that can be accessed by an entire program—in this case, a game. C# doesn't directly support global variables, but the concept is useful in certain cases, which we'll cover in *Chapter 10*.
- **Class scope** or **member scope** refers to a variable that is accessible anywhere in its containing class.
- **Local scope** refers to a variable that is only accessible inside the specific method or block of code it's created in.

Take a look at the following screenshot. You don't need to put this into LearningCurve right now, it's just to help you visualize what's happening:

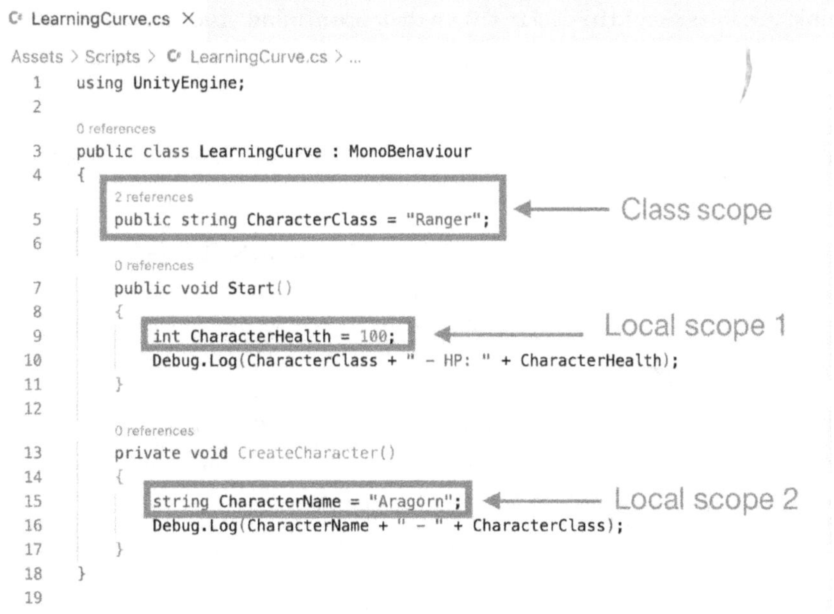

Figure 3.9: Diagram of different scopes in the LearningCurve script

When we talk about code blocks, we're referring to the area inside any set of curly brackets. These brackets serve as a kind of visual hierarchy in programming; the farther right-indented they are, the deeper they are nested in the class.

Let's break down the class and local scope variables in *Figure 3.9*:

- `CharacterClass` is declared at the very top of the class, which means we can reference it by name anywhere inside `LearningCurve`. You might hear this concept referred to as **variable visibility**, which is a good way of thinking about it.
- `CharacterHealth` is declared inside the `Start()` method, which means it is only visible inside that block of code. We can still access `CharacterClass` from `Start()` with no issue, but if we attempted to access `CharacterHealth` from anywhere but `Start()`, we would receive an error.
- `CharacterName` is in the same boat as `CharacterHealth`; it can only be accessed from the `CreateCharacter()` method. This was just to illustrate that there can be multiple, even nested, local scopes in a single class.

If you spend enough time around programmers, you'll hear discussions (or arguments, depending on the time of day) about the best place to declare a variable. The answer is simpler than you might think: variables should be declared with their use in mind. If you have a variable that needs to be accessed throughout a class, make it a class variable. If you only need a variable in a specific section of code, declare it as a local variable.

Note that only class variables can be viewed in the **Inspector** window, which isn't an option for local or global variables.

With naming and scope in our toolbox, let's transport ourselves back to middle school math class and relearn how arithmetic operations work all over again!

Introducing operators

Operator symbols in programming languages represent the *arithmetic, assignment, relational*, and *logical* functionality that types can perform. Arithmetic operators represent basic math functions, while assignment operators perform math and assignment functions together on a given value. Relational and logical operators evaluate conditions between multiple values, such as *greater than, less than*, and *equal to*.

C# also offers bitwise and miscellaneous operators, but these won't come into play for you until you're well on your way to creating more complex applications. At this point, it only makes sense to cover arithmetic and assignment operators; we'll get to relational and logical functionality when it becomes relevant in *Chapter 4*.

You're already familiar with the arithmetic operator symbols from school:

- + for addition
- – for subtraction
- / for division
- * for multiplication

C# operators follow the conventional order of operations, that is, evaluating parentheses first, then exponents, then multiplication, then division, then addition, and finally, subtraction.

For instance, the following equations will provide different results, even though they contain the same values and operators:

```
5 + 4 - 3 / 2 * 1 = 8
5 + (4 - 3) / 2 * 1 = 5
```

Operators work the same when applied to variables as they do with literal values. Assignment operators can be used as a shorthand replacement for any math operation by using any arithmetic and equals symbol together. For example, if we wanted to multiply a variable, you could use the following code:

```
int CurrentAge = 32;
CurrentAge = CurrentAge * 2;
```

The second, alternative, way to do this is shown here:

```
int CurrentAge = 32;
CurrentAge *= 2;
```

The equals symbol is also considered an assignment operator in C#. The other assignment symbols follow the same syntax pattern as our preceding multiplication example: +=, -=, and /= for add and assign, subtract and assign, and divide and assign, respectively.

Strings are a special case when it comes to operators as they can use the addition symbol to create patchwork text. For example, put the following code into the `Start()` method:

```
string FullName = "Harrison " + "Ferrone";
```

This will produce the following when logged in to the **Console** panel:

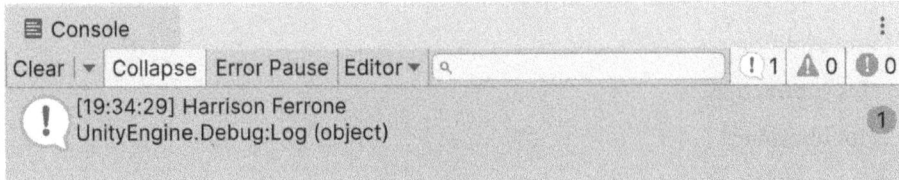

Figure 3.10: Using operators on strings

This approach tends to produce clunky code, making string interpolation the preferred method for putting together different bits of text in most cases.

Take note that arithmetic operators don't work on all data types. For example, the * and / operators don't work on string values, and none of these operators work on Booleans. Having learned that types have rules that govern what kind of operations and interactions they can have, we'll give it a shot in the *Understanding methods* section.

Let's do a little experiment. We'll try to multiply our `string` and `float` variables together, as we did earlier with our numbers:

Figure 3.11: Visual Studio incorrect type operation error message

Look at Visual Studio Code and you'll see we've got an error message letting us know that a `string` type and a `float` type can't be multiplied. This error will also show up in the Unity **Console** window and won't let the project build.

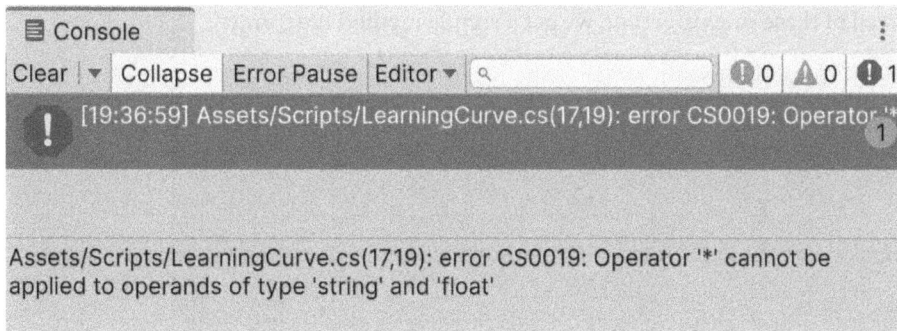

Figure 3.12: Console showing operator errors on incompatible data types

Whenever you see this type of error, go back and inspect your variable types for incompatibilities.

We must clean up this example, as the compiler won't allow us to run our game at this point. Choose between a pair of backslashes (//) at the beginning of the `Debug.Log(FirstName*Pi)` line, or delete it altogether.

That's as far as we need to go in terms of variables and types for the moment. Be sure to test yourself on the quiz at the end of this chapter before moving on!

Understanding methods

In the previous chapter, we briefly touched on the role that methods play in our programs; namely, they store and execute instructions, just like variables store values. Now, we need to understand the syntax of method declarations and how they drive action and behavior in our classes.

As with variables, method declarations have their basic requirements, which are as follows:

- The type of data that will be returned by the method (methods don't all have to return anything, so this can be void)
- A unique name, starting with a capital letter
- A pair of parentheses following the method name
- A pair of curly brackets marking the method body (where instructions are stored)

Putting all of these rules together, we get a simple method blueprint:

```
returnType UniqueName()
{
    method body
}
```

Let's break down the default `Start()` method in `LearningCurve` as a practical example:

```
void Start()
{
}
```

In the preceding output, we can see the following:

- The method starts with the void keyword, which is used as the method's return type if it doesn't return anything.
- The method has a unique name within the class. You can use the same name in different classes, but you should aim to always make your names unique no matter what.
- The method has a pair of parentheses after its name to hold any potential parameters.
- The method body is defined by a set of curly brackets.

In general, if you have a method that has an empty method body, it's good practice to delete it from the class. You always want to be pruning your scripts of unused code.

Like variables, methods can also have security levels. However, they can also have input parameters, both of which we'll be discussing next!

Declaring methods

Methods can also have the same four access modifiers that are available to variables, as well as input parameters. Parameters are variable placeholders that can be passed into methods and accessed inside them. The number of input parameters you can use isn't limited, but each one needs to be separated by a comma, show its data type, and have a unique name.

Think of method parameters as variable placeholders whose values can be used inside the method body. If we apply these options, our updated blueprint will look like this:

```
accessModifier returnType UniqueName(parameterType parameterName)
{
    method body
}
```

If there is no explicit access modifier, the method defaults to private. A private method, like a private variable, cannot be called from other scripts. To call a method (meaning to run or execute its instructions), we simply use its name, followed by a pair of parentheses, with or without parameters, and cap it off with a semicolon:

```
// Without parameters
UniqueName();
// With parameters
UniqueName(parameterVariable);
```

Like variables, every method has a fingerprint that describes its access level, return type, and parameters. This is called its **method signature**. Essentially, a method's signature marks it as unique to the compiler so Visual Studio knows what to do with it.

Now that we understand how methods are structured, let's create one of our own.

The *Methods are placeholders too* section in *Chapter 2* had you blindly copy a method called ComputeAge() into LearningCurve without you knowing what you were getting into. This time, let's purposefully create a method:

1. Declare a public method with a void return type called GenerateCharacter():

    ```
    public void GenerateCharacter()
    {
    }
    ```

2. Add a simple Debug.Log() inside the new method and print out a character name from your favorite game or movie:

    ```
    Debug.Log("Character: Spike");
    ```

3. Call GenerateCharacter() inside the Start() method:

    ```
    void Start()
    {
        GenerateCharacter();
    }
    ```

4. Hit **Play** to see the output in the following figure:

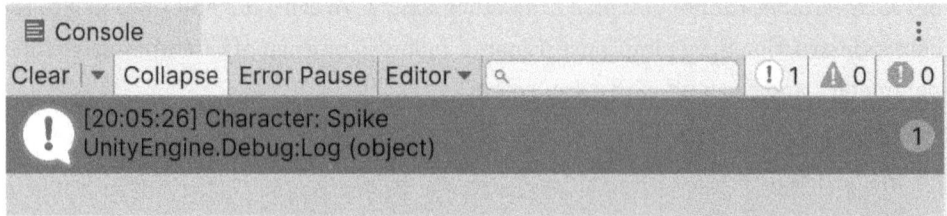

Figure 3.13: Console showing results of the GenerateCharacter method

When the game starts up, Unity automatically calls Start(), which, in turn, calls our
GenerateCharacter() method and prints the result to the **Console** window.

If you have read enough documentation, you'll see different terminology related to methods.
Throughout the rest of this book, when a method is created or declared, I'll refer to this as *defining*
a method. Similarly, I'll refer to running or executing a method as *calling* that method.

The power of naming is integral to the entirety of the programming landscape, so it shouldn't be
a surprise that we're going to revisit naming conventions for methods before moving on.

Naming methods

Like variables, methods need unique, meaningful names to distinguish them in code. Methods drive
actions, so it's a good practice to name them with that in mind. For example, GenerateCharacter()
sounds like a command, which reads well when you call it in a script, whereas a name such as
Summary() is bland and doesn't paint a very clear picture of what the method will accomplish.
Like variables, method names are written in Pascal case.

Methods as logic detours

We've seen that lines of code execute sequentially in the order they're written, but bringing
methods into the picture introduces a unique situation. Calling a method tells the program to
take a detour into the method instructions, run them one by one, and then resume sequential
execution where the method was called.

Look at the following screenshot and see whether you can figure out in what order the debug
logs will be printed out to the console. Again, adding the following code to the LearningCurve.
cs script is optional; it's mainly an analytical exercise:

```
8        // Start is called once before the first execution of Update after
         0 references
9   ∨    void Start()
10       {
11           Debug.Log("Choose a character ->");
12           GenerateCharacter();
13           Debug.Log("A fine choice!");
14       }
15

         1 reference
16  ∨    public void GenerateCharacter()
17       {
18           Debug.Log("Character: Spike");
19       }
```

Figure 3.14: Considering the order of debug logs

These are the steps that occur:

1. "Choose a character ->" prints out first because it's the first line of code.

2. When GenerateCharacter() is called, the program jumps to *line 21*, prints out Character: Spike, and then resumes execution at *line 17*.

3. "A fine choice!" prints out last, after all the lines in GenerateCharacter() have finished running.

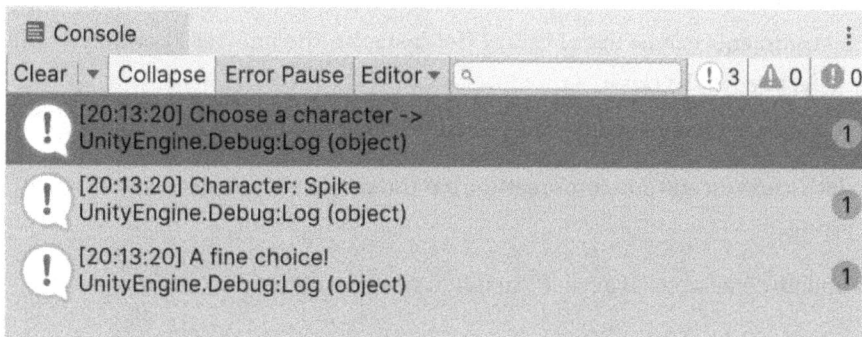

Figure 3.15: Console showing the output of character-building code

Now, methods in themselves wouldn't be very useful beyond simple examples like these if we couldn't add parameter values to them, which is what we'll do next.

Specifying parameters

Chances are your methods aren't always going to be as simple as `GenerateCharacter()`. To pass in additional information, we'll need to define parameters that our method can accept and work with. Every method parameter is an instruction and needs to have two things:

- An explicit type
- A unique name

Does this sound familiar? Method parameters are essentially stripped-down variable declarations and perform the same function. Each parameter acts like a local variable, only accessible inside their specific method.

You can have as many parameters as you need. Whether you're writing custom methods or using built-in ones, the parameters that are defined are what the method requires to perform its specified task.

If parameters are the blueprint for the types of values a method can accept, then arguments are the values themselves. To break this down further, consider the following:

- The argument that's passed into a method needs to match the parameter type, just like a variable type and its value.
- Arguments can be literal values (for instance, the number 2) or other variables you've declared in the class.
- Argument names and parameter names don't need to match to compile.

Now, let's move on and add some method parameters to make `GenerateCharacter()` a bit more interesting.

Let's update `GenerateCharacter()` so that it can take in two parameters:

1. Add two method parameters—one for a character's name of the `string` type, and another for a character's level of the `int` type:

   ```
   public void GenerateCharacter(string name, int level)
   {

   }
   ```

2. Update `Debug.Log()` inside `GenerateCharacter()` to use the new parameters:

   ```
   Debug.LogFormat("Character: {0} - Level: {1}", name, level);
   ```

3. Add arguments to the `GenerateCharacter()` method call in `Start()`, which can be either literal values or declared variables (I'm going to use one of each):

```
int CharacterLevel = 35;
GenerateCharacter("Spike", CharacterLevel);
```

Your code should look like the following:

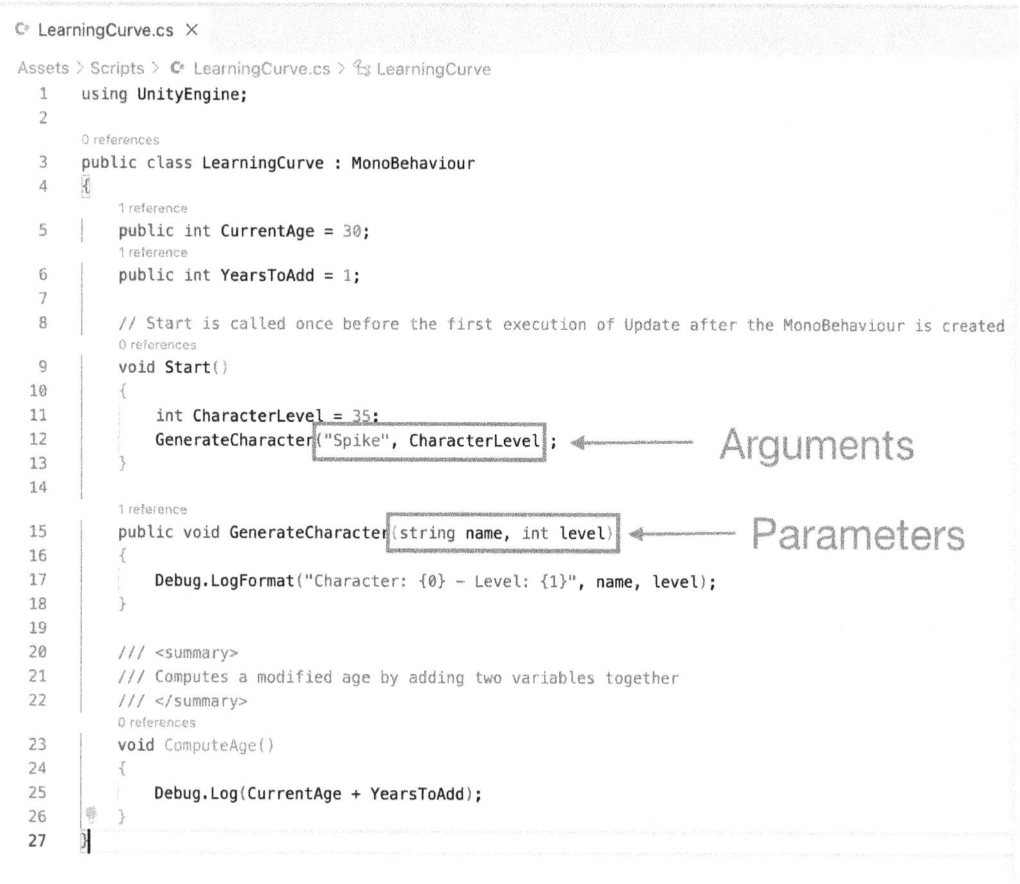

```
C⁺ LearningCurve.cs ×

Assets > Scripts > C⁺ LearningCurve.cs > ⅗ LearningCurve
 1   using UnityEngine;
 2
     0 references
 3   public class LearningCurve : MonoBehaviour
 4   {
         1 reference
 5       public int CurrentAge = 30;
         1 reference
 6       public int YearsToAdd = 1;
 7
 8       // Start is called once before the first execution of Update after the MonoBehaviour is created
         0 references
 9       void Start()
10       {
11           int CharacterLevel = 35;
12           GenerateCharacter("Spike", CharacterLevel);         ←——————  Arguments
13       }
14
         1 reference
15       public void GenerateCharacter(string name, int level)   ←——————  Parameters
16       {
17           Debug.LogFormat("Character: {0} - Level: {1}", name, level);
18       }
19
20       /// <summary>
21       /// Computes a modified age by adding two variables together
22       /// </summary>
         0 references
23       void ComputeAge()
24       {
25           Debug.Log(CurrentAge + YearsToAdd);
26       }
27   }
```

Figure 3.16: Updating the GenerateCharacter() method

Here, we defined two parameters, name (string) and level (int), and used them inside the GenerateCharacter() method, just like local variables. When we called the method inside Start(), we added argument values for each parameter with corresponding types.

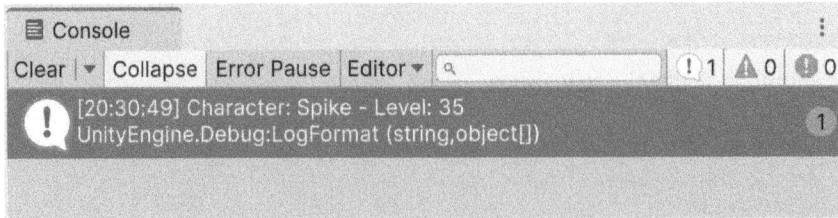

Figure 3.17: Console showing the output from method parameters

Going even further with methods, you might be wondering how we can pass values from inside the method and back out again. This brings us to our next section on return values.

Specifying return values

Aside from accepting parameters, methods can return values of any C# type. All of our previous examples have used the void type, which doesn't return anything, but being able to write instructions and pass back computed results is where methods shine.

According to our blueprints, method return types are specified after the access modifier. In addition to the type, the method needs to contain the return keyword, followed by the return value. A return value can be a variable, a literal value, or even an expression, as long as it matches the declared return type.

Methods that have a return type of void can still use the return keyword with no value or expression assigned.

Once the line with the return keyword is reached, the method will stop executing. This is useful in cases where you want to check whether a value or values exist before continuing or guard against program crashes.

Next, add a return type to GenerateCharacter() and learn how to capture it in a variable. Let's update the GenerateCharacter() method so that it returns an integer.

Change the return type in the method declaration from void to int, and set the return value to level += 5 using the return keyword:

```
public int GenerateCharacter(string name, int level)
{
```

```
    Debug.LogFormat("Character: {0} - Level: {1}", name, level);

    return level += 5;
}
```

GenerateCharacter() will now return an integer. This is computed by adding 5 to the level argument. We haven't specified how, or if, we want to use this return value, which means that right now, the script won't do anything new.

Now, the question becomes how do we capture and use the newly added return value? Well, we'll discuss that very topic in the following section.

Using return values

When it comes to using return values, there are two approaches available:

- Create a local variable to capture (store) the returned value.
- Use the calling method itself as a stand-in for the returned value, using it just like a variable. The calling method is the actual line of code that fires the instructions, which, in our example, would be GenerateCharacter("Spike", CharacterLevel). You can even pass a calling method into another method as an argument if needed.

The first option is preferred in most programming circles for its readability. Throwing around method calls as variables can get messy fast, especially when we use them as arguments in other methods.

Let's give this a try in our code by capturing and debugging the return value that GenerateCharacter() returns.

We're going to use both ways of capturing and using return variables with two simple debug logs:

1. Create a new int variable in the Start() method called NextSkillLevel and assign it to the return value of the GenerateCharacter() method call we already have in place:

    ```
    int NextSkillLevel = GenerateCharacter("Spike", CharacterLevel);
    ```

2. Add a debug log to print out the next skill level after a character is created:

    ```
    Debug.Log(NextSkillLevel);
    ```

Your code should look like the following:

```
void Start()
{
    int CharacterLevel = 32;
    int NextSkillLevel = GenerateCharacter("Spike", CharacterLevel);
    Debug.Log("Next skill level -> " + NextSkillLevel);
}

public int GenerateCharacter(string name, int level)
{
    Debug.LogFormat("Character: {0} - Level: {1}", name, level);
    return level += 5;
}
```

3. Save the file and hit **Play** in Unity:

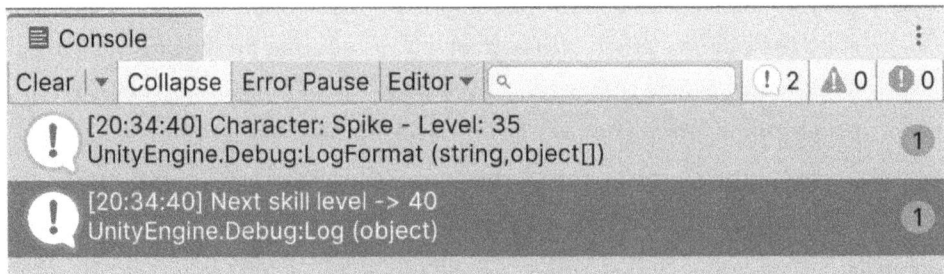

Figure 3.18: Console output from the character generation code

That was a lot to take in, especially given the exponential possibilities of methods with parameters and return values. However, we'll ease off the throttle here for a minute and consider some of Unity's most common methods to catch a little breathing room.

But first, see whether you can handle a challenge in the next *Hero's trial*!

Hero's trial: methods as arguments

If you're feeling brave, why not try creating a new method that takes in an int parameter and simply prints it out to the console? No return type is necessary. When you've got that, call the method in Start(), pass in a GenerateCharacter() method call as its argument, and take a look at the output.

Dissecting common Unity methods

We're now at a point where we can realistically discuss the most common default methods that come with any new Unity C# script: Start() and Update(). Unlike the methods we define ourselves, methods belonging to the MonoBehaviour class are called automatically by the Unity engine according to their respective rules. In most cases, it's important to have at least one MonoBehaviour method in a script to kick off your code.

You can find a complete list of all available MonoBehaviour methods and their descriptions at https://docs.unity3d.com/ScriptReference/MonoBehaviour.html. You can also find the order in which each method is executed at https://docs.unity3d.com/Manual/ExecutionOrder.html.

Just like stories, it's always a good idea to start at the beginning. So, naturally, we should take a look at every Unity script's first default method—Start().

The Start() method

Unity calls the Start() method on the first frame where a script is enabled for the first time. Since MonoBehaviour scripts are almost always attached to **GameObjects** in a scene, their attached scripts are enabled at the same time they are loaded when you hit **Play**. In our project, LearningCurve is attached to the **Main Camera** GameObject, which means that its Start() method runs when the camera is loaded into the scene. Start() is primarily used to set up variables or perform logic that needs to happen before Update() runs for the first time.

The examples we've worked on so far have all used Start(), even though they weren't performing setup actions, which isn't normally the way it would be used. However, it only fires once, making it an excellent tool to use for displaying one-time-only information on the console.

Other than Start(), there's one other major Unity method that you'll run into by default: Update(). Let's familiarize ourselves with how it works in the following section before we finish this chapter.

The Update() method

If you spend enough time looking at the sample code in the *Unity Scripting Reference* (https://docs.unity3d.com/ScriptReference/), you'll notice that a vast majority of the code is executed using the Update() method. As your game runs, the **Scene** window is displayed many times per second, which is called the **frame rate** or **frames per second (FPS)**.

After each frame is displayed, the Update() method is called by Unity, making it one of the most executed methods in your game. This makes it ideal for detecting mouse and keyboard input or running gameplay logic.

If you're curious about the FPS rating on your machine, hit **Play** in Unity and click the **Stats** tab in the upper-right corner of the **Game** view:

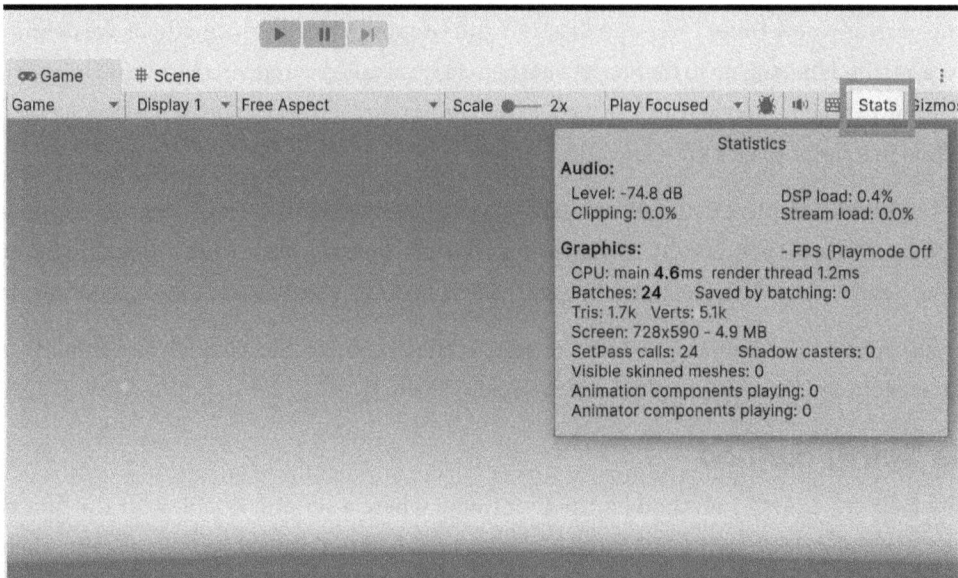

Figure 3.19: Unity editor showing the Stats panel with graphics FPS count

When you hit **Play**, the **Statistics** pop-up window will update in real time to show you all the information relating to how the game is running!

You'll be using the Start() and Update() methods in the lion's share of your initial C# scripts, so get acquainted with them. That being said, you've reached the end of this chapter with a pocketful of the most fundamental building blocks that programming with C# has to offer.

Summary

This chapter has been a fast descent from the basic theory of programming and its building blocks into the strata of real code and C# syntax. We've seen good and bad forms of code formatting, learned how to debug information in the Unity **Console** window, and created our first variables.

C# types, access modifiers, and variable scope weren't far behind, as we worked with member variables in the **Inspector** window and started venturing into the realm of methods and actions.

Methods helped us to understand written instructions in code, but more importantly, how to properly harness their power into useful behaviors. Input parameters, return types, and method signatures are all important topics, but the real gift they offer is the potential for new kinds of actions to be performed.

You're now armed with the two fundamental building blocks of programming—variables and methods; almost everything you'll do from now on will be an extension or application of these two concepts.

In the next chapter, we'll take a look at a special subset of C# types called collections, which can store groups of related data, and learn how to write decision-based code.

Pop quiz: Variables and methods

a. What is the proper way to write a variable name in C#?

b. How do you make a variable appear in Unity's **Inspector** window?

c. What are the four access modifiers available in C#?

d. When are explicit conversions needed between types?

e. What are the minimum requirements for defining a method?

f. What is the purpose of the parentheses at the end of the method name?

g. What does a return type of void mean in a method definition?

h. How often is the Update() method called by Unity?

Don't forget to check your answers against mine in the *Pop Quiz Answers* appendix to see how you did!

Subscribe to Game Dev Assembly Newsletter!

We are excited to introduce Game Dev Assembly, our brand-new newsletter dedicated to everything game development. Whether you're a programmer, designer, artist, animator, or studio lead, you'll get exclusive insights, industry trends, and expert tips to help you build better games and grow your skills. Sign up today and become part of a growing community of creators, innovators, and game changers: https://packt.link/gamedev-newsletter

Scan the QR code to join instantly!

Join our community on Discord

Join our community's Discord space for discussions with the authors and other readers: `https://packt.link/gamedevelopment`

4

Control Flow and Collection Types

One of the central duties of a computer is to control what happens when predetermined conditions are met. When you click on a folder, you expect it to open; when you type on the keyboard, you expect the text to mirror your keystrokes. Writing C# code for applications or games is no different—they both need to behave in a certain way in one state, and in another when conditions change. In programming terms, this is called **control flow**, which is apt because it controls the flow of how code is executed in different scenarios.

In addition to working with control statements, we'll be taking a hands-on look at collection data types. Collections are a category of types that allow multiple values, and groupings of values, to be stored in a single variable.

We'll break the chapter down into the following topics:

- Selection statements
- Working with array, dictionary, and list collections
- Iteration statements with for, foreach, and while loops
- Fixing infinite loops

Selection statements

The most complex programming problems can often be boiled down to sets of simple choices that a game or program evaluates and acts on. Since Visual Studio and Unity can't make those choices by themselves, writing out those decisions is up to you.

The if-else and switch selection statements allow you to specify branching paths, based on one or more conditions, and the actions you want to be taken in each case. Traditionally, these conditions include the following:

- Detecting user input
- Evaluating expressions and Boolean logic
- Comparing variables or literal values

Let's start with the simplest of these conditional statements, if-else, in the following section.

The if-else statement

if-else statements are the most common way of making decisions in code. When stripped of all its syntax, the basic idea behind an if-else statement is *If my condition is met, execute this block of code; if it's not, execute this other block of code.* Think of if-else statements as gates, or doors, with the conditions as their keys. To pass through, the key needs to be valid. Otherwise, entry will be denied and the code will be sent to the next possible door. Let's take a look at the syntax for declaring one of these gates.

A valid if-else statement requires the following:

- The if keyword at the beginning of the line
- A pair of parentheses to hold the condition
- A statement body inside curly brackets

It looks like this:

```
if(condition is true)
{
    Execute block of code
}
```

Optionally, an else statement can be added to store the action you want to take when the if statement condition fails. The same rules apply for the else statement:

```
else
{
    Execute another block of code
}
```

In blueprint form, the syntax almost reads like a sentence, which is why this is the recommended approach:

```
if(condition is true)
{
    Execute this code
    block
}
else
{
    Execute this code
    block
}
```

Since these are great introductions to logical thinking, at least in programming, we'll break down the three different if-else variations in more detail (adding this code to your LearningCurve. cs script is optional right now).

A single if statement can exist by itself in cases where you don't care about what happens if the condition isn't met. In the following example, if HasDungeonKey is set to true, then a debug log will print out; if set to false, no code will execute:

```
public class LearningCurve: MonoBehaviour
{
    public bool HasDungeonKey = true;
    void Start()
    {
        if(hasDungeonKey)
        {
            Debug.Log("You possess the sacred key: enter.");
        }
    }
}
```

When referring to a condition as being met, I mean that it evaluates to true, which is often referred to as a *passing condition*.

In cases where an action needs to be taken, whether the condition is true or false, an else statement is added. If HasDungeonKey were false in the following example, the if statement would fail and the code execution would jump to the else statement:

```
public class LearningCurve: MonoBehaviour
{
    public bool HasDungeonKey = true;
    void Start()
    {
        if(HasDungeonKey)
        {
            Debug.Log("You possess the sacred key: enter.");
        }
        else
        {
            Debug.Log("You have not proved yourself yet.");
        }
    }
}
```

For cases where you need to have more than two possible outcomes, add an else-if statement with its parentheses, conditions, and curly brackets. This is best shown rather than explained, which we'll do in the next exercise with the Thievery() method.

Keep in mind that if statements can be used by themselves, but the other statements cannot exist on their own. You can also create more complex conditions with basic math operations, such as:

- > (greater than)
- < (less than)
- >= (greater than or equal to)
- <= (less than or equal to)
- == (equivalent)

For example, a condition of (2 > 3) will return false and fail, while a condition of (2 < 3) will return true and pass. Let's write out an if-else statement that checks the amount of money in a character's pocket, returning different debug logs for three different cases—greater than 50, less than 15, and anything else:

1. Open up LearningCurve and add a new public int variable named CurrentGold to the top of the script and set its value to between 1 and 100:

   ```
   public int CurrentGold = 32;
   ```

2. Create a public method with no return value, called Thievery():

   ```
   public void Thievery()
   {

   }
   ```

3. Inside the new function, add an if statement to check whether CurrentGold is greater than 50, and print a message to the console if this is true:

   ```
   if(CurrentGold > 50)
   {
       Debug.Log("You're rolling in it!");
   }
   ```

4. Add an else-if statement to check whether CurrentGold is less than 15 with a different debug log:

   ```
   else if (CurrentGold < 15)
   {
       Debug.Log("Not much there to steal...");
   }
   ```

5. Add an else statement with no condition and a final default log:

   ```
   else
   {
       Debug.Log("Looks like your purse is in the sweet spot.");
   }
   ```

6. Call the Thievery() method inside Start:

   ```
   void Start()
   {
       Thievery();
   }
   ```

7. Save the file, check that your method matches the following code, and click **Play**:

```
public void Thievery()
{
    if(CurrentGold > 50)
    {
        Debug.Log("You're rolling in it!");
    }
    else if (CurrentGold < 15)
    {
        Debug.Log("Not much there to steal...");
    }
    else
    {
        Debug.Log("Looks like your purse is in the sweet spot.");
    }
}
```

With CurrentGold set to 32 in my example, we can break down the code sequence as follows:

1. The if statement and debug log are skipped because CurrentGold is not greater than 50.

2. The else-if statement and debug log are also skipped because CurrentGold is not less than 15.

3. Since 32 is not less than 15 or greater than 50, neither of the previous conditions was met, so the else statement executes and the third debug log is displayed:

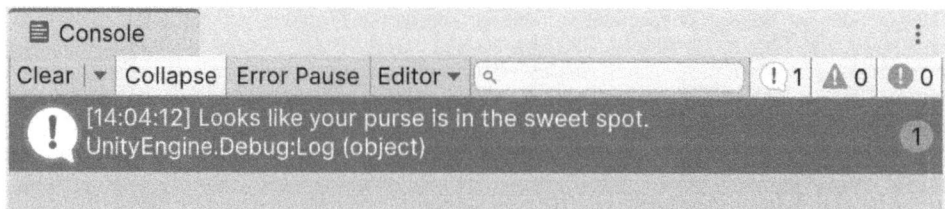

Figure 4.1: Screenshot of the console showing the debug output

Note

To provide a complete view of the Unity editor, all our screenshots are taken in full-screen mode. For color versions of all book images, use the following link: https://packt.link/gbp/9781805808718.

After trying out some other values for `CurrentGold` on your own, let's discuss what happens if we want to test a failing condition.

Using the NOT operator

Use cases won't always require checking for a positive, or `true`, condition, which is where the NOT operator comes in. Represented by typing a single exclamation point, the `NOT` operator allows negative, or `false`, conditions to be met by `if` or `else-if` statements. This means that the following conditions are the same:

```
if(variable == false)
// AND
if(!variable)
```

As you already know, you can check for Boolean values, literal values, or expressions in an `if` condition. So, naturally, the `NOT` operator has to be adaptable.

Take a look at the following example of two different negative values, `HasDungeonKey` and `WeaponType`, used in an `if` statement:

```
public class LearningCurve : MonoBehaviour
{
    public bool HasDungeonKey = false;
    public string WeaponType = "Arcane Staff";

    void Start()
    {
        if(!HasDungeonKey)
        {
            Debug.Log("You may not enter without the sacred key.");
        }

        if(WeaponType != "Longsword")
        {
            Debug.Log("You don't appear to have the right type
                of weapon...");
        }
    }
}
```

We can evaluate each statement as follows:

1. The first statement can be translated to *If* HasDungeonKey *is false, the* if *statement evaluates to* true *and executes its code block.*

    If you're asking yourself how a false value can evaluate to true, think of it this way: the if statement is not checking whether the value is true, but whether the expression itself is true. HasDungeonKey might be set to false, but that's what we're checking for, so it's true in the context of the if condition.

2. The second statement can be translated to *If the string value of* WeaponType *is not equal to* Longsword, *then execute this code block.*

    If you were to put this code into LearningCurve.cs, the results would match the following screenshot:

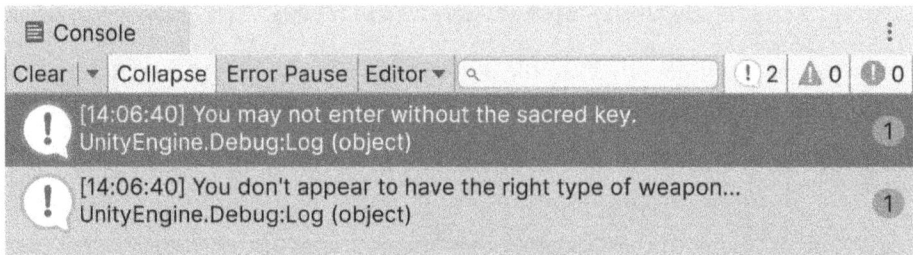

Figure 4.2: Screenshot of the console showing the NOT operator output

> 🔍 **Quick tip**: Need to see a high-resolution version of this image? Open this book in the next-gen Packt Reader or view it in the PDF/ePub copy.
>
> 📖 **The next-gen Packt Reader** and a **free PDF/ePub copy** of this book are included with your purchase. Scan the QR code OR visit https://packtpub.com/unlock, then use the search bar to find this book by name. Double-check the edition shown to make sure you get the right one.

However, if you're still confused, copy the code we've looked at in this section into LearningCurve. cs and play around with the variable values until it makes sense.

So far, our branching conditions have been fairly simple, but C# also allows conditional statements to be nested inside each other for more complex situations.

Nesting statements

One of the most valuable functions of if-else statements is that they can be nested inside each other, creating complex logic routes through your code. In programming, we call them decision trees. Just like a real hallway, there can be doors behind other doors, creating a labyrinth of possibilities:

```
public class LearningCurve : MonoBehaviour
{
    public bool WeaponEquipped = true;
    public string WeaponType = "Longsword";

    void Start()
    {
        if(WeaponEquipped)
        {
            if(WeaponType == "Longsword")
            {
                Debug.Log("For the Queen!");
            }
        }
        else
        {
            Debug.Log("Fists aren't going to work against armor...");
        }
    }
}
```

Let's break down the preceding example:

1. The first if statement checks whether we have WeaponEquipped. At this point, the code only cares whether it's true, not what type of weapon it is.
2. The second if statement checks WeaponType and prints out the associated debug log.

If the first `if` statement evaluates to `false`, the code would jump to the `else` statement and its debug log. If the second `if` statement evaluates to `false`, nothing is printed because there is no `else` statement.

The responsibility of handling logic outcomes is 100% on the programmer. It's up to you to determine the possible branches or outcomes your code can take.

What you've learned so far will get you through simple use cases with no problem. However, you'll quickly find yourself in need of more complex statements, which is where evaluating multiple conditions comes into play.

Evaluating multiple conditions

In addition to nesting statements, it's also possible to combine multiple condition checks into a single `if` or `else-if` statement with `AND` `OR` logic operators:

- `AND` is represented by two ampersand characters, `&&`. Any condition using the `AND` operator means that all conditions need to evaluate to `true` for the `if` statement to execute.

- `OR` is represented with two pipe characters, `||`. An `if` statement using the `OR` operator will execute if one or more of its conditions are `true`.

Conditions are always evaluated from left to right.

In the following example, the `if` statement has been updated to check for both `WeaponEquipped` and `WeaponType`, both of which need to be `true` for the code block to execute:

```
if(WeaponEquipped && WeaponType == "Longsword")
{
    Debug.Log("For the Queen!");
}
```

The `AND` `OR` operators can be combined to check multiple conditions in any order. There is also no limit to how many operators you can combine—just be careful when using them together that you don't create logic conditions that will never execute.

It's time to put everything we've learned so far about `if` statements to the test. So, review this section if you need to, and then move on to the next section.

Putting it all together

Let's cement this topic with a little treasure chest experiment:

1. Declare three variables at the top of LearningCurve:

    - PureOfHeart is a Boolean and should be true
    - HasSecretIncantation is also a Boolean and should be false
    - RareItem is a string, and its value is up to you

    ```
    public bool PureOfHeart = true;
    public bool HasSecretIncantation = false;
    public string RareItem = "Relic Stone";
    ```

2. Create a public method at the bottom of the script with no return value called OpenTreasureChamber:

    ```
    public void OpenTreasureChamber()
    {
    }
    ```

3. Inside OpenTreasureChamber, declare an if-else statement to check whether PureOfHeart is true *and* that RareItem matches the string value you assigned to it:

    ```
    if(PureOfHeart && RareItem == "Relic Stone")
    {
    }
    ```

4. Create a nested if-else statement inside the first, checking whether HasSecretIncantation is false:

    ```
    if(!HasSecretIncantation)
    {
        Debug.Log("You have the spirit, but not the knowledge.");
    }
    ```

5. Add debug logs for each if-else case.

6. Call the OpenTreasureChamber() method inside Start():

    ```
    void Start()
    {
        OpenTreasureChamber();
    }
    ```

7. Save, check that your code matches the following code, and click **Play**:

```
public class LearningCurve : MonoBehaviour
{
    public bool PureOfHeart = true;
    public bool HasSecretIncantation  = false;
    public string RareItem = "Relic Stone";

    void Start()
    {
        OpenTreasureChamber();
    }
    public void OpenTreasureChamber()
    {
        if(PureOfHeart && RareItem == "Relic Stone")
        {
            if(!HasSecretIncantation)
            {
                Debug.Log("You have the spirit, but not
                    the knowledge.");
            }
            else
            {
                Debug.Log("The treasure is yours, worthy hero!");
            }
        }
        else
        {
            Debug.Log("Come back when you have what it takes.");
        }
    }
}
```

If you matched the variable values to the preceding screenshot, the nested if statement debug log will be printed out. This means that our code got past the first if statement checking for two conditions, but failed the third:

Figure 4.3: Screenshot of the debug output in the console

Now, you could stop here and use even bigger if-else statements for all your conditional needs, but that's not going to be efficient in the long run. Good programming is about using the right tool for the right job, which is where the switch statement comes in.

The switch statement

if-else statements are a great way to write decision logic. However, when you have more than three or four branching actions, they just aren't feasible. Before you know it, your code can end up looking like a tangled knot that's hard to follow, and a headache to update.

switch statements take in expressions and let us write out actions for each possible outcome, but in a much more concise format than if-else.

switch statements require the following elements:

- The switch keyword followed by a pair of parentheses holding its condition
- A pair of curly brackets
- A case statement for each possible path ending with a colon: individual lines of code or methods, followed by the break keyword and a semicolon
- A default case statement ending with a colon: individual lines of code or methods, followed by the break keyword and a semicolon

In blueprint form, it looks like this:

```
switch(matchExpression)
{
    case matchValue1:
        Executing code block
        break;
    case matchValue2:
        Executing code block
```

```
        break;
    default:
        Executing code block
        break;
}
```

The highlighted keywords in the preceding blueprint are the important bits. When a case state-ment is defined, anything between its colon and break keyword acts like the code block of an if-else statement. The break keyword just tells the program to exit the switch statement entirely after the selected case fires. Now, let's discuss how the statement determines which case gets executed, which is called pattern matching.

Pattern matching

In switch statements, **pattern matching** refers to how a **match expression** is validated against multiple case statements. A match expression can be of any type that isn't null or nothing; all case statement values need to match the type of the match expression.

For example, if we had a switch statement that was evaluating an integer variable, each case statement would need to specify an integer value for it to check against.

The case statement with a value that matches the expression is the one that is executed. If no case is matched, the default case fires.

That was a lot of new syntax and information, but it helps to see it in action. Let's try this out for ourselves! Let's create a simple switch statement for different actions a character could take:

1. Create a new public string variable named CharacterAction and set its value to "Attack":

    ```
    public string CharacterAction = "Attack";
    ```

2. Create a public method with no return value called PrintCharacterAction():

    ```
    public void PrintCharacterAction()
    {
    }
    ```

3. Declare a switch statement inside the new method and use CharacterAction as the match expression:

    ```
    switch(CharacterAction)
    {
    }
    ```

4. Create two case statements for "Heal" and "Attack" with different debug logs. Don't forget to include the break keyword at the end of each:

```
case "Heal":
    Debug.Log("Potion sent.");
    break;
case "Attack":
    Debug.Log("To arms!");
    break;
```

5. Add a default case with a debug log and break:

```
default:
    Debug.Log("Shields up.");
    break;
```

6. Call the PrintCharacterAction method inside Start():

```
void Start()
{
    PrintCharacterAction();
}
```

7. Save the file, make sure your script matches the following code, and click **Play**:

```
public string CharacterAction = "Attack";
void Start()
{
    PrintCharacterAction();
}
public void PrintCharacterAction()
{
    switch(CharacterAction)
    {
        case "Heal":
            Debug.Log("Potion sent.");
            break;
        case "Attack":
            Debug.Log("To arms!");
            break;
        default:
```

```
                    Debug.Log("Shields up.");
                    break;
            }
        }
```

Since CharacterAction is set to "Attack", the switch statement executes the second case and prints out its debug log:

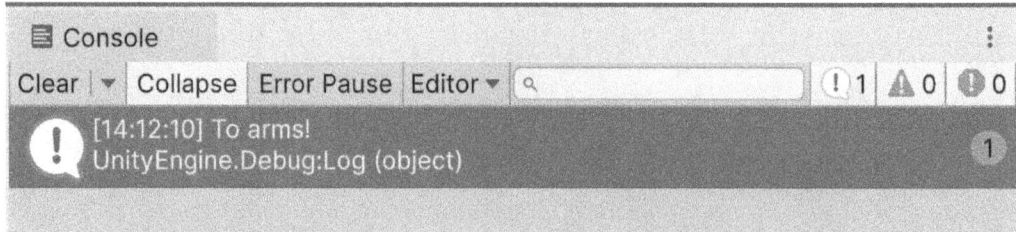

Figure 4.4: Screenshot of the switch statement output in the console

Change the CharacterAction string variable to either "Heal" or an undefined action to see the first and default cases in action.

There are going to be times where you need several, but not all, switch cases to perform the same action. These are called fall-through cases and are the subject of our next section.

Fall-through cases

switch statements can execute the same action for multiple cases, similar to how we specified several conditions in a single if statement. The term for this is **fall-through** or, sometimes, **fall-through cases**. Fall-through cases let you define a single set of actions for multiple cases. If a case block is left empty or has code without the break keyword, it will fall through to the case directly beneath it. This helps keep your switch code clean and efficient, without duplicated case blocks.

Cases can be written in any order, so creating fall-through cases greatly increases code readability and efficiency.

Let's simulate a tabletop game scenario with a switch statement and fall-through case, where a dice roll determines the outcome of a specific action:

1. Create a public int variable named Dice and assign it a value of 7:

    ```
    public int Dice = 7;
    ```

2. Create a `public` method with no return value called `RollDice()`:

```
public void RollDice()
{
}
```

3. Add a `switch` statement with `Dice` as the match expression:

```
switch(Dice)
{
}
```

4. Add three cases for possible dice rolls at 7, 15, and 20, with a default `case` statement at the end.

   Cases 15 and 20 should have their own debug logs and `break` statements, while case 7 should fall through to case 15:

```
case 7:
case 15:
    Debug.Log("Mediocre damage, not bad.");
    break;
case 20:
    Debug.Log("Critical hit, the creature goes down!");
    break;
default:
    Debug.Log("You completely missed and fell on your face.");
    break;
```

5. Call the `RollDice()` method inside `Start()`:

```
void Start()
{
    RollDice();
}
```

6. Save the file and run it in Unity.

If you want to see the fall-through case in action, try adding a debug log to case 7, but without the `break` keyword.

With `Dice` set to 7, the `switch` statement will match with the first case, which will fall through and execute case 15 because it lacks a code block and a `break` statement. If you change `Dice` to 15 or 20, the console will show their respective messages, and any other value will fire off the default case at the end of the statement:

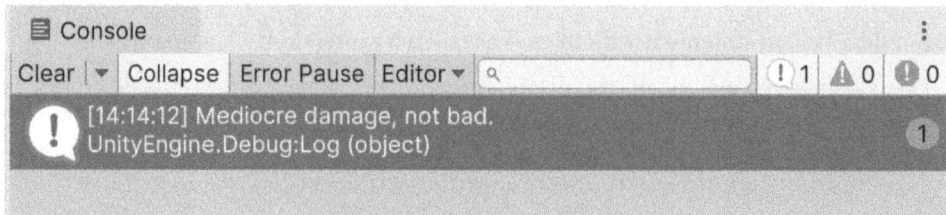

Figure 4.5: Screenshot of fall-through switch statement code

`switch` statements are extremely powerful and can simplify even the most complex decision logic. If you want to dig deeper into `switch` pattern matching, refer to `https://docs.microsoft.com/en-us/dotnet/csharp/language-reference/keywords/switch`.

That's all we need to know about conditional logic for the moment. So, review this section if you need to, and then test yourself on the following quiz before moving on to collections!

Pop quiz 1: if, and, or but

Test your knowledge with the following questions:

    a.   What values are used to evaluate `if` statements?

    b.   Which operator can turn a true condition `false` or a false condition `true`?

    c.   If two conditions need to be `true` for an `if` statement's code to execute, what logical operator would you use to join the conditions?

    d.   If only one of two conditions needs to be `true` to execute an `if` statement's code, what logical operator would you use to join the two conditions?

Don't forget to check your answers against mine in the *Pop Quiz Answers* appendix to see how you did!

With that done, you're ready to step into the world of collection data types. These types are going to open up a whole new subset of programming functionality for your games and C# programs!

Collections at a glance

So far, we've only needed variables to store a single value, but there are many conditions where a group of values will be required. **Collection types** in C# include arrays, lists, and dictionaries— each has its strengths and weaknesses, which we'll discuss in the following sections.

Arrays

Arrays are the most basic collection that C# offers. Think of them as containers for a group of values, called **elements** in programming terminology, each of which can be accessed or modified individually:

- Arrays can store any type of value; all the elements need to be of the same type.
- The length, or the number of elements an array can have, is set when it's created and can't be modified afterward.
- If no initial values are assigned when it's created, each element will be given a default value. Arrays storing number types default to zero, while any other type gets set to null or nothing.
- Arrays are the least flexible collection type in C#. This is mainly because elements can't be added or removed after they have been created. However, they are particularly useful when storing information that isn't likely to change. That lack of flexibility makes them faster compared to other collection types.

Declaring an array is similar to other variable types we've worked with, but has a few modifications:

- Array variables require a specified element type, a pair of square brackets, and a unique name.
- The new keyword is used to create the array in memory, followed by the value type and another pair of square brackets. The reserved memory area is the exact size of the data you're intending to store in the new array.
- The number of elements the array will store goes inside the second pair of square brackets.

In blueprint form, it looks like this:

```
elementType[] name = new elementType[numberOfElements];
```

Let's take an example where we need to store the top three high scores in our game:

```
int[] TopPlayerScores = new int[3];
```

Broken down, `TopPlayerScores` is an array of integers that will store three integer elements. Since we didn't add any initial values, each of the three values in `TopPlayerScores` is 0. However, if you change the array size, the contents of the original array are lost, so be careful.

You can assign values directly to an array when it's created by adding them inside a pair of curly brackets at the end of the variable declaration. C# has a longhand and shorthand way of doing this, but both are equally valid:

```
// Longhand initializer
int[] TopPlayerScores = new int[] {713, 549, 984};
// Shortcut initializer
int[] TopPlayerScores = { 713, 549, 984 };
```

Initializing arrays with the shorthand syntax is very common, so I'll be using it for the rest of the book. However, if you want to remind yourself of the details, feel free to use the explicit longhand initializer syntax as shown previously.

Now that the declaration syntax is no longer a mystery, let's talk about how array elements are stored and accessed.

Indexing and subscripts

Each array element is stored in the order it's assigned, which is referred to as its **index**. Arrays are zero-indexed, meaning that the element order starts at 0 instead of 1. Think of an element's index as its reference, or location.

In `TopPlayerScores`, the first integer, 452, is located at index 0, 713 at index 1, and 984 at index 2:

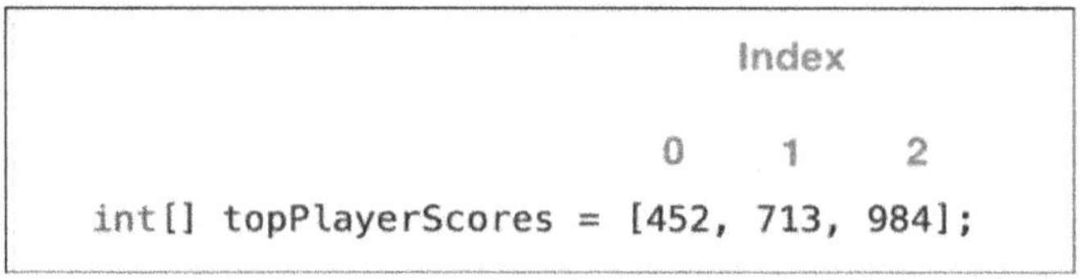

Figure 4.6: Array indexes mapped to their values

Individual values are located by their index using the **subscript operator**, which is a pair of square brackets that contains the index of the elements.

For example, to retrieve and store the second array element in `TopPlayerScores`, we would use the array name followed by subscript brackets and index 1:

```
// The value of score is set to 713
int score = TopPlayerScores[1];
```

The subscript operator can also be used to directly modify an array value just like any other variable, or even passed around as an expression by itself:

```
TopPlayerScores[1] = 1001;
```

The values in `TopPlayerScores` would then be 452, 1001, and 984.

Multidimensional arrays

Arrays are also a great way to store elements in a table format—think rows and columns in the real world. These are called **multidimensional arrays** because each added element brings another dimension to the data. The preceding array examples only hold one element per index, so they are one-dimensional. If we wanted an array to hold, say, an x and y coordinate in each element like in middle-school math class, we could create a two-dimensional array like so:

```
// The Coordinates array has 3 rows and 2 columns
int[,] Coordinates = new int[3,2];
```

Notice we used a comma inside the square brackets to mark the array as two-dimensional, and we added two initialization fields, which are also separated by a comma.

We can also directly initialize a multidimensional array with values, so creating a table of x and y coordinates like the preceding one could be shortened to the following:

```
int[,] Coordinates = new int[3,2]
{
    {5,4},
    {1,7},
    {9,3}
};
```

You can see that we have three rows, or elements, each containing two columns of data for the x and y values. Now, here's the tricky bit of mental gymnastics—you need to think of multidimensional arrays as *arrays of arrays*. In the preceding example, each element is still stored at an index starting with 0 and moving up, but each element is an array instead of a single value.

To put this in concrete terms, the value of 4 in the first column of the first row is located at index 0, and the actual value of 4 is located at the second element in that row's array, or 1:

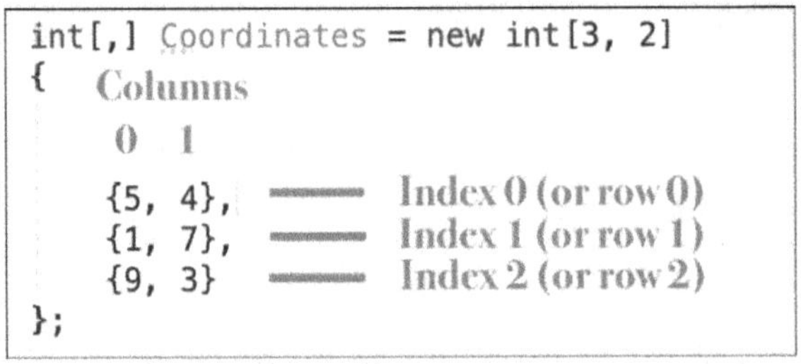

Figure 4.7: Multidimensional array mapped with indexes

In code, we would use the following subscript, using the row subscript first, followed by the column index:

```
// Finding the value in the first row, first column
int coordinateValue = Coordinates[0, 1];
```

Changing a value in a multidimensional array is the same as with a regular array. We use the subscript of the value we want to update and then assign a new value:

```
// Value in the first row, first column is now 10
Coordinates[0, 1] = 10;
```

A C# array can have up to 32 dimensions, which is a lot, but the rules for creating them are the same — add an extra comma for every dimension inside the type brackets at the beginning of the variable and an extra comma and number of elements in the initialization. For instance, a three-dimensional array would look like this:

```
int[,,] Coordinates = new int[3,3,2];
```

This is a bit advanced for our needs, but you can get into more complex multidimensional array code at https://learn.microsoft.com/dotnet/csharp/programming-guide/arrays/multidimensional-arrays.

Range exceptions

When arrays are created, the number of elements is set and unchangeable, which means we can't access an element that doesn't exist. In the TopPlayerScores example, the array length is 3, so the range of valid indices is from 0 to 2.

For example, let's say we tried to run the following code:

```
Debug.Log(TopPlayerScores[3]);
```

The console would print an aptly-named `IndexOutOfRangeException` error in the console because any index of 3 or higher is out of the array's range:

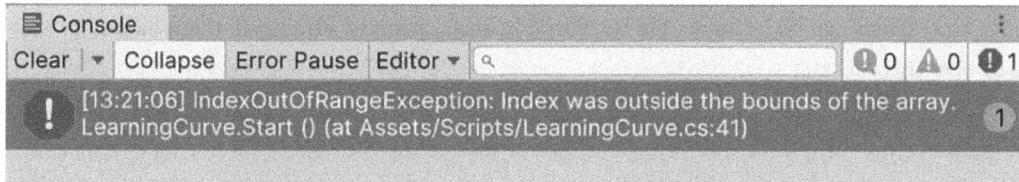

Figure 4.8: Screenshot of index-out-of-range exception

Good programming habits dictate that we avoid range exceptions by checking whether the value we want is within an array's index range, which we'll cover in the *Iteration statements* section.

You can always check the length of an array—that is, how many items it contains—with the `Length` property:

```
TopPlayerScores.Length;
```

Arrays aren't the only collection types C# has to offer. In the next section, we'll deal with lists, which are more flexible and more common in the programming landscape.

Lists

Lists are closely related to arrays, collecting multiple values of the same type in a single variable. They're much easier to deal with when it comes to adding, removing, and updating elements, but their elements aren't stored sequentially. They are also mutable, meaning you can change the length or number of items you're storing, without overwriting the whole variable. This can, sometimes, lead to a higher performance cost over arrays.

Performance cost refers to how much of a computer's time and energy a given operation takes up. Nowadays, computers are fast, but they can still get overloaded by big games or applications.

A list-type variable needs to meet the following requirements:

- The `List` keyword, its element type inside left and right arrow characters, and a unique name
- The `new` keyword to initialize the list in memory, with the `List` keyword and element type between arrow characters
- A pair of parentheses capped off by a semicolon

In blueprint form, it reads as follows:

```
List<elementType> name = new List<elementType>();
```

List length can always be modified, so there is no need to specify how many elements it will eventually hold when created.

Like arrays, lists can be initialized in the variable declaration by adding element values inside a pair of curly brackets:

```
List<elementType> name = new List<elementType>() { value1, value2 };
```

Elements are stored in the order they are added (instead of the sequential order of the values themselves), are zero-indexed like arrays, and can be accessed using the subscript operator.

Setting up a list

Let's start setting up a list of our own to test out the basic functionality this class has on offer.

We'll start with a warm-up exercise by creating a list of party members in a fictional role-playing game:

1. Add a using declaration at the top of the `LearningCurve.cs` script to access the `List` type (namespaces are an intermediate topic we'll cover at the end of *Chapter 10*):

    ```
    using System.Collections.Generic;


    public class LearningCurve : MonoBehaviour
    {
        //... No other changes needed ...
    }
    ```

2. Create a new list of the string type inside `Start()` called `QuestPartyMembers`, and initialize it with the names of three characters:

    ```
    List<string> QuestPartyMembers = new List<string>()
    {
        "Grim the Barbarian",
        "Merlin the Wise",
        "Sterling the Knight"
    };
    ```

3. Add a debug log to print out the number of party members in the list using the `Count` method:

```
Debug.LogFormat("Party Members: {0}", QuestPartyMembers.Count);
```

4. Save the file and play it in Unity.

We initialized a new list, called `QuestPartyMembers`, which now holds three string values, and used the `Count` method from the `List` class to print out the number of elements.

Notice that you use `Count` for lists, but `Length` for arrays.

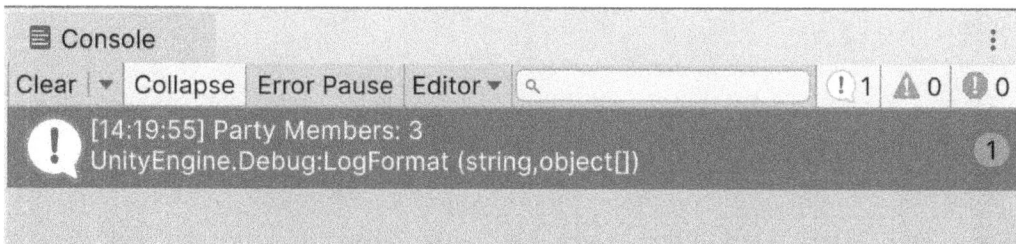

Figure 4.9: Screenshot of list item output in the console

Knowing how many elements are in a list is highly useful; however, in most cases, that information is not enough. We want to be able to modify our lists as needed, which we'll discuss next.

Accessing and modifying lists

List elements can be accessed and modified like arrays with a subscript operator and index, as long as the index is within the `List` class's range. However, the `List` class has a variety of methods that extend its functionality, such as adding, inserting, and removing elements.

Sticking with the `QuestPartyMembers` list, let's add a new member to the team in the `LearningCurve.cs` script:

```
QuestPartyMembers.Add("Craven the Necromancer");
```

The `Add()` method appends the new element at the end of the list, which brings the `QuestPartyMembers` count to four and the element order to the following:

```
{
    "Grim the Barbarian",
    "Merlin the Wise",
    "Sterling the Knight",
    "Craven the Necromancer"
};
```

To add an element to a specific spot in a list, we can pass the index and the value that we want to add to the `Insert()` method:

```
QuestPartyMembers.Insert(1, "Tanis the Thief");
```

When an element is inserted at a previously occupied index, all the elements in the list have their indices increased by 1. In our example, `"Tanis the Thief"` is now at index 1, meaning that `"Merlin the Wise"` is now at index 2 instead of 1, and so on:

```
{
    "Grim the Barbarian",
    "Tanis the Thief",
    "Merlin the Wise ",
    "Sterling the Knight",
    "Craven the Necromancer"
};
```

Removing an element is just as simple; all we need is the index or the literal value, and the `List` class does the work:

```
// Both of these methods would remove the required element
QuestPartyMembers.RemoveAt(0);
QuestPartyMembers.Remove("Grim the Barbarian");
```

At the end of our edits, `QuestPartyMembers` now contains the following elements indexed from 0 to 3:

```
{
    "Tanis the Thief",
    "Merlin the Wise",
    "Sterling the Knight",
    "Craven the Necromancer"
};
```

If you run the game now, you'll also see the party list length is 4 instead of 3!

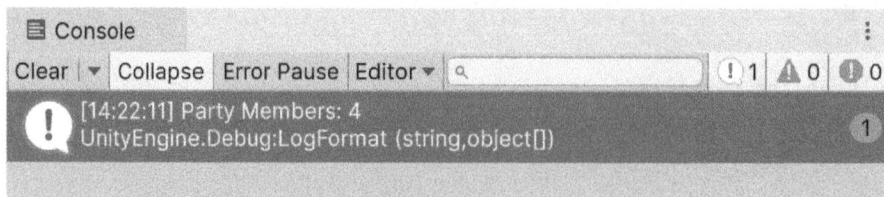

Figure 4.10: Screenshot of modified list items in the console

There are many more `List` class methods that allow for value checks, finding and sorting elements, and working with ranges. A full method list, with descriptions, can be found here: `https://docs.microsoft.com/en-us/dotnet/api/system.collections.generic.list-1?view=netframework-4.7.2`.

While lists are great for single-value elements, there are cases where you'll need to store information or data containing more than one value. This is where dictionaries come into play.

Dictionaries

The `Dictionary` type steps away from arrays and lists by storing value pairs in each element, instead of single values. These elements are referred to as key-value pairs: the key acts as the index, or lookup value, for its corresponding value. Unlike arrays and lists, dictionaries are unordered. However, they can be sorted and ordered in various configurations after they are created.

Declaring a dictionary is almost the same as declaring a list, but with one added detail—both the key and the value type need to be specified inside the arrow symbols:

```
Dictionary<keyType, valueType> name = new
Dictionary<keyType, valueType>();
```

To initialize a dictionary with key-value pairs, do the following:

- Use a pair of curly brackets at the end of the declaration.
- Add each element within its pair of curly brackets, with the key and the value separated by a comma.
- Separate elements with a comma, except the last element where the comma is optional.

It looks like this:

```
Dictionary<keyType, valueType> name = new
Dictionary<keyType, valueType>()
{
    {key1, value1},
    {key2, value2}
};
```

An important note to consider when picking key values is that each key must be unique, and they cannot be changed. If you need to update a key, then you need to change its value in the variable declaration or remove the entire key-value pair and add another in the code, which we'll look at in the next section on dictionaries.

Just like with arrays and lists, dictionaries can be initialized on a single line with no problems from Visual Studio. However, writing out each key-value pair on its line, as in the preceding example, is a good habit to get into—both for readability and your sanity.

Creating a dictionary

Let's create a dictionary to store items that a character might carry:

1. Declare a dictionary with a key type of `string` and a value type of `int` called `ItemInventory` in the `Start()` method and initialize it with three key-value pairs of your choice. Make sure each element is in its pair of curly brackets:

    ```
    Dictionary<string, int> ItemInventory = new
    Dictionary<string, int>()
    {
        { "Potion", 5 },
        { "Antidote", 7 },
        { "Aspirin", 1 }
    };
    ```

2. Add a debug log to print out the `ItemInventory.Count` property so that we can see how items are stored:

    ```
    Debug.LogFormat("Items: {0}", ItemInventory.Count);
    ```

3. Save the file and play.

Here, a new dictionary, called `ItemInventory`, was created and initialized with three key-value pairs. We specified the keys as strings, with corresponding values as integers, and printed out how many elements `ItemInventory` currently holds:

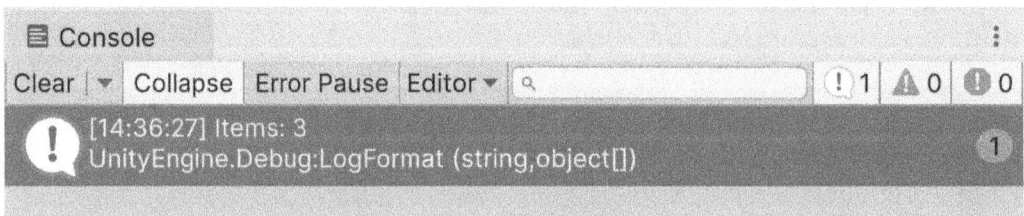

Figure 4.11: Screenshot of dictionary count in console

Like lists, we need to be able to do more than just print out the number of key-value pairs in a given dictionary. We'll explore adding, removing, and updating these values in the following section.

Working with dictionary pairs

Key-value pairs can be added, removed, and accessed from dictionaries using both subscript and class methods. To retrieve an element's value, use the subscript operator with the element's key—in the following example, numberOfPotions would be assigned a value of 5:

```
int numberOfPotions = ItemInventory["Potion"];
```

An element's value can be updated using the same method—the value associated with "Potion" would now be 10:

```
ItemInventory["Potion"] = 10;
```

Elements can be added to dictionaries in two ways: with the Add() method and with the subscript operator. The Add() method takes in a key and a value and creates a new key-value element, as long as their types correspond to the dictionary declaration:

```
ItemInventory.Add("Throwing Knife", 3);
```

If the subscript operator is used to assign a value to a key that doesn't exist in a dictionary, the compiler will automatically add it as a new key-value pair. For example, if we wanted to add a new element for "Bandage", we could do so with the following code:

```
ItemInventory["Bandage"] = 5;
```

This brings up a crucial point about referencing key-value pairs: it's better to be certain that an element exists before trying to access it, to avoid mistakenly adding new key-value pairs. Pairing the ContainsKey() method with an if statement is the simple solution since ContainsKey returns a Boolean value based on whether the key exists. In the following example, we make sure that the "Aspirin" key exists using an if statement before modifying its value:

```
if(ItemInventory.ContainsKey("Aspirin"))
{
    ItemInventory["Aspirin"] = 3;
}
```

Finally, a key-value pair can be deleted from a dictionary using the Remove() method, which takes in a key parameter:

```
ItemInventory.Remove("Antidote");
```

Like lists, dictionaries offer a variety of methods and functionality to make development easier, but we can't cover them all here. If you're curious, the official documentation can be found at `https://docs.microsoft.com/en-us/dotnet/api/system.collections.generic.dictionary-2?view=netframework-4.7.2`.

Collections are safely in our toolkit, so it's time for another quiz to make sure you're ready to move on to the next big topic: iteration statements.

Pop quiz 2: all about collections

Test your knowledge with the following questions:

    a.   What is an element in an array or list?

    b.   What is the index number of the first element in an array or list?

    c.   Can a single array or list store different types of data?

    d.   How can you add more elements to an array to make room for more data?

Don't forget to check your answers against mine in the *Pop Quiz Answers* appendix to see how you did!

Since collections are groups or lists of items, they need to be accessible in an efficient manner. Luckily, C# has several iteration statements, which we'll talk about in the following section.

Iteration statements

We've accessed individual collection elements through the subscript operator, along with collection type methods, but what do we do when we need to go through the entire collection element by element? In programming, this is called **iteration**, and C# provides several statement types that let us loop through (or iterate over, if you want to be technical) collection elements. Iteration statements are like methods, in that they store a block of code to be executed; however, unlike methods, they can repeatedly execute their code blocks as long as their conditions are met.

for loops

The for loop is most commonly used when a block of code needs to be executed a certain number of times before the program continues. The statement itself takes in three expressions, each with a specific function to perform before the loop executes. Since for loops keep track of the current iteration, they are best suited to arrays and lists.

Take a look at the following looping statement blueprint:

```
for (initializer; condition; iterator)
{
    code block;
}
```

Let's break this down:

- The `for` keyword starts the statement, followed by a pair of parentheses.
- Inside the parentheses are the gatekeepers: the initializer, condition, and iterator expressions.
- The loop starts with the initializer expression, which is a local variable created to keep track of how many times the loop has executed—this is usually set to 0 because collection types are zero-indexed.
- Next, the condition expression is checked and, if `true`, proceeds to the iterator.

The iterator expression is used to either increase or decrease (**increment** or **decrement**) the initializer, meaning the next time the loop evaluates its condition, the initializer will be different.

Increasing and decreasing a value by 1 is called **incrementing** and **decrementing**, respectively (`--` will decrease a value by 1, and `++` will increase it by 1).

That all sounds like a lot, so let's look at a practical example with the `QuestPartyMembers` list we created earlier. Add the following code to `LearningCurve.cs`:

```
int listLength = QuestPartyMembers.Count;
for (int i = 0; i < listLength; i++)
{
    Debug.LogFormat("Index: {0} - {1}", i, QuestPartyMembers[i]);
}
```

Let's go through the loop again and see how it works:

1. First, the initializer in the `for` loop is set as a local `int` variable named i with a starting value of 0.

2. Second, we store the list of the list in a variable so the loop doesn't need to check the length every time through, which is best practice for performance.

3. To ensure we never get an out-of-range exception, the `for` loop makes sure that the loop only runs another time if `i` is less than the number of elements in `QuestPartyMembers`:

   - With arrays, we use the `Length` property to determine how many items it has.
   - With lists, we use the `Count` property.

4. Finally, `i` is increased by 1 each time the loop runs with the `++` operator.

Inside the `for` loop, we've just printed out the index and the list element at that index using `i`.

Notice that `i` is in step with the index of the collection elements, since both start at 0:

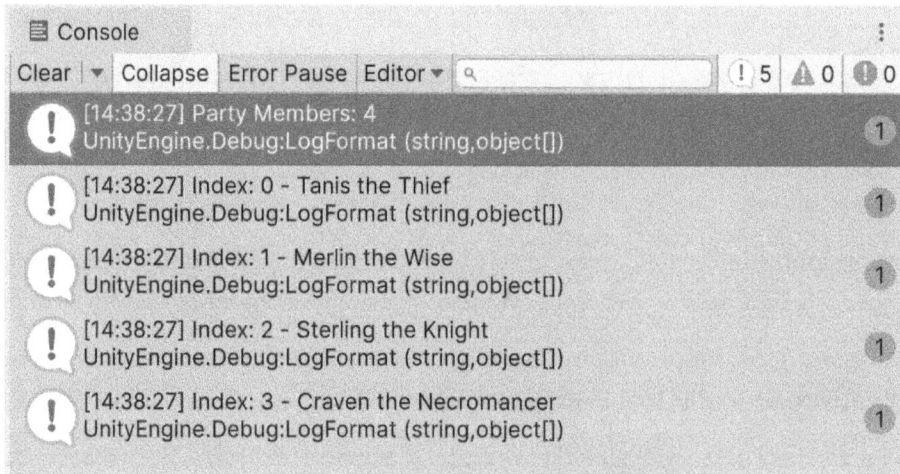

Figure 4.12: Screenshot of list values printed out with a for loop

Traditionally, the letter `i` is used as the initializer variable name. If you happen to have nested `for` loops, the variable names used should be the letters `j`, `k`, `l`, and so on.

Let's try out our new iteration statements on one of our existing collections.

While we loop through `QuestPartyMembers`, let's see whether we can identify when a certain element is iterated over and add a special debug log just for that case:

1. Move the `QuestPartyMembers` list and `for` loop into a public function called `FindPartyMember` and call it in `Start`.

2. Add an `if` statement below the debug log in the `for` loop to check whether the current `questPartyMember()` list matches `"Merlin the Wise"`:

   ```
   if(QuestPartyMembers[i] == "Merlin the Wise")
   {
   ```

```
        Debug.Log("Glad you're here Merlin!");
    }
```

3. If it does, add a debug log of your choice, check that your script matches the following code, and hit **Play**:

```
void Start()
{
    FindPartyMember();
}
public void FindPartyMember()
{
    List<string> QuestPartyMembers = new
    List<string>()
    {
        "Grim the Barbarian",
        "Merlin the Wise",
        "Sterling the Knight"
    };
    QuestPartyMembers.Add("Craven the Necromancer");
    QuestPartyMembers.Insert(1, "Tanis the Thief");
    QuestPartyMembers.RemoveAt(0);
    //QuestPartyMembers.Remove("Grim the Barbarian");

    int listLength = QuestPartyMembers.Count;
    Debug.LogFormat("Party Members: {0}", listLength);
    for(int i = 0; i < listLength; i++)
    {
        Debug.LogFormat("Index: {0} - {1}", i,
QuestPartyMembers[i]);
        if(QuestPartyMembers[i] == "Merlin the Wise")
        {
            Debug.Log("Glad you're here Merlin!");
        }
    }
}
```

The console output should look almost the same, except that there is now an extra debug log—one that only printed once when it was Merlin's turn to go through the loop. More specifically, when i was equal to 1 on the second loop, the if statement fired and two logs were printed out instead of just one:

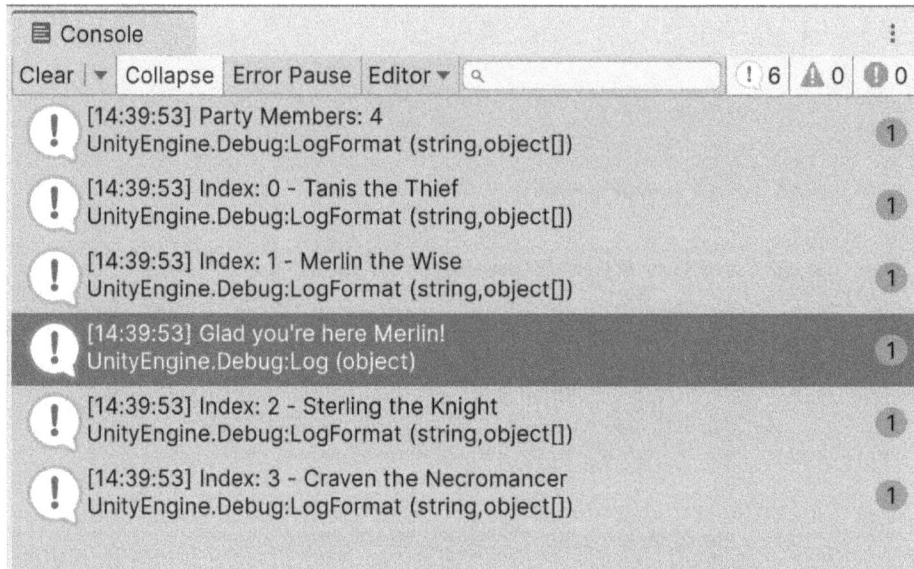

Figure 4.13: Screenshot of the for loop printing out list values and matching if statements

Using a standard for loop can be highly useful in the right situation, but there's seldom just one way to do things in programming, which is where the foreach statement comes into play.

foreach loops

foreach loops take each element in a collection and store each one in a local variable, making it accessible inside the statement. The local variable type must match the collection element type to work properly. foreach loops can be used with arrays and lists, but they are especially useful with dictionaries, since dictionaries are key-value pairs instead of numeric indexes.

In blueprint form, a foreach loop looks like this:

```
foreach(elementType localName in collectionVariable)
{
    code block;
}
```

Let's stick with the QuestPartyMembers list example and do a roll call for each of its elements. Replace the for loop in FindPartyMembers with the following code:

```
foreach(string partyMember in QuestPartyMembers)
{
    Debug.LogFormat("{0} - Here!", partyMember);
}
```

You can also use the var keyword to automatically determine the type of collection you're looping through, like so:

```
foreach(var partyMember in QuestPartyMembers)
{
    Debug.LogFormat("{0} - Here!", partyMember");
}
```

We can break this down as follows:

- The element type is declared as a string, which matches the values in QuestPartyMembers.
- A local variable, called partyMember, is created to hold each element as the loop repeats.

The in keyword, followed by the collection we want to loop through, in this case, QuestPartyMembers, finishes things off:

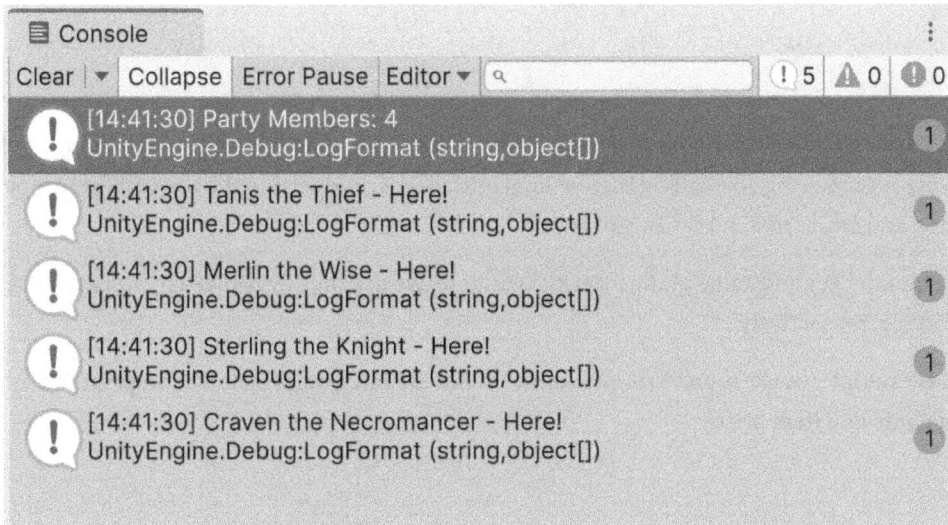

Figure 4.14: Screenshot of a foreach loop printing out list values

This is a good deal simpler than the for loop. However, when dealing with dictionaries, there are important differences we need to mention—namely, how to deal with key-value pairs as local variables.

Looping through key-value pairs

To capture a key-value pair in a local variable, we need to use the aptly named KeyValuePair type, assigning both the key and value types to match the dictionary's corresponding types. Since KeyValuePair is its type, it acts just like any other element type, as a local variable.

For example, let's loop through the ItemInventory dictionary we created earlier in the *Dictionaries* section and debug each key-value like a shop item description:

```
Dictionary<string, int> ItemInventory = new
Dictionary<string, int>()
{
    { "Potion", 5},
    { "Antidote", 7},
    { "Aspirin", 1}
};

foreach(KeyValuePair<string, int> kvp in ItemInventory)
{
    Debug.LogFormat("Item: {0} - {1}g", kvp.Key, kvp.Value);
}
```

We've specified a local variable of KeyValuePair, called kvp, which is a common naming convention in programming, like calling the for loop initializer i, and setting the key and value types to string and int to match ItemInventory.

To access the key and value of the local kvp variable, we use the KeyValuePair properties of Key and Value, respectively.

In this example, the keys are strings and the values are integers, which we can print out as the item name and item price:

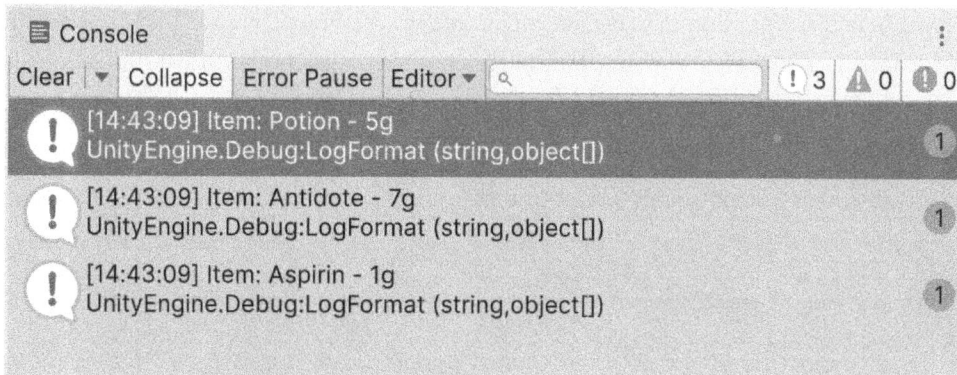

Figure 4.15: Screenshot of a foreach loop printing out dictionary key-value pairs

If you're feeling particularly adventurous, try out the following optional challenge to drive home what you've just learned.

Hero's trial: finding affordable items

Using the preceding script, create a variable to store how much gold your fictional character has, and see whether you can add an if statement inside the foreach loop to check for items that you can afford.

Hint: use kvp.Value to compare prices with what's in your wallet.

while loops

while loops are similar to if statements in that they run as long as a single expression or condition is true.

Value comparisons and Boolean variables can be used as while conditions, and they can be modified with the NOT operator.

The while loop syntax says, *While my condition is true, keep running my code block indefinitely*:

```
Initializer
while (condition)
{
    code block;
    iterator;
}
```

With while loops, it's common to declare an initializer variable, as in a for loop, and manually increment or decrement it at the end of the loop's code block. We do this to avoid an infinite loop, which we will discuss at the end of the chapter. Depending on your situation, the initializer is usually part of the loop's condition.

while loops are very useful when coding in C#, but they are not considered good practice in Unity because they can negatively impact performance and routinely need to be manually managed.

Let's take a common use case where we need to execute code while the player is alive, and then debug when that's no longer the case:

1. Create a public variable called PlayerLives of the int type and set it to 3:

    ```
    public int PlayerLives = 3;
    ```

2. Create a new public function called HealthStatus:

    ```
    public void HealthStatus()
    {
    }
    ```

3. Declare a while loop with the condition checking whether PlayerLives is greater than 0 (that is, the player is still alive):

    ```
    while(PlayerLives > 0)
    {
    }
    ```

4. Inside the while loop, debug something to let us know the character is still kicking, then decrement PlayerLives by 1 using the -- operator:

    ```
    Debug.Log("Still alive!");
    PlayerLives--;
    ```

5. Add a debug log after the while loop curly brackets to print something when our lives run out:

    ```
    Debug.Log("Player KO'd...");
    Call the HealthStatus method inside Start():void Start()
    {
        HealthStatus();
    }
    ```

6. Your code should look like the following:

```
public int PlayerLives = 3;
void Start()
{
    HealthStatus();
}
public void HealthStatus()
{
    while(PlayerLives > 0)
    {
        Debug.Log("Still alive!");
        PlayerLives--;
    }
    Debug.Log("Player KO'd...");
}
```

With PlayerLives starting out at 3, the while loop will execute three times. During each loop, the "Still alive!" debug log fires, and a life is subtracted from PlayerLives.

When the while loop goes to run a fourth time, our condition fails because PlayerLives is 0, so the code block is skipped, and the final debug log prints out:

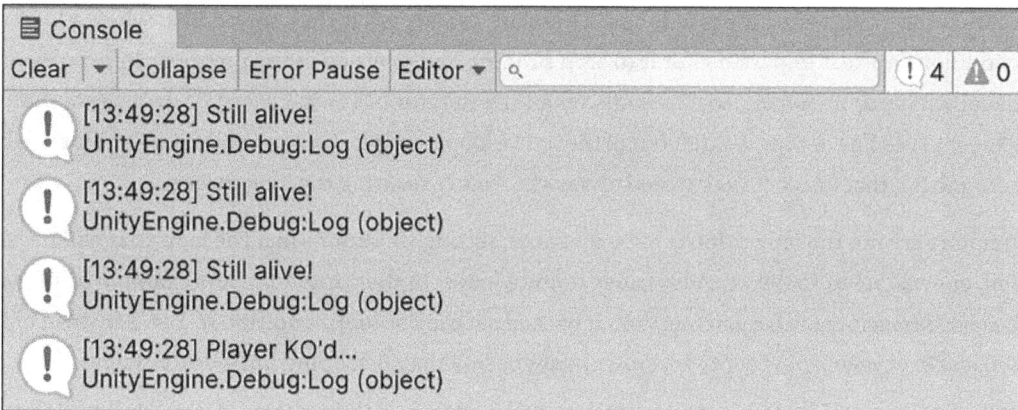

Figure 4.16: Screenshot of while loop output in the console

If you're not seeing multiple Still alive! debug logs, make sure the **Collapse** button in the
Console toolbar isn't selected:

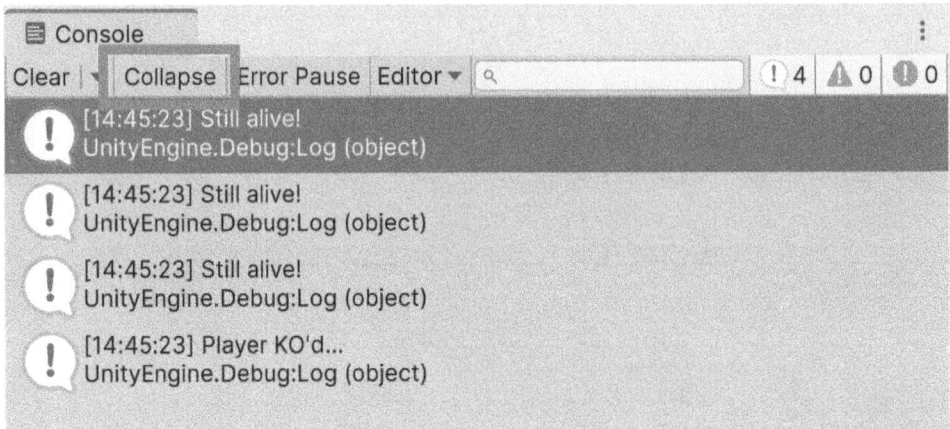

Figure 4.17: Screenshot of console messages with the Collapse option unchecked

The question now is what happens if a loop never stops executing? We'll discuss this issue in the
following section.

To infinity and beyond

Before finishing this chapter, we need to understand one extremely vital concept when it comes
to iteration statements: **infinite loops**. These are exactly what they sound like: when a loop's
conditions make it impossible for it to stop running and move on in the program. Infinite loops
usually happen in for and while loops when the iterator is not increased or decreased; if the
PlayerLives line of code was left out of the while loop example, Unity would freeze and/or crash,
recognizing that PlayerLives would always be 3 and executing the loop forever.

Iterators are not the only culprits to be aware of; setting conditions in a for loop that will never
fail, or evaluate to false, can also cause infinite loops. In the party members example from the
Looping through key-value pairs section, if we had set the for loop condition to i < 0 instead of i
< QuestPartyMembers.Count, i would always be less than 0, looping until Unity crashed.

Summary

As we bring the chapter to a close, we should reflect on how much we've accomplished and what
we can build with that new knowledge. We know how to use simple if-else checks and more
complex switch statements, allowing decision-making in code. We can create variables that hold
collections of values with arrays and lists or key-value pairs with dictionaries.

This allows complex and grouped data to be stored efficiently. We can even choose the right looping statement for each collection type, while carefully avoiding infinite-loop crashes.

If you're feeling overloaded, that's perfectly OK—logical, sequential thinking is all part of exercising your programming brain.

The next chapter will complete the basics of C# programming with a look at classes, structs, and **object-oriented programming (OOP)**. We'll be putting everything we've learned so far into these topics, preparing for our first real dive into understanding and controlling objects in the Unity engine.

Subscribe to Game Dev Assembly Newsletter!

We are excited to introduce **Game Dev Assembly**, our brand-new newsletter dedicated to everything game development. Whether you're a programmer, designer, artist, animator, or studio lead, you'll get exclusive insights, industry trends, and expert tips to help you build better games and grow your skills. Sign up today and become part of a growing community of creators, innovators, and game changers: https://packt.link/gamedev-newsletter

Scan the QR code to join instantly!

Unlock this book's exclusive benefits now

UNLOCK NOW

Scan this QR code or go to https://packtpub.com/unlock, then search this book by name.

Note: Keep your purchase invoice ready before you start.

5

Working with Classes, Structs, and OOP

For obvious reasons, the goal of this book isn't to give you a splitting headache from information overload, but these next topics will take you out of the beginner's cubicle and into the open air of object-oriented programming (OOP). Up to this point, we've been relying exclusively on predefined variable types that are part of the C# language: under-the-hood strings, lists, and dictionaries that are classes, which is why we can create them and use their properties through dot notation. However, relying on built-in types has one glaring weakness—the inability to deviate from the blueprints that C# has already set.

Creating your classes gives you the freedom to define and configure blueprints of your design, capturing information and driving action that is specific to your game or application. In essence, custom classes and OOP are the keys to the programming kingdom; without them, unique programs will be few and far between.

In this chapter, you'll get hands-on experience creating classes from scratch and using the inner workings of class variables, constructors, and methods. You'll also be introduced to the differences between reference and value type objects, and how these concepts can be applied in Unity. The following topics will be discussed in more detail as you move along:

- Introducing OOP
- Defining classes
- Declaring structs

- Understanding reference and value types
- Integrating the object-oriented mindset
- Applying OOP in Unity

Introducing OOP

Object-Oriented Programming (OOP) is the main programming paradigm that you'll use when coding in C#. If classes and structs are the blueprints of our programs, then OOP is the architecture that holds everything together. When we refer to OOP as a programming paradigm, we are saying that it has specific principles for how the overall program should work and communicate.

Essentially, OOP focuses on objects rather than pure sequential logic—the data they hold, how they drive action, and, most importantly, how they communicate with each other.

Defining classes

Back in *Chapter 2*, we talked briefly about how classes are blueprints for objects (in this case, objects in code, not GameObjects in Unity) and mentioned that they can be treated as custom variable types. We also learned that the LearningCurve script is a class, but a special one that Unity can attach to objects in the scene. The main thing to remember with classes is that they are reference types—that is, when they are assigned or passed to another variable, the original object is referenced, not a new copy. We'll get into this after we discuss structs in the *Declaring structs* section. However, before any of that, we need to understand the basics of creating classes.

Creating a class

For now, we're going to set aside how classes and scripts work in Unity and focus on how they are created and used in C#. Classes are created using the class keyword, as follows:

```
accessModifier class UniqueName
{
    Variables
    Constructors
    Methods
}
```

Any variables or methods declared inside a class belong to that class and are accessed through its unique class name.

To make the examples as cohesive as possible throughout this chapter, we'll be creating and modifying a simple Character class that a typical game would have. We'll also be moving away from code screenshots to get you accustomed to reading and interpreting code as you would see it *"in the wild."* However, the first thing we need is a custom class of our own, so let's create one.

We'll need a class to practice with before we can understand their inner workings, so let's create a new C# script and start from scratch:

1. Right-click on the Scripts folder that you created in *Chapter 1* and choose **Create | Scripting | Empty C# Script**.

2. Name the script Character and open it up in Visual Studio Code.

3. Your code should exactly match the following code:

```
using UnityEngine;

public class Character
{
}
```

Character is now registered as a public class blueprint. This means that any class in the project can use it to create characters. However, these are just the instructions—to create a character takes an additional step. This creational step is called **instantiation** and is the subject of the next section.

Instantiating class objects

Instantiation is the act of creating an object from a specific set of instructions, which is called an instance. If classes are blueprints, instances are the houses built from their instructions; every new instance of Character is its object, just as two houses built from the same instructions are still two different physical structures. What happens to one doesn't have any repercussions for the other.

In *Chapter 4*, we created lists and dictionaries, which are default classes that come with C#, using their types and the new keyword. We can do the same thing for custom classes such as Character, which you'll do next.

We declared the Character class as public, which means you can create a Character instance in any other class. Since we have LearningCurve working already, let's declare a new character in the Start() method.

Open LearningCurve and declare a new Character type variable, called hero, in the Start() method:

```
Character hero = new Character();
```

Let's break this down one step at a time:

1. The variable type is specified as Character, meaning that the variable is an instance of that class.

2. The variable is named hero, and it is created using the new keyword, followed by the Character class name and two parentheses ( ). This is where the actual instance is created in the program's memory, even if the class is empty right now.

3. We can use the hero variable just like any other object we've worked with so far. When the Character class gets variables and methods of its own, we can access them from hero using dot notation.

You could just as easily have used an inferred declaration when creating the hero variable, like so:

```
var hero = new Character();
```

Now, our character class can't do much without any class fields to work with. You'll be adding class fields and more in the next few sections.

Adding class fields

Adding variables, or fields, to a custom class is no different from what we've already been doing with LearningCurve. The same concepts apply, including access modifiers, variable scope, and value assignments. However, any variables belonging to a class are created with the class instance, meaning that if there are no values assigned, they will default to zero or null. In general, choosing to set initial values comes down to what information they will store:

- If a variable needs to have the same starting value whenever a class instance is created, setting an initial value is a solid idea. This would be useful for something such as experience points or the starting score.

- If a variable needs to be customized in every class instance, like CharacterName, leave its value unassigned and use a class constructor (a topic that we'll get to in the *Using constructors* section).

Every Character class is going to need a few basic fields; it's your job to add them.

Let's incorporate two variables to hold the character's name and the number of starting experience points:

1. Add two public variables inside the Character class's curly braces—a string variable for the name and an integer variable for the experience points.

2. Leave both variables uninitialized (they will use their default values):

```
public class Character
{
    public string Name;
    public int Exp;
}
```

3. Add a debug log in LearningCurve right after the Character instance was initialized. Use it to print out the new character's Name and Exp variables using dot notation:

```
Character hero = new Character();
Debug.LogFormat("Hero: {0} - {1} EXP", hero.Name, hero.Exp);
```

4. Click **Play** and run the game.

When hero is initialized, Name is assigned a null value that shows up as an empty space in the debug log, while Exp prints out as 0. Notice that we didn't have to attach the Character script to any GameObjects in the scene; we just referenced them in LearningCurve and Unity did the rest. The console will now debug our character information, which is referenced as follows:

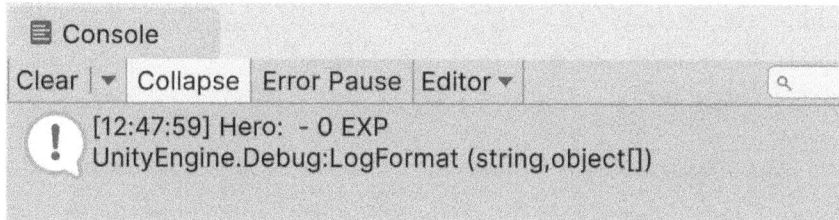

Figure 5.1: Screenshot of custom class properties printed in the console

Note

To provide a complete view of the Unity editor, all our screenshots are taken in fullscreen mode. For color versions of all book images, use this link: https://packt.link/gbp/9781805808718.

At this point, our class is working, but it's not very practical with these empty values. You'll need to fix that with what's called a class constructor.

Using constructors

Class constructors are special methods that fire automatically when a class instance is created, which is similar to how the Start() method runs in LearningCurve. Constructors build the class according to its blueprint:

- If a constructor is not specified, C# generates a default one. The default constructor sets any variables to their default type values—numeric values are set to 0, Booleans to false, and reference types (classes) to null.
- Custom constructors can be defined with parameters, just like any other method, and are used to set class variable values at initialization.
- A class can have multiple constructors.

Constructors are written like regular methods but with a few differences; for instance, they need to be public, have no return type, and the method name is always the class name. As an example, let's add a basic constructor with no parameters to the Character class and set the Name field to something other than null.

Add this new code directly underneath the class variables, as follows:

```
public class Character
{
    public string Name;
    public int Exp;
    public Character()
    {
        Name = "Not assigned";
    }
}
```

Run the project in Unity and you'll see the hero instance using this new constructor. The debug log will show the hero's name as **Not assigned** instead of a null value:

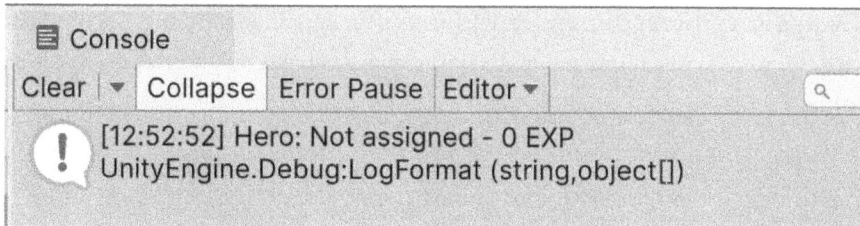

Figure 5.2: Screenshot of unassigned custom class variables printed to the console

This is good progress, but we need the class constructor to be more flexible. This means that we need to be able to pass in values so that they can be used as starting values, which you'll do next.

1. Now, the Character class is starting to behave more like a real object, but we can make this even better by adding a second constructor to take in a name at initialization and set it to the name field.

2. Add another constructor to Character that takes in a string parameter, called name. Having multiple constructors in a single class is called **constructor overloading**.

3. Assign the parameter to the class's Name variable using the this keyword:

```
public class Character
{
        public string Name;
        public int Exp;
        public Character()
        {
            Name = "Not assigned";
        }
        public Character(string name)
        {
            this.Name = name;
        }
}
```

For convenience, constructors will often have parameters that share a name with a class variable. In these cases, use the this keyword to specify which variable belongs to the class. In the example here, this.Name refers to the class's name variable, while name is the parameter; without the this keyword, the compiler will throw a warning because it won't be able to tell them apart. For clarity, you could also have used the this keyword in the default constructor where we set the Name property to Not assigned.

4. Create a new Character instance in LearningCurve, called heroine. Use the custom con-
    structor to pass in a name when it's initialized and print out the details in the console:

    ```
    Character heroine = new Character("Agatha");
    Debug.LogFormat("Hero: {0} - {1} EXP", heroine.Name,
            heroine.Exp);
    ```

5. When a class has multiple constructors or a method has multiple variations, Visual Studio
    Code will show a set of arrows in the autocomplete popup that can be scrolled through
    using the arrow keys:

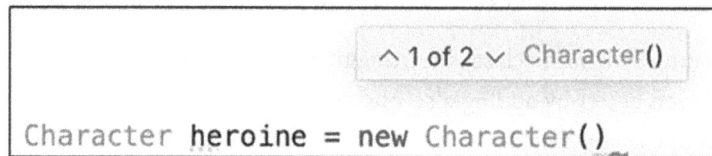

Figure 5.3: Screenshot of multiple method constructors in Visual Studio Code

6. We can now choose between the basic and custom constructors when we initialize a
    new Character class. The Character class itself is now far more flexible when it comes
    to configuring different instances for different situations:

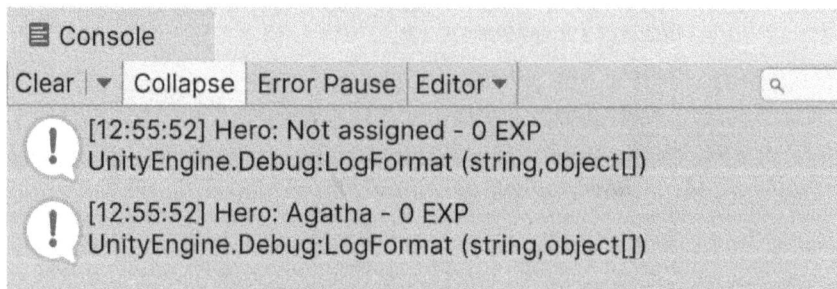

Figure 5.4: Screenshot of multiple custom class instances printed in the console

Now the real work starts; our class needs methods to be able to do useful things besides acting
as a storage facility for variables. Your next task is to put this into practice.

Declaring class methods

Adding methods to custom classes is no different from adding them to LearningCurve. However,
this is a good opportunity to talk about a staple of good programming—**Don't Repeat Yourself**
(DRY). DRY is a benchmark of all well-written code. Essentially, if you find yourself writing the
same line, or lines, over and over, it's time to rethink and reorganize.

This usually takes the form of a new method to hold the repeated code, making it easier to modify and call that functionality elsewhere in the current script or even from other scripts. In programming terms, you'll see this referred to as **abstracting** a method or feature.

We have a fair bit of repeated code already, so let's take a look and see where we can increase the legibility and efficiency of our scripts.

Our repeated debug logs are a perfect opportunity to abstract out some code directly into the Character class:

1. Add a new public method with a void return type, called PrintStatsInfo(), to the Character class.

    a. Copy and paste the debug log from LearningCurve into the method body.

    b. Change the variables to Name and Exp, since they can now be referenced from the class directly:

    ```
    public void PrintStatsInfo()
    {
        Debug.LogFormat("Hero: {0} - {1} EXP", this.Name, this.
    Exp);
    }
    ```

2. Replace the character debug log that we previously added to LearningCurve with method calls to PrintStatsInfo():

    ```
    Character hero = new Character();
    hero.PrintStatsInfo();
    Character heroine = new Character("Agatha");
    heroine.PrintStatsInfo();
    ```

3. Run the game and everything in the console will work the same (but with better code).

Now that the Character class has a method, any instance can freely access it using dot notation. Since hero and heroine are both separate objects, PrintStatsInfo() debugs their respective Name and Exp values to the console.

This behavior is better than having the debug logs directly in LearningCurve. It's always a good idea to group functionality into a class and drive action through methods. This makes the code more readable—as our Character objects are giving a command when printing out the debug logs, instead of repeating code.

The entire `Character` class should look like the following code:

```
using UnityEngine;

public class Character
{
    public string Name;
    public int Exp;

    public Character()
    {
        Name = "Not assigned";
    }

    public Character(string name)
    {
        this.Name = name;
    }

    public void PrintStatsInfo()
    {
        Debug.LogFormat("Hero: {0} - {1} EXP", this.Name, this.Exp);
    }
}
```

With classes covered, you're well on your way to writing modularized code that's readable, light-weight, and reusable. Now it's time to tackle the class's cousin object—the struct!

Declaring structs

Structs are similar to classes in that they are also blueprints for objects you want to create in your programs. The main difference is that they are value types, meaning they are passed by value instead of reference, like classes are. When structs are assigned or passed to another variable, a new copy of the struct is created, so the original isn't referenced at all. We'll go into this in more detail in the next section. First, we need to understand how structs work and the specific rules that apply when creating them.

Structs are declared in the same way as classes, and can hold fields, methods, and constructors. A good rule of thumb is to only store other value types inside of your structs; while you can store reference types in a struct, this often defeats the purpose and advantages of using structs instead of classes.

```
accessModifier struct UniqueName
{
    Variables
    Constructors
    Methods
}
```

Like classes, any variables and methods belong exclusively to the struct and are accessed by its unique name.

However, structs have a few limitations:

- Variables cannot be initialized with values inside the struct declaration unless they're marked with the static or const modifier—you can read more about this in *Chapter 10*. For example, the following code would throw an error:

```
public struct Author
    {
        string Name = "Harrison";
        int Age = 32;
    }
```

- Constructors without parameters aren't permitted (as will not assigning all constructor variables). For example, the following code would also throw an error:

```
public struct Author
{
    public Author()
        {
        }
}
```

- Structs come with a default constructor that will automatically set all variables to their default values according to their type.

Every character requires a good weapon, and these weapons are the perfect fit for a struct object over a class. We'll discuss why that is in the *Understanding reference and value types* section of this chapter. However, first, you're going to create one to play around with.

Our characters are going to need good weapons to see them through quests, which are good candidates for a simple struct:

1. Right-click on the Scripts folder and choose **Create | Scripting | Empty C# Script**.

2. Name it Weapon, open it up in Visual Studio Code, and delete all the generated code after using UnityEngine.

3. Declare a public struct called Weapon, followed by a set of curly braces, and add a field for Name of type string and another field for Damage of type int.

4. You can have classes and structs nested within each other, but this is generally frowned upon because it clutters up the code:

```
using UnityEngine;
public struct Weapon
{
    public string Name;
    public int Damage;
}
```

5. Declare a constructor with the Name and Damage parameters, and set the struct fields using the this keyword:

```
public Weapon(string name, int damage)
{
    this.Name = name;
    this.Damage = damage;
}
```

6. Add a debug method below the constructor to print out the weapon information:

```
public void PrintWeaponStats()
{
    Debug.LogFormat("Weapon: {0} - {1} DMG", this.Name, this.
Damage);
}
```

7. In `LearningCurve`, create a new `Weapon` struct using the custom constructor and the new
    keyword, then use the `PrintWeaponStats()` method to debug the struct values:

    ```
    Weapon huntingBow = new Weapon("Hunting Bow", 105);
    huntingBow.PrintWeaponStats();
    ```

8. Click **Play** and take a look at the new debug log!

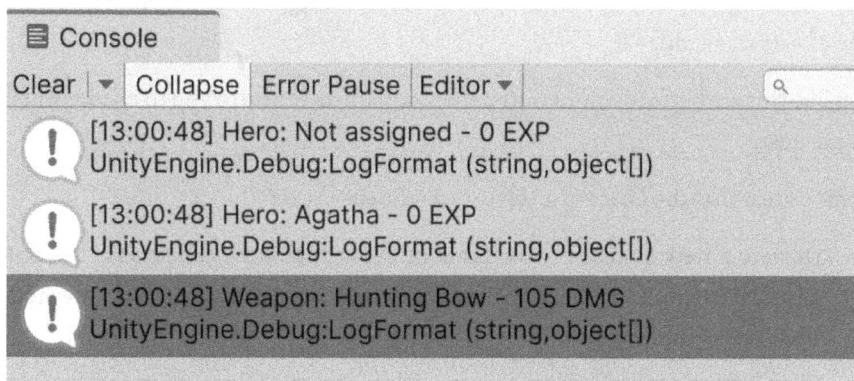

Figure 5.5: Screenshot of weapon struct properties printed to the console

Our new `huntingBow` object uses the custom constructor and provides values for both fields on
initialization. It's a good idea to limit scripts to a single class, but it's fairly common to see structs
that are used exclusively by a class included in the file.

Now that we have an example of both reference (class) and value (struct) objects, it's time to get
acquainted with each of their finer points. More specifically, you'll need to understand how each
of these objects is passed and stored in memory.

Understanding reference and value types

Other than keywords and initial field values, we haven't seen much difference between classes
and structs so far. Classes are best suited for grouping together complex actions and data that
will change throughout a program; structs are a better choice for simple objects and data that
will remain constant for the most part, such as values that stay the same throughout the entire
project. Besides their uses, they are fundamentally different in one key area—that is, how they are
passed or assigned between variables. Classes are reference types, meaning that they are passed
by reference; structs are value types, meaning that they are passed by value.

Reference types

When the instances of our Character class are initialized, the hero and heroine variables don't hold their class information—instead, they hold a reference to where the object is located in the program's memory. If we assigned hero or heroine to another variable in the same class, the memory reference is assigned, not the character data. This has several implications, the most important being that if we have multiple variables storing the same memory reference, a change to one affects them all.

Topics like this are better demonstrated than explained; it's up to you to try this out in a practical example next.

It's time to test that the Character class is a reference type:

1. Declare a new Character variable in LearningCurve called assistantHero. Assign assistantHero to the hero variable and use the PrintStatsInfo() method to print out both sets of information.

2. Click **Play** and take a look at the two debug logs that show up in the console:

    ```
    Character hero = new Character();
    Character assistantHero= hero;

    hero.PrintStatsInfo();
    assistantHero.PrintStatsInfo();
    ```

    The two debug logs will be identical because assistantHero was assigned to hero when it was created. At this point, both hero and assistantHero point to where hero is stored in memory:

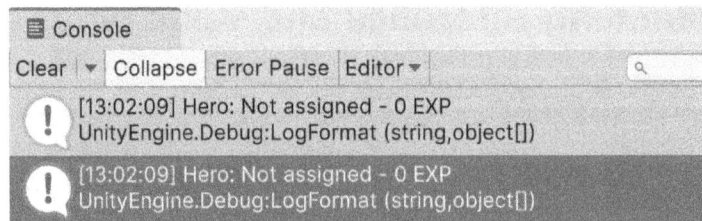

Figure 5.6: Screenshot of the struct stats printed to the console

3. Now, change the name of assistantHero to something fun *before* printing out the stats and click **Play** again:

```
Character assistantHero = hero;
assistantHero.Name = "Sir Kane the Bold";
```

4. You'll see that both hero and assistantHero now have the same name, even though only one of our characters' data was changed:

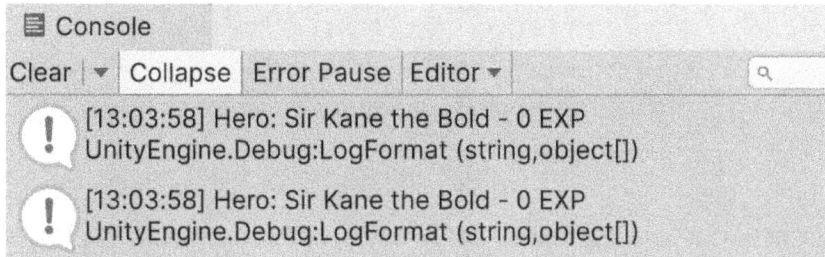

Figure 5.7: Screenshot of class instance properties printed to the console

The lesson here is that reference types need to be treated carefully and not copied when assigned to new variables. Any change to one reference trickles through all other variables holding the same reference.

If you're trying to copy a class, either create a new, separate instance or reconsider whether a struct might be a better choice for your object blueprint. You'll get a better glimpse of value types in the following section.

Value types

When a struct object is created, all of its data is stored in its corresponding variable with no references or connections to its memory location. This makes structs useful for creating objects that need to be copied quickly and efficiently, while still retaining their separate identities. Try this out with our Weapon struct in the following exercise.

Let's create a new weapon object by copying huntingBow into a new variable and updating its data to see whether the changes affect both structs:

1. Declare a new Weapon struct in LearningCurve, and assign huntingBow as its initial value:

```
Weapon huntingBow = new Weapon("Hunting Bow", 105);
Weapon warBow = huntingBow;
```

2. Print out each weapon's data using the debug method:

```
huntingBow.PrintWeaponStats();
warBow.PrintWeaponStats();
```

3. The way they're set up now, both huntingBow and warBow will have the same debug logs, just like our two characters did before we changed any data:

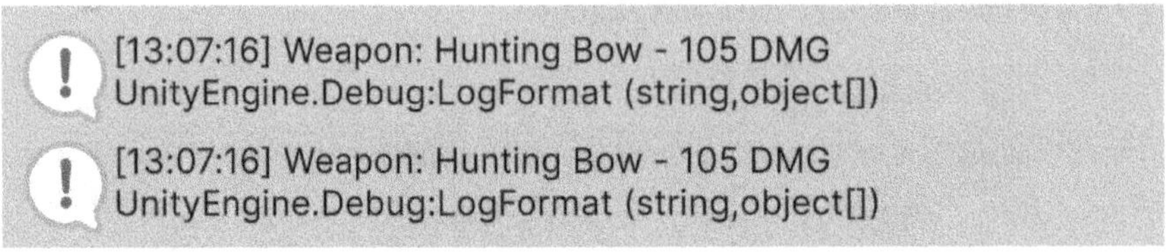

> **!** [13:07:16] Weapon: Hunting Bow - 105 DMG
> UnityEngine.Debug:LogFormat (string,object[])
>
> **!** [13:07:16] Weapon: Hunting Bow - 105 DMG
> UnityEngine.Debug:LogFormat (string,object[])

Figure 5.8: Screenshot of the struct instances printed to the console

4. Change the Name and Damage fields to values of your choice and click on **Play** again:

```
Weapon warBow = huntingBow;
warBow.Name = "War Bow";
warBow.Damage = 155;
```

The console will show that only the data relating to warBow was changed, and that huntingBow retains its original data.

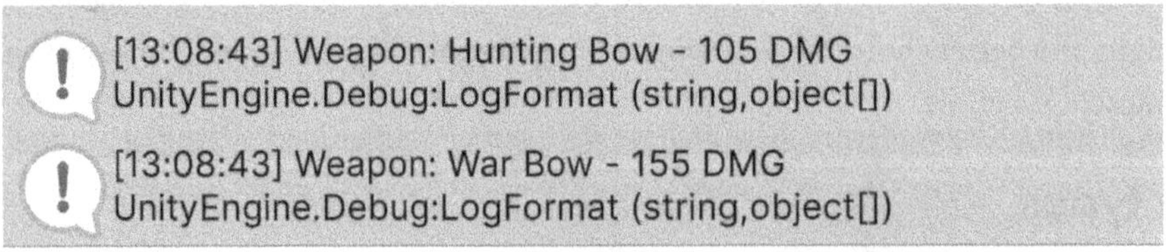

> **!** [13:08:43] Weapon: Hunting Bow - 105 DMG
> UnityEngine.Debug:LogFormat (string,object[])
>
> **!** [13:08:43] Weapon: War Bow - 155 DMG
> UnityEngine.Debug:LogFormat (string,object[])

Figure 5.9: Screenshot of updated struct properties printed to the console

The takeaway from this example is that structs are easily copied and modified as their separate objects, unlike classes, which retain references to an original object.

Now that we understand a little more about how structs and classes work under the hood and have confirmed how reference and value types behave in their natural habitat, we're in a good place to start talking about one of the most important coding topics, OOP, and how it fits into the programming landscape.

Integrating the object-oriented mindset

Things in the physical world operate on a similar level to OOP; when you want to buy a soft drink, you grab a can of soda, not the liquid itself. The can is an object, grouping related information and actions together in a self-contained package. However, there are rules when dealing with objects, both in programming and the grocery store—for instance, who can access them. Different variations and generic actions all play into the nature of the objects all around us.

In programming terms, these rules are the main tenets of OOP: **encapsulation**, **inheritance**, and **polymorphism**. Let's discuss these topics in the next few sections!

Encapsulation

One of the best things about OOP is that it supports **encapsulation**—defining how accessible an object's variables and methods are to outside code (this is sometimes referred to as calling code). Take our soda can as an example—in a vending machine, the possible interactions are limited.

Since the machine is locked, not just anyone can come up and grab one; if you happen to have the right change, you'll be allowed provisional access to it, but in a specified quantity. If the machine itself is locked inside a room, only someone with the door key will even know the soda can exists.

The question you're asking yourself now is, how do we set these limitations? The simple answer is that we've been using encapsulation this entire time by specifying access modifiers for our object variables and methods.

If you need a refresher, go back and visit the *Access modifiers* section in *Chapter 3*.

Let's try out a simple encapsulation example to understand how this works in practice. Our Character class is public, as are its fields and methods. However, what if we wanted a method that could reset a character's data to its initial values? This could come in handy, but could prove disastrous if it were accidentally called, making it a perfect candidate for a private object member:

1. In Character.cs, create a private method called Reset(), with no return value inside the Character class. Set the Name and Exp variables back to "Not assigned" and 0, respectively:

    ```
    private void Reset()
    {
        this.Name = "Not assigned";
        this.Exp = 0;
    }
    ```

2. Try and call `Reset()` from the `assistantHero` instance in `LearningCurve`:

```
assistantHero.Reset();
```

If you're wondering whether Visual Studio Code is broken, it's not. Marking a method or variable as private will make it inaccessible using dot notation; it can only be called from within the class or struct it belongs to. If you manually type it in and hover over `Reset()`, you'll see an error message regarding the method being protected, as shown in the following screenshot:

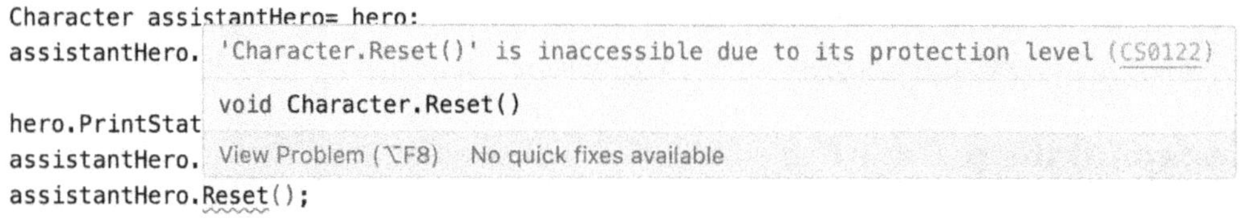

```
Character assistantHero= hero:
assistantHero.  'Character.Reset()' is inaccessible due to its protection level (CS0122)

                void Character.Reset()
hero.PrintStat
assistantHero.  View Problem (⌥F8)   No quick fixes available
assistantHero.Reset();
```

Figure 5.10: Screenshot of an inaccessible method in the Character class

This method can only be called from within the `Character` class, so, for example, we could reset our data in the default constructor:

```
public Character()
{
    Reset();
}
```

Encapsulation does allow more complex accessibility setups with objects; however, for now, we're going to stick with `public` and `private` members. As we begin to flesh out our game prototype in the next chapter, we'll add different modifiers as needed.

Now, let's talk about inheritance, which is going to be your best friend when creating class hierarchies in your future games.

Inheritance

A C# class can be created in the image of another class, sharing its member variables and methods, but able to define its unique data. In OOP, we refer to this as inheritance, and it's a powerful way of creating related classes without having to repeat code. Take the soda example again—there are generic sodas on the market that have all the same basic properties, and then there are special sodas. The special sodas share the same basic properties but have different branding, or packaging, that sets them apart. When you look at both side by side, it's obvious that they're both cans of soda—but they're also obviously not the same.

The original class is usually called the base or parent class, while the inheriting class is called the derived or child class. Any base class members marked with the public, protected, or internal access modifiers are automatically part of the derived class—except for constructors. Class constructors always belong to their containing class, but they can be used from derived classes to keep repeated code to a minimum. Don't worry too much about the different base class scenarios right now. Instead, let's try out a simple game example.

Most games have more than one type of character, so let's create another type of character:

1. Right-click on the Scripts folder and choose **Create | Scripting | Empty C# Script**.

2. Name it Paladin, open it up in Visual Studio Code, and declare a new class to inherit from the Character class:

```
using UnityEngine;

public class Paladin : Character
{

}
```

Just as LearningCurve inherits from MonoBehaviour, all we need to do is add a colon : and the base class we want to inherit from, and C# does the rest. Now, any Paladin instances will have access to a name property and an exp property along with a PrintStatsInfo method.

This is great, but how do inherited classes handle their construction? You can find out in the following section.

Base constructors

When a class inherits from another class, they form a pyramid of sorts with member variables flowing down from the parent class to any of its derived children. The parent class isn't aware of any of its children, but all children are aware of their parent. However, parent class constructors can be called directly from child constructors with a simple syntax modification:

```
public class ChildClass: ParentClass
{
    public ChildClass(): base()
    {
    }
}
```

The base keyword stands in for the parent constructor—in this case, the default constructor. However, since base is standing in for a constructor, and a constructor is a method, a child class can pass parameters up the pyramid to its parent constructor.

Since we want all Paladin objects to have a name variable, and Character already has a construc-tor that handles this, we can call the base constructor directly from the Paladin class and save ourselves the trouble of rewriting a constructor:

1. Add a constructor to the Paladin class that takes in a string parameter, called name. Use a colon (:) and the base keyword to call the parent constructor, passing in name:

```
public class Paladin: Character
{
    public Paladin(string name): base(name)
    {

    }
}
```

2. In LearningCurve, create a new Paladin instance called knight. Use the base constructor to assign a value. Call PrintStatsInfo() from knight and take a look at the console:

```
Paladin knight = new Paladin("Sir Arthur");
knight.PrintStatsInfo();
```

3. The debug log will be the same as our other Character instances, but with the name that we assigned to the Paladin constructor:

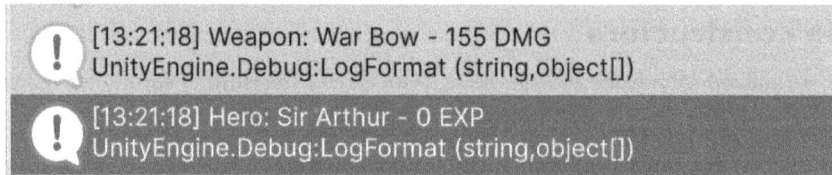

Figure 5.11: Screenshot of base character constructor properties

When the Paladin constructor fires, it passes the name parameter to the Character constructor, which sets the name value. Essentially, we used the Character constructor to do the initialization work for the Paladin class, making the Paladin constructor only responsible for initializing its unique properties, which it doesn't have at this point.

Aside from inheritance, there will be times when you want to make new objects out of a combination of other existing objects. Think of LEGO®; you don't start building from nothing—you already have different colored blocks and structures to work with. In programming terms, this is called composition, which we'll discuss in the following section.

Composition

Aside from inheritance, classes can be composed of other classes. Take our Weapon struct, for example. Paladin can easily contain a Weapon variable inside itself and have access to all its properties and methods.

Let's do that by updating Paladin to take in a starting weapon and assign its value in the constructor:

```
public class Paladin: Character
{
    public Weapon PrimaryWeapon;

    public Paladin(string name, Weapon weapon): base(name)
    {
        this.PrimaryWeapon = weapon;
    }
}
```

Since PrimaryWeapon is unique to Paladin and not Character, we need to set its initial value in the constructor. We also need to update the knight instance to include a Weapon variable. So, let's go back into LearningCurve.cs and use huntingBow:

```
Paladin knight = new Paladin("Sir Arthur", huntingBow);
```

You *must* declare knight *after* instantiating huntingBow to be able to use it in the Paladin class constructor—huntingBow has to exist before we can use it! If you run the game now, you won't see anything different because we're using the PrintStatsInfo() method from the Character class, which doesn't know about the Paladin class's weapon property. To tackle this problem, we need to talk about **polymorphism**.

Polymorphism

Polymorphism is the Greek word for *many-shaped* and applies to OOP in two distinct ways:

- Derived class objects are treated the same as parent class objects. For example, an array of Character objects could also store Paladin objects, as they derive from Character.

- Parent classes can mark methods as virtual, meaning that their instructions can be modified by derived classes using the override keyword. In the case of Character and Paladin, it would be useful if we could debug different messages from PrintStatsInfo() for each one.

Polymorphism allows derived classes to keep the structure of their parent class while also having the freedom to tailor actions to fit their specific needs. Any method you mark as virtual will give you the freedom of object polymorphism.

Let's take this new knowledge and apply it to our character debug method.

Let's modify Character and Paladin to print out different debug logs using PrintStatsInfo:

1. In Character.cs, change PrintStatsInfo() in the Character class by adding the virtual keyword between public and void:

```
public virtual void PrintStatsInfo()
{
    Debug.LogFormat("Hero: {0} - {1} EXP", this.Name, this.Exp);
}
```

2. Declare the PrintStatsInfo() method in the Paladin class using the override keyword. Add a debug log to print out the Paladin properties in whatever way you like:

```
public override void PrintStatsInfo()
{
    Debug.LogFormat("Hail {0} - take up your {1}!", this.Name,
        this.PrimaryWeapon.Name);
}
```

3. This might look like repeated code, which we already said is bad form, but this is a special case. What we've done by marking PrintStatsInfo() as virtual in the Character class is to tell the compiler that this method can have many shapes according to the calling class.

4. When we declared the overridden version of `PrintStatsInfo()` in `Paladin`, we added the custom behavior that only applies to that class. Thanks to polymorphism, we don't have to choose which version of `PrintStatsInfo()` we want to call from a `Character` or `Paladin` object—the compiler already knows:

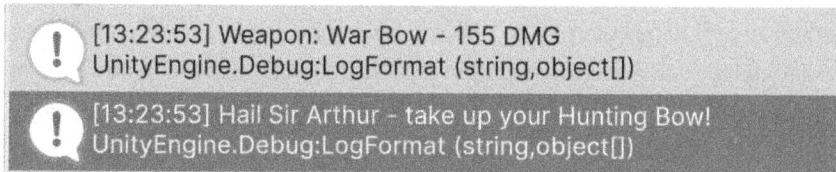

    > ! [13:23:53] Weapon: War Bow - 155 DMG
    >   UnityEngine.Debug:LogFormat (string,object[])
    >
    > ! [13:23:53] Hail Sir Arthur - take up your Hunting Bow!
    >   UnityEngine.Debug:LogFormat (string,object[])

Figure 5.12: Screenshot of polymorphic character properties

This was a lot to take in, I know. So, let's review some of the main points of OOP as we approach the finish line:

*   OOP is all about grouping related data and actions into objects—objects that can communicate and act independently of each other.
*   Access to class members can be set using access modifiers, just like variables.
*   Classes can inherit from other classes, creating trickle-down hierarchies of parent/child relationships.
*   Classes can have members of other class or struct types.
*   Classes can override any parent methods marked as `virtual`, allowing them to perform custom actions while retaining the same blueprint.

OOP is not the only programming paradigm that can be used with C#—you can find practical explanations of the other main approaches here: `http://cs.lmu.edu/~ray/notes/paradigms`.

All the OOP you've learned in this chapter is directly applicable to the C# world. However, we still need to put this into perspective with Unity, which is what you'll spend the rest of the chapter focusing on.

Applying OOP in Unity

If you're around OOP languages enough, you'll eventually hear the phrase *"everything is an object"* whispered like a secret prayer between developers. Following OOP principles, everything in a program should be an object, but GameObjects in Unity can represent your classes and structs. However, that's not to say all objects in Unity have to be in the physical scene, so we can still use our newfound programmed classes behind the scenes.

Objects are a class act

Back in *Chapter 2*, we discussed how a script is transformed into a component when it's added to a GameObject in Unity. Think of this in terms of the OOP principle of composition—GameObjects are the parent containers, and they can be made up of multiple components. This might sound contradictory to the idea of one C# class per script but, in truth, that's more of a guideline for better readability than an actual requirement. Classes can be nested inside one another—it just gets messy fast. However, having multiple script components attached to a single GameObject can be very useful, especially when dealing with manager classes or behaviors.

Always try to boil down objects to their most basic elements, and then use composition to build bigger, more complex objects out of those smaller classes. It's easier to modify a GameObject made out of small, interchangeable components than a large, clunky one.

Let's take a look at **Main Camera** to see this in action:

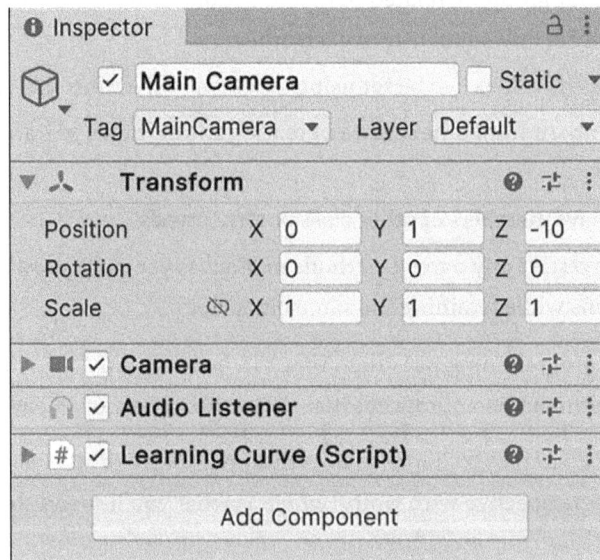

Figure 5.13: Screenshot of the Main Camera object in the Inspector

Each component in the preceding screenshot (Transform, Camera, Audio Listener, and the Learning Curve script) started as a class in Unity. Like instances of Character or Weapon, these components become objects in computer memory when we click on **Play**, complete with their member variables and methods.

If we were to attach LearningCurve (or any script or component) to 1,000 GameObjects and click on **Play**, 1,000 separate instances of LearningCurve would be created and stored in memory.

We can even create our instances of these components using their component name as the data type. Like classes, Unity component classes are reference types and can be created like any other variable. However, finding and assigning these Unity components is slightly different than what you've seen so far. For that, you'll need to understand a little more about how GameObjects work in the following section.

Accessing components

Now that we know how components act on GameObjects, how do we go about accessing their specific instances? Lucky for us, all GameObjects in Unity inherit from the GameObject class, which means we can use their member methods to find anything we need in a scene. There are two ways to assign or retrieve GameObjects that are active in the current scene:

1. Through the GetComponent() or Find() method in the GameObject class, which work with public and private variables. However, it's important to be careful with these two methods; for optimal performance and best practices, the result of the GetComponent() call should always be saved in its own variables and Find() should be used sparingly and never in an Update() loop.

2. By dragging and dropping the GameObjects themselves from the Project panel directly into variable slots in the **Inspector** tab. This option only works with public variables in C#, since they are the only ones that will appear in the **Inspector**. If you decide you need a private variable displayed in the **Inspector**, you can mark it with the SerializeField attribute.

You can learn more about attributes and SerializeField in the Unity documentation: https:// docs.unity3d.com/ScriptReference/SerializeField.html.

Let's take a look at the syntax of the first option.

Accessing components in code

Using GetComponent() is fairly simple, but its method signature is slightly different from other methods that we've seen so far:

```
GameObject.GetComponent<ComponentType>();
```

All we need is the component type that we're looking for, and the GameObject class will return the component if it exists and null if it doesn't. There are other variations of the GetComponent method, but this one is the simplest because we don't need to know specifics about the GameObject class that we're looking for.

This is called a generic method, which we'll discuss further in *Chapter 13*. However, for now, let's just work with the camera's **Transform**.

Since LearningCurve is already attached to the Main Camera object, let's grab the camera's **Transform** component and store it in a public variable. The **Transform** component controls an object's position, rotation, and scale in Unity, so it's a handy example:

1. In LearningCurve, add a new public Transform type variable, called CamTransform:

    ```
    public Transform CamTransform;
    ```

2. Initialize CamTransform in Start() using the GetComponent method from the GameObject class. Use the this keyword, since LearningCurve is attached to the same GameObject component as the **Transform** component.

    a. Access and debug the localPosition property of CamTransform using dot notation (notice we're storing the component in its own variable for performance):

    ```
    void Start()
    {
        CamTransform = this.GetComponent<Transform>();
        Debug.Log(CamTransform.localPosition);
    }
    ```

3. We've added an uninitialized public Transform variable at the top of LearningCurve and initialized it using the GetComponent method inside Start(). GetComponent() finds the Transform component attached to this GameObject component and returns it to CamTransform. With CamTransform now storing a Transform object, we have access to all its class properties and methods—including localPosition in the following screenshot:

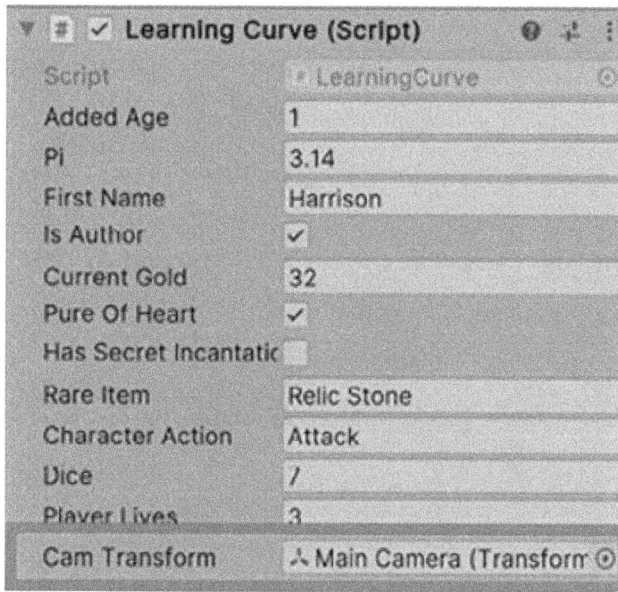

Figure 5.14: Screenshot of the Transform position printed to the console

The GetComponent() method is fantastic for quickly retrieving components, but it only has access to components on the GameObject that the calling script is attached to. For instance, if we use GetComponent() from the LearningCurve script attached to the **Main Camera**, we'll only be able to access the **Transform, Camera,** and **Audio Listener** components.

If we wanted to reference a component on a separate GameObject, such as **Directional Light**, we would need to get a reference to the object first using the Find method. All it takes is the name of a GameObject and Unity will kick back the appropriate GameObject for us to store or manipulate.

For reference, the name of each GameObject can be found at the top of the **Inspector** tab with the object selected:

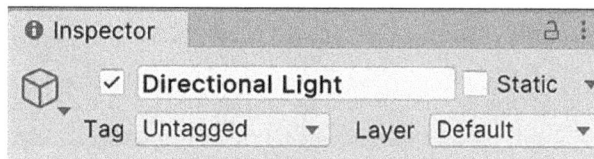

Figure 5.15: Screenshot of the Directional Light object in the Inspector

Finding objects in your game scenes is crucial in Unity, so you'll need to practice. Let's take the objects we have to work with and practice finding and assigning their components.

Let's take the `Find` method out for a spin and retrieve the **Directional Light** object from `LearningCurve`:

1. Add two variables to `LearningCurve` underneath `CamTransform`—one of type `GameObject` and one of type `Transform`:

    ```
    public GameObject DirectionLight;
    public Transform LightTransform;
    ```

2. Find the **Directional Light** component by name, and use it to initialize `DirectionLight` inside the `Start()` method:

    ```
    void Start()
    {
        DirectionLight = GameObject.Find("Directional Light");
    }
    ```

3. Set the value of `LightTransform` to the `Transform` component attached to `DirectionLight` and debug its `localPosition`. Since `DirectionLight` is its GameObject now, `GetComponent` works perfectly:

    ```
    LightTransform = DirectionLight.GetComponent<Transform>();
    Debug.Log(LightTransform.localPosition);
    ```

Before running the game, it's important to understand that method calls can be chained together to cut down the number of code steps. For instance, we could initialize `LightTransform` in a single line by combining `Find` and `GetComponent()` without having to go through `DirectionLight`:

```
GameObject.Find("Directional Light").GetComponent<Transform>();
```

A word of warning—long lines of chained code can lead to poor readability and confusion when working on complex applications. It's a good rule of thumb to avoid lines longer than this example.

While finding objects in code always works, you can also simply drag and drop the objects themselves into the **Inspector** tab. Let's demonstrate how to do that in the following section.

Drag and drop

Now that we've covered the code-intensive way of doing things, let's take a quick look at Unity's drag and drop functionality. Although dragging and dropping is much faster than using the GameObject class in code, Unity sometimes loses the connections between objects and variables made this way when saving or exporting projects, or when Unity updates.

When you need to assign a few variables quickly, then, by all means, take advantage of this feature. For most cases, I'd advise sticking with code.

Let's change LearningCurve to show how to assign a GameObject component using drag and drop:

1. Comment the following line of code, where we used GameObject.Find() to retrieve and assign the Directional Light object to the DirectionLight variable:

   ```
   //DirectionLight = GameObject.Find("Directional Light");
   ```

2. Select the Main Camera GameObject, drag Directional Light to the Direction Light field in the Learning Curve component, and click on **Play**:

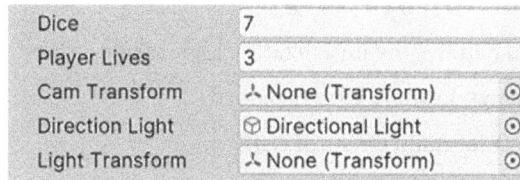

Dice	7	
Player Lives	3	
Cam Transform	⟁ None (Transform)	⊙
Direction Light	⊘ Directional Light	⊙
Light Transform	⟁ None (Transform)	⊙

Figure 5.16: Screenshot of dragging Directional Light to the script property

3. The Directional Light GameObject is now assigned to the DirectionLight variable. No code was involved because Unity assigned the variable internally, with no change to the LearningCurve class.

It is important to understand a few things when deciding whether to assign variables using drag and drop or GameObject.Find(). First, the Find() method is marginally slower, leaving your game open to performance issues if you are calling the method multiple times in multiple scripts.

Second, you need to be sure your GameObjects all have unique names in the scene hierarchy; if they don't, it may lead to some nasty bugs in situations where you have several objects of the same name or change the object names themselves.

Summary

Our journey into classes, structs, and OOP marks the end of the first section on the fundamentals of C#. You've learned how to declare your classes and structs, which is the scaffolding for every application or game you'll ever make. You've also identified the differences in how these two objects are passed and accessed and how they relate to OOP. Finally, you got hands-on with the tenets of OOP—creating classes using inheritance, composition, and polymorphism.

Identifying related data and actions, creating blueprints to give them shape, and using instances to build interactions are strong foundations for approaching any program or game. Add the ability to access components to the mix, and you've got the makings of a Unity developer.

The next chapter will segue into the basics of game development and scripting object behavior directly in Unity. We'll start by fleshing out the requirements of a simple open-world adventure game, work with GameObjects in the scene, and finish off with a white-boxed environment ready for our characters.

Pop quiz: All things OOP

    a.   What method handles the initialization logic inside a class?

    b.   Being value types, how are structs passed?

    c.   What are the three main tenets of OOP?

    d.   Which GameObject class method would you use to find a component on the same object as the calling class?

Don't forget to check your answers against mine in the *Pop Quiz Answers* appendix to see how you did!

Subscribe to Game Dev Assembly Newsletter!

We are excited to introduce **Game Dev Assembly**, our brand-new newsletter dedicated to everything game development. Whether you're a programmer, designer, artist, animator, or studio lead, you'll get exclusive insights, industry trends, and expert tips to help you build better games and grow your skills. Sign up today and become part of a growing community of creators, innovators, and game changers: `https://packt.link/gamedev-newsletter`

Scan the QR code to join instantly!

Join our community on Discord

Join our community's Discord space for discussions with the authors and other readers: `https://packt.link/gamedevelopment`

6

Getting Your Hands Dirty with Unity

Creating a game involves much more than just simulating actions in code. Design, story, environment, lighting, and animation all play an important part in setting the stage for your players. A game is, first and foremost, an experience—something that code alone can't deliver.

Unity has placed itself at the forefront of game development over the past decade by bringing advanced tools to programmers and non-programmers alike. Animation and effects, audio, environment design, and much more are all available directly from the Unity Editor without a single line of code, including XR/AR/VR features, AI integrations, and performance improvements with Unity 6. We'll discuss these topics as we define the requirements, environment, and game mechanics of our game. However, first, we need a topical introduction to game design.

Game design theory is a large area of study, and learning all its secrets can consume an entire career. However, we'll only be getting hands-on with the basics; everything else is up to you to explore! This chapter will set us up for the rest of the book and will cover the following topics:

- A game design primer
- Building a level
- Lighting basics
- Animating in Unity

A game design primer

Before jumping into any game project, it's important to have a blueprint of what you want to build. Sometimes, ideas will start crystal clear in your mind, but the minute you start creating character classes or environments, things seem to drift away from your original intention. This is where the game's design allows you to plan out the following touchpoints:

- **Concept:** The big-picture idea and design of a game, including its genre and play style.
- **Story:** The underlying narrative that fuels a game, creating empathy and a connection between players and the game world they play in.
- **Art style:** The game's overarching look and feel, consistent across everything from characters and menu art to the levels and environments.
- **Core mechanics:** The playable features or interactions that a character can take in-game. Common gameplay mechanics include jumping, shooting, puzzle-solving, or driving.
- **Control schemes:** A map of the buttons and/or keys that give players control over their character, environment interactions, and other executable actions.
- **Win/lose conditions:** The rules that govern how the game is won or lost, usually consisting of objectives or goals that carry the weight of potential failure.

These topics are by no means an exhaustive list of what goes into designing a game. However, they're a good place to start fleshing out something called a **game design document**, which is your next task!

Game design documents

Googling game design documents will result in a flood of templates, formatting rules, and content guidelines that can leave a new programmer ready to give it all up. The truth is, design documents are tailored to the team or company that creates them, making them much easier to draft than the internet would have you think.

In general, there are three types of design documentation, as follows:

- **Game design document (GDD):** The GDD houses everything from how the game is played to its atmosphere, story, and the experience it's trying to create. Depending on the game, this document can be a few pages long or several hundred.
- **Technical design document (TDD):** This document focuses on all the technical aspects of the game, from the hardware it will run on to how the classes and program architecture need to be built out. Like a GDD, the length will vary based on the project.

- **One-page document**: Usually used for marketing or promotional situations, a one-page document is essentially a snapshot of your game. As the name suggests, it should only take up a single page.

There's no right or wrong way to format a GDD, so it's a good place to let your brand of creativity thrive (and check out the original design document for **Grand Theft Auto** for reference at https://www.gamedevs.org/uploads/grand-theft-auto.pdf). Throw in pictures of reference material that inspires you; get creative with the layout—this is your place to define your vision.

The **Hero Born** game we'll be working on throughout the rest of this book is fairly simple and won't require anything as detailed as a GDD or TDD. Instead, we'll create a one-pager to keep track of our project objectives and some background information.

The Hero Born one-pager

To keep us on track going forward, I've put together a simple table that lays out the basics of our game prototype:

Concept	Game prototype focused on stealthily avoiding enemies and collecting health items, with a little FPS on the side.
Story	A lone hero trapped in a strange and unknown arena. Collecting items and avoiding enemy sightings is the only way out!
Art style	Level and character styles will be primitive GameObjects for fast and efficient prototyping. These can be swapped out at a later date with 3D models or terrain environments if needed.
Core mechanics	Uses line-of-sight to stay one step ahead of patrolling enemies and collecting required items. Combat consists of shooting projectiles at enemies, which will automatically trigger an attack response.
Control schemes	*WASD* for movement and arrow keys to control the camera. The *J* key will control player jumps, and the spacebar will control shooting mechanics. Item collection will work on collisions with a simple UI to display items collected, remaining lives, and game messages.
Win/lose conditions	Players win when all items are collected; they lose when their health drops to zero.

Table 6.1: Hero Born one-page document

> **Note**
>
> To provide a complete view of the Unity Editor, all our screenshots are taken in full-screen mode. For color versions of all book images, use the following link: `https://packt.link/gbp/9781805808718`.

Now that you have a high-level view of the pillars of our game, you're ready to start building a prototype level to house the game experience.

Building a level

When building your game levels, it's always a good idea to try to see things from the perspective of your players. How do you want them to see the environment, interact with it, and feel while walking around in it? You're literally building the world your game exists in, so be consistent.

With Unity, you can use basic 3D shapes to block out simple environments, the more advanced ProBuilder tool, or a mixture of the two. You can even import 3D models from other programs, such as Blender, to use as objects in your scenes.

Unity has a great introduction to the ProBuilder tool at `https://unity.com/features/probuilder`.

You can also use tools such as Blender to create your game assets, which you can find at `https://www.blender.org/features/modeling/`.

For *Hero Born*, we'll stick with a simple indoor arena-like setting that's easy to get around, but with a few corners to hide in. You'll cobble all this together using **primitives**—base object shapes provided in Unity—because of how easy they are to create, scale, and position in a scene.

Creating primitives

Looking at games you might play regularly, you're probably wondering how you'll ever create models and objects that look so realistic that it seems you could reach through the screen and grab them. Fortunately, Unity has a set of primitive GameObjects that you can select from to prototype faster. These won't be super fancy or high-definition, but they are a lifesaver when you're learning the ropes or don't have a 3D artist on your development team.

If you open up Unity, you can go into the **Hierarchy** panel and click on + | **3D Object**, and you'll see all the available options, but only about half of these are primitives or common shapes, indicated in the following screenshot:

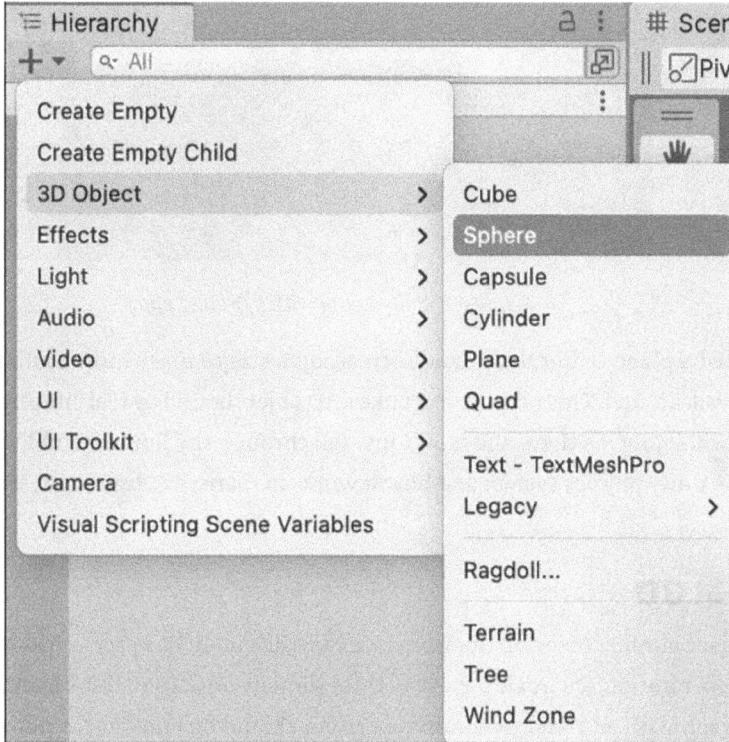

Figure 6.1: Unity Hierarchy window with the 3D Object option selected

Other **3D Object** options, such as **Terrain, Wind Zone**, and **Tree**, are a bit too advanced for what we need, but feel free to experiment with them if you're interested.

You can find out more about building Unity environments at https://docs.unity3d.com/Manual/CreatingEnvironments.html.

Before we jump too far ahead, it's usually easier to walk around when you've got a floor underneath you, so let's start by creating a ground plane for our arena using the following steps:

1.   In the **Hierarchy** panel, click on + | **3D Object** | **Plane**.

2.   Select the new object in the **Hierarchy** tab and rename the GameObject to Ground in the **Inspector** tab or by pressing *Enter*.

3. In the **Inspector**, find the **Scale** variable in the **Transform** section and change it to 3 in the **X**, **Y**, and **Z** axes:

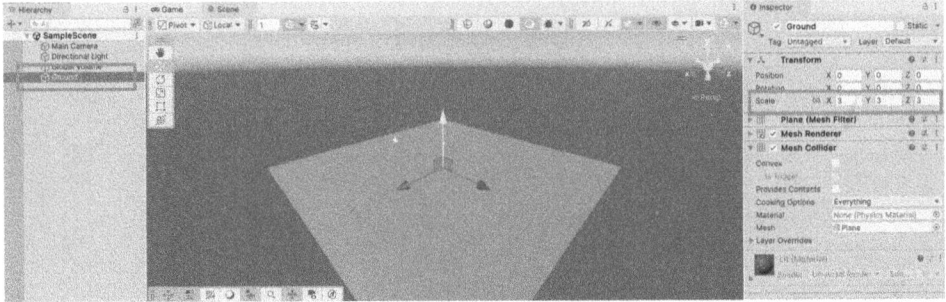

Figure 6.2: Unity Editor with a Ground plane

Here, we created a plane GameObject, and increased its size to make more room for our future characters to walk around. This plane will act like a 3D object bound by real-life physics, meaning other objects will know it's there and won't just fall through the floor into oblivion. We'll talk more about the Unity physics system and how it works in *Chapter 7*. Right now, we need to start thinking in 3D.

Thinking in 3D

Now that we have our first object in the scene, we can talk about 3D space—specifically, how an object's position, rotation, and scale behave in three dimensions. If you think back to high school geometry, a graph with an *x* and *y* coordinate system should be familiar. To put a point on the graph, you need an *x* value and a *y* value.

Unity supports both 2D and 3D game development, and if we were making a 2D game, we could leave our explanation there. However, when dealing with 3D space in the Unity Editor, we have an extra axis, called the *z* axis. The *z* axis maps depth, or perspective, giving our space and the objects in it their 3D quality.

This might be confusing at first, but Unity has some nice visual aids to help you get your head on straight. In the top-right corner of the **Scene** panel, you'll see a geometric-looking icon with the *x*, *y*, and *z* axes marked in red, green, and blue, respectively. All GameObjects in the scene will show their axis arrows when they're selected in the **Hierarchy** window:

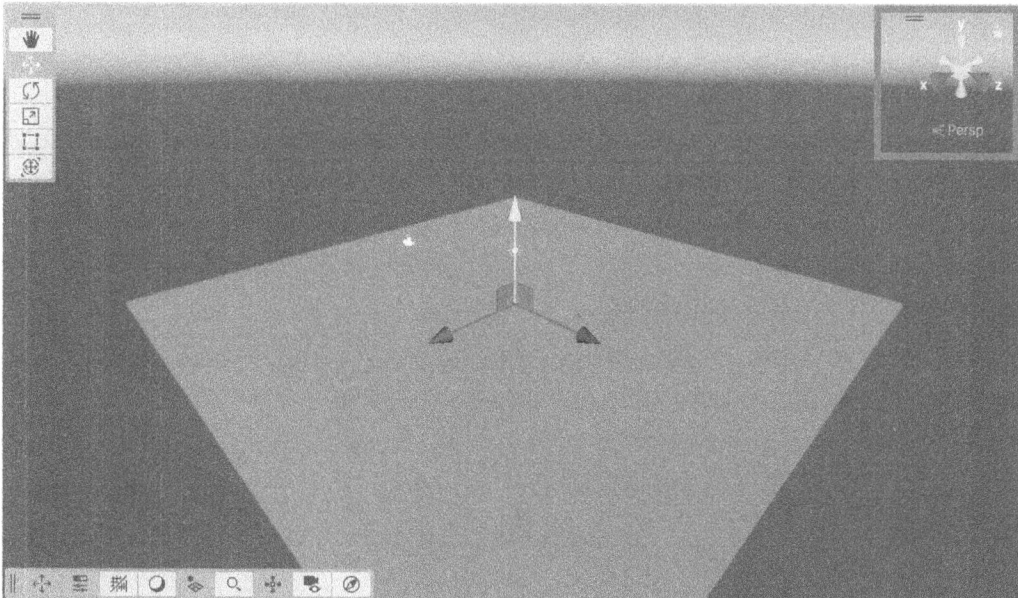

Figure 6.3: Scene view with the orientation gizmo highlighted

This will always show the current orientation of the scene and the objects placed inside it. Clicking on any of the colored axes will switch the scene orientation to the selected axis. Give this a go yourself to get comfortable with switching perspectives.

If you take a look at the Ground object's **Transform** component in the **Inspector** window, you'll see that the position, rotation, and scale are all determined by these three axes.

The position determines where the object is placed in the scene, its rotation governs how it's angled, and its scale takes care of its size. These values can be changed at any time in the **Inspector** pane or in a C# script:

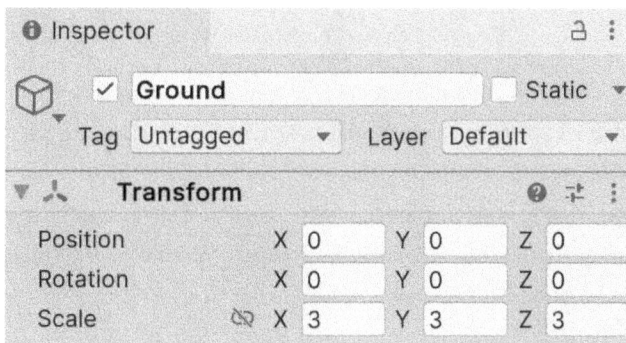

Figure 6.4: The Ground object selected in the Hierarchy

Right now, the ground is looking a little boring. Let's change that with a material.

Applying materials

Our ground plane isn't very interesting right now, but we can use **materials** to breathe a little life into the level. Materials are in charge of setting GameObject properties such as color and texture; the material is passed to the shader, which uses the shader to render the material properties onscreen. Think of shaders as being responsible for combining lighting and texture data into a representation of how the material looks.

Each GameObject starts with a default material and shader—in our case, new objects use the default **Lit** shader in the **Inspector** panel, as shown in the following figure:

Figure 6.5: Default material on an object

To change an object's color, we need to create a material and drag it to the object that we want to modify. Remember, everything is an object in Unity—materials are no different. Materials can be reused on as many GameObjects as needed, but any change to a material will also carry through to any objects the material is attached to. If we had several enemy objects in the scene with a material that set them all to red, and we changed that base material color to blue, all our enemies would then be blue.

Blue is eye-catching; let's change the color of the ground plane to match, and create a new material to turn the ground plane from a dull white to a dark and vibrant blue:

1. Create a new folder in the **Project** panel by right-clicking and selecting **Create | Folder** and name it Materials.

2. Inside the Materials folder, right-click and select **Create | Material**, and name it Ground_ Mat.

3. Select Ground_Mat in the **Project** panel and look at its properties in the **Inspector**:

    1. Find the **Surface Inputs** section and click on the color box next to **Base Map**.

    2. Select your color from the color picker window that pops up (the big square in the middle sets the actual color), and then close it:

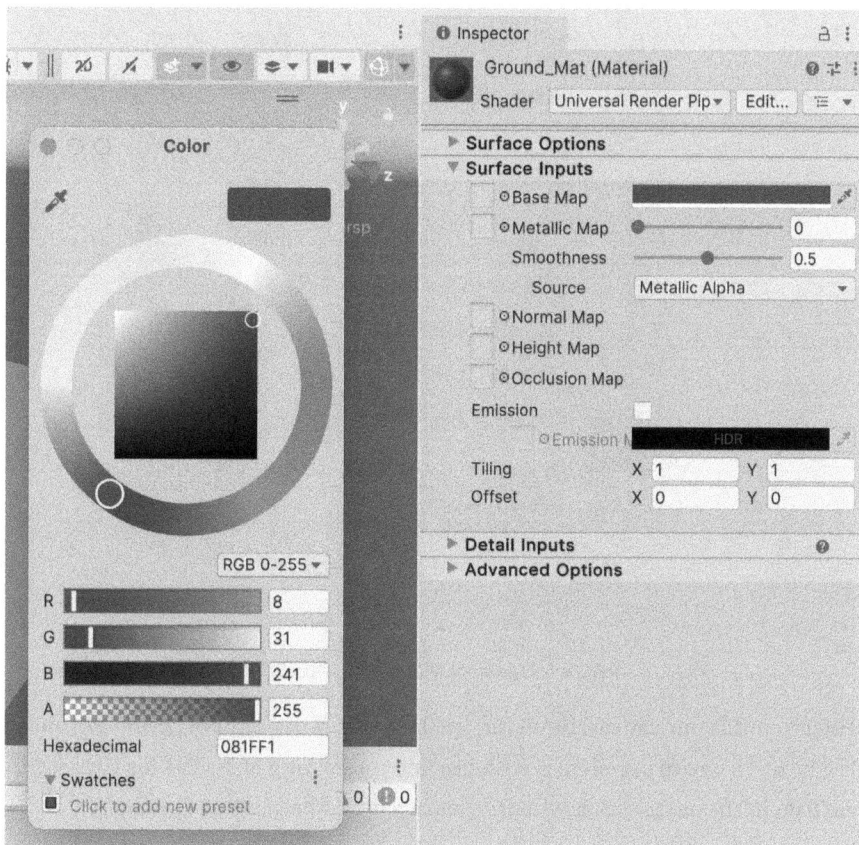

Figure 6.6: Material color picker

4. Drag the Ground_Mat object from the **Project** panel and drop it onto the Ground GameObject in the **Hierarchy** panel.

The new material you created is now a project asset. Dragging and dropping Ground_Mat from the **Project** panel onto the Ground GameObject in the **Hierarchy** panel changed the color of the plane, which means any changes to Ground_Mat will be reflected in the Ground GameObject.

If you select Ground in the **Hierarchy** panel, you'll also see that the Ground_Mat (Material) component at the very bottom is now being used by **Standard Shader** to render the plane's color property:

Figure 6.7: Ground plane with the updated color material

The ground is our canvas; however, in 3D space, it can support other 3D objects on its surface. It'll be up to you to populate it with fun and interesting obstacles for your future players, which we'll do in the next section when we learn a little about white-boxing!

White-boxing

White-boxing is a design term for laying out ideas using placeholders, usually with the intent of replacing them with finished assets at a later date. In level design, the practice of white-boxing is to block out an environment with primitive GameObjects to get a sense of how you want it to look. This is a great way to start things off, especially during the prototyping stages of your game.

Before diving into Unity, I'd like to start with a simple sketch of the basic layout and position of my level. This gives us a bit of direction and will help to get our environment laid out quicker.

In the following drawing, you'll be able to see the arena I have in mind, with a raised platform in the middle that is accessible by ramps, complete with small turrets in each corner:

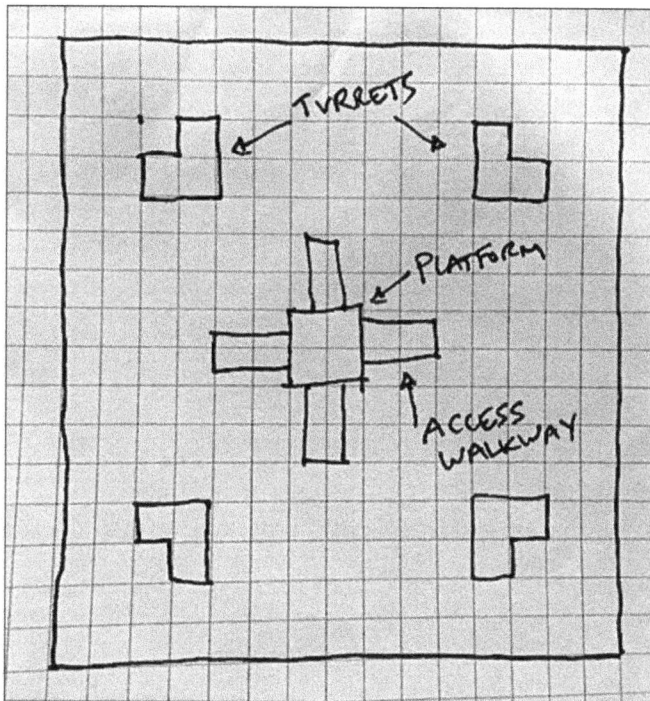

Figure 6.8: Sketch of the Hero Born level arena

Don't worry if you're not an artist—neither am I. The important thing is to get your ideas down on paper to solidify them in your mind and work out any kinks before getting busy in Unity.

Before you go full steam ahead and put this sketch into production, you'll need to familiarize yourself with a few Unity Editor shortcuts to make white-boxing easier.

Editor tools

When we discussed the Unity interface in *Chapter 1*, we skimmed over some of the **Toolbar** functionality, which we need to revisit so that we know how to efficiently manipulate GameObjects. You can find these in the upper-left corner of the Unity Editor:

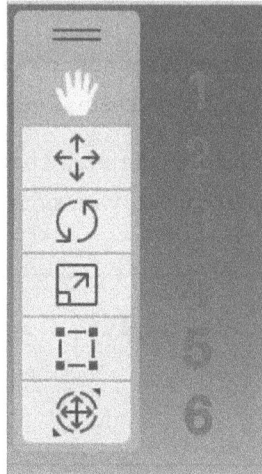

Figure 6.9: Unity Editor Toolbar

Let's break down the different tools that are available to us from the Toolbar in the preceding screenshot:

1. **View**: This allows you to pan and change your position in the scene by clicking and dragging your mouse.
2. **Move**: This lets you move objects along the x, y, and z axes by dragging their respective arrows.
3. **Rotate**: This lets you adjust an object's rotation by turning or dragging its respective markers.
4. **Scale**: This lets you modify an object's scale by dragging it to specific axes.
5. **Rect Transform**: This combines the **Move**, **Rotate**, and **Scale** tool functionality into one package.
6. **Transform**: This gives you access to the position, rotation, and scale of an object all at once.

You can find more information about navigating and positioning GameObjects in the **Scene** panel at https://docs.unity3d.com/Manual/PositioningGameObjects.html. It's also worth noting that you can move, position, and scale objects using the **Transform** component, as we discussed earlier in the *Thinking in 3D* section.

Panning and navigating the scene can be done with similar tools, although not from the Unity Editor itself:

- To look around, hold down the right mouse button and drag it to pan the camera around.
- To move around while using the camera, continue to hold the right mouse button and use the *W*, *S*, *A*, and *D* keys to move forward, back, left, and right, respectively. If you're on a Mac and using your trackpad instead of a mouse, click-and-hold two fingers while pressing the *W*, *S*, *A*, and *D* keys.
- Hit the *F* key to zoom in and focus on a GameObject that has been selected in the **Hierarchy** panel.

This kind of scene navigation is more commonly known as **fly-through mode**, so when I ask you to focus on or navigate to a particular object or viewpoint, use a combination of these features.

Getting around the **Scene** view can be a task all on its own, but it all comes down to repeated practice. For a more detailed list of scene navigation features, visit `https://docs.unity3d.com/Manual/SceneViewNavigation.html`.

Even though the ground plane won't allow our character to fall through it, we could still walk off the edge at this point. Now, your job is to wall in the arena so that the player has a confined locomotion area.

Hero's trial: putting up drywall

Using primitive cubes and the toolbar, position four walls around the level using the **Move**, **Rotate**, and **Scale** tools to section off the main arena:

1. In the **Hierarchy** panel, select **+** | **3D Object** | **Cube** to create the first wall and name it `Wall`.
2. Set its **Scale** value to `30` for the *x* axis, `1.5` for the *y* axis, and `0.2` for the *z* axis.

> Note that planes operate on a scale 10 times larger than objects—so our plane with a length of 3 is the same length as any other object of length 30.

3. In the `Materials` folder, right-click and select **Create** | **Material** and name it `Wall_Mat`, then change the **Base Map** color to white and drag the material onto the `Wall` object in the **Hierarchy** panel.

4. With the Wall object selected in the **Hierarchy** panel, switch to the **Position** tool in the upper-left corner and use the red, green, and blue arrows to position the wall at the edge of the ground plane.

5. Repeat *steps 1–3* until you have four walls surrounding your area or duplicate the Wall object with *cmd + D* on a Mac or *Ctrl + D* on Windows. When you create duplicate objects in the **Hierarchy** panel, Unity will automatically add a number to the object name to differentiate the duplicates. You'll see in *Figure 6.10* that our three duplicate walls are named Wall (1), Wall (2), and Wall (3). You can rename any of these if you want, but I'll be leaving them as-is to use Unity's default naming convention:

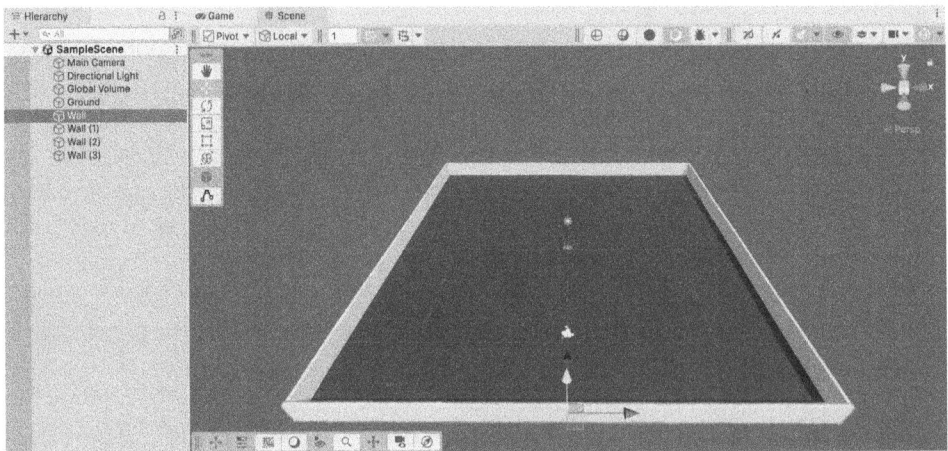

Figure 6.10: Level arena with four walls and a ground plane

Note

From this chapter onward, I'll be giving some basic values for wall position, rotation, and scale, but feel free to be adventurous and use your own creativity. I want you to experiment with the Unity Editor tools so you get comfortable faster.

That was a bit of construction, but the arena is starting to take shape! Before we move on to adding obstacles and platforms, you'll want to get into the habit of cleaning up your object hierarchy. We'll talk about how that works in the following section.

Keeping the hierarchy clean

Normally, I would put this sort of advice in a blurb at the end of a section, but making sure your project hierarchy is as organized as possible is so important that it needs its own subsection. Ideally, you'll want all related GameObjects to be under a single **parent object**. Right now, it's not a risk because we only have a few objects in the scene; however, when that gets into the hundreds on a big project, you'll be struggling.

The easiest way to keep your hierarchy clean is to store related objects in a parent object, just as you would with files inside a folder on your desktop. Our level has a few objects that could use some organization, and Unity makes this easy by letting us create empty GameObjects. An empty object is a perfect container (or folder) for holding related groups of objects because it doesn't come with any components attached—it's a shell.

Let's take our ground plane and four walls and group them all under a common empty GameObject:

1. Select + | **Create Empty** in the **Hierarchy** panel and name the new object Environment.
2. Select the Environment empty object and check that its **X**, **Y**, and **Z** positions are all set to 0.
3. Drag and drop the ground plane and the four walls into Environment, making them child objects:

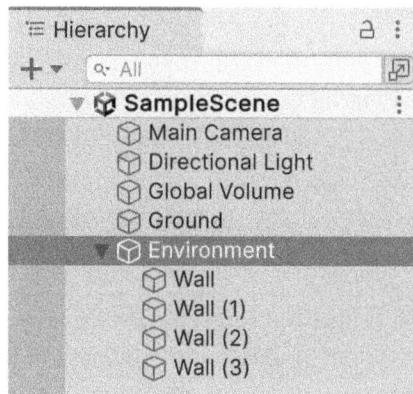

Figure 6.11: The Hierarchy panel showing the empty GameObject parent

The environment exists in the **Hierarchy** tab as a parent object, with the arena objects as its children. Now, we're able to expand or close the Environment object drop-down list with the arrow icon, making the **Hierarchy** panel less cluttered.

Important note

It's important to set the `Environment` object's **X**, **Y**, and **Z** positions to 0 because the child object positions are now relative to the parent position. This leads to an interesting question: what are the origin points of these positions, rotations, and scales that we're setting? The answer is that they depend on what relative space we're using, which, in Unity, is either **World** or **Local**:

- **World space** uses a set origin point in the scene as a constant reference for all GameObjects. In Unity, this origin point is $(0, 0, 0)$, or 0 on the x, y, and z axes.
- **Local space** uses the object's parent `Transform` component as its origin, essentially changing the perspective of the scene. Unity also sets this local origin to $(0, 0, 0)$. Think of this as the parent `Transform` being the center of the universe, with everything else orbiting in relation to it.

Both of these orientations are useful in different situations, but right now, resetting it at this point starts everyone on an even playing field.

Working with Prefabs

Prefabs are one of the most powerful components you'll come across in Unity. They come in handy not only in level building but in scripting as well. Think of Prefabs as GameObjects that can be saved and reused with every child object, component, C# script, and property setting intact. Once created, a Prefab is like a class template; each copy used in a scene is a separate instance of that Prefab. Consequently, any change to the base Prefab will also change all the unaltered active instances in the scene.

The arena looks a little too simple and completely wide open, making it a perfect place to test out creating and editing Prefabs. Since we want four identical turrets in each corner of the arena, they're a perfect case for a Prefab.

Again, I haven't included any precise barrier position, rotation, or scale values because I want you to get up close and personal with the Unity Editor tools.

Going forward, when you see a task ahead of you that doesn't include specific position, rotation, or scale values, I'm expecting you to learn by doing.

Let's create the turrets with the following steps:

1. Select the `Environment` parent object, right-click and select **Create Empty**, and name it `Barrier`.

2. Select `Barrier`, then right-click and select **3D Object | Cube** *twice*, then position and scale them as a v-shaped base.

    a. Drag the **Wall_Mat** material onto each new **Cube** object.

    b. Change **Y Position** to `0.5`.

    c. Change **X Scale** of the first cube to 3 and the second cube to 4 if you're not sure how big they should be.

3. Create two more **Cube** primitives (no need to rescale them) and place them on top of the ends of the turret base:

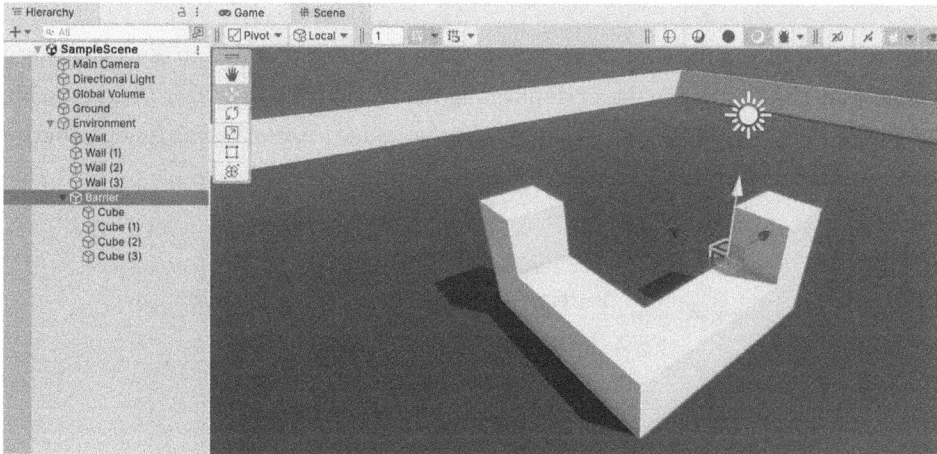

Figure 6.12: Screenshot of the turret composed of cubes

4. In the main `Assets` folder, create a new folder named `Prefabs` and drag the `Barrier` GameObject from the **Hierarchy** panel to the `Prefabs` folder in the **Project** view:

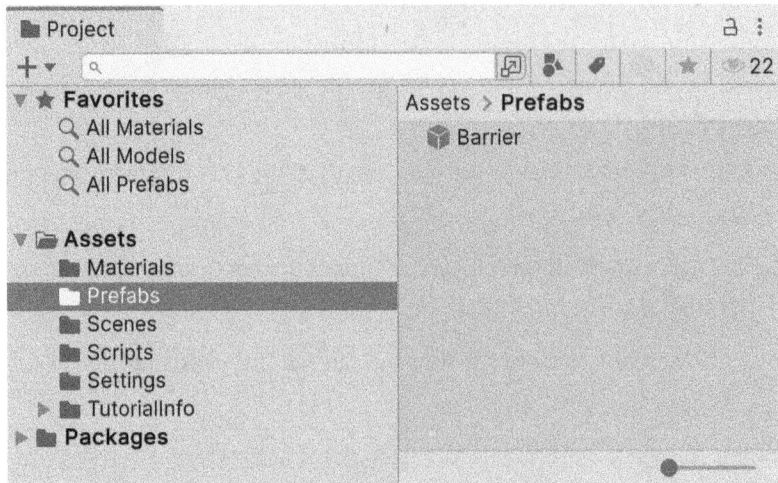

Figure 6.13: The Barrier Prefab in the Prefabs folder

Barrier, and all its child objects, are now Prefabs, meaning that we can reuse them by dragging copies from the `Prefabs` folder or duplicating the one in the scene. `Barrier` turned blue in the **Hierarchy** tab to signify its status change, and also added a row of **Prefab** function buttons in the **Inspector** tab underneath its name:

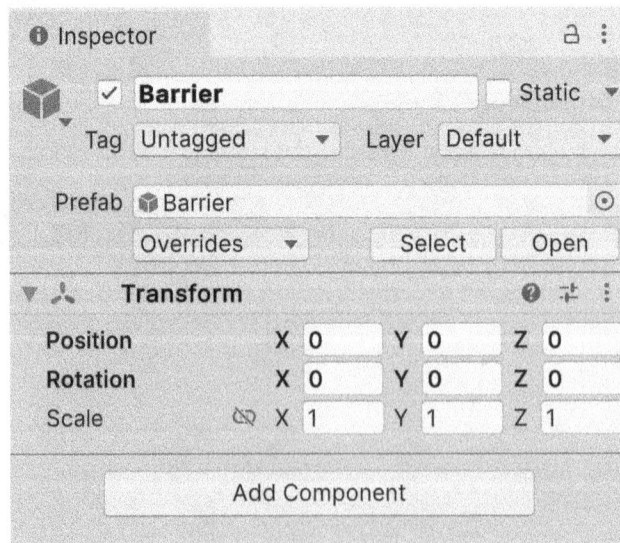

Figure 6.14: The Barrier Prefab highlighted in the Inspector pane

Any edits to the original Prefab object, `Barrier`, will now affect any copies in the scene. Since we need a fifth cube to complete the barrier, let's update and save the Prefab to see this in action.

Now our turret has a huge gap in the middle (see *Figure 6.12*), which isn't ideal for covering our character, so let's update the `Barrier` Prefab by adding another cube and applying the change:

1. In the **Hierarchy** pane, create one last **Cube** primitive and place it at the intersection of the turret base.

   The new **Cube** primitive will be marked as gray with a little + icon next to its name in the **Hierarchy** tab. This means it's not officially part of the Prefab yet:

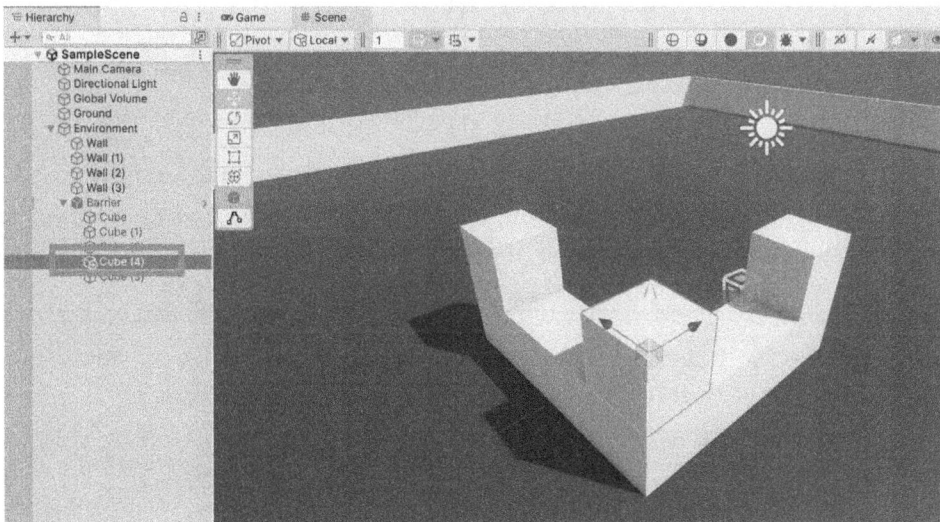

Figure 6.15: New Prefab update marked in the Hierarchy window

2. Right-click on the new **Cube** primitive in the **Hierarchy** panel and select **Added Game-Object | Apply to Prefab 'Barrier'**:

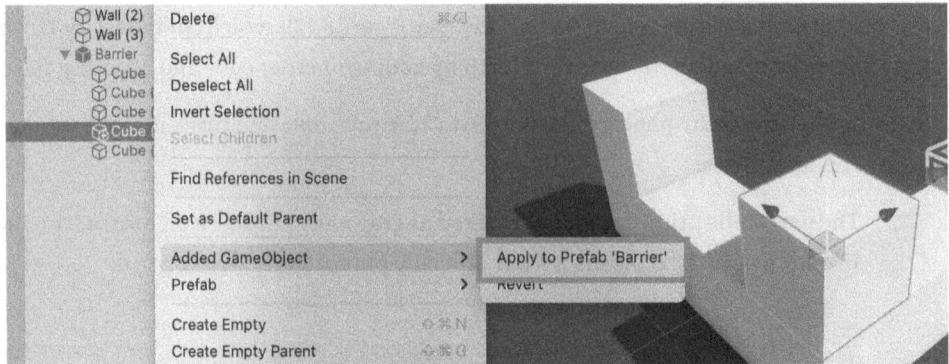

Figure 6.16: Option to apply Prefab changes to the base Prefab

The Barrier Prefab is now updated to include the new cube, and the entire Prefab hierarchy should be blue again. You now have a turret Prefab that looks like *Figure 6.17* or, if you're feeling adventurous, something more creative. However, we want these to be in every corner of the arena.

Duplicate the Barrier Prefab three times and place each one in a different corner of the arena. You can do this by dragging multiple Barrier objects from the Prefabs folder into the scene, or right-clicking on Barrier in the **Hierarchy** pane and selecting **Duplicate**.

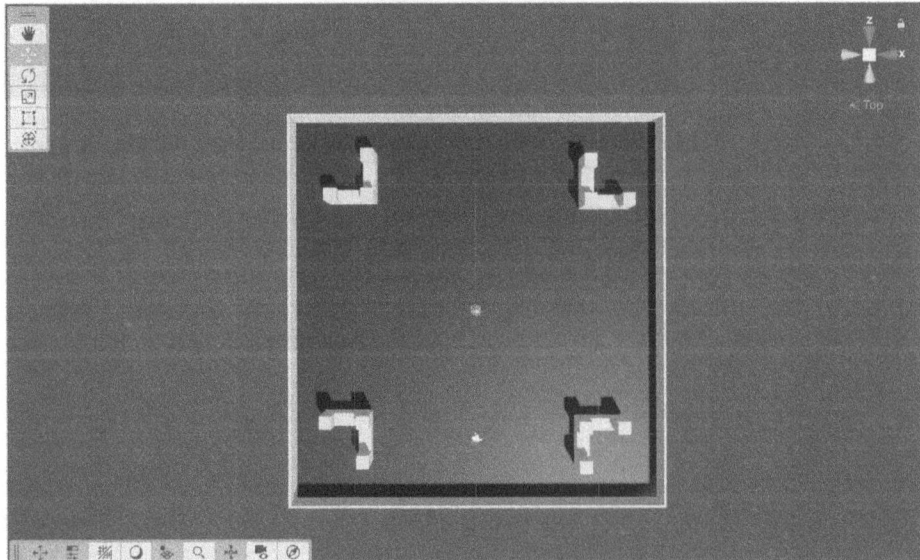

Figure 6.17: Barriers placed in the corners of the arena

Now that we've got a reusable `Barrier` Prefab, let's build out the rest of the level to match the rough sketch in *Figure 6.8*:

1. Create a new empty GameObject inside the `Environment` parent object, name it `Platform`, and set its position in the *x*, *y*, and *z* axes to 0.

2. Create a **Cube** object as a child object of `Platform`, name it `Center`, and scale it ($x = 5, y = 2$, and $z = 5$) to form a platform, as shown in *Figure 6.18*:

    a. Drag the **Wall_Mat** material onto the `Center` object.

3. Now, create a **Plane** object, name it `Ramp`, and scale it into a ramp ($\mathbf{x = 1, y = 1}$, and $\mathbf{z = 0.5}$):

    a. Drag the **Wall_Mat** material onto the `Ramp` object.

> **Hint**: Rotate the plane around the *z* axis to create an angled plane, then position it so that it connects the platform to the ground with enough room to walk onto it

4. Duplicate the `Ramp` object by using *cmd + D* on a Mac, or *Ctrl + D* on Windows. Then, repeat the rotation and positioning steps.

5. Repeat *step 4* two more times, until you have four ramps in total, leading to the platform:

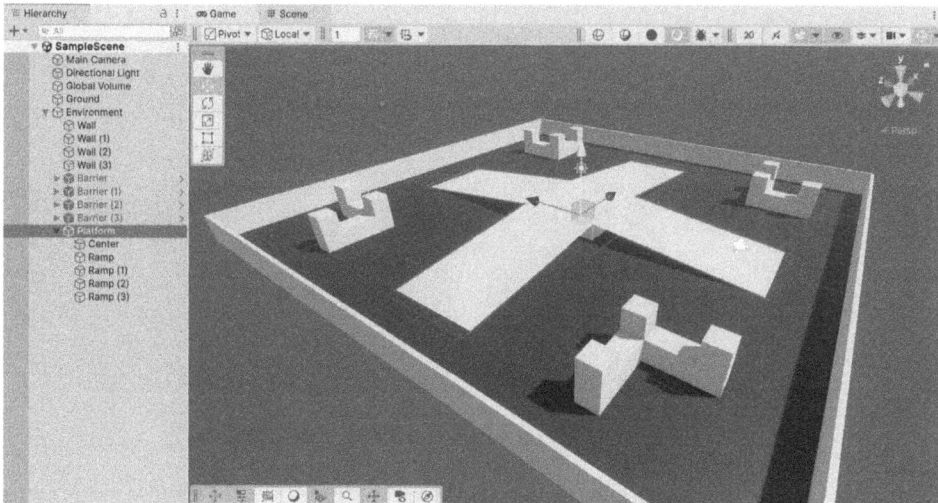

Figure 6.18: Platform parent GameObject

You've now successfully white-boxed your first game level! Don't get too caught up in it yet, though—we're just getting started. All good games have items that players can pick up or interact with. In the following challenge, it's your job to create a health item and make it a Prefab.

Hero's trial: creating a health pickup

Putting together everything we've learned so far in this chapter might take you a few minutes, but it's well worth the time. Create the pickup item as follows:

1. Create a **Capsule** GameObject by selecting **+** | **3D Object** | **Capsule** and name it Health_ Pickup.

2. Set **Scale** to 0.3 for the **x**, **y**, and **z** axes, and then switch to the **Move** tool and position it near one of your barriers.

3. Create and attach a new yellow-colored material to the Health_Pickup object.

4. Drag the Health_Pickup object from the **Hierarchy** pane into the Prefabs folder.

Refer to the following screenshot for an example of what the finished product should look like:

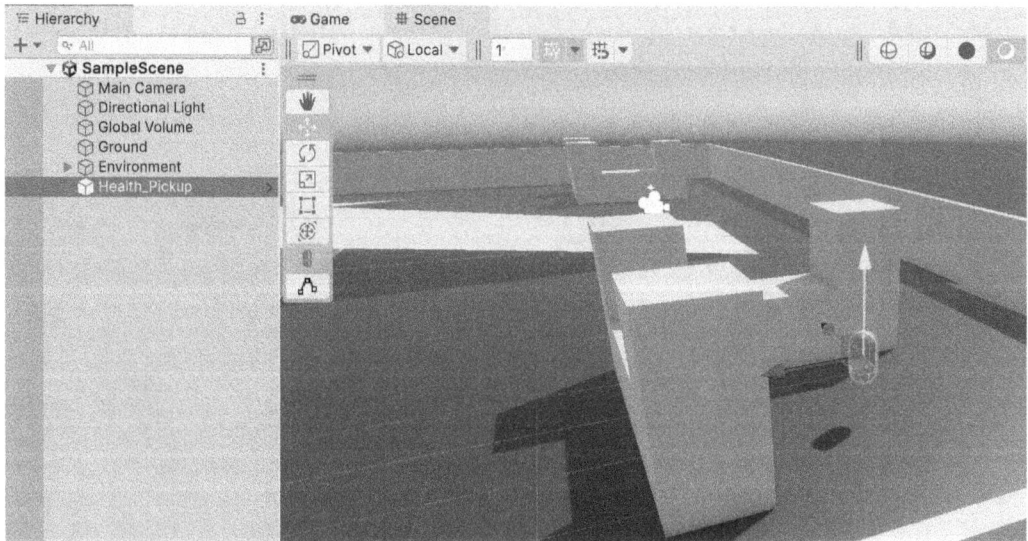

Figure 6.19: Pickup item and Barrier Prefab in Scene

That wraps up our work with level design and layout for now. Next up, you're going to get a crash course in lighting with Unity, and we'll learn about animating our item later on in the chapter.

Lighting basics

Lighting in Unity is a broad topic, but it can be boiled down into two categories: real-time and precomputed. Both types of lights take into account properties such as the color and intensity of the light, as well as the direction it is facing in the scene, which can all be configured in the **Inspector** pane. The difference is how the Unity engine computes how the lights act:

- **Real-time lighting** is computed in every frame, meaning that any object that passes in its path will cast realistic shadows and generally behave like a real-world light source. However, this can significantly slow down your game and cost an exponential amount of computing power, depending on the number of lights in your scene.

- **Precomputed lighting**, on the other hand, stores the scene's lighting in a texture called a **lightmap**, which is then applied, or baked, into the scene. While this saves computing power, baked lighting is static. This means that it doesn't react realistically or change when objects move in the scene.

There is also a mixed type of lighting called **Precomputed Realtime Global Illumination**, which bridges the gap between real-time and precomputed processes. This is an advanced Unity-specific topic, so we won't cover it in this book, but feel free to view the documentation at `https://docs.unity3d.com/Manual/GIIntro.html`.

Let's now take a look at how to create light objects in the Unity scene itself.

Creating lights

By default, every scene comes with a directional light component to act as a main source of illumination, but lights can be created in the **Hierarchy** pane like any other GameObject. Even though the idea of controlling light sources might be new to you, they are objects in Unity, which means they can be positioned, scaled, and rotated to fit your needs.

You can find a complete list of available light objects by clicking + | **Light** in **Hierarchy**:

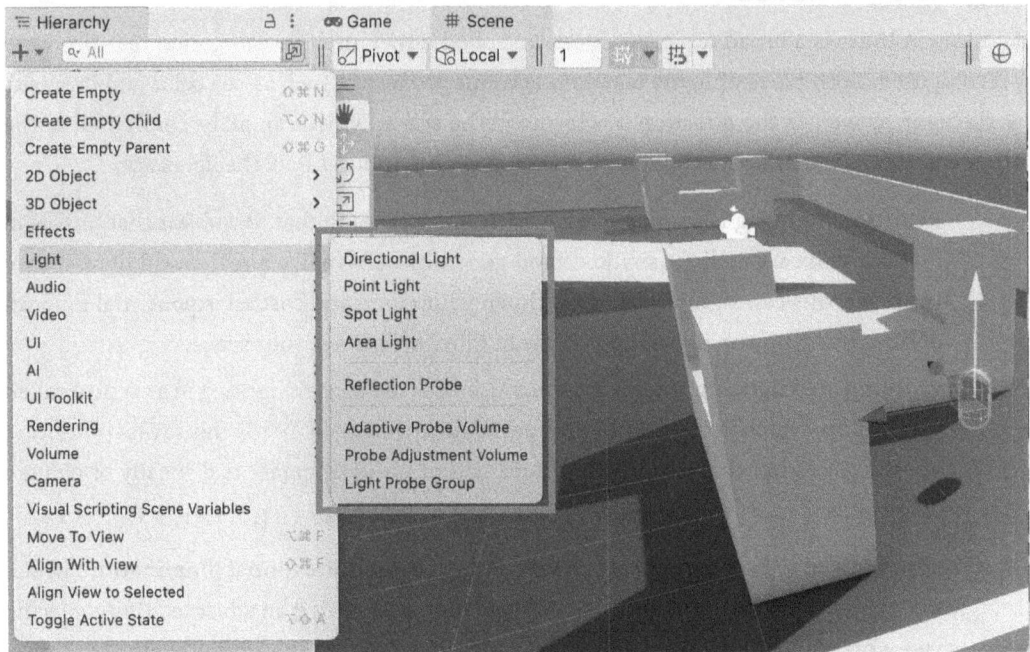

Figure 6.20: Lighting creation menu option

Let's take a look at some examples of real-time light objects and their performance:

- **Directional lights** are great for simulating natural light, such as sunshine. They don't have an actual position in the scene, but their light hits everything as if it's always pointed in the same direction.

- **Point lights** are essentially floating globes, sending light rays out from a central point in all directions. These have defined positions and intensities in the scene.

- **Spotlights** send light out in a given direction, but they are locked in by their angle and focused on a specific area of the scene. Think of these as spotlights or floodlights in the real world.

- **Area lights** are shaped like rectangles, sending out the light from their surface from a single side of the rectangle.

> **More information**
>
> **Reflection probes** and **light probe groups** are beyond what we need for *Hero Born*; however, if you're interested, you can find out more at https://docs.unity3d.com/Manual/ReflectionProbes.html and https://docs.unity3d.com/Manual/LightProbes.html, respectively.

Like all GameObjects in Unity, lights have properties that can be adjusted to give a scene a specific ambiance or theme.

Light component properties

The following screenshot shows the **Light** component on the directional light in our scene. All of these properties can be configured to create immersive environments, but the basic ones we need to be aware of are **Mode**, **Light Appearance**, and **Intensity**. These properties govern the light's tint, real-time or computed effects, and general strength:

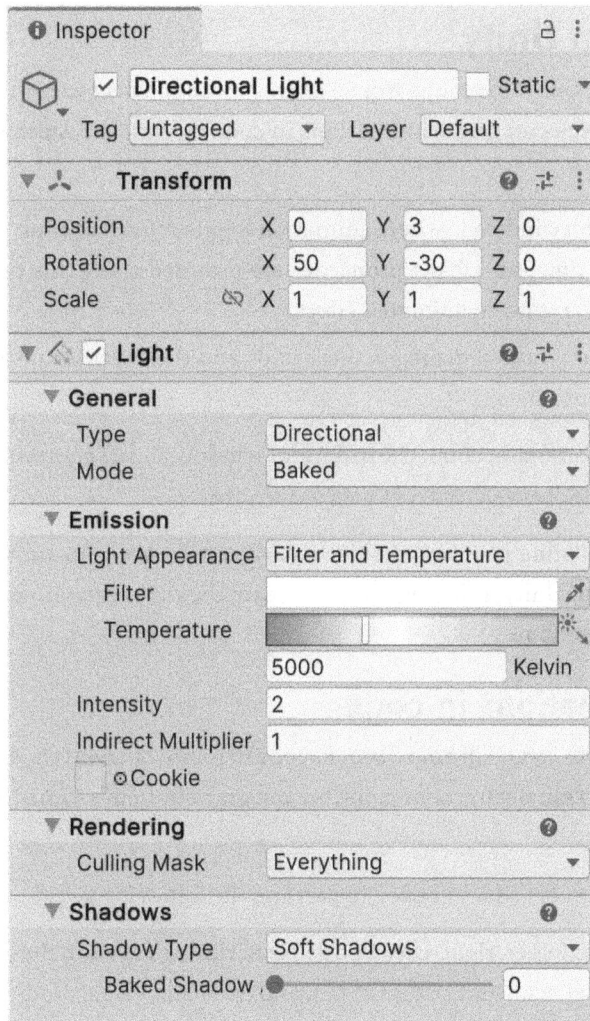

Figure 6.21: The Light component in the Inspector window

Like other Unity components, these properties can be accessed through scripts and the `Light` class, which can be found at `https://docs.unity3d.com/ScriptReference/Light.html`.

Try this out for yourself by selecting + | **Light** | **Point Light** and seeing how it affects the area lighting. After you've played around with the settings, delete the point light by right-clicking on it in the **Hierarchy** panel and choosing **Delete**.

Now that we know a little more about what goes into lighting up a game scene, let's turn our attention to adding some animations!

Animating in Unity

Animating objects in Unity can range from a simple rotation effect to complex character movements and actions. You can create animations in code or with the **Animation** and **Animator** windows:

- The **Animation** window is where animation segments, called **clips**, are created and managed using a timeline. Object properties are recorded along this timeline and are then played back to create an animated effect.

- The **Animator** window manages these clips and their transitions using objects called animation controllers.

You can find more information about the **Animator** window and its controllers at `https://docs.unity3d.com/Manual/class-AnimatorController.html`.

Creating and manipulating your target objects in clips will have your game moving in no time. For our short trip into Unity animations, we'll create the same rotation effect in code, and by using the **Animator** window.

Creating animations in code

To start, we're going to create an animation in code to rotate our `Health_Pickup` item. Since all GameObjects have a **Transform** component, we can grab our item's **Transform** component and rotate it indefinitely.

To create an animation in code, you need to perform the following steps:

1. In the `Scripts` folder, right-click and select **Scripting** | **MonoBehaviour Script** to create a new C# script, name it `ItemRotation`, and open it in Visual Studio Code.

2. At the top of the new class, add a public `int` variable containing the value `100` called
    `RotationSpeed`, and a private `Transform` variable called `_itemTransform`. If you don't
    specify an access level, Visual Studio Code assumes it's private, but the best practice is to
    use explicit access modifiers to make sure your code is crystal clear:

```
public int RotationSpeed = 100;
private Transform _itemTransform;
```

> ♀ **Quick tip:** Enhance your coding experience with the **AI Code Explainer**
> and **Quick Copy** features. Open this book in the next-gen Packt Reader. Click
> the **Copy** button
>
> **(1)** to quickly copy code into your coding environment, or click the **Explain**
> button
>
> **(2)** to get the AI assistant to explain a block of code to you.

```
                                                    Copy      Explain
function calculate(a, b) {
    return {sum: a + b};                             1          2
};
```

> 🔖 **The next-gen Packt Reader** is included for free with the purchase of this
> book. Scan the QR code OR go to `https://packtpub.com/unlock`, then use
> the search bar to find this book by name. Double-check the edition shown
> to make sure you get the right one.

3. Inside the `Start()` method body, grab the GameObject's `Transform` component and as-
    sign it to `_itemTransform`:

```
_itemTransform = this.GetComponent<Transform>();
```

4. Inside the Update() method body, call _itemTransform.Rotate. This Transform class method takes in three axes, one for the *x*, *y*, and *z* rotations you want to execute. Since we want the item to rotate end over end, we'll use the *x* axis and leave the others set to 0:

    ```
    _itemTransform.Rotate(RotationSpeed * Time.deltaTime, 0, 0);
    ```

    You'll notice that we're multiplying RotationSpeed by something called Time.deltaTime. This is the standard way of normalizing movement effects in Unity so that they look smooth no matter how fast or slow the player's computer is running. In general, you should always multiply your movement or rotation speeds by Time.deltaTime.

5. Back in Unity, select the Health_Pickup object in the Prefabs folder in the **Projects** pane and scroll down to the bottom of the **Inspector** window. Click **Add Component**, search for the ItemRotation script, and then press *Enter*:

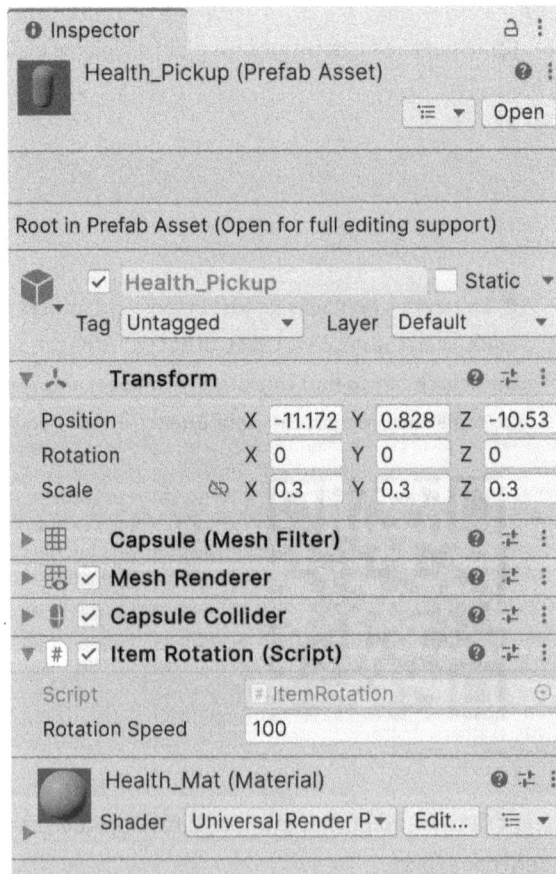

Figure 6.22: The Add Component button in the Inspector panel

6. Now that our Prefab is updated, move **Main Camera** so that you can see the Health_Pickup object and click on **Play**!

Figure 6.23: Screenshot of the camera focused on the health item

As you can see, the health pickup now spins around its *x* axis in a continuous and smooth animation! Now that you've animated the item in code, we'll duplicate our animation using Unity's built-in animation system.

Creating animations in the Unity Animation window

Before we go any further, it's important to choose either the code method or Unity's animation system for *a single animation*—not both. Otherwise, the two systems will end up fighting each other.

Any GameObject that you want to apply an animation clip to needs to be attached to an **Animator** component with an **Animation Controller** set. If there is no controller in the project when a new clip is created, Unity will create one and save it in the **Project** panel, which you can then use to manage your clips. Your next challenge is to create a new animation clip for the pickup item.

We're going to start animating the Health_Pickup Prefab by creating a new animation clip, which will spin the object around in an infinite loop. To create a new animation clip, we need to perform the following steps:

1. Navigate to **Window | Animation | Animation** and drag and drop the **Animation** tab next to the **Game** tab:

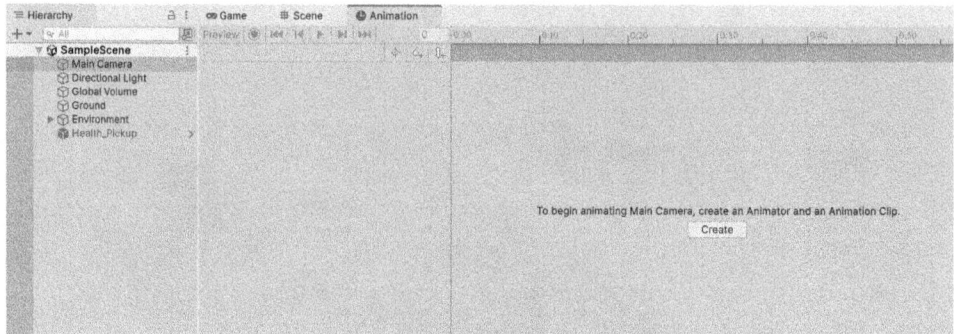

Figure 6.24: Screenshot of the Unity Animation window

2. Make sure the Health_Pickup item is selected in **Hierarchy** and then click on **Create** in the **Animation** panel.

3. Create a new folder under Assets from the following drop-down list, name it Animations, and then name the new clip Spin.

   Make sure the new clip shows up in the **Animation** panel:

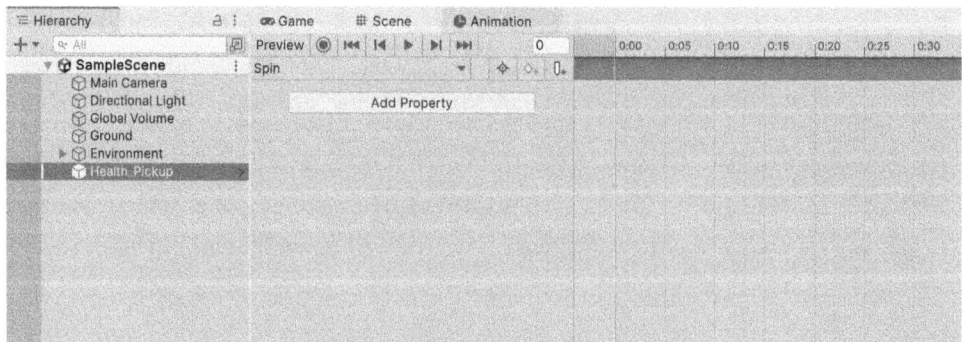

Figure 6.25: Screenshot of the Animation window with a clip selected

4. Since we didn't have any **Animator** controllers, Unity created one for us in the Animations folder called Health_Pickup (along with the animation itself).

With `Health_Pickup` selected, note in the **Inspector** pane that when we created the clip, an **Animator** component was also added to the Prefab for us, but hasn't been officially saved to the Prefab yet with the `Health_Pickup` controller set.

5. In **Inspector**, notice that the + icon is showing at the top left of the **Animator** component, meaning it's not yet part of the `Health_Pickup` Prefab:

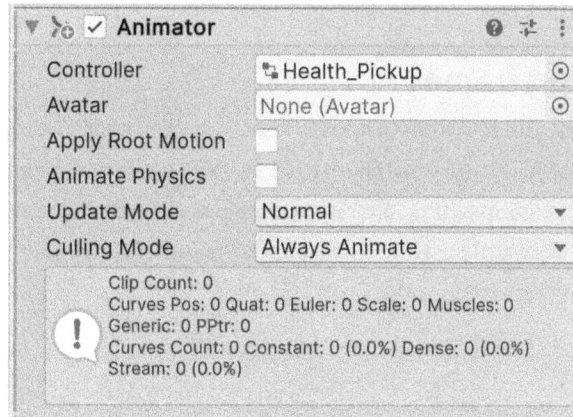

Figure 6.26: The Animator component in the Inspector panel

6. Select the three-vertical-dots icon at the top right and choose **Added Component | Apply to Prefab 'Health_Pickup'**:

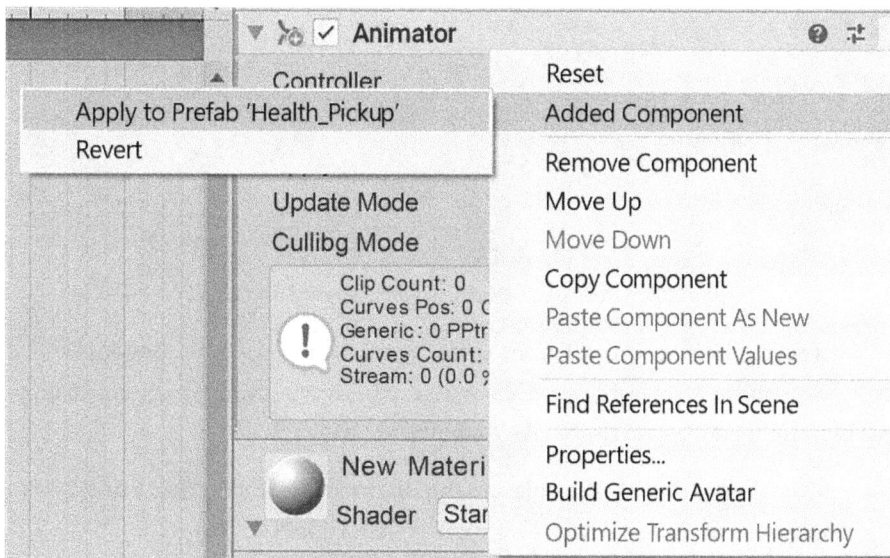

Figure 6.27: Screenshot of a new component being applied to the Prefab

Now that you've created and added an **Animator** component to the Health_Pickup Prefab, it's time to start recording some animation frames.

When you think of motion clips, as in movies, you may think of frames. As the clip moves through its frames, the animation advances, giving the effect of movement. It's no different in Unity; we need to record our target object in different positions throughout different frames so that Unity can play the clip.

Recording keyframes

Now that we have a clip to work with, you'll see a blank timeline in the **Animation** window. Essentially, when we modify our Health_Pickup Prefab's z rotation, or any other property that can be animated, the timeline will record those changes as keyframes. Unity then assembles those keyframes into your complete animation, similar to how individual frames on analog film play together into a moving picture.

Take a look at the following screenshot and remember the locations of the **Record** button and the timeline:

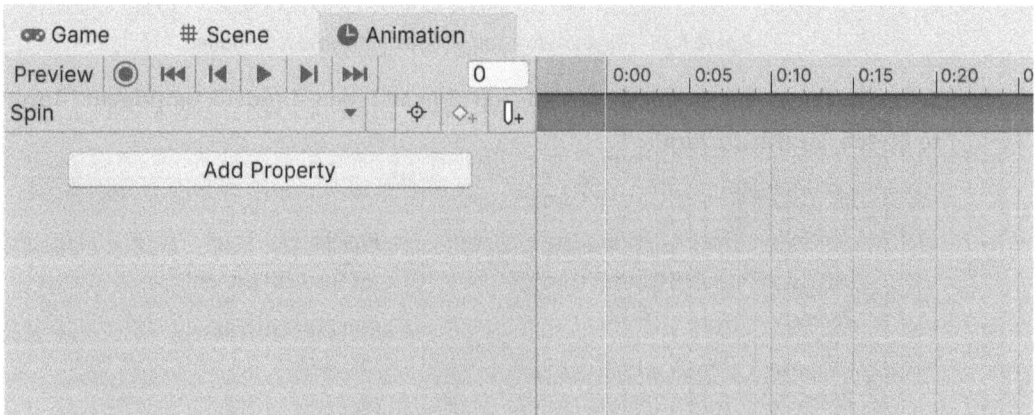

Figure 6.28: Screenshot of the Animation window and keyframe timeline

Now, let's get our item spinning. For the spinning animation, we want the Health_Pickup Prefab to make a complete 360-degree rotation on its z axis every second, which can be done by setting three keyframes and letting Unity take care of the rest:

1. Select the Health_Pickup object in the **Hierarchy** window, choose **Add Property** | **Transform**, and then click on the + sign next to **Rotation**:

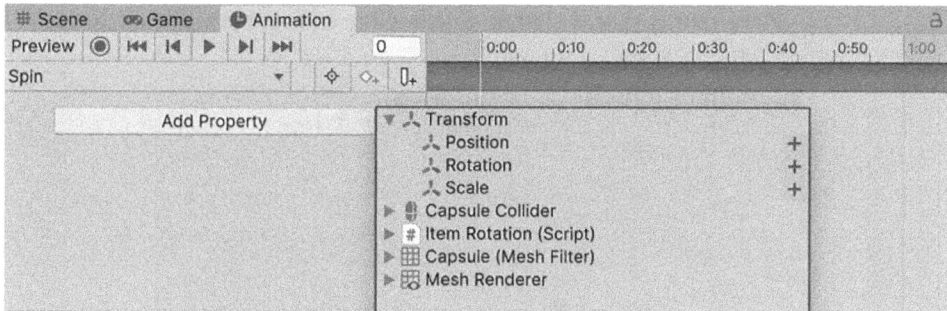

Figure 6.29: Screenshot of adding a Transform property for animation

2. Click on the **Record** button to start the animation:

    a. Place your cursor at 0:00 on the timeline, but leave the Health_Pickup Prefab's z rotation at 0 in **Inspector**—the modifiable fields will appear in red so you don't accidentally animate a property:

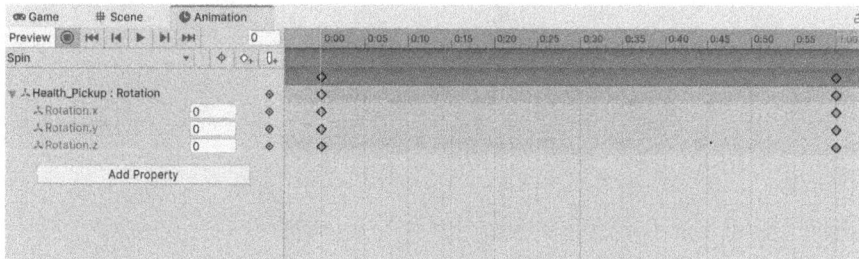

Figure 6.30: Screenshot of animatable property in Inspector with the cursor at 0.00 and z rotation set to 0

    b. Place your cursor at 0:30 on the timeline and set the z rotation to 180:

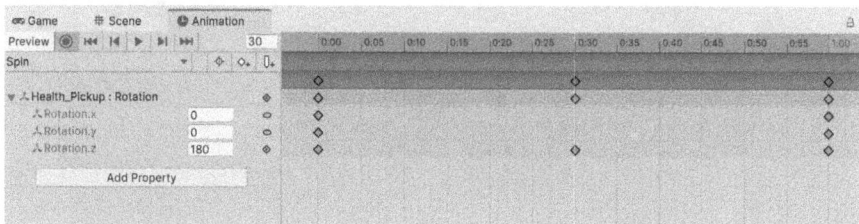

Figure 6.31: Screenshot of animatable property in Inspector with the cursor at 0.30 and z rotation set to 180

    c.   Place your cursor at 1:00 on the timeline and set the *z* rotation to 360:

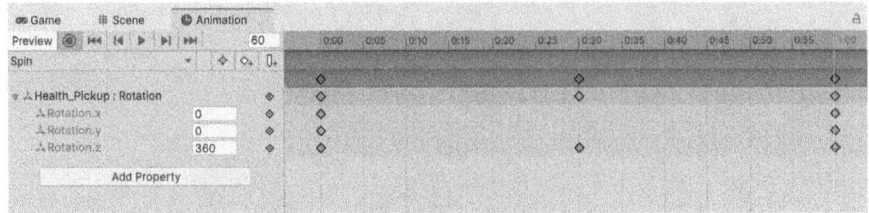

Figure 6.32: Screenshot of Animation keyframes being recorded

3.   Click on the **Record** button to finish the animation.

4.   Click on the **Play** button to the right of the **Record** button to see the animation loop:

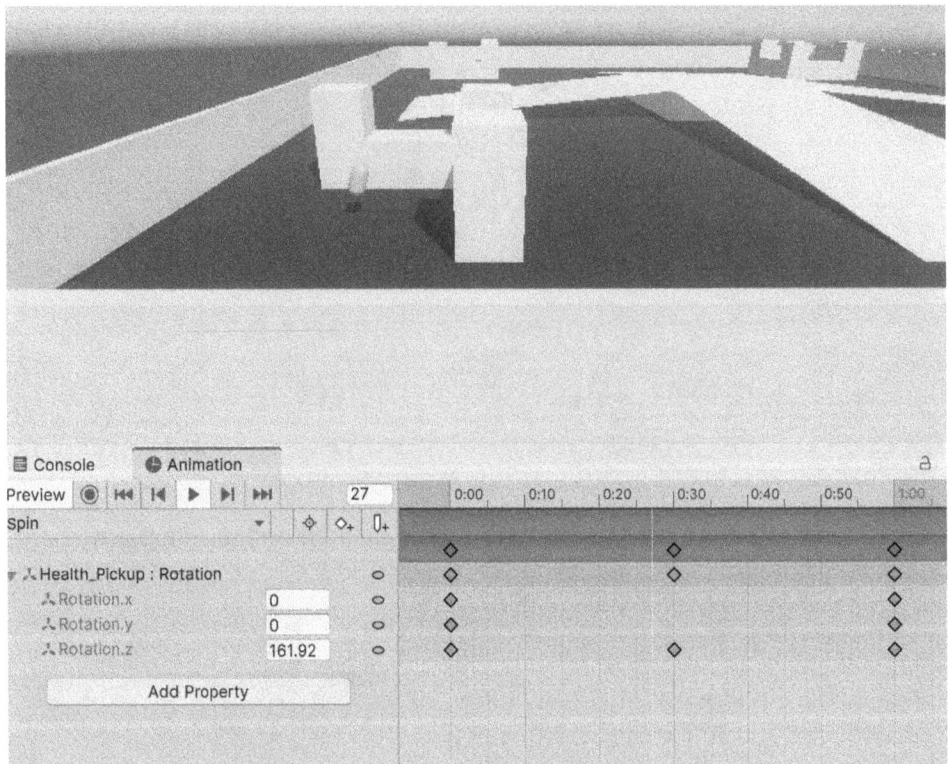

Figure 6.33: Screenshot of the animation playing

You'll notice that our **Animator** animation overrides the one we wrote in code earlier. Don't worry; this is expected behavior. You can click the small checkbox to the right of any component in the **Inspector** panel to activate or deactivate it. If you deactivate the **Animator** component, Health_Pickup will rotate around the *x* axis again using our code.

The `Health_Pickup` object now rotates on the *z* axis between 0, 180, and 360 degrees every second, creating the looping spin animation. If you play the game now, the animation will run indefinitely.

All animations have curves, which determine specific properties of how an animation executes. We won't be doing too much with these, but it's important to understand the basics.

Curves and tangents

In addition to animating an object property, Unity lets us manage how the animation plays out over time with animation curves. So far, we've been in **Dopesheet** mode, which you can change at the bottom of the **Animation** window.

If you click on the **Curves** view (pictured in the following screenshot), you'll see a different graph with accent points in place of our recorded keyframes.

We want the spinning animation to be smooth—what we call **linear**—so we'll leave everything as is. However, speeding up, slowing down, or altering the animation at any point in its run can be done by dragging or adjusting the points on the curve graph in any direction:

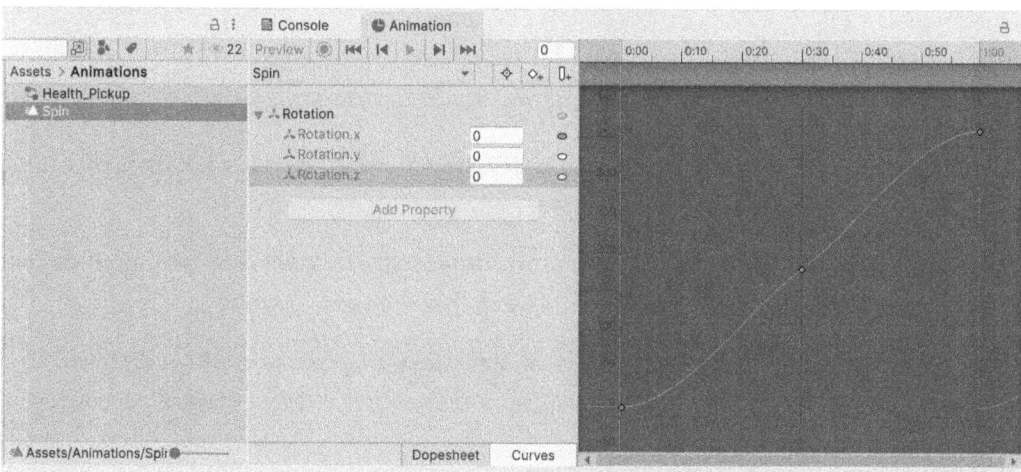

Figure 6.34: Screenshot of an animation playing in the Animation window

Both curves and tangents are intermediate/advanced, so we won't be delving too deeply into them. If you're interested, you can take a look at the documentation on animation curves and tangent options at https://docs.unity3d.com/Manual/animeditor-AnimationCurves.html.

If you play the spinning animation as it is now, there's a slight pause between when the item completes its full rotation and starts a new one. Your job is to smooth that out, which is the subject of the next challenge.

Let's adjust the tangents on the first and last frames of the animation so that the spinning animation blends seamlessly together when it repeats:

1. Switch back to the **Dopesheet** mode, right-click on the first and last keyframes' diamond icons on the animation timeline, and select **Auto**:

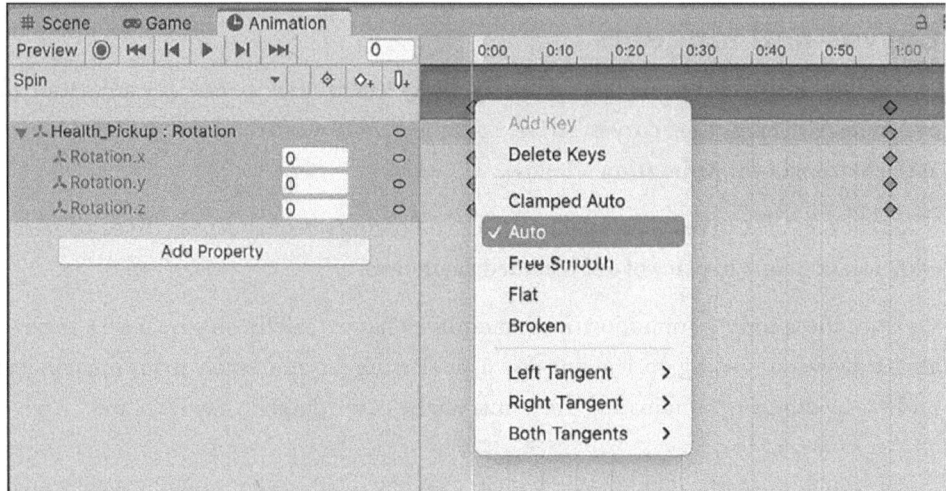

Figure 6.35: Changing keyframe smoothing options

2. If you haven't already done so, move **Main Camera** so that you can see the Health_Pickup object, and click on **Play**.

Changing the first and last keyframe tangents to **Auto** tells Unity to make their transitions smooth, which eliminates the jerky stop/start motion when the animation loops.

That's all the animation you'll need for this book, but I'd encourage you to check out the full toolbox that Unity offers in this area. Your games will be more engaging and your players will thank you!

Summary

We made it to the end of another chapter that had a lot of moving parts, which might have been a lot for those of you who are new to Unity.

Even though this book is focused on the C# language and its implementation in Unity, we still need to take time to get an overview of game development, documentation, and the non-scripting features of the engine. While we didn't have time for in-depth coverage of the lighting and animation, it's worth getting to know them if you're thinking about continuing to create Unity projects.

In the next chapter, we'll be switching our focus back to programming *Hero Born*'s core mechanics, starting with setting up a moveable player object, controlling the camera, and understanding how Unity's physics system governs the game world.

Pop quiz: Basic Unity features

Try and answer the following questions:

a. Cubes, capsules, and spheres are examples of what kind of GameObject?

b. What axis does Unity use to represent depth, which gives scenes their 3D appearance?

c. How do you turn a GameObject into a reusable Prefab?

d. What unit of measurement does the Unity animation system use to record object animations?

Don't forget to check your answers against mine in the *Pop Quiz Answers* appendix to see how you did!

Subscribe to Game Dev Assembly Newsletter!

We are excited to introduce **Game Dev Assembly**, our brand-new newsletter dedicated to everything game development. Whether you're a programmer, designer, artist, animator, or studio lead, you'll get exclusive insights, industry trends, and expert tips to help you build better games and grow your skills. Sign up today and become part of a growing community of creators, innovators, and game changers: https://packt.link/gamedev-newsletter

Scan the QR code to join instantly!

Unlock this book's exclusive benefits now

UNLOCK NOW

Scan this QR code or go to `https://packtpub.com/unlock`,
then search this book by name.

Note: Keep your purchase invoice ready before you start.

7

Movement, Camera Controls, and Collisions

One of the first things a player does when starting a new game is to try out character movement (if, of course, the game has a movable character) and camera controls. Not only is this exciting, but it lets your player know what kind of gameplay they can expect. The character in *Hero Born* will be a capsule object that can be moved and rotated using the *W*, *A*, *S*, *D*, and arrow keys.

We'll start by learning how to manipulate the player object's **Transform** component and then replicate the same player control scheme using applied force. This produces a more realistic movement effect. When we move the player, the camera will follow along from a position that is slightly behind and above the player, making aiming easier when we implement the shooting mechanic. Finally, we'll explore how collisions and physical interactions are handled by Unity's physics system by working with our item pickup prefab.

All of this will come together at a playable level, albeit without any shooting mechanics just yet. It's also going to give us our first taste of C# being used to program game features by tying together the following topics:

- Managing player movement
- Moving the player with the **Transform** component
- Scripting camera behavior
- Working with the Unity physics system

Managing player movement

When you're deciding on how best to move your player character around your virtual world, consider what's going to look the most realistic and not run your game into the ground with expensive computations. This is somewhat of a trade-off in most cases, and Unity is no different.

The three most common ways of moving a GameObject and their results are as follows:

- **Option A**: Use a GameObject's **Transform** component for movement and rotation. This is the easiest solution and the one we'll be working with first.

- **Option B**: Use real-world physics by attaching a **Rigidbody** component to a GameObject and applying force in code. **Rigidbody** components add simulated real-world physics to any GameObject they are attached to. This solution relies on Unity's physics system to do the heavy lifting, delivering a far more realistic effect. We'll update our code to use this approach later on in this chapter to get a feel for both methods.

    Unity suggests sticking to a consistent approach when moving or rotating a GameObject; manipulate either an object's **Transform** or **Rigidbody** component, but never both at the same time.

- **Option C**: Attach a ready-made Unity component or Prefab, such as **Character Controller** or **First-Person Controller**. This cuts out the boilerplate code and still delivers a realistic effect while speeding up the prototyping time.

We won't be doing any work with **Option C**, but there are tons of assets in the **Asset Store** and out in the Unity community for you to explore!

You can find more information on the **Character Controller** component and its uses at https://docs.unity3d.com/ScriptReference/CharacterController.html.

The **First-Person Controller** Prefab is available from the **Standard Assets** package, which you can download from https://assetstore.unity.com/packages/essentials/asset-packs/standard-assets-32351.

Since you're just getting started with player movement in Unity, you'll start off using the player **Transform** component in the next section, and then move on to **Rigidbody** physics later in the chapter.

Moving the player with the Transform component

We want a third-person adventure setup for *Hero Born*, so we'll start with a capsule that can be controlled with keyboard input and a camera to follow the capsule as it moves. Even though these two GameObjects will work together in the game, we'll keep them and their scripts separate for better control.

Before we can do any scripting, you'll need to add a player capsule to the scene, which is your next task.

We can create a nice player capsule in just a few steps:

1. Click on + | **3D Object** | **Capsule** from the **Hierarchy** panel and name it Player.
2. Position the player capsule in the level wherever you like, but I like to put it close to one of the central ramps. It's also important to position the capsule above the ground plane, so be sure to set the **Transform Y** position value to 1 in the **Inspector**.
3. Select the Player GameObject and click on **Add Component** at the bottom of the **Inspector** tab. Search for **Rigidbody** and hit *Enter* to add it. We won't use this component until later, but it's good to set things up properly at the beginning.

4. At the bottom of the **Rigidbody** component, expand the **Constraints** property:

    a. Check the boxes for **Freeze Rotation** on the x, y, and z axes so the player can't be rotated by accident during collisions or other physics interactions. We want to limit rotation to the code we'll write later:

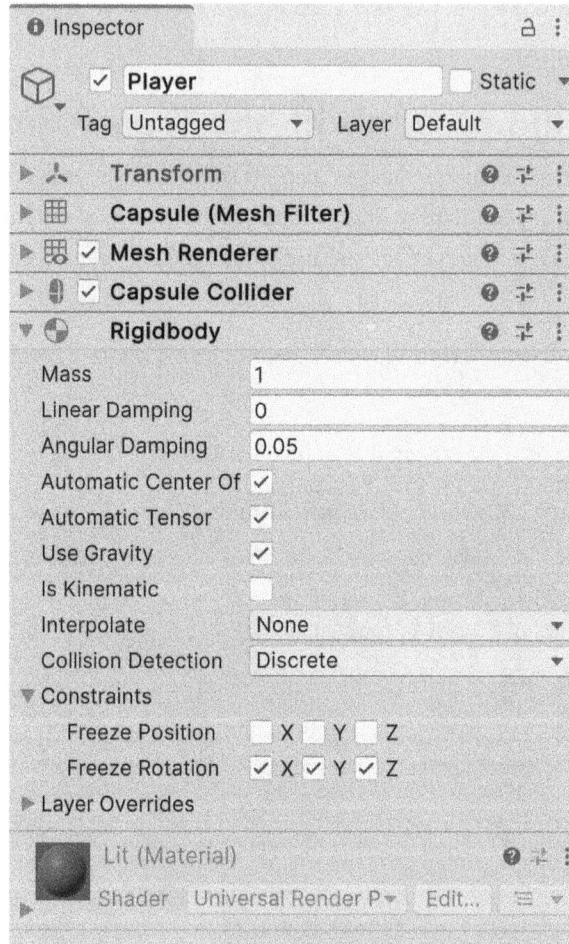

Figure 7.1: Rigidbody component

> **Note**
>
> To provide a complete view of the Unity Editor, all our screenshots are taken in full-screen mode. For color versions of all book images, use this link: https://packt.link/gbp/9781805808718.

5. Select the Materials folder in the **Project** panel and right-click and select **Create | Material**. Name it Player_Mat.

6. Select Player_Mat in the **Hierarchy**, then change the **Base Map** property in the **Inspector** to a bright green.

7. Drag the material to the Player object in the **Hierarchy** panel:

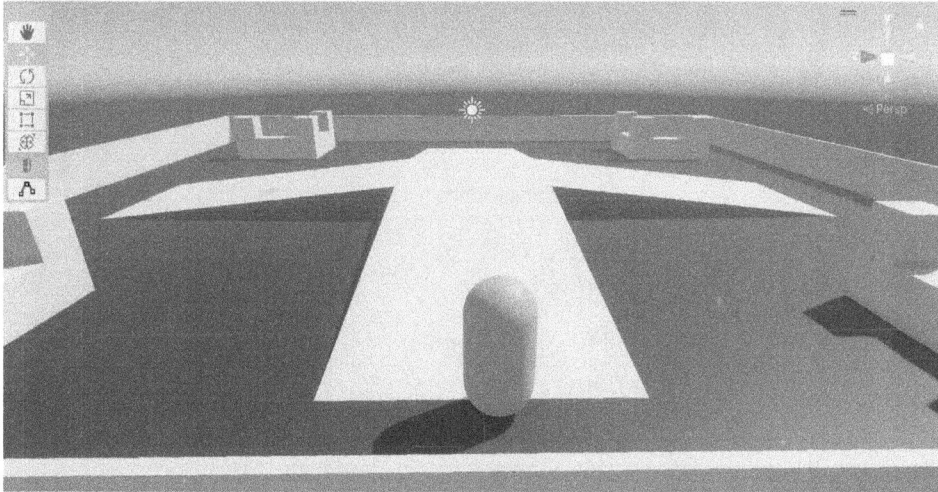

Figure 7.2: Player material attached to a capsule

You've created the Player object out of a capsule primitive, a **Rigidbody** component, and a new bright green material. Don't worry about what the **Rigidbody** component is just yet—all you need to know right now is that it allows our capsule to interact with the physics system. We'll go into more detail in the *Working with the Unity physics system* section at the end of this chapter. Before we get to that, we need to talk about a very important subject in 3D space: *vectors*.

Understanding vectors

Now that we have a player capsule set up, we can start looking at how to move and rotate a GameObject using its **Transform** component. Every **Transform** component has a Translate() and Rotate() method that are part of the Transform class that Unity provides, and each needs a vector parameter to perform its given function.

In Unity, vectors are used to hold position and direction data in 2D and 3D spaces, which is why they come in two varieties—Vector2 and Vector3. These can be used like any other variable type we've seen; they just hold different information. Since our game is in 3D, we'll be using Vector3 objects, which means we'll need to construct them using x, y, and z values.

For 2D vectors, only the *x* and *y* positions are required. Remember, the most up-to-date orientation in your 3D scene will be displayed in the upper-right graphic that we discussed in the previous chapter, *Chapter 6*:

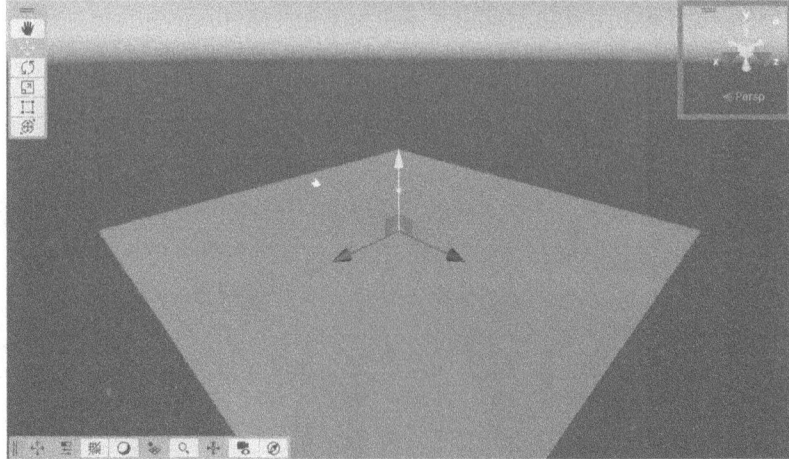

Figure 7.3: Vector gizmos in Unity Editor

If you would like more information about vectors in Unity, refer to the documentation and scripting reference at `https://docs.unity3d.com/ScriptReference/Vector3.html`.

For instance, if we wanted to create a new vector to hold a position in our scene, we could use the following code:

```
Vector3 Origin = new Vector3(1f, 1f, 1f);
```

All we've done here is create a new `Vector3` variable and initialize it with a 1 for the *x* position, 1 for the *y* position, and 1 for the *z* position, in that order. Float values can be written with or without a decimal, but they always need to end with a lowercase `f`.

We can also create directional vectors by using the `Vector2` or `Vector3` class properties:

```
Vector3 ForwardDirection = Vector3.forward;
```

Instead of holding a position, `ForwardDirection` references the *forward* direction in our scene along the *z* axis in the 3D space. The neat thing about using the `Vector3` direction is that no matter which way we make the player look, our code will always know which way is forward. We'll look at using vectors later in this chapter, but for now, just get used to thinking about 3D movement in terms of *x*, *y*, and *z* positions and directions.

Don't worry if the concept of vectors is new to you—it's a complicated topic. Unity's vector cookbook is a great place to start: `https://docs.unity3d.com/Manual/VectorCookbook.html`.

Now that you understand vectors a bit more, you can start implementing the basics of moving the player capsule. For that, you'll need to gather player input from the keyboard, which is the topic of the following section.

Getting player input

Positions and directions are useful in themselves, but they can't generate movement without input from the player. This is where the `Input` class comes in, which handles everything from keystrokes and mouse position to acceleration (applied force in a direction) and gyroscopic data (rotation).

We're going to be using the *W, A, S, D,* and arrow keys for movement in *Hero Born*, coupled with a script that allows the camera to follow where the player points the mouse. To do that, we'll need to understand how input axes work.

First, go to **Edit** | **Project Settings** | **Input Manager** to open the **Input Manager** tab shown in *Figure 7.4*:

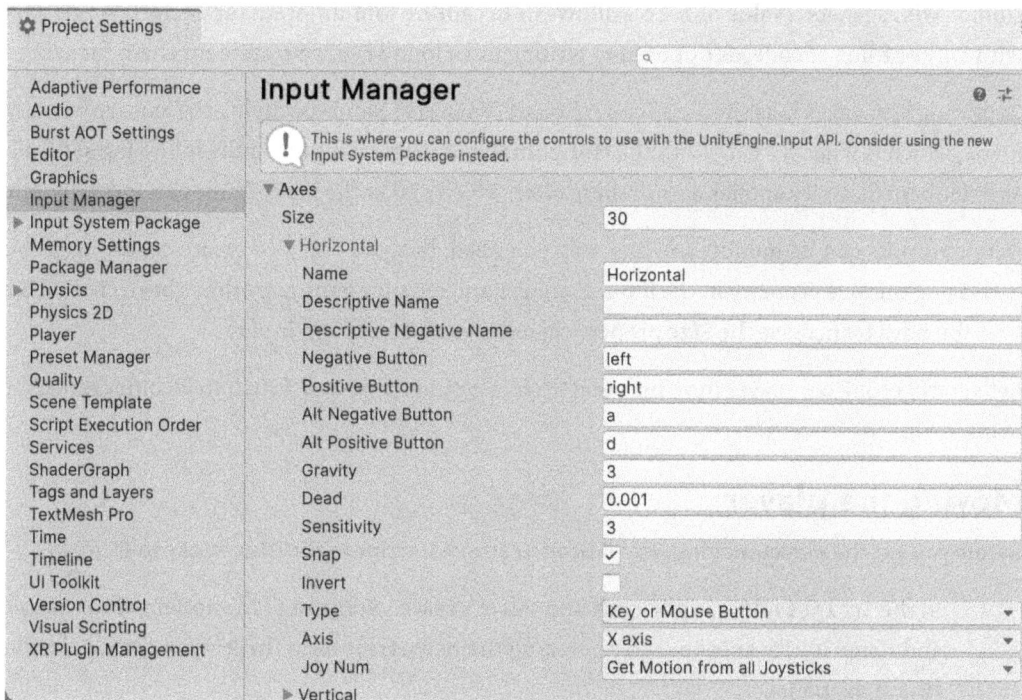

Figure 7.4: Input Manager window

Deciding how to handle player input in Unity has become more complicated in the last few years because Unity introduced a new input system that removes a lot of setup and coding work by wrapping input handling into a component you can use from the editor. I've chosen to stay with the older, programmatic approach in this chapter to avoid introducing topics such as delegates and actions too early, which are necessary with the new Input System.

However, once you finish this book and are comfortable with your C# skills, I recommend diving into the new Input System for your future projects to keep up with the times. You can find more documentation on the new **Input System** at https://unity.com/features/input-system and a great tutorial at https://learn.unity.com/project/using-the-input-system-in-unity.

You'll see a long list of Unity's default inputs already configured, but let's take the **Horizontal** axis as an example. You can see that the **Horizontal** input axis has the **Positive** and **Negative** buttons set to left and right, and the **Alt Negative** and **Alt Positive** buttons set to the *A* and *D* keys.

Whenever an input axis is queried from the code, its value will be between -1 and 1. For example, when the left arrow or *A* key is pushed down, the horizontal axis registers a -1 value. When those keys are released, the value returns to 0. Likewise, when the right arrow or *D* key is used, the horizontal axis registers a value of 1. This allows us to capture four different inputs for a single axis with only one line of code, as opposed to writing out a long if-else statement chain for each.

Capturing input axes is as simple as calling Input.GetAxis() and specifying the axis we want by name, which is what we'll do with the **Horizontal** and **Vertical** inputs in the following sections. As a side benefit, Unity applies a smoothing filter, which makes the input frame rate independent.

Default inputs can be modified in any way you need, but you can also create custom axes by increasing the **Size** property in the input manager and renaming the copy that's been created for you. You have to increase the **Size** property in order to add a custom input.

Let's start getting our player moving using Unity's input system and a custom locomotion script of our own.

Moving the player

Before you get the player moving, you'll need to attach a script to the Player capsule:

1. In the Scripts folder, right-click and select **Create** | **Scripting** | **MonoBehaviour Script** and name it PlayerBehavior, then drag the new script onto the Player capsule in the **Hierarchy** panel.

2. Add the following code and save:

```
using System.Collections;
using System.Collections.Generic;
using UnityEngine;
public class PlayerBehavior : MonoBehaviour
{
    // 1
    public float MoveSpeed = 10f;
    public float RotateSpeed = 75f;
    // 2
    private float _vInput;
    private float _hInput;
    void Update()
    {
        // 3
        _vInput = Input.GetAxis("Vertical") * MoveSpeed;
        // 4
        _hInput = Input.GetAxis("Horizontal") * RotateSpeed;
        // 5
        this.transform.Translate(Vector3.forward * _vInput *
        Time.deltaTime);
        // 6
        this.transform.Rotate(Vector3.up * _hInput *
        Time.deltaTime);
    }
}
```

Using the this keyword is optional. Visual Studio may suggest that you remove it to simplify the code, but I prefer leaving it in so my code is always super clear. When you have empty methods, such as Start(), in this case, it's common to delete them for clarity.

Here's a breakdown of the preceding code:

1. We declare two public variables to be used as multipliers:

    *   MoveSpeed for how fast we want the player to go forward and backward
    *   RotateSpeed for how fast we want the player to rotate left and right

2. We then declare two private variables to hold inputs from the player; initially set with no value:

    - _vInput will store the vertical axis input

    - _hInput will store the horizontal axis input

3. Input.GetAxis("Vertical") detects when the up arrow, down arrow, *W*, or *S* key is pressed and multiplies that value by MoveSpeed:

    - The up arrow and *W* keys return a value of 1, which will move the player in the forward (positive) direction

    - The down arrow and *S* keys return a value of -1, which moves the player backward (negative) direction

4. Input.GetAxis("Horizontal") detects when the left arrow, right arrow, *A*, or *D* key is pressed and multiplies that value by RotateSpeed:

    - The right arrow and *D* keys return a value of 1, which will rotate the capsule to the right

    - The left arrow and *A* keys return a value of -1, rotating the capsule to the left

    If you're wondering whether it's possible to do all the movement calculations on one line, the simple answer is *yes*. However, it's better to have your code broken down, even if you're the only one reading it.

5. We use the Translate() method, which takes in a Vector3 parameter, to move the capsule's **Transform** component:

    Remember that the this keyword specifies the GameObject the current script is attached to, which, in this case, is the player capsule.

    - Vector3.forward multiplied by _vInput and Time.deltaTime supplies the direction and speed the capsule needs to move forward or back along the *z* axis at the speed we've calculated.

    - Time.deltaTime will always return the value in seconds since the last frame of the game was executed. It's commonly used to smooth values that are captured or run in the Update method instead of letting it be determined by the device's frame rate.

6. Finally, we use the `Rotate()` method to rotate the capsule's **Transform** component relative to the vector we pass in as a parameter:

   - `Vector3.up` multiplied by `_hInput` and `Time.deltaTime` gives us the left/right rotation axis we want

   - We use the `this` keyword and `Time.deltaTime` here for the same reasons

As we discussed earlier, using direction vectors in the `Translate` and `Rotate` functions is only one way to go about this. We could have created new `Vector3` variables from our axis inputs and used them as parameters just as easily.

When you click **Play**, you'll be able to move the capsule forward and backward using the up/down arrow keys and the *W/S* keys, while rotating or turning with the left/right arrow keys and the *A/D* keys. Since the camera doesn't follow our player yet, you may need to move the camera to a higher position to see the capsule move when you press the input keys.

With these few lines of code, you've set up two separate controls that are frame-rate independent and easily modified. However, our camera doesn't follow the capsule as it moves around, so let's fix that in the following section.

Scripting camera behavior

The easiest way to get one GameObject to follow another is to make one of them a child of the other. When an object is a child of another, the child object's position and rotation are relative to the parent. This means that any child object will move and rotate with the parent object.

However, this approach means that any kind of movement or rotation that happens to the player capsule also affects the camera (like a waterfall affects the water downstream), which is something we don't necessarily want. We always want the camera to be positioned a set distance behind our player and always rotate to look at it, no matter what. Luckily, we can easily set the position and rotation of the camera relative to the capsule with methods from the `Transform` class. It's your task to script out the camera logic in the next challenge.

Since we want the camera behavior to be entirely separate from how the player moves, we'll be controlling where the camera is positioned relative to a target we can set from the **Inspector** tab:

1. In the `Scripts` folder, create a new **MonoBehaviour** script, name it `CameraBehavior`, and drag it into **Main Camera** in the **Hierarchy** panel.

2. Add the following code and save it:

```
using System.Collections;
using System.Collections.Generic;
using UnityEngine;
public class CameraBehavior : MonoBehaviour
{
    // 1
    public Vector3 CamOffset= new Vector3(0f, 1.2f, -2.6f);
    // 2
    private Transform _target;
    void Start()
    {
        // 3
        _target = GameObject.Find("Player").transform;
    }
    // 4
    void LateUpdate()
    {
        // 5
        this.transform.position = _target.TransformPoint(CamOffset);
        // 6
        this.transform.LookAt(_target);
    }
}
```

Here's a breakdown of the preceding code:

1. We declare a `Vector3` variable to store the distance we want between **Main Camera** and the `Player` capsule:

    *   We'll be able to manually set the x, y, and z positions of the camera offset in the **Inspector** because it's public.

    *   These default values are what I think look best, but feel free to experiment.

2. We then create a variable to hold the player capsule's `Transform` information:

   - This will give us access to its position, rotation, and scale.
   - We don't want any other script to be able to change the camera's target, which is why it's private.

3. We use `GameObject.Find` to locate the capsule by name and retrieve its `Transform` property from the scene:

   - This means the capsule's *x*, *y*, and *z* positions are updated and stored in the `_target` variable every frame.
   - Finding objects in the scene is a computationally expensive task, so it's good practice to only do it once in the `Start()` method and store the reference. Never use `GameObject.Find` in the `Update()` method, as that will try to continually find the object you're looking for and potentially crash the game.

4. `LateUpdate()` is a `MonoBehaviour` method, like `Start()` or `Update()`, that executes after `Update()`:

   - Since our `PlayerBehavior` script moves the capsule in its `Update()` method, we want the code in `CameraBehavior` to run after the movement happens; this guarantees that `_target` has the most up-to-date position to reference.

5. We set the camera's position to `_target.TransformPoint(CamOffset)` for every frame, which creates the following effect:

   - The `TransformPoint()` method calculates and returns a relative position in the world space.
   - In this case, it returns the position of the target (our capsule) offset by `0` on the *x* axis, `1.2` on the *y* axis (putting the camera above the capsule), and `-2.6` on the *z* axis (putting the camera slightly behind the capsule).

6. The LookAt() method updates the capsule's rotation at every frame, focusing on the Transform parameter we pass in, which, in this case, is _target:

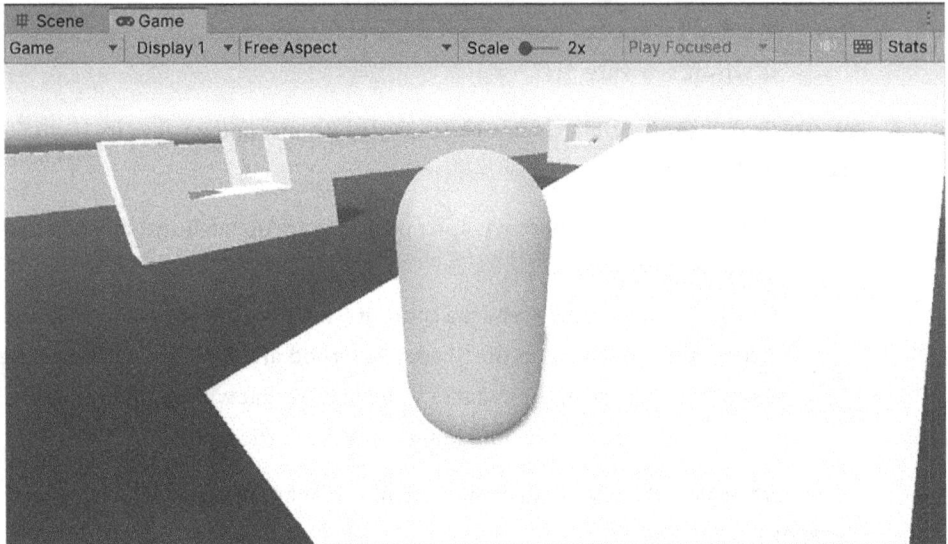

Figure 7.5: Capsule and following camera in Play mode

This was a lot to take in, but it's easier to process if you break it down into its chronological steps:

1. We created an offset position for the camera.

2. We found and stored the player capsule's position.

3. We manually updated its position and rotation every frame so that it's always following at a set distance and looking at the player.

When using class methods that deliver platform-specific functionality, always remember to break things down to their most basic steps. This will help you to stay above water in new programming environments.

While the code you've written to manage player movement is perfectly functional, you might have noticed that it's a little jerky in places. To create a smoother, more realistic movement effect, you'll need to understand the basics of the Unity physics system, which you'll dive into next.

Working with the Unity physics system

Up to this point, we haven't talked about how the Unity engine works or how it manages to create lifelike interactions and movement in a virtual space. We'll spend the rest of this chapter learning the basics of Unity's physics system.

The two main components that power Unity's **NVIDIA PhysX** engine are as follows:

- **Rigidbody** components, which allow GameObjects to be affected by gravity and add properties such as **Mass** and **Drag**. **Rigidbody** components can also be affected by an applied force if they have a **Collider** component attached, which generates more realistic movement:

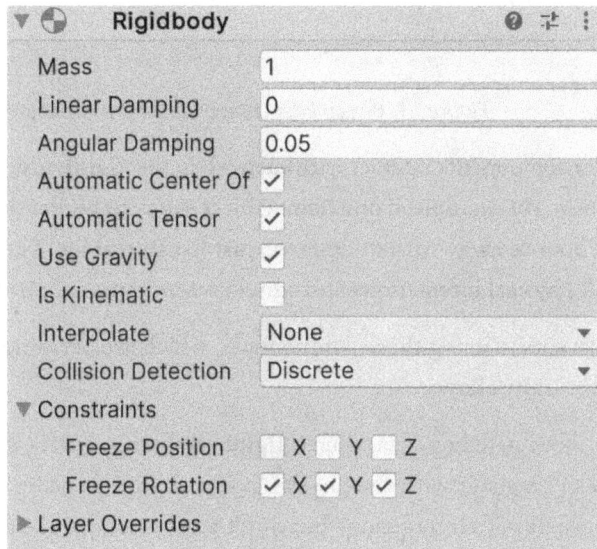

Figure 7.6: Rigidbody component in the Inspector pane

- **Collider** components, which determine how and when GameObjects enter and exit each other's physical space or simply collide and bounce away. While there should only be one **Rigidbody** component attached to a given GameObject, there can be several **Collider** components if you need different shapes or interactions.

This is commonly referred to as a **compound collider setup**:

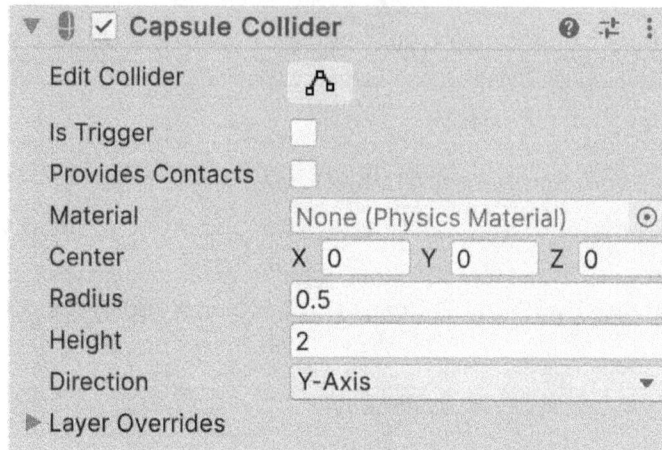

Figure 7.7: Box collider component in the Inspector pane

When two **Collider** components interact with each other, the **Rigidbody** properties determine the resulting interaction. For example, if one GameObject's mass is higher than the other, the lighter GameObject will bounce away with more force, just like in real life. These two components are responsible for all physical interactions and simulated movement in Unity.

There are some caveats to using these components, which are best understood in terms of the types of movement Unity allows:

- *Kinematic* movement happens when a **Rigidbody** component is attached to a GameObject, but it doesn't register with the physics system in the scene. In other words, kinematic objects have physics interactions but don't react to them, like a wall in real life. This is only used in certain cases and can be enabled by checking the **Is Kinematic** property of a **Rigidbody** component. Since we want our capsule to interact with the physics system, we won't be using this kind of motion.

- *Non-kinematic* movement is when a **Rigidbody** component is moved or rotated by applying force rather than manually changing a GameObject's **Transform** properties. Our goal for this section is to update the PlayerBehavior script to implement this type of motion.

The setup we have now, that is, manipulating the capsule's **Transform** component while using a **Rigidbody** component to interact with the physics system, was meant to get you thinking about movement and rotation in a 3D space. However, it's not meant for production, and Unity suggests avoiding a mix of kinematic and non-kinematic movement in your code.

Your next task is to use applied force to convert the current movement system into a more realistic locomotion experience.

Rigidbody components in motion

Since our player has a **Rigidbody** component attached, we should let the physics engine control our movement instead of manually translating and rotating the **Transform**. There are two options when it comes to applying force:

- You can do it directly by using `Rigidbody` class methods such as `AddForce()` and `AddTorque()` to move and rotate an object, respectively. This approach has its drawbacks and often requires additional code to compensate for unexpected physics behavior such as unwanted torque or applied force during collisions.
- Alternatively, you can use other `Rigidbody` class methods such as `MovePosition()` and `MoveRotation()`, which still use applied force.

We'll take the second route in the next section so that Unity takes care of the applied physics for us, but if you're curious about manually applying force and torque to your GameObjects, then start here: `https://docs.unity3d.com/ScriptReference/Rigidbody.AddForce.html`.

Either of these will give the player a more lifelike feel and allow us to add jumping and dashing mechanics in *Chapter 8*.

If you're curious about what happens when a moving object without a **Rigidbody** component interacts with pieces of the environment that have them equipped, remove the component from `Player` and run around the arena. Congratulations—you're a ghost and can walk through walls! Don't forget to add the **Rigidbody** component back, though!

The player capsule already has a **Rigidbody** component attached, which means that you can access and modify its properties. First, though, you'll need to find and store the component, which is your next challenge.

You'll need to access and store the **Rigidbody** component on the `Player` capsule before modifying it. Update `PlayerBehavior` with the following changes:

```
using System.Collections;
using System.Collections.Generic;
using UnityEngine;
public class PlayerBehavior : MonoBehaviour
{
    public float MoveSpeed = 10f;
```

```
public float RotateSpeed = 75f;
private float _vInput;
private float _hInput;
// 1
private Rigidbody _rb;
// 2
void Start()
{
    // 3
    _rb = GetComponent<Rigidbody>();
}
// 4
void Update()
{
  _vInput = Input.GetAxis("Vertical") * MoveSpeed;
  _hInput = Input.GetAxis("Horizontal") * RotateSpeed;
  /*
  this.transform.Translate(Vector3.forward * _vInput *
  Time.deltaTime);
  this.transform.Rotate(Vector3.up * _hInput * Time.deltaTime);
  */
}
}
```

Here's a breakdown of the preceding code:

1. Adds a private variable of type Rigidbody that will contain a reference to the capsule's **Rigidbody** component.

2. The Start() method fires when a script is initialized in a scene, which happens when you click on **Play**, and should be used any time variables need to be set at the beginning of a class.

3. The GetComponent method checks whether the component type we're looking for – in this case, Rigidbody – exists on the GameObject the script is attached to and returns it:

    a. If the component isn't attached to the GameObject, the method will return null, but since we know there's one on the player, we won't worry about error checking right now.

4. Comments out the `Transform()` and `Rotate()` method calls in the Update function so that we won't be running two different kinds of player controls:

    a. We want to keep our code that captures player input so that we can still use it later on.

You've initialized and stored the **Rigidbody** component on the player capsule and commented out the obsolete `Transform` code to set the stage for physics-based movement. The character is now ready for the next challenge, which is to add force.

Use the following steps to move and rotate the **Rigidbody** component. Add the following code to `PlayerBehavior` underneath the Update method, and then save the file:

```
// 1
void FixedUpdate()
{
    // 2
    Vector3 rotation = Vector3.up * _hInput;
    // 3
    Quaternion angleRot = Quaternion.Euler(rotation *
        Time.fixedDeltaTime);
    // 4
    _rb.MovePosition(this.transform.position +
        this.transform.forward * _vInput * Time.fixedDeltaTime);
     // 5
    _rb.MoveRotation(_rb.rotation * angleRot);
}
```

Here's a breakdown of the preceding code:

1. Any physics- or `Rigidbody`-related code always goes inside the `FixedUpdate()` method, rather than `Update()` or the other `MonoBehaviour` methods:

    •   `FixedUpdate` is frame rate independent and is used for all physics code.

2. We create a new `Vector3` variable to store our left and right rotations:

    •   `Vector3.up * _hInput` is the same rotation vector we used with the `Rotate()` method in the previous example.

3. Quaternion.Euler takes a Vector3 parameter and returns a rotation value in Euler angles:

    -   We need a quaternion value instead of a Vector3 parameter to use the MoveRotation() method. This is just a conversion to the rotation type that Unity prefers.

    -   You can read more about how Unity handles object rotations and orientation at https://docs.unity3d.com/Documentation/Manual/QuaternionAndEulerRot ationsInUnity.html.

    We multiply by Time.fixedDeltaTime for the same reason we used Time.deltaTime in Update().

4. We call MovePosition() on our _rb component, which takes in a Vector3 parameter and applies force accordingly:

    -   The vector that's used can be broken down as follows: the capsule's Transform position in the forward direction, multiplied by the vertical inputs and Time. fixedDeltaTime.

    -   The **Rigidbody** component takes care of applying movement force to satisfy our vector parameter.

5. We call the MoveRotation() method on the _rb component, which also takes in a Vector3 parameter and applies the corresponding forces under the hood:

    -   angleRot already has the horizontal inputs from the keyboard, so all we need to do is multiply the current Rigidbody rotation by angleRot to get the same left and right rotation.

Be aware that MovePosition() and MoveRotation() work differently for non-kinematic Game-Objects. You can find more information in the **Rigidbody** scripting reference at https://docs. unity3d.com/ScriptReference/Rigidbody.html.

If you click on **Play** now, you'll be able to move forward and backward in the direction you're looking, as well as to rotate around the *y* axis.

Applied force produces stronger effects than translating and rotating a **Transform** component, so you may need to fine-tune the MoveSpeed and RotateSpeed variables in the **Inspector** pane. You've now recreated the same type of movement scheme as before, just with more realistic physics.

If you run up a ramp or drop off the central platform, you might see the player launch into the air or slowly drop to the ground. Even though the **Rigidbody** component is set to use gravity, it's fairly weak. We'll tackle applying our gravity to the player in the next chapter, when we implement the jump mechanic. For now, your job is to get comfortable with how **Collider** components handle collisions in Unity.

Colliders and collisions

Collider components not only allow GameObjects to be recognized by Unity's physics system, but they also make interactions and collisions possible. Think of colliders as invisible force fields that surround GameObjects; they can be passed through or bumped into depending on their settings, and they come with a host of methods that execute during different interactions.

Unity's physics system works differently for 2D and 3D games, so we will only be covering the 3D topics in this book. If you're interested in making 2D games, refer to the Rigidbody2D component at `https://docs.unity3d.com/Manual/class-Rigidbody2D.html` and the list of available 2D colliders at `https://docs.unity3d.com/Manual/Collider2D.html`.

Take a look at the following screenshot of the `Capsule` in the `Health_Pickup` object. If you want to see the **Capsule** collider a little better, increase the **Radius** property:

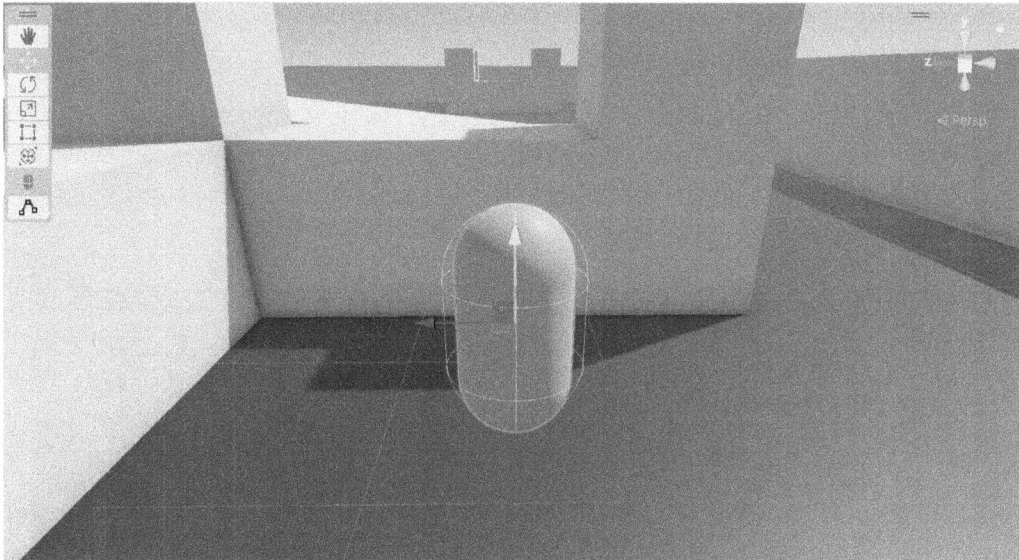

Figure 7.8: Capsule collider component attached to pickup item

The green shape around the object is the **Capsule** collider, which can be moved and scaled using the **Center**, **Radius**, and **Height** properties.

When a primitive is created, the collider matches the primitive's shape by default; since we created a capsule primitive, it comes with a **Capsule** collider.

Colliders also come in **Box**, **Sphere**, and **Mesh** shapes and can be manually added from the **Component | Physics** menu or from the **Add Component** button in the **Inspector**.

When a collider comes into contact with other components, it sends out what's called a **message**, or **broadcast**. Any script that adds one or more of those methods will receive a notification when the collider sends out a message. This is called an **event**, which is a topic that we'll cover in more detail in *Chapter 14*.

For example, when two GameObjects with colliders come into contact, both objects register an OnCollisionEnter event, complete with a reference to the object they ran into. Think of an event like a message being sent out—if you choose to listen for it, you'll get notified when a collision happens in this case. This information can be used to track a variety of interactive events, but the simplest one is picking up an item. For cases where you want objects to be able to pass through others, you can use collision triggers, which we'll talk about in the next section.

A complete list of **Collider** notifications can be found underneath the **Messages** header at https://docs.unity3d.com/ScriptReference/Collider.html.

Collision and trigger events are only sent out when the colliding objects belong to a specific combination of **Collider**, **Trigger**, and **RigidBody** components and kinematic or non-kinematic motion. You can find details under the **Collision action matrix** section at https://docs.unity3d.com/Manual/CollidersOverview.html.

The health item you previously created is a perfect place to test out how collisions work. You'll tackle that in the next challenge.

Picking up an item

To update the Health_Pickup object using collision logic, you need to do the following:

1. In the Scripts folder, create a new MonoBehaviour script, name it ItemBehavior, and then drag it onto the Health_Pickup object in the **Hierarchy** panel:

    *   Any script that uses collision detection *must* be attached to a GameObject with a **Collider** component, even if it's the child of a prefab.

2. Select `Health_Pickup` in the **Hierarchy** panel, click the three-vertical-dots icon in the **Inspector** to the right of the **Item Behavior (Script)** component, and choose **Added Component | Apply to Prefab 'Health_Pickup'**:

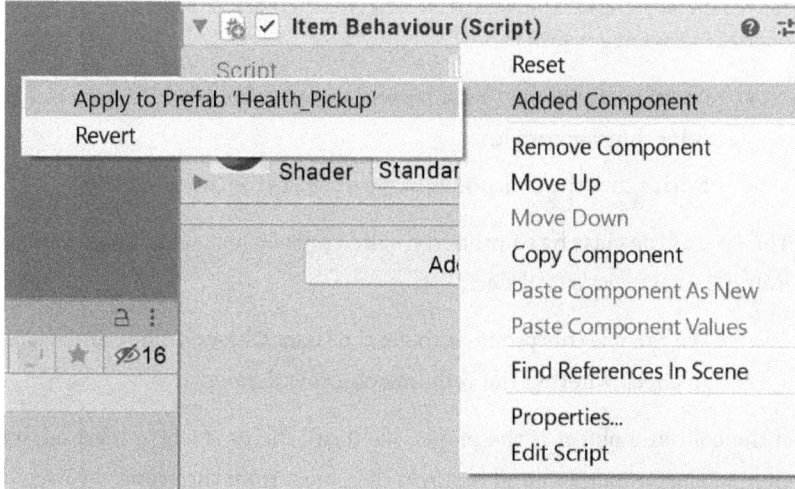

Figure 7.9: Applying prefab changes to a pickup item

3. Replace the default code in `ItemBehavior` with the following, and then save it:

```
using System.Collections;
using System.Collections.Generic;
using UnityEngine;
public class ItemBehavior : MonoBehaviour
{
    // 1
    void OnCollisionEnter(Collision collision)
    {
        // 2
        if(collision.gameObject.name == "Player")
        {
            // 3
            Destroy(this.transform.gameObject);
            // 4
            Debug.Log("Item collected!");
        }
    }
}
```

4. Click on **Play** and move the player over the capsule to pick it up!

Here's a breakdown of the preceding code:

1. When another object runs into the Item prefab, Unity automatically calls the OnCollisionEnter() method:

   - OnCollisionEnter() comes with a parameter that stores a reference to the **Collider** that ran into it.
   - Notice that the collision is of type Collision, not Collider.

2. The Collision class has a property, called gameObject, that holds a reference to the colliding GameObject's **Collider**:

   - We can use this property to get the GameObject's name and use an if statement to check whether the colliding object is the player.

3. If the colliding object is the player, we'll call the Destroy() method, which takes in a GameObject parameter and removes the object from the scene.

4. It then prints out a simple log to the console that we have collected an item:

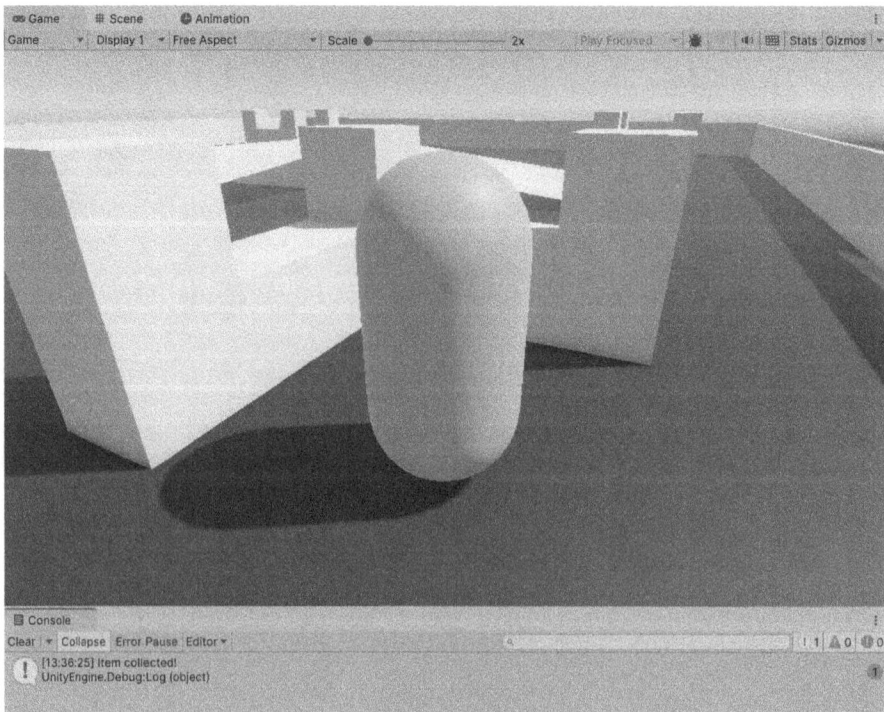

Figure 7.10: Example of GameObjects being deleted from a scene

We've set up `ItemBehavior` to essentially listen for any collisions with the `Health_Pickup` object prefab. Whenever a collision occurs, `ItemBehavior` uses `OnCollisionEnter()` and checks whether the colliding object is the player and, if so, destroys (or collects) the item.

If you're feeling lost, think of the collision code we wrote as a receiver for notifications from `Health_Pickup`; any time it's hit, the code fires.

It's also important to understand that we could have created a similar script with an `OnCollisionEnter()` method, attached it to the player, and then checked whether the colliding object was a `Health_Pickup` prefab. Collision logic depends on the perspective of the object being collided with.

Now the question is, how would you set up a collision without stopping the colliding objects from moving through each other? We'll tackle that in the next section.

Using Collider triggers

By default, colliders are set with the **isTrigger** property unchecked, meaning that the physics system treats them as solid objects and will raise a collision event on impact. However, in some cases, you'll want to be able to pass through a **Collider** component without it stopping your GameObject. This is where triggers come in. With **isTrigger** checked, a GameObject can pass through it, but the collider will send out the **OnTriggerEnter**, **OnTriggerExit**, and **OnTriggerStay** notifications instead.

Triggers are most useful when you need to detect when a GameObject enters a certain area or passes a certain point. We'll use this to set up the areas around our enemies; if the player walks into the trigger zone, the enemies will be alerted, and, later on, attack the player. For now, we're going to focus just on the enemy logic in the following challenge.

Creating an enemy

Use the following steps to create an enemy:

1. Create a new primitive using + | **3D Object** | **Capsule** in the **Hierarchy** panel and name it Enemy.

2. Inside the `Materials` folder, use + | **Material**, name it Enemy_Mat, and set its **Base Map** property to a bright red:

    a. Drag and drop Enemy_Mat into the Enemy GameObject

3. With Enemy selected, click on **Add Component**, search for **Sphere** collider, and hit *Enter* to add it:

    a. Check the **isTrigger** property box and change **Radius** to 8:

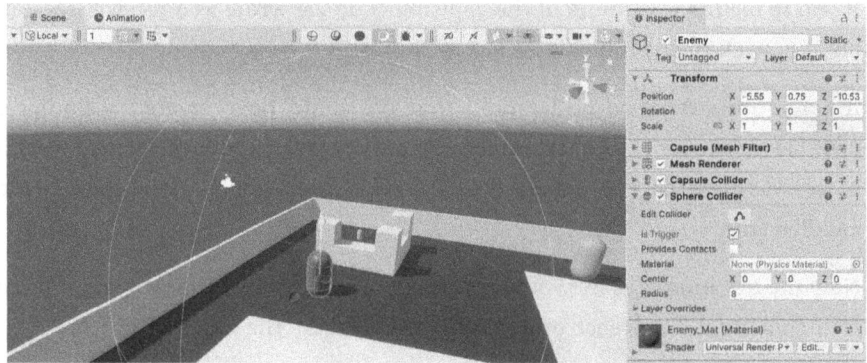

Figure 7.11: Sphere collider component attached to an enemy object

Our new Enemy primitive is now surrounded by an 8-unit trigger radius shaped like a sphere. Any time another object enters, stays inside, or exits that area, Unity will send out notifications that we can capture, just like we did with collisions. Your next challenge will be to capture that notification and act on it in code.

To capture trigger events, you'll need to create a new script by following these steps:

1. In the Scripts folder, create a new MonoBehaviour script, name it EnemyBehavior, and then drag it into Enemy.

2. Add the following code and save the file:

```
using System.Collections;
using System.Collections.Generic;
using UnityEngine;

public class EnemyBehavior : MonoBehaviour
{
    // 1
    void OnTriggerEnter(Collider other)
    {
        //2
        if(other.name == "Player")
        {
```

```
                    Debug.Log("Player detected - attack!");
        }
    }
    // 3
    void OnTriggerExit(Collider other)
    {
        // 4
        if(other.name == "Player")
        {
            Debug.Log("Player out of range, resume patrol");
        }
    }
}
```

3. Click **Play** and walk over to the enemy to set off the first notification, then walk away from the enemy to set off the second notification.

Here's a breakdown of the preceding code:

1. OnTriggerEnter() is fired whenever an object enters the enemy's **Sphere** collider radius:

    - Similar to OnCollisionEnter(), OnTriggerEnter() stores a reference to the trespassing object's **Collider** component.

    - Note that other is of type Collider, not Collision.

2. We can use other to access the name of the colliding GameObject, and check whether it's the player with an if statement.

    - If it is, the console prints out a log that the player is in the danger zone:

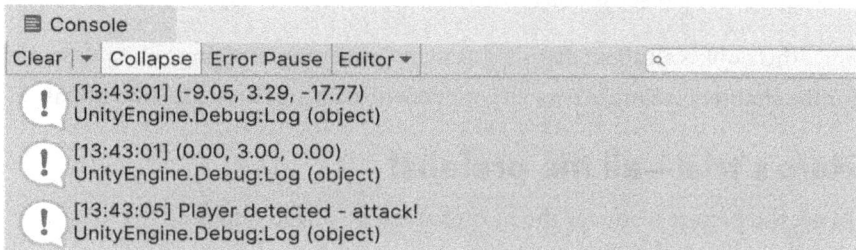

Figure 7.12: Collision detection between player and enemy objects

3. `OnTriggerExit()` is fired when an object leaves the enemy's **Sphere** collider radius:

    •   This method also has a reference to the colliding object's **Collider** component.

4. We check the object leaving the **Sphere** collider radius by name using another `if` statement:

    •   If it's `Player`, we print out another log to the console saying that they're safe:

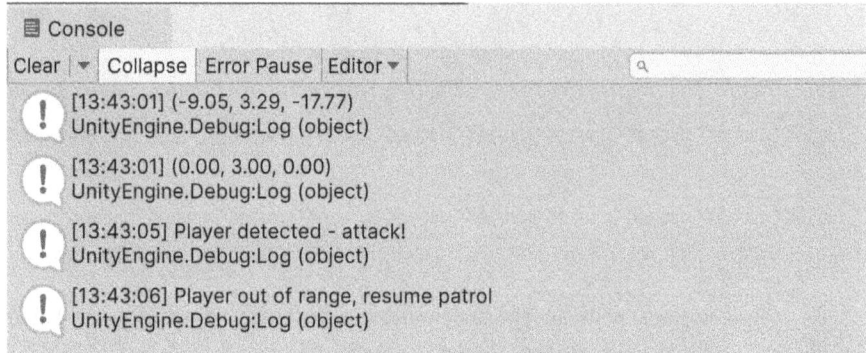

Figure 7.13: Example of collision triggers

The **Sphere** collider on our Enemy sends out notifications when its area is invaded, and the `EnemyBehavior` script captures two of those events. Whenever the player enters or exits the collision radius, a debug log appears in the console to let us know that the code is working. We'll continue to build on this in *Chapter 9*.

Unity makes use of something called the **Component Design Pattern**. Without going into too much detail, that's a fancy way of saying objects (and, by extension, their classes) should be responsible for their behavior as opposed to having all the code in one huge file. This is why we put separate collision scripts on the pickup item and enemy instead of having a single class handle everything. We'll discuss this further in *Chapter 14*.

Since this book is all about instilling as many good programming habits as possible, your last task for the chapter is to make sure all your core objects are converted into prefabs.

Hero's trial—all the prefabs!

To get the project ready for the next chapter, go ahead and drag the `Player` and `Enemy` objects into the `Prefabs` folder.

Remember, from now on, you always need to right-click on the **Prefab** in the **Hierarchy** panel, switch to the **Inspector** panel, and select the three-vertical-dots icon, then choose **Added Component** | **Apply to Prefab** to solidify any changes you make to these GameObjects.

With that done, continue to the *Physics roundup* section and make sure that you've internalized all the major topics we've covered before moving on.

Physics roundup

Before we wrap up the chapter, here are a few high-level concepts to cement what we've learned so far:

- **Rigidbody** components add simulated real-world physics to the GameObjects they are attached to.
- **Collider** components interact with each other, as well as objects, using **Rigidbody** components:
    - If a **Collider** component is not a trigger, it acts as a solid object.
    - If a **Collider** component is a trigger, it can be walked through.
- An object is *kinematic* if it uses a **Rigidbody** component and has **Is Kinematic** checked, telling the physics system to ignore it.
- An object is *non-kinematic* if it uses a **Rigidbody** component and force or torque is applied to power its movement and rotation.
- Colliders send out notifications based on their interactions. These notifications depend on whether the **Collider** component is set to be triggered or not. Notifications can be received from either colliding party, and they come with reference variables that hold an object's collision information.

Remember, a topic as broad and complex as the Unity physics system isn't learned in a day. Use what you've learned here as a springboard to launch yourself into more intricate topics!

Summary

This wraps up your first experience of creating independent gameplay behaviors and tying them all together into a cohesive, albeit simple, game prototype. You've used vectors and basic vector math to determine positions and angles in a 3D space, and you're familiar with player input and the two main methods of moving and rotating GameObjects. You've even gone down into the bowels of the Unity physics system to get comfortable with Rigidbody physics, collisions, triggers, and event notifications. All in all, *Hero Born* is off to a great start.

In the next chapter, we'll start tackling more game mechanics, including jumping, dashing, shooting projectiles, and interacting with parts of the environment. This will give you more hands-on experience in using force with **Rigidbody** components, gathering player input, and executing logic.

Pop quiz: Player controls and physics

a. What data type would you use to store 3D movement and rotation information?

b. What built-in Unity component allows you to track and modify player controls?

c. Which component adds real-world physics to a GameObject?

d. What method does Unity suggest using to execute physics-related code on GameObjects?

Don't forget to check your answers against mine in the *Pop Quiz Answers* appendix!

Subscribe to Game Dev Assembly Newsletter!

We are excited to introduce **Game Dev Assembly,** our brand-new newsletter dedicated to everything game development. Whether you're a programmer, designer, artist, animator, or studio lead, you'll get exclusive insights, industry trends, and expert tips to help you build better games and grow your skills. Sign up today and become part of a growing community of creators, innovators, and game changers: https://packt.link/gamedev-newsletter

Scan the QR code to join instantly!

Join our community on Discord

Join our community's Discord space for discussions with the authors and other readers: https://packt.link/gamedevelopment

8

Scripting Game Mechanics

In the last chapter, we focused on using code to move the player and camera, with a trip into Unity physics on the side. However, controlling a playable character isn't enough to make a compelling game; in fact, it's probably the one area that remains fairly constant across different titles.

A game's unique spark comes from its core mechanics, and the feeling of power and agency those mechanics give to the players. Without fun and engrossing ways to affect the virtual environment you've created, your game doesn't stand a chance of repeat play, to say nothing of fun. As we venture into implementing the game's mechanics, we'll also be upgrading our knowledge of C# and its intermediate-level features.

This chapter will build upon the *Hero Born* prototype by focusing on individually implemented game mechanics, as well as the basics of system design and **user interfaces** (**UIs**). You'll be diving into the following topics:

- Making the player jump
- Shooting projectiles
- Creating a game manager
- Adding a user interface

Making the player jump

Remember from the last chapter that `Rigidbody` components add simulated real-world physics to GameObjects, and `Collider` components interact with each other using `Rigidbody` objects.

Another great thing that we didn't discuss in the previous chapter about using a `Rigidbody` component to control player movement is that we can easily add in different mechanics that rely on applied force, such as jumping. In this section, we'll get our player jumping and write our first utility function.

A **utility function** is a class method that performs some kind of grunt work so that we don't clutter up gameplay code, such as wanting to check whether the player capsule is touching the ground to jump.

Before that, you'll need to get acquainted with a new data type called enumerations, which you'll do in the following section.

Introducing enumerations

By definition, an **enumeration type** is a set, or collection, of named constants that belong to the same variable. These are useful when you want a collection of different values, but with the added benefit of them all being of the same parent type.

It's easier to show rather than tell with enumerations, so let's take a look at their syntax in the following code snippet:

```
enum PlayerAction { Attack, Defend, Flee };
```

Let's break down how this works, as follows:

- The enum keyword declares the type, followed by the variable name.
- The different values an enum type can have are written inside curly brackets, separated by a comma (except for the last item).
- The enum type has to end with a semicolon, just like all other data types we've worked with.

In this case, we're declaring a variable called `PlayerAction` of the enum type, which can be set to one of three values: `Attack`, `Defend`, or `Flee`.

To declare an enumeration variable, we use the following syntax:

```
PlayerAction CurrentAction = PlayerAction.Defend;
```

Again, we can break this down as follows:

- The type is set as `PlayerAction`, since our enumeration is just like any other type, such as a string or integer.
- The variable is named `currentAction` and is set equal to a `PlayerAction` value.
- Each enum constant can be accessed using dot notation.

Our `currentAction` variable is now set to `Defend`, but it can be changed to `Attack` or `Flee` at any time.

Enumerations may look simple at first glance, but they are extremely powerful in the right situations. One of their most useful features is the ability to store underlying types, which is the next subject you'll be jumping into.

Underlying types

Enums come with an **underlying type**, meaning that each constant inside the curly brackets has an associated value. The default underlying type is `int` and starts at `0`, just like arrays, with each sequential constant getting the next highest number.

Not all types are created equal—underlying types for enumerations are limited to `byte`, `sbyte`, `short`, `ushort`, `int`, `uint`, `long`, and `ulong`. These are called integral types and are used to specify the size of numeric values that a variable can store.

This is a bit advanced for this book, but you'll be using `int` in most cases. More information on these types can be found here: `https://docs.microsoft.com/en-us/dotnet/csharp/language-reference/keywords/enum`.

For example, our `PlayerAction` enumeration values right now are listed as follows, even though they aren't explicitly written out:

```
enum PlayerAction { Attack = 0, Defend = 1, Flee = 2 };
```

There's no rule that says underlying values need to start at `0`; in fact, all you have to do is specify the first value, and then C# increments the rest of the values for you, as illustrated in the following code snippet:

```
enum PlayerAction { Attack = 5, Defend, Flee };
```

In the preceding example, `Defend` equals 6, and `Flee` equals 7 automatically. However, if we wanted the `PlayerAction` enum to hold non-sequential values, we could explicitly add them in, like this:

```
enum PlayerAction { Attack = 10, Defend = 5, Flee = 0};
```

We can even change the underlying type of `PlayerAction` to any of the approved types by adding a colon after the enum name, as follows:

```
enum PlayerAction :  byte { Attack, Defend, Flee };
```

Retrieving an enum's underlying type takes an explicit conversion, but we've already covered those, so the following syntax shouldn't be a surprise:

```
enum PlayerAction { Attack = 10, Defend = 5, Flee = 0};
PlayerAction CurrentAction = PlayerAction.Attack;
int ActionCost = (int)CurrentAction;
```

Since CurrentAction is set to Attack, ActionCost would be 10 in the preceding example code.

Enumerations are extremely powerful tools in your programming arsenal. Your next challenge is to use your knowledge of enumerations to gather more specific user input from the keyboard.

Now that we have a basic grasp of enum types, we can capture keyboard input using the KeyCode enum. Update the PlayerBehavior script with the following code, save it, and hit **Play**:

```
public class PlayerBehavior : MonoBehaviour
{
    // ... No other variable changes needed ...


    // 1
    public float JumpVelocity = 5f;
    private bool _isJumping;

    void Start()
    {
        // ... No other changes needed ...
    }

    void Update()
    {
        // 2
        _isJumping |= Input.GetKeyDown(KeyCode.J);
        // ... No other changes needed ...
    }

    void FixedUpdate()
    {
        // 3
        if(_isJumping)
        {
```

```
                    // 4
                    _rb.AddForce(Vector3.up * JumpVelocity, ForceMode.Impulse);
            }
            // 5
            _isJumping = false;
            // ... No other changes needed ...
        }
    }
```

Let's break down this code as follows:

1. First, we create two new variables—a public variable to hold the amount of applied jump force we want and a private Boolean to check whether our player should be jumping.

2. We set the value of _isJumping to the Input.GetKeyDown() method, which returns a bool value depending on whether a specified key is pressed during the current frame and will only fire once, even if held down:

    a. We use the |= operator to set _isJumping, which is the logical or condition. This operator makes sure that we don't have consecutive input checks overriding each other when the player is jumping.

    b. The method accepts a key parameter as either a string or KeyCode, which is an enum type. We specify that we want to check for KeyCode.J, or the *J* key being pressed.

3. Checking for inputs in FixedUpdate can sometimes lead to input loss or even double inputs because it doesn't run once per frame. To avoid this problem, we're checking for inputs in Update and then applying force or setting the velocity in FixedUpdate, which is where physics are applied.

4. We use an if statement to check whether _isJumping is true and trigger the jump mechanic if it is.

5. Since we already have the Rigidbody component stored, we can pass the Vector3 and ForceMode parameters to RigidBody.AddForce() and make the player jump:

    a. We specify that the vector (or applied force) should be in the up direction, multiplied by JumpVelocity.

    b. The ForceMode parameter determines how the force is applied and is also an enum type. Impulse applies instant force to an object while taking its mass into account, which is perfect for a jump mechanic.

Other `ForceMode` choices can be useful in different situations, all of which are detailed here: `https://docs.unity3d.com/ScriptReference/ForceMode.html`.

6. At the end of every `FixedUpdate` frame, we reset `_isJumping` to `false` so the input check knows that a complete jump and the landing cycle have been completed.

If you play the game now, you'll be able to move around and jump when you hit the *J* key. However, the mechanic allows you to keep jumping indefinitely, which isn't what we want. We'll work on limiting our jump mechanic to one at a time in the next section, using something called a **layer mask**.

Working with layer masks

Think of layer masks as invisible groups that a GameObject can belong to, used by the physics system to determine anything from navigation to intersecting `Collider` components. While more advanced uses of layer masks are outside the scope of this book, we'll create and use one to perform a simple check—whether the player capsule is touching the ground—in order to limit the player to one jump at a time.

Before we can check that the player capsule is touching the ground, we need to add all the environment objects in our level to a custom layer mask. This will let us perform the actual collision calculation with the `CapsuleCollider` component that's already attached to the player, in order to detect when the player lands on the ground. Proceed as follows:

1. In the **Hierarchy** panel, drag **Ground** onto the **Environment** parent object.

2. Select the **Environment** GameObject in **Hierarchy**, and in the corresponding **Inspector** pane, click on **Layer | Add Layer...**, as illustrated in *Figure 8.1*:

Figure 8.1: Selecting layers in the Inspector pane

Note

To provide a complete view of the Unity editor, all our screenshots are taken in full-screen mode. For color versions of all book images, use this link: https://packt.link/gbp/9781805808718.

3. Add a new layer called Ground by typing the name into the first available slot, which is **Layer 6**. Layers 0–5 are reserved for Unity's default layers, even though **Layer 3** is empty, as illustrated in *Figure 8.2*:

Figure 8.2: Adding layers in the Inspector pane

4.   Select the **Environment** parent GameObject in **Hierarchy**, click on the **Layer** dropdown, and select **Ground**:

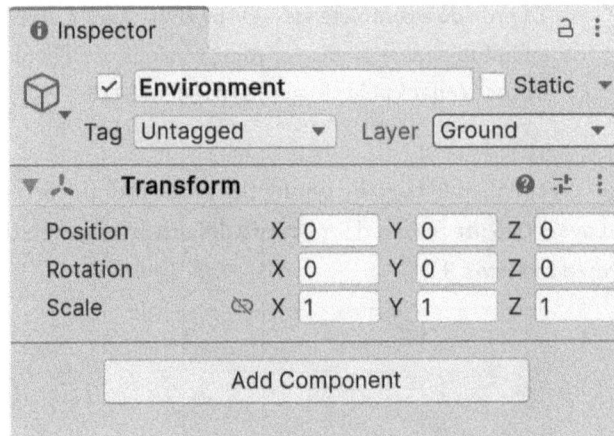

Figure 8.3: Setting a custom layer

After you have selected the **Ground** option shown in the preceding screenshot, click **Yes, change children** when a dialog appears asking you whether you want to change all child objects. You've now defined a new layer called Ground and assigned every child object of Environment to that layer. Even though we can't jump off the walls of the arena, marking all our Environment objects with the Ground layer is easier than going through each child object.

Going forward, all the objects on the Ground layer can be checked to see whether they intersect with a specific object. You'll use this in the following challenge to make sure the player can per-form a jump if it's on the ground; no unlimited jump hacks here.

Since we don't want code cluttering up the Update() method, we'll do our layer mask calculations in a utility function and return a true or false value based on the outcome. To do so, proceed as follows:

1.   Add the following code to PlayerBehavior and play the scene again:

```
public class PlayerBehavior : MonoBehaviour
{
    // 1
    public float DistanceToGround = 0.1f;
    // 2
    public LayerMask GroundLayer;
    // 3
```

```
        private CapsuleCollider _col;
        // ... No other variable changes needed ...


        void Start()
        {
            _rb = GetComponent<Rigidbody>();


            // 4
            _col = GetComponent<CapsuleCollider>();
        }


        void Update()
        {
            // ... No changes needed ...
        }


        void FixedUpdate()
        {
            // 5
            if(IsGrounded() && _isJumping)
            {
                _rb.AddForce(Vector3.up * JumpVelocity,
                    ForceMode.Impulse);
            }
            _isJumping = false;


            // ... No other changes needed …
        }


    // 6
    private bool IsGrounded()
    {
        // 7
        Vector3 capsuleBottom = new Vector3(_col.bounds.center.x,
            _col.bounds.min.y, _col.bounds.center.z);


        // 8
```

```
        bool grounded = Physics.CheckCapsule(_col.bounds.center,
            capsuleBottom, DistanceToGround, GroundLayer,
                QueryTriggerInteraction.Ignore);


        // 9
        return grounded;
    }
}
```

2. With the **PlayerBehavior** script selected, set **Ground Layer** in the **Inspector** pane to
    Ground from the **Ground Layer** dropdown, as illustrated in *Figure 8.4*:

Figure 8.4: Setting the Ground Layer option

Let's break down the preceding code as follows:

1. We create a new variable for the distance we'll check between the player's `CapsuleCollider` component and any **Ground Layer** object.

2. We create a `LayerMask` variable that we can set in **Inspector** and use for the collider detection.

3. We create a variable to store the player's `CapsuleCollider` component.

4. We use `GetComponent()` to find and return the `CapsuleCollider` component attached to the player.

5. We update the `if` statement to check whether `IsGrounded` returns `true` and the *J* key is pressed before executing the jump code.

6. We declare the `IsGrounded()` method with a `bool` return type.

7. We create a local `Vector3` variable to store the position at the bottom of the player's `CapsuleCollider` component, which we'll use to check for collisions with any objects on the **Ground** layer:

    - All `Collider` components have a bounds property, which gives us access to the `min`, `max`, and `center` positions of their *x*, *y*, and *z* axes.
    - The bottom of `Collider` is the 3D point at `center x`, `min y`, and `center z`.

8. We create a local `bool` to store the result of the `CheckCapsule()` method that we call from the `Physics` class, which takes in the following five arguments:

    - The start of the capsule, which we set to the middle of `CapsuleCollider` since we only care about checking whether the bottom touches the ground.
    - The end of the capsule, which is the `capsuleBottom` position that we've already calculated.
    - The radius of the capsule, which is the `DistanceToGround` value already set.
    - The layer mask we want to check collisions on, set to **Ground Layer** in **Inspector**.
    - The query trigger interaction, which determines whether the method should ignore colliders that are set as triggers. Since we want to ignore all triggers, we use the `QueryTriggerInteraction.Ignore` enum.

    We could also use the `Distance()` method from the `Vector3` class to determine how far we are from the ground, since we know the height of the player capsule. However, we're going to stick with using the `Physics` class, since that's the focus of this chapter.

9. We return the value stored in grounded at the end of the calculation.

We could have done the collision calculation manually, but that would require more complex 3D math than we have time to cover here. However, it's always a good idea to use built-in methods when available.

That was an involved piece of code that we just added into `PlayerBehavior`, but when you break it down, the only new thing we did was use a method from the `Physics` class. In plain English, we supplied `CheckCapsule()` with a start point and end point, a collision radius, and a layer mask. If the end point gets closer than the collision radius to an object on the layer mask, the method returns `true`, meaning the player is touching the ground. If the player is in a mid-jump position, `CheckCapsule()` returns `false`.

Since we're checking `IsGround` in the `if` statement every frame in `Update()`, our player's jump skills are only allowed when touching the ground.

That's all you're going to do with the jump mechanic, but the player still needs a way to interact and defend themself against the hordes of enemies that will eventually populate the arena. In the following section, you'll fix that gap by implementing a simple shooting mechanic.

Shooting projectiles

Shooting mechanics are so common that it's hard to think of a first-person game without some variation present, and *Hero Born* is no different. In this section, we'll talk about how to instantiate GameObjects from Prefabs while the game is running and use the skills we've learned to propel them forward using Unity physics.

Instantiating objects

The concept of instantiating a GameObject in the game is similar to instantiating an instance of a class—both require starting values so that C# knows what kind of object we want to create and where it needs to be created. To create objects in the scene at runtime, we use the `GameObject.Instantiate()` method and provide a `Prefab` object, a starting position, and a starting rotation.

Essentially, we can tell Unity to create a given object with all its components and scripts at this spot, looking in this direction, and then manipulate it as needed once it's born in the 3D space. Before we instantiate an object, you'll need to create the `Prefab` object itself, which is your next task.

Before we can shoot any projectiles, we'll need a Prefab to use as a reference, so let's create that now, as follows:

1. Select **+** | **3D Object** | **Sphere** in the **Hierarchy** panel and name it `Bullet`. Change its **Scale** value to `0.15` in the *x*, *y*, and *z* axes in the **Transform** component.

2. Select the **Bullet** object in **Inspector** and use the **Add Component** button at the bottom to search for and add a **Rigidbody** component, leaving all default properties as they are.

3. Create a new material in the `Materials` folder using **Create** | **Material**, and name it `Bullet_Mat`:

    a. Change the **Albedo** property to a deep yellow.

    b.   Drag and drop the material from the Materials folder onto the **Bullet** GameObject in the **Hierarchy** pane:

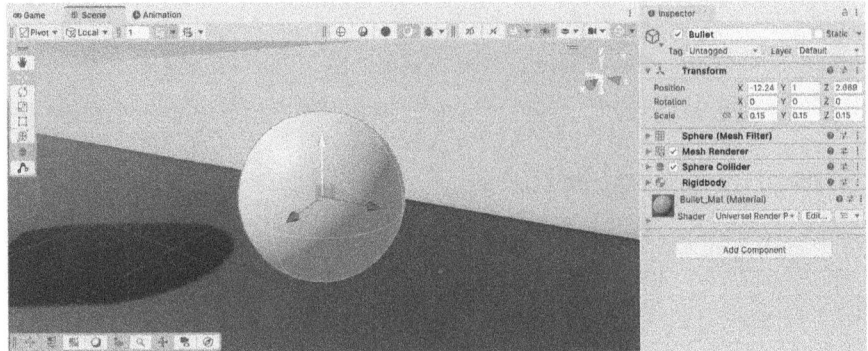

Figure 8.5: Setting projectile properties

4.   Select **Bullet** in the **Hierarchy** panel and drag it into the Prefabs folder in the **Project** panel (you can always tell when an object in **Hierarchy** is a Prefab because it turns blue). Then, delete it from **Hierarchy** to clean up the scene:

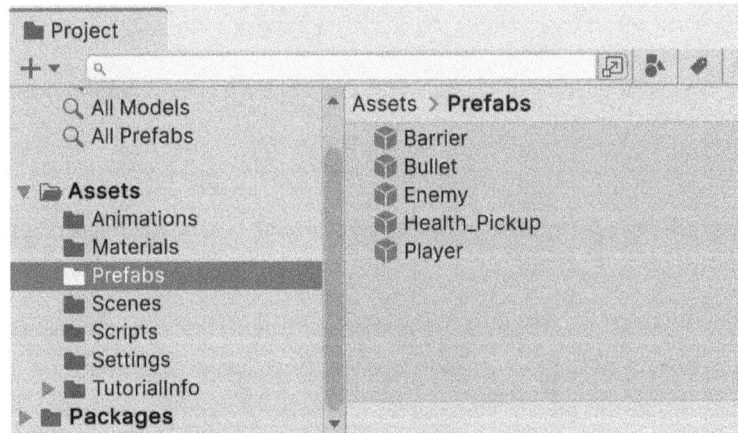

Figure 8.6: Creating a projectile Prefab

You created and configured a Bullet Prefab GameObject that can be instantiated as many times as you need in the game and updated as needed. This means you're ready for the next challenge—shooting projectiles.

Adding the shooting mechanic

Now that we have a Prefab object to work with, we can instantiate and move copies of the Prefab whenever we hit the spacebar key to create a shooting mechanic, as follows:

1. Update the `PlayerBehavior` script with the following code:

```
public class PlayerBehavior : MonoBehaviour
{
    // 1
    public GameObject Bullet;
    public float BulletSpeed = 100f;

    // 2
    private bool _isShooting;

    // ... No other variable changes needed ...
    void Start()
    {
        // ... No changes needed ...
    }

    void Update()
    {
        // 3
        _isShooting |= Input.GetKeyDown(KeyCode.Space);
        // ... No other changes needed ...
    }

    void FixedUpdate()
    {
        // ... No other changes needed ...

        // 4
        if (_isShooting)
        {
            // 5
            Vector3 spawnPos = transform.position +
                                    transform.forward * 1f;
            // 6
            GameObject newBullet = Instantiate(Bullet, spawnPos,
                                    this.transform.rotation);
```

```
        // 7
        Rigidbody bulletRB =
            newBullet.GetComponent<Rigidbody>();

        // 8
        bulletRB.linearVelocity = this.transform.forward *
                                    BulletSpeed;
    }
    // 9
    _isShooting = false;
}


private bool IsGrounded()
{
    // ... No changes needed ...
}
}
```

2. In **Inspector**, drag the **Bullet** Prefab from the **Project** panel into the **Bullet** property of **Player Behavior**, as illustrated in *Figure 8.7*:

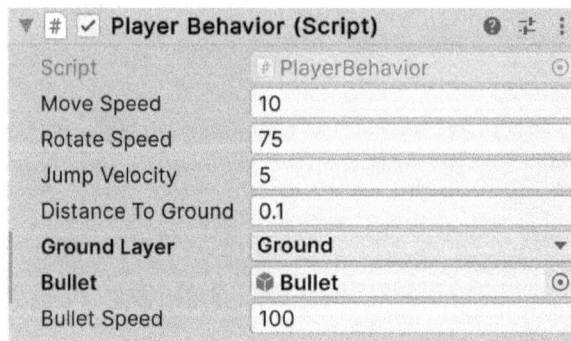

Figure 8.7: Setting the Bullet Prefab

3. Play the game and use the spacebar to fire projectiles in the direction the player is facing!

Let's break down the code as follows:

1. We create two variables: one to store the Bullet Prefab, the other to hold the projectile speed. The best practice is to always declare new variables as private unless there's a good reason to make them public.

2. Like our jumping mechanic, we use a Boolean in the Update() method to check whether our player should be shooting.

3. We set the value of _isShooting using the or logical operator and Input. GetKeyDown(KeyCode.Space), just like we did for the jumping mechanic. Then, we check whether our player is supposed to be shooting using the _isShooting variable.

4. We check whether _isShooting is true, meaning the player has pressed the spacebar.

5. We create a new Vector3 spawning position that is always directly in front of the player in whatever direction you're currently facing.

6. We create a new Bullet GameObject using the Instantiate method and passing in the Bullet Prefab, spawnPos, and the current Player rotation.

7. We call GetComponent() to return and store the Rigidbody component on newBullet.

8. We set the velocity property of the Rigidbody component to the player's transform. forward direction multiplied by BulletSpeed. Changing the velocity instead of using AddForce() ensures that gravity doesn't pull our bullets down in an arc when fired.

9. Finally, we set the _isShooting value to false so our shooting input is reset for the next input event.

Again, you've significantly upgraded the logic that the player script is using. You should now be able to use the mouse to shoot projectiles that fly straight out from the player's position.

However, the problem now is that your game scene and **Hierarchy** are flooded with spent Bullet objects. Your next task is to clean those objects up once they've been fired, to avoid any performance issues.

Managing object build-up

Whether you're writing a completely code-based application or a 3D game, it's important to make sure that unused objects are regularly deleted to avoid overloading the program. Our bullets don't exactly play an important role after they are shot; they just keep existing on the floor near whatever wall or object they collided with.

With a mechanic such as shooting, this could result in hundreds, if not thousands, of bullets down the line, which is something we don't want. Your next challenge is to destroy each bullet after a set delay time.

For this task, we can take the skills we've already learned and make the bullets responsible for their self-destructive behavior, as follows:

1. In the Scripts folder, create a new MonoBehaviour script and name it BulletBehavior.

2. In the Prefabs folder, drag and drop the BulletBehavior script onto the Bullet Prefab and add the following code:

```
using System.Collections;
using System.Collections.Generic;
using UnityEngine;
public class BulletBehavior : MonoBehaviour
{
    // 1
    public float OnscreenDelay = 3f;

    void Start ()
    {
        // 2
        Destroy(this.gameObject, OnscreenDelay);
    }
}
```

Let's break down this code as follows:

1. We declare a float variable to store how long we want the Bullet Prefabs to remain in the scene after they are instantiated.

2. We use the Destroy() method to delete the GameObject:

   - Destroy() always needs an object as a parameter. In this case, we use the this keyword to specify the object that the script is attached to.

   - Destroy() can optionally take an additional float parameter as a delay, which we use to keep the bullets on the screen for a short amount of time.

Play the game again, shoot some bullets, and watch as they are deleted from the **Hierarchy** panel by themselves in the scene after a specific delay. This means that the bullet executes its defined behavior, without another script having to tell it what to do, which is an ideal application of the *Component* design pattern.

Now that our housekeeping is done, you're going to learn about a key component of any well-designed and organized project—the manager class.

Creating a game manager

A common misconception when learning to program is that all variables should automatically be made public, but in general, this is not a good idea. In my experience, variables should be thought of as protected and private from the start and only made public if necessary. One way you'll see experienced programmers protect their data is through manager classes, and since we want to build good habits, we'll be following suit. Think of manager classes as a funnel where important variables and methods can be accessed safely.

When I say safely, I mean just that, which might seem unfamiliar in a programming context. However, when you have different classes communicating and updating data with each other, things can get messy. That's why having a single contact point, such as a manager class, can keep this to a minimum. We'll get into how to do that effectively in the following section.

Tracking player properties

Hero Born is a simple game, so the only two data points we need to keep track of are how many items the player has collected and how much health they have left. We want these variables to be private so that they can only be modified from the manager class, giving us control and safety. Your next challenge is to create a game manager for *Hero Born* and populate it with helpful functionality.

Game manager classes will be a constant facet of any project you develop in the future, so let's learn how to properly create one, as follows:

1. In the Scripts folder, create a new MonoBehaviour script and name it GameBehavior.

> **Note**
>
> Usually, this script would be named GameManager, but Unity reserves that name for its own scripts. If you ever create a script and a cogwheel icon shows up next to its name instead of the C# file icon, that tells you it's restricted.

2. Create a new empty GameObject in the **Hierarchy** panel by using + | **Create Empty**, and name it Game Manager.

3. Drag and drop the `GameBehavior.cs` script from the `Scripts` folder onto the **Game Man-ager** object, as illustrated in *Figure 8.8*:

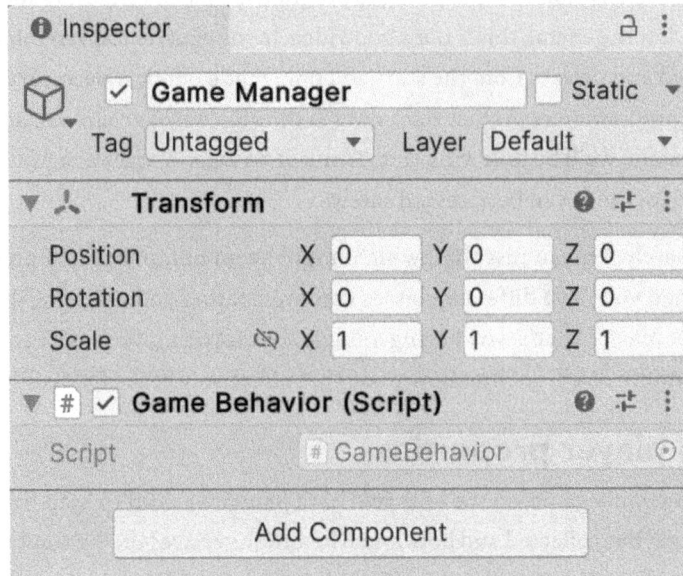

Figure 8.8: Attaching the game manager script

Manager scripts and other non-game files are set up on empty objects to put them in the scene, even though they don't interact with the actual 3D space.

4. Add the following code to the top of `GameBehavior.cs`:

```
public class GameBehavior : MonoBehaviour
{
    private int _itemsCollected = 0;
    private int _playerHP = 10;
}
```

Let's break down this code. We added two new `private` variables to hold the number of items picked up and how many lives the player has left; these are private because they should only be modifiable in this class. If they were made public, other classes could change them at will, which could lead to the variables storing incorrect or concurrent data.

Having these variables declared as `private` means that you are responsible for how they are accessed. The following topic on `get` and `set` properties will introduce you to a standard, safe way to accomplish this task going forward.

The get and set properties

We've got our manager script and `private` variables set up, but how do we access them from other classes if they're private? While we could write separate `public` methods in `GameBehavior` to handle passing new values to the `private` variables, let's see whether there is a better way of doing things.

In this case, C# provides all variables with get and set properties, which are perfectly suited to our task. Think of these as methods that are automatically fired by the C# compiler, whether we explicitly call them or not, similar to how `Start()` and `Update()` are executed by Unity when a scene starts.

The get and set properties can be added to any variable, with or without an initial value, as illustrated in the following code snippet:

```
public string FirstName { get; set; };
// OR
public string LastName { get; set; } = "Smith";
```

However, using them like this doesn't add any additional benefits; for that, you need to include a code block for each property, as illustrated in the following code snippet:

```
public string FirstName
{
    get {
        // Code block executes when variable is accessed
    }
    set {
        // Code block executes when variable is updated
    }
}
```

Now, the get and set properties are set up to execute additional logic, depending on where it's needed. We're not done yet, though, as we still need to handle the new logic.

Every get code block needs to return a value, while every set block needs to assign a value; this is where having a combination of a `private` variable, called a **backing variable**, and a `public` variable with get and set properties comes into play.

The private variable remains protected, while the public variable allows controlled access from other classes, as shown in the following code snippet:

```
private string _firstName
public string FirstName {
    get {
        return _firstName;
    }
    set {
        _firstName = value;
    }
}
```

Let's break this down as follows:

- We can return the value stored in the private variable from the get property anytime another class needs it, without actually giving that outside class direct access.
- We can update the private variable anytime an outside class assigns a new value to the public variable, keeping them in sync.
- The value keyword is a stand-in for whatever new value is assigned.

This can seem a little esoteric without an actual application, so let's update GameBehavior with public variables with get and set properties to go along with our existing private variables.

Now that we understand the syntax of the get and set property accessors, we can implement them in our manager class for greater efficiency and code readability.

Update the code in GameBehavior as follows:

```
public class GameBehavior : MonoBehaviour
{
    private int _itemsCollected = 0;
    private int _playerHP = 10;

    // 1
    public int Items
    {
        // 2
        get { return _itemsCollected; }
        // 3
```

```
            set {

                    _itemsCollected = value;

                    Debug.LogFormat("Items: {0}", _itemsCollected);

            }

        }

        // 4

        public int HP

        {

            get { return _playerHP; }

            set {

                    _playerHP = value;

                    Debug.LogFormat("Lives: {0}", _playerHP);

            }

        }

    }
```

Let's break down the code as follows:

1. We declare a new `public` variable called `Items` with `get` and `set` properties.

2. We use the `get` property to return the value stored in `_itemsCollected` whenever `Items` is accessed from an outside class.

3. We use the `set` property to assign `_itemsCollected` to the new value of `Items` whenever it's updated, with an added `Debug.LogFormat()` call to print out the modified value of `_itemsCollected`.

4. We set up a `public` variable called `HP` with `get` and `set` properties to complement the private `_playerHP` backing variable.

Both `private` variables are now readable, but only through their `public` counterparts; they can only be changed in `GameBehavior`. With this setup, we ensure that our private data can only be accessed and modified from specific contact points. This makes it easier to communicate with `GameBehavior` from our other mechanical scripts, as well as to display the real-time data in the simple UI we'll create at the end of the chapter.

Let's test this out by updating the `Items` property when we successfully interact with an item pickup in the arena.

Updating item collection

Now that we have our variables set up in GameBehavior, we can update Items every time we collect an item in the scene, as follows:

1. Add the following code to the ItemBehavior script:

```
public class ItemBehavior : MonoBehaviour
{
    // 1
    public GameBehavior GameManager;
    void Start()
    {
        // 2
        GameManager = GameObject.Find("Game Manager")
            .GetComponent<GameBehavior>();
    }
    void OnCollisionEnter(Collision collision)
    {
        if (collision.gameObject.name == "Player")
        {
            Destroy(this.gameObject);
            Debug.Log("Item collected!");
            // 3
            GameManager.Items += 1;
        }
    }
}
```

2. Hit **Play** and collect the pickup item to see the new console log printout from the manager script, as illustrated in *Figure 8.9*:

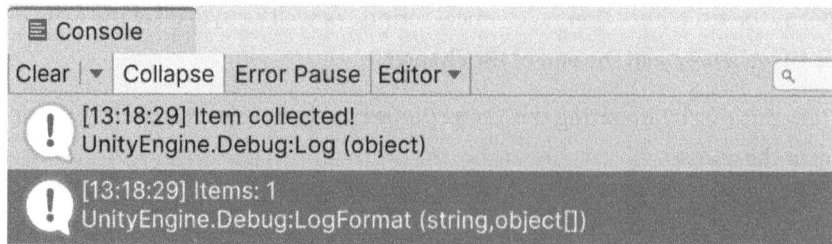

Figure 8.9: Collecting a pickup item

Let's break down the code as follows:

1. We create a new variable of the `GameBehavior` type to store a reference to the attached script.

2. We use `Start()` to initialize `GameManager` by looking it up in the scene with `Find()` and adding a call to `GetComponent()`.

    You'll see this kind of code done in a single line quite often in Unity documentation and community projects. This is done for simplicity, but if you feel more comfortable writing out the `Find()` and `GetComponent()` calls separately, go right ahead; there's nothing wrong with clear, explicit formatting.

3. We increment the `Items` property using the `GameManager` class instance in `OnCollisionEnter()` after the `Item` Prefab is destroyed.

Since we already set up `ItemBehavior` to take care of collision logic, it's easy to modify `OnCollisionEnter()` to communicate with our manager class when an item is picked up by the player. Keep in mind that separating functionality like this is what makes the code more flexible and less likely to break as you make changes during development.

The last piece that *Hero Born* is missing is some kind of interface that displays game data to the player. In programming and game development, this is called a UI. Your final task in this chapter is to familiarize yourself with how Unity creates and handles the UI code.

Creating a GUI

At this point, we have several scripts working together to give players access to movement, jumping, collecting, and shooting mechanics. However, we're still missing any kind of display or visual cue that shows our player's stats, as well as a way to win and lose the game. We'll focus on these two topics as we close out this last section.

Displaying player stats

UIs are the visual components of any computer system. The cursor, folder icons, and programs on your laptop are all UI elements. For our game, we want a simple display to let our players know how many items they've collected and their current health, and a textbox to give them updates when certain events happen.

UI elements in Unity can be added in the following two ways:

- Unity UI (uGUI)
- UI Toolkit

uGUI is an older UI system in Unity, but we're going to use it over UI Toolkit because it's based on GameObjects that can be easily manipulated right in the **Scene** view like any other object.

We'll be going over the basics in this chapter, but you can find more information at `https://docs.unity3d.com/Packages/com.unity.ugui@2.0/manual/index.html`.

While UI Toolkit is a newer addition to the Unity Engine, it uses **UI Documents (UXML)**, which is based on standard web technologies and isn't written in C#. Since we want to keep things squarely focused on C# as much as possible, we'll be opting for uGUI instead.

If you're interested in learning about the newest Unity features when it comes to UIs, check out the UI Toolkit documentation at `https://docs.unity3d.com/6000.1/Documentation/Manual/UIElements.html`.

If you're curious about the comparison specifics between the different UI options in Unity, check out `https://docs.unity3d.com/6000.3/Documentation/Manual/UI-system-compare.html`.

Your next task is to add a simple UI to the game scene that displays the items collected, player health, and progress information variables that are stored in `GameBehavior.cs`.

First, let's create three text objects in our scene. UIs in Unity work off a canvas, which is exactly what it sounds like. Think of the canvas as a blank painting that you can draw on that Unity will render on top of the game world for you. Whenever you create your first **UI** element in the **Hierarchy** panel, a **Canvas** parent object is created along with it:

1. Right-click in the **Hierarchy** panel and select **UI | Text - TextMeshPro**. When the **TMP Importer** window pops up and asks you to import the missing assets, select **Import TMP Essentials**:

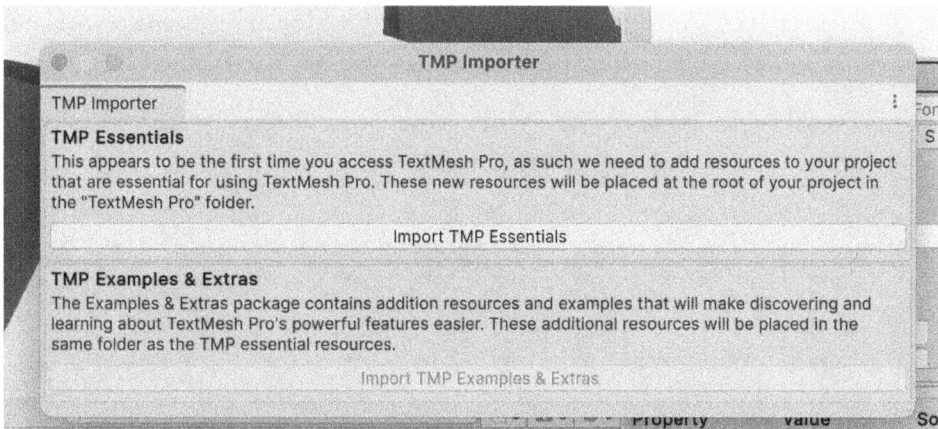

Figure 8.10: Importing TextMeshPro assets

More information

TextMeshPro is Unity's system for handling, rendering, and styling text. This topic is a little advanced for us to get into here, but if you're interested, you can read the documentation at https://docs.unity3d.com/Manual/com.unity.textmeshpro.html.

2.   Select the new **Text(TMP)** object in **Hierarchy**, hit *Enter*, and name it Health. Notice that a **Canvas** parent object and the new **Text(TMP)** object were created for you all at once:

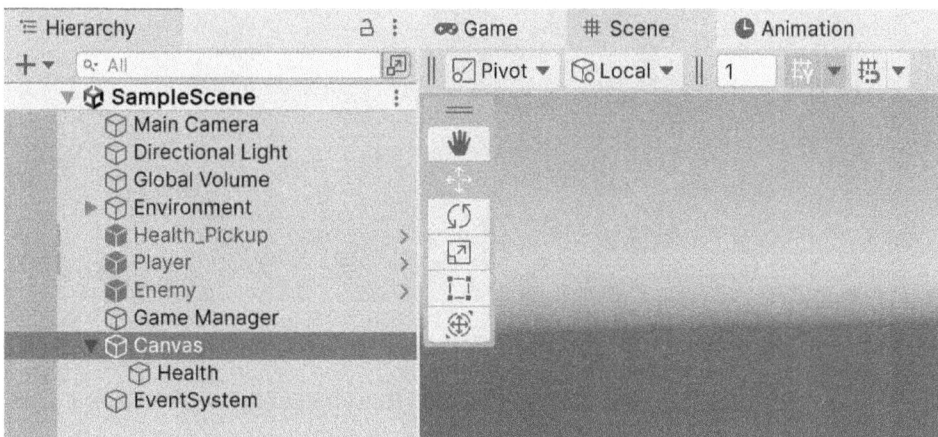

Figure 8.11: Creating a Text element

3.   To see the canvas correctly, select **2D** mode at the top of the **Scene** tab. From this view, our entire level is the tiny white line in the lower-left-hand corner:

Even though **Canvas** and the level don't overlap in the scene, when the game plays, Unity will automatically overlay them correctly:

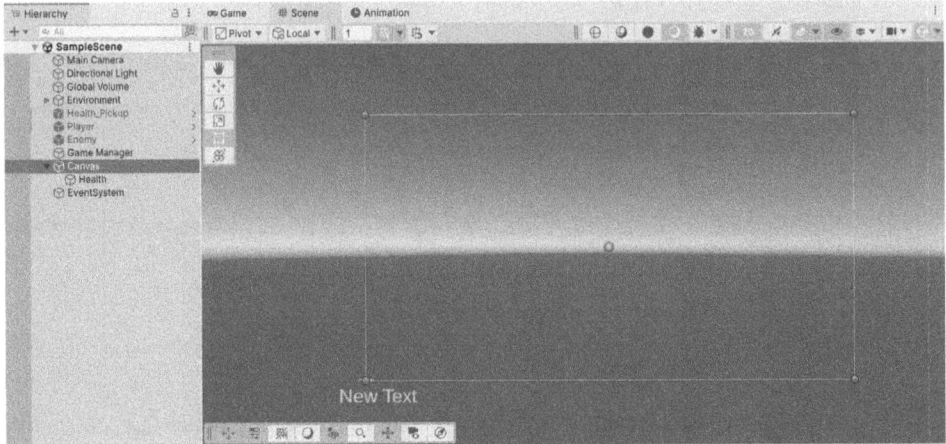

Figure 8.12: Canvas in the Unity editor

4.   If you select the **Health** object in **Hierarchy**, you'll see that the new Text object was created in the lower-left corner of the canvas by default, and it has a whole list of customizable properties, such as text and color, in the **Inspector** pane:

Figure 8.13: Text element on the Unity Canvas

5.   With the **Health** object selected in the **Hierarchy** pane, click on the **Anchor** presets in the **Rect Transform** component of **Inspector** and choose **Top Left**.

Anchors set a UI element's point of reference on the canvas, meaning that, whatever the size of the device screen, our health points will always be anchored to the top left of the screen:

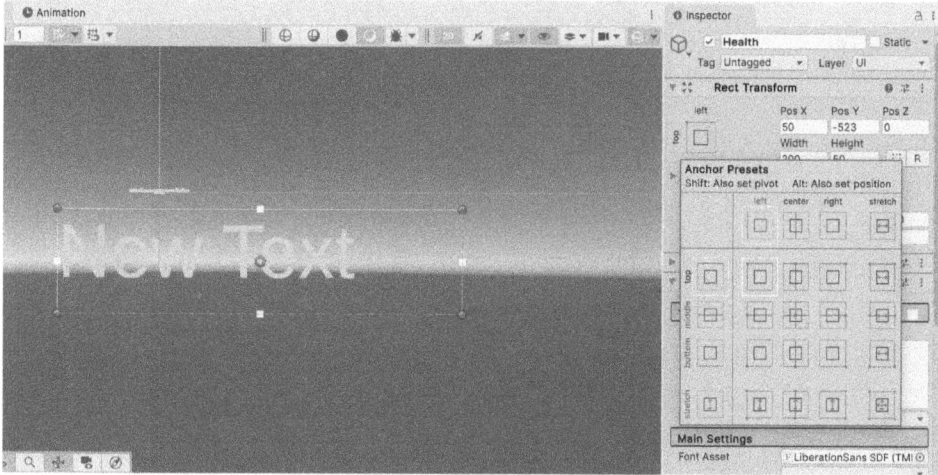

Figure 8.14: Setting anchor presets

6. With the **Health** object still selected in **Hierarchy**, scroll down in **Inspector** to **Main Settings**, click on the color bar to the right of **Vertex Color**, and change it to black:

Figure 8.15: Setting text color properties

7. In the **Inspector** pane, change the **Rect Transform** position to 110 on the **X** axis and –35 on the **Y** axis to position the text in the upper-right corner. Also, change the **Text** property to say Health:. We'll be setting the actual value in code in a later step:

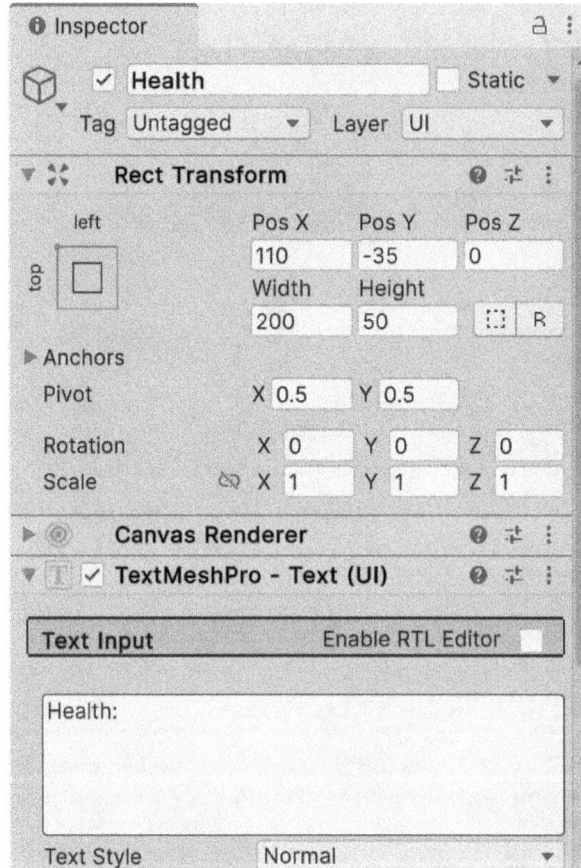

Figure 8.16: Setting text properties

8. Repeat *steps 1–6* to create a new UI Text object and name it Items:

    a. Set the anchor presets to **Top Left, Pos X** to 110, and **Pos Y** to –85.

    b. Set **Text** to Items:

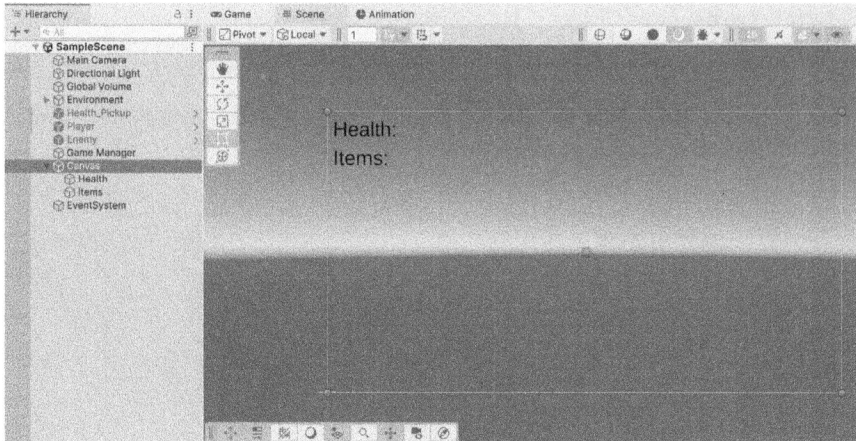

Figure 8.17: Creating another Text element

9. Repeat *steps 1–6* to create a new UI Text object and name it Progress:

    a. Set the anchor presets to **Bottom Center**, **Pos X** to 0, **Pos Y** to 15, and **Width** to 435.

    b. Set **Text** to Collect all the items to win!

    c. Set the text alignment to **center**:

Figure 8.18: Creating a progress text element

Now that we have our UI set up, let's connect the variables we already have in our game manager script. Proceed as follows:

1. Update GameBehavior with the following code to collect an item and display onscreen text when items are collected:

```
// 1
using TMPro;

public class GameBehavior : MonoBehaviour
{
    // 2
    public int MaxItems = 4;
    // 3
    public TMP_Text HealthText;
    public TMP_Text ItemText;
    public TMP_Text ProgressText;
    // 4
    void Start()
    {
        ItemText.text += _itemsCollected;
        HealthText.text += _playerHP;
    }
    private int _itemsCollected = 0;
    public int Items
    {
        get { return _itemsCollected; }
        set {
            _itemsCollected = value;
            // 5
            ItemText.text = "Items: " + Items;
            // 6
            if(_itemsCollected >= MaxItems)
            {
                ProgressText.text = "You've found all the items!";
            }
            else
            {
```

```
                    ProgressText.text = "Item found, only " +
                        (MaxItems - _itemsCollected) + " more!";
            }
        }
    }


    private int _playerHP = 10;
    public int HP
    {
        get { return _playerHP; }
        set {
            _playerHP = value;
            // 7
            HealthText.text = "Health: " + HP;
            Debug.LogFormat("Lives: {0}", _playerHP);
        }
    }
}
```

2. Select **Game Manager** in **Hierarchy** and drag over our three text objects one by one into their corresponding GameBehavior script fields in **Inspector**:

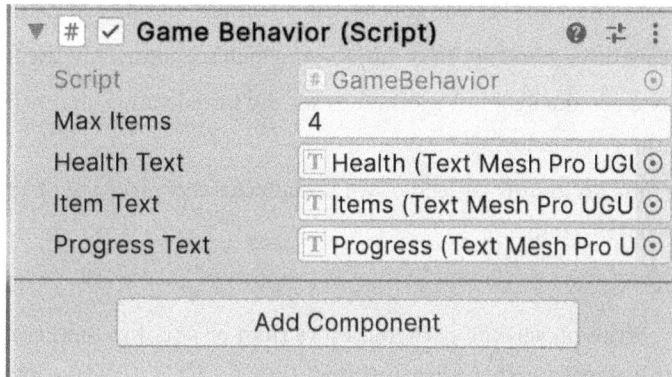

Figure 8.19: Dragging text elements to script components

3. Run the game and take a look at our new onscreen GUI boxes, shown in *Figure 8.20*:

Figure 8.20: Testing UI elements in play mode

Let's break down the code as follows:

1. We add the TMPro namespace so we have access to the TMP_Text variable type, which is what our text objects in the **Hierarchy** panel are.

2. We create a new public variable for the maximum number of items in the level.

3. We create three new TMP_Text variables, which we connect in the **Inspector** panel.

4. Then, we use the Start() method to set the initial values of our health and items text using the += operator.

5. Every time an item is collected, we update the text property of ItemText to show the updated item count.

6. We declare an if statement in the set property of _itemsCollected:

    • If the player has gathered more than or equal to MaxItems, they've won, and ProgressText.text is updated.

    • Otherwise, ProgressText.text shows how many items are still left to collect.

Every time the player's health is damaged, which we'll cover in the next chapter, we update the text property of HealthText with the new value.

When we play the game now, our three UI elements show up with the correct values; when Health_Pickup is collected, the ProgressText and _itemsCollected counts update, as illustrated in *Figure 8.21*:

Figure 8.21: Updating the UI text

Every game can either be won or lost. In the last section of this chapter, your task is to implement those conditions and the UI that goes along with them.

Win and loss conditions

We've implemented our core game mechanics and a simple UI, but *Hero Born* is still missing an important game design element: its win and loss conditions. These conditions will manage how the player wins or loses the game and execute different code depending on the situation.

Back in the game document from *Chapter 6*, we set out our win and loss conditions as follows:

- Collecting all items in the level with at least one health point remaining to win
- Taking damage from enemies until health points are at 0 to lose

These conditions are going to affect both our UI and game mechanics, but we've already set up GameBehavior to handle this efficiently. Our get and set properties will handle any game-related logic and changes to the UI when a player wins or loses.

We're going to implement the win condition logic in this section because we have the pickup system already in place. When we get to the enemy AI behavior in the next chapter, we'll add in the loss condition logic. Your next task is to determine when the game is won in code.

We always want to give players clear and immediate feedback, so we'll start by adding in the logic for a win condition, as follows:

1. Update `GameBehavior` to match the following code:

```csharp
//1
using UnityEngine.UI;
public class GameBehavior : MonoBehaviour
{
    // 2
    public Button WinButton;

    private int _itemsCollected = 0;
    public int Items
    {
        get { return _itemsCollected; }
        set
        {
            _itemsCollected = value;
            ItemText.text = "Items: " + Items;

            if (_itemsCollected >= MaxItems)
            {
                ProgressText.text = "You've found all the items!";

                // 3
                WinButton.gameObject.SetActive(true);
            }
            else
            {
                ProgressText.text = "Item found, only " +
                    (MaxItems - _itemsCollected) + " more to go!";
            }
        }
    }
}
```

2. Right-click in the **Hierarchy** panel and select **UsI** | **Button - TextMeshPro**, then name it
   Win Condition:

   a. Select **Win Condition** and set **Pos X** and **Pos Y** to 0, **Width** to 225, and **Height** to 115.

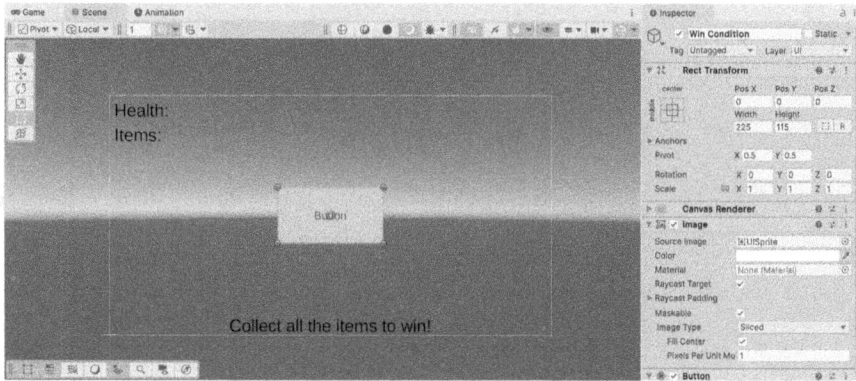

Figure 8.22: Creating a UI button

3. Click on the arrow to the right of the **Win Condition** button to expand its text child object,
   then change the text to say You won!:

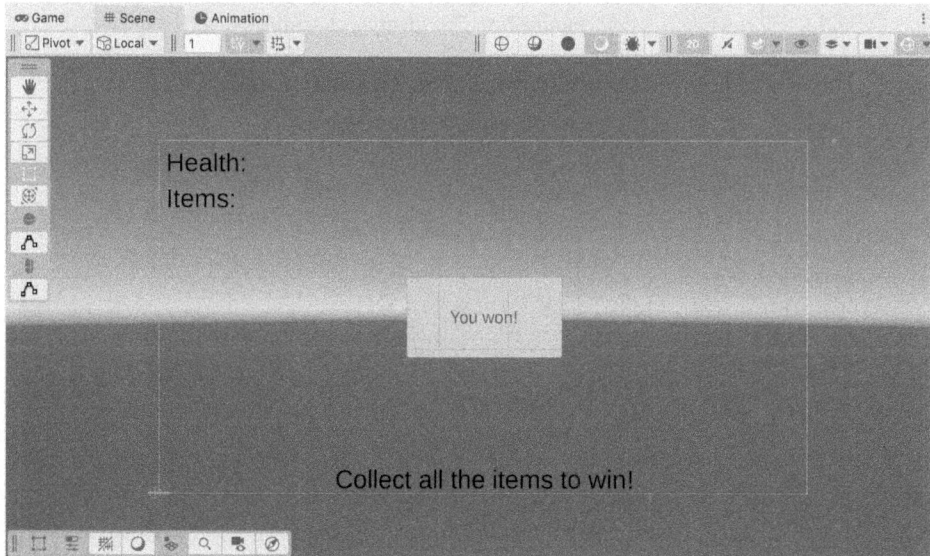

Figure 8.23: Updating button text

4. Select the **Win Condition** parent object again and click the checkmark icon at the upper right of **Inspector**:

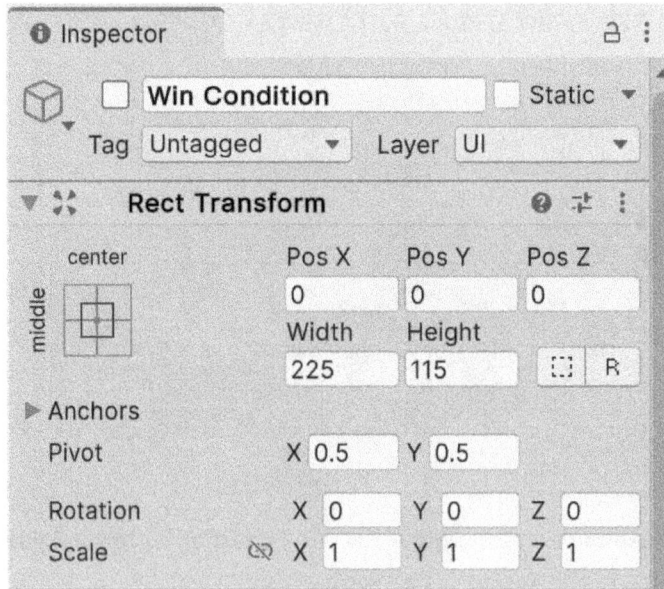

Figure 8.24: Deactivating the GameObject

This will hide the button until we've won the game:

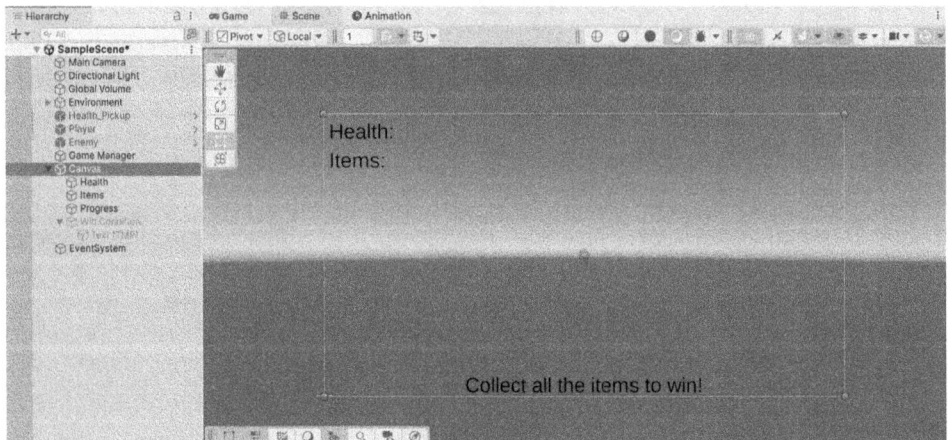

Figure 8.25: Testing the hidden UI button

5. Select **Game Manager** in the **Hierarchy** panel, change **Max Items** to 1, and drag **Win Condition (Button)** from the **Hierarchy** panel to **Game Behavior (Script)**:

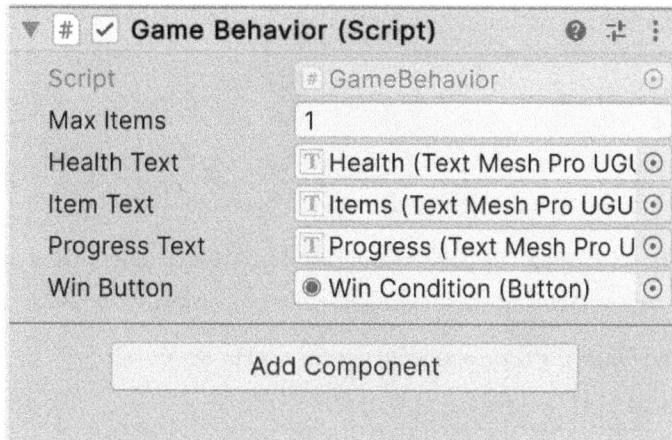

Figure 8.26: Dragging the UI button onto the script component

Let's break down the code as follows:

1. We added the using directive for UnityEngine.UI to access the Button class.
2. We created a UI button variable to connect to **Win Condition (Button)** in the **Hierarchy** panel.
3. Since we set **Win Condition (Button)** as **Hidden** when the game starts, we reactivate it when the game is won.

With **Max Items** set to 1, **Win Button** will show up on collecting the only pickup item in the scene. Clicking the button doesn't do anything right now, but we'll address that in the following section.

Pausing and restarting the game with using directives and namespaces

Right now, our win condition works as expected, but the player still has control over the capsule and doesn't have a way of restarting the game once it's over. Unity provides a property in the Time class called timeScale, which, when set to 0, freezes the game scene. However, to restart the game, we need access to a namespace called SceneManagement that isn't accessible from our classes by default.

A namespace collects and groups a set of classes under a specific name to organize large projects and avoid conflicts between scripts that may share the same names. A using directive needs to be added to a class to access a namespace's classes.

All C# scripts created from Unity come with three default using directives, shown in the following code snippet:

```
using System.Collections;
using System.Collections.Generic;
using UnityEngine;
```

These allow access to common namespaces, but Unity and C# offer plenty more that can be added with the using keyword followed by the name of the namespace.

Since our game will need to be paused and restarted when a player wins or loses, this is a good time to use a namespace that isn't included in new C# scripts by default:

1. Add the following code to GameBehavior and play:

    ```
    using UnityEngine;
    using TMPro;
    using UnityEngine.UI;

    // 1
    using UnityEngine.SceneManagement;

    public class GameBehavior : MonoBehaviour
    {
        // ... No changes needed ...
        private int _itemsCollected = 0;
        public int Items
        {
            get { return _itemsCollected; }
            set {
                _itemsCollected = value;

                if (_itemsCollected >= MaxItems)
                {
    ```

```
                    ProgressText.text = "You've found all the items!";
                    WinButton.gameObject.SetActive(true);

                    // 2
                    Time.timeScale = 0f;
            }
            else
            {
                    ProgressText.text= "Item found, only " +
                        (MaxItems - _itemsCollected) + " more to go!";
            }
        }
    }
    public void RestartScene()
    {
        // 3
        SceneManager.LoadScene(0);
        // 4
        Time.timeScale = 1f;
    }

    // ... No other changes needed ...
}
```

2. Select **Win Condition** from the **Hierarchy** panel, scroll down in the **Inspector** panel to the **OnClick** section of the **Button** component, and hit the plus (+) icon:

   - Every Button component has an OnClick event, which means you can assign a method from a script to execute when the button is pushed.

- You can have multiple methods fire when a button is clicked, but we only need one in this case:

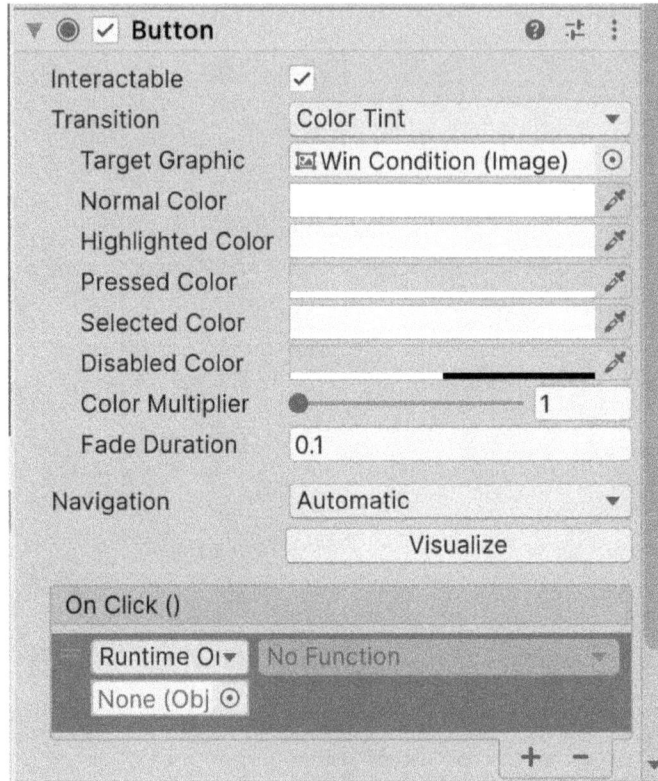

Figure 8.27: OnClick section of the button

3. From the **Hierarchy** panel, drag the **Game Manager** GameObject into the slot underneath **Runtime** to tell the button we want to choose a method from our manager script to fire when the button is pushed:

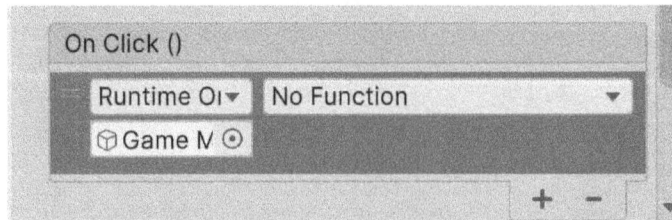

Figure 8.28: Setting the Game_Manager object in On Click()

4. Select **GameBehavior | RestartScene ()** to set the method we want the button to execute:

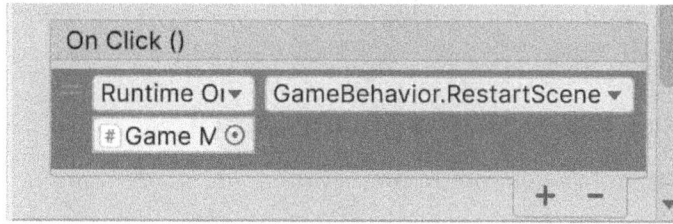

Figure 8.29: Choosing the restart method for the button click

Let's break down the code as follows:

1. We add the `SceneManagement` namespace with the `using` keyword, which handles all scene-related logic, such as creating and loading scenes.

2. We set `Time.timeScale` to 0 to pause the game when the win screen is displayed, which disables any input or movement.

3. We create a new method called `RestartScene()` and call `LoadScene()` when the win screen button is clicked:

    *   `LoadScene()` takes in a scene index as an `int` parameter
    *   Because there is only one scene in our project, we use index 0 to restart the game from the beginning

4. We reset `Time.timeScale` to the default value of 1 so that when the scene restarts, all controls and behaviors will be able to execute again.

Now, when you collect an item and click on the win screen button, the level restarts, with all scripts and components restored to their original values and set up for another round!

Summary

Congratulations! *Hero Born* is now a playable prototype. We implemented jumping and shooting mechanics, managed physics collisions and spawning objects, and added a few basic UI elements to display feedback. We even got as far as resetting the level when the player wins.

A lot of new topics were introduced in this chapter, and it's important to go back and make sure you understand what went into the code we wrote. Pay special attention to our discussions on enumerations, get and set properties, and namespaces. From here on, the code is only going to get more complex as we dive further into the possibilities of the C# language.

In the next chapter, we'll start working on getting our enemy GameObjects to take notice of our player when we get too close, resulting in a follow-and-shoot protocol that will up the stakes for our player.

Pop quiz: Working with mechanics

a.   What type of data do enumerations store?

b.   How would you create a copy of a Prefab GameObject in an active scene?

c.   Which variable properties allow you to add functionality when their values are referenced or modified?

d.   Which Unity method displays all UI objects in the scene?

Don't forget to check your answers against mine in the *Pop Quiz Answers* appendix to see how you did!

Subscribe to Game Dev Assembly Newsletter!

We are excited to introduce Game Dev Assembly, our brand-new newsletter dedicated to everything game development. Whether you're a programmer, designer, artist, animator, or studio lead, you'll get exclusive insights, industry trends, and expert tips to help you build better games and grow your skills. Sign up today and become part of a growing community of creators, innovators, and game changers: https://packt.link/gamedev-newsletter

Scan the QR code to join instantly!

Unlock this book's exclusive benefits now

UNLOCK NOW

Scan this QR code or go to https://packtpub.com/unlock, then search this book by name.

Note: Keep your purchase invoice ready before you start.

9

Basic AI and Enemy Behavior

Virtual scenarios need conflicts, consequences, and potential rewards to feel real. Without these three things, there's no incentive for the player to care about what happens to their in-game character, much less continue to play the game. While there are plenty of game mechanics that deliver on one or more of these conditions, nothing beats an enemy that will seek you out and try to end your session.

Programming an intelligent enemy is no easy task and often goes hand in hand with long working hours and frustration. However, Unity has built-in features, components, and classes we can use to design and implement AI systems in a more user-friendly way. These tools will push the first playable iteration of *Hero Born* over the finish line and provide a springboard for more advanced C# topics.

In this chapter, we'll focus on the following topics:

- The Unity navigation system
- Working with a navigation mesh
- Navigation agents
- Procedural programming and logic
- Taking and dealing damage
- Adding a loss condition
- Refactoring and keeping it DRY

Let's get started!

Navigating 3D space in Unity

When we talk about navigation in real life, it's usually a conversation about how to get from point A to point B. Navigating around virtual 3D space is largely the same, but how do we account for the experiential knowledge we humans have accumulated since the day we first started crawling? Everything from walking on a flat surface to climbing stairs and jumping off curbs is a skill we learned by doing; how can we possibly program all that into a game without going insane?

Before you can dive into the answers to these questions, you'll need to know what navigation components Unity has to offer.

Unity's navigation components

The short answer is that Unity has spent a lot of time perfecting its navigation system and delivering components that we can use to govern how playable and non-playable characters can get around. Each of the following components is included with the new Unity AI Navigation package and has complex features already built in:

- **NavMeshSurface**: This is essentially a map of the walkable surfaces in a given level; the NavMeshSurface component itself is created from the level geometry in a process called **baking**. Baking a NavMeshSurface component into your level creates a unique project asset that holds the navigation data.

- **NavMeshAgent**: If NavMeshSurface is the level map, then NavMeshAgent is the moving piece on the board. Any object with a NavMeshAgent component attached will automatically avoid other agents or obstacles it comes into contact with.

- **NavMeshObstacle**: The navigation system needs to be aware of any moving or stationary objects in the level that could cause NavMeshAgent to alter its route. Adding NavMeshObstacle components to those objects lets the system know that they need to be avoided.

While this description of the Unity navigation system is far from complete, it's enough for us to move forward with our enemy behavior. For this chapter, we'll be focusing on adding NavMeshSurface to our level, setting up the Enemy prefab as a NavMeshAgent, and getting the Enemy prefab to move along a predefined route in a seemingly intelligent way.

You can find more information on the navigation system at `https://docs.unity3d.com/Packages/com.unity.ai.navigation@1.1/manual/NavigationSystem.html`.

Let's set up an "intelligent" enemy using Unity 6's **AI Navigation** package.

Adding a NavMeshSurface

The **AI Navigation** package comes pre-installed with Unity 6, but let's make triple sure by going to **Window | Package Manager** and checking that **AI Navigation** is there:

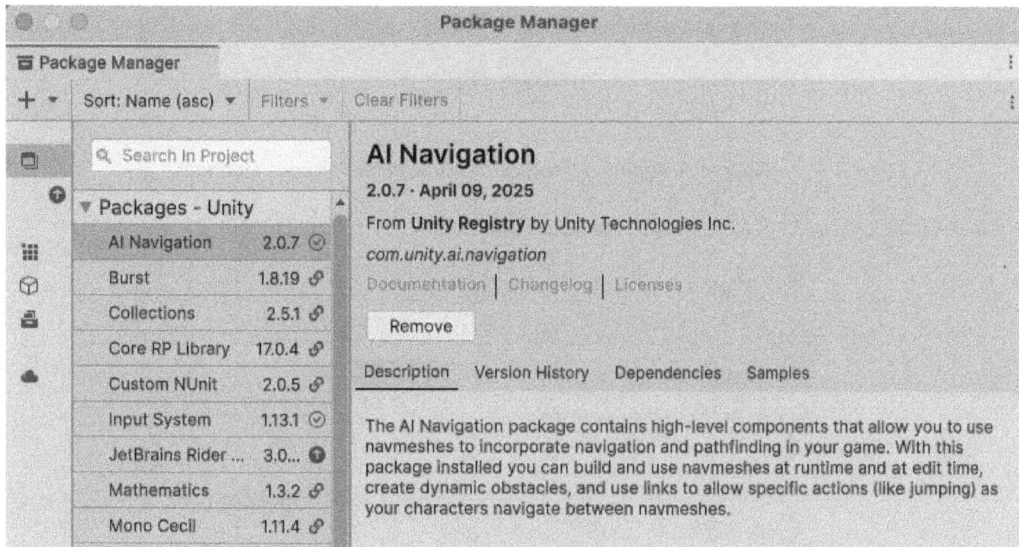

Figure 9.1: Checking the AI Navigation package in the Package Manager

> **Note**
>
> To provide a complete view of the Unity editor, all our screenshots are taken in full-screen mode. For color versions of all images in the book, use this link: `https://packt.link/gbp/9781805808718`.

If you don't see the AI Navigation package in your project for any reason, you can add it by following these steps:

1. Click the + sign in the upper-left corner and select **Add package by name...**:

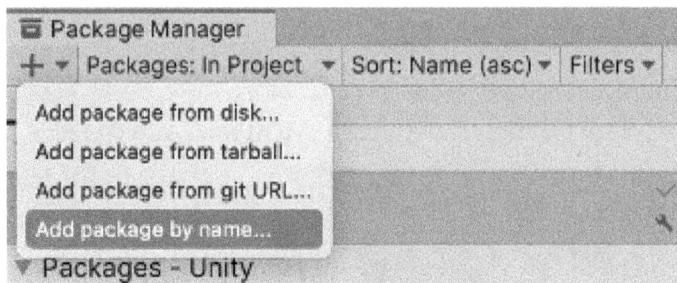

Figure 9.2: Adding a package by name in the Package Manager

2. Enter com.unity.ai.navigation and click **Add**:

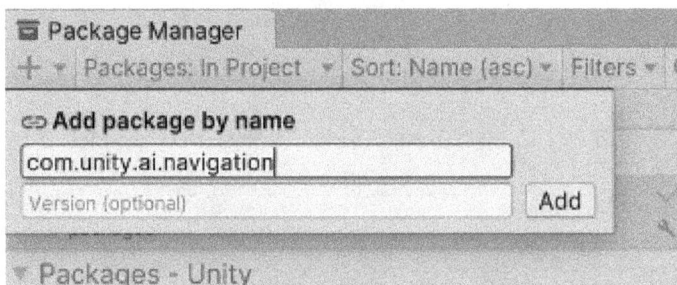

Figure 9.3: Entering a package name manually

Your first task in setting up an "intelligent" enemy is to create a NavMeshSurface over the arena's walkable areas. Let's set up and configure our level's NavMeshSurface:

1. Select the Environment GameObject, click on **Add Component** in the **Inspector** window, and choose **NavMesh Surface**:

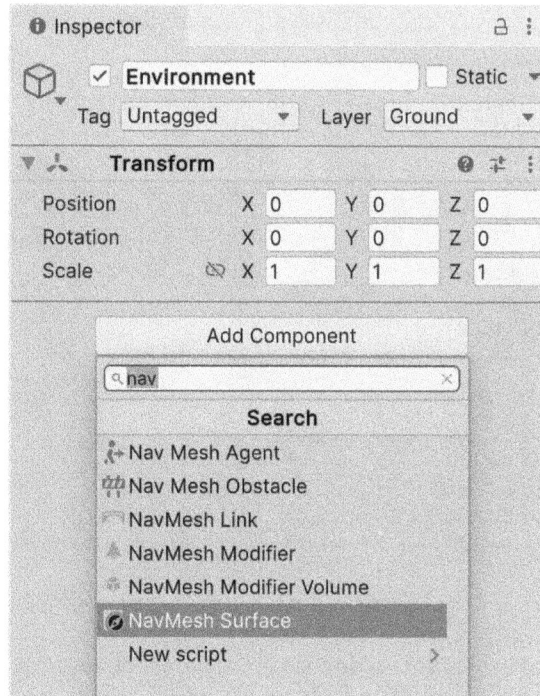

Figure 9.4: Adding a NavMeshSurface component

2. In the **Inspector** window, leave everything set to the default values and click **Bake** in the
NavMesh Surface component:

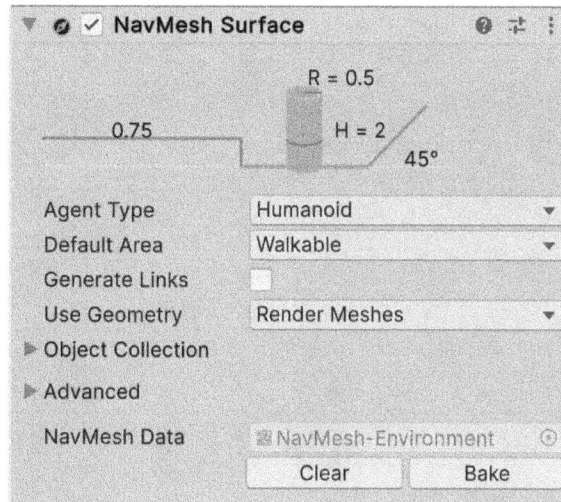

Figure 9.5: NavMeshSurface component added in the Inspector

3. Once baking is finished, you'll see a new **SampleScene** folder inside the **Scenes** folder with our new navigation mesh data:

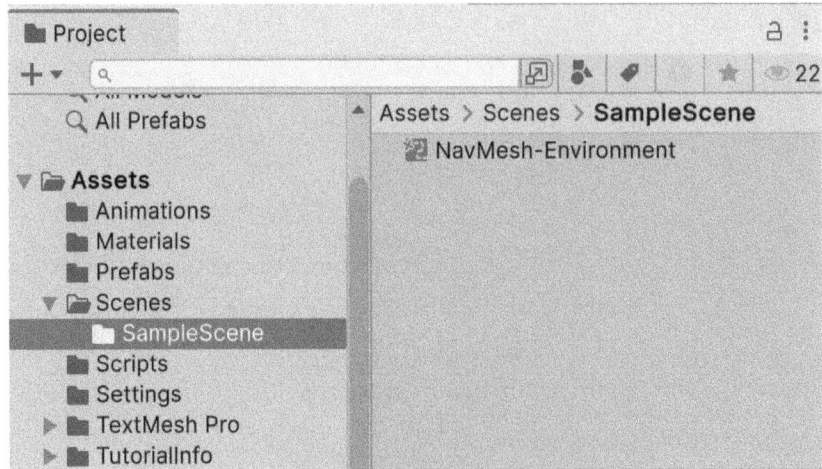

Figure 9.6: NavMeshSurface baking data under Assets

Our newly baked NavMeshSurface is now set up for us to interact with, and a light blue overlay has been added to show all the walkable surfaces to which a NavMeshAgent component is attached:

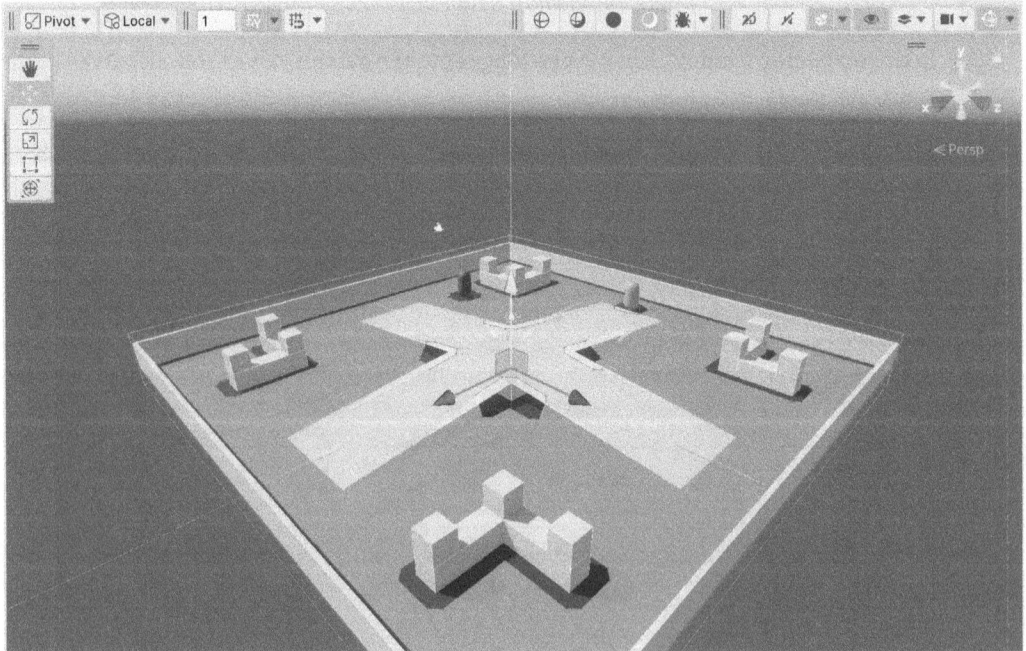

Figure 9.7: NavMeshSurface overlay on the environment object

It's somewhat hard to see on our blue floor, but NavMeshSurface is covering the entire surface. Your next task is to get the Enemy prefab walking around using the built-in navigation system!

Setting up enemy agents

Let's register the Enemy prefab as a NavMeshAgent:

1. In the Prefabs folder, select the Enemy prefab, click **Add Component** in the **Inspector** window, and search for NavMeshAgent:

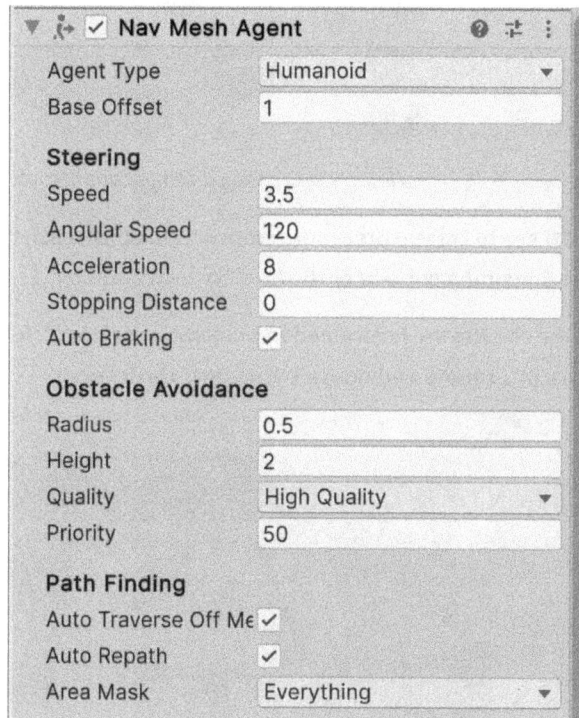

Figure 9.8: Adding a NavMeshAgent component

2. Click + | **Create Empty** from the **Hierarchy** window and name the GameObject Patrol Route:

    a. Select **Patrol Route**, click + | **Create Empty** to add a child GameObject, name it Corner, and position it in one of the corners of the level—make sure there's enough room between the barriers and the wall on each side to let the enemy walk past:

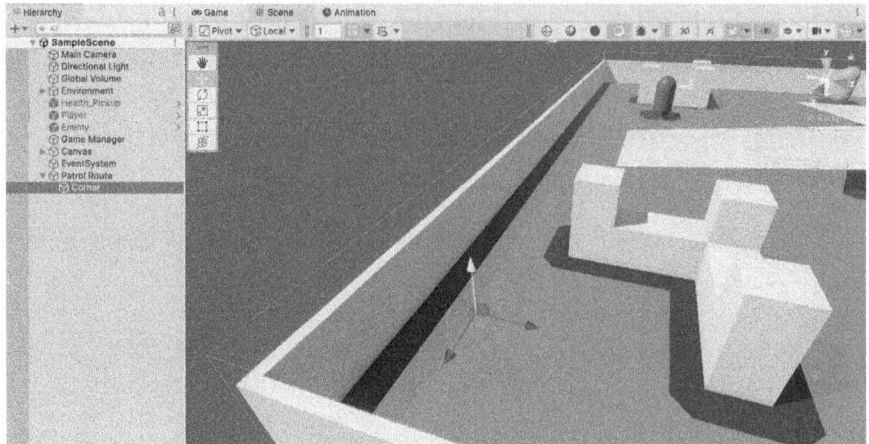

Figure 9.9: Creating an empty patrol route object

3. Duplicate Corner to create three more empty child objects in Patrol Route and position them in the remaining corners of the level to form a square.

    Make sure the corners are positioned in a clockwise or counterclockwise sequence so the enemy walks in a square and doesn't crisscross the level:

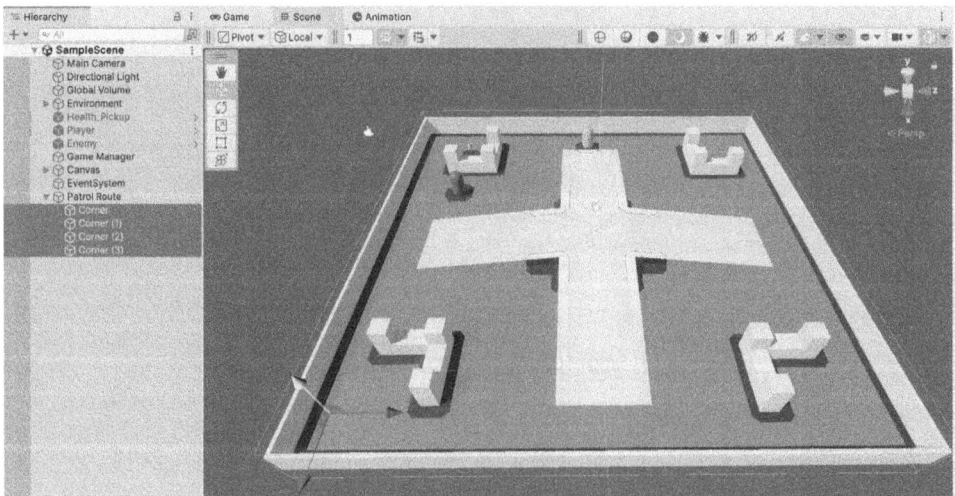

Figure 9.10: Creating all empty patrol route objects

Adding a NavMeshAgent component to Enemy tells the NavMeshSurface component to take notice and register it as an object that has access to its autonomous navigation features. Creating the four empty GameObjects in each corner of the level lays out the simple route we want our enemies to eventually patrol; grouping them in an empty parent object makes it easier to reference them in code and makes for a more organized **Hierarchy** window. All that's left is the code to make the enemy walk the patrol route, which you'll add in the next section.

Moving enemy agents

Our patrol locations are set, and the Enemy prefab has a NavMeshAgent component, but now we need to figure out how to reference those locations and get the enemy moving on its own. To do that, we'll first need to talk about an important concept in the world of software development: procedural programming.

Procedural programming

Even though it's in the name, the idea behind procedural programming can be elusive until you get your head around it; once you do, you'll never see a code challenge the same way.

Any task that executes the same logic on one or more sequential objects is the perfect candidate for procedural programming. You already did a little procedural programming when you debugged arrays, lists, and dictionaries with for and foreach loops. Each time those looping statements were executed, you performed the same call to Debug.Log(), iterating over each item sequentially. The idea now is to use that skill to get a more useful outcome.

One of the most common uses of procedural programming is adding items from one collection to another, often modifying them along the way. This works great for our purposes since we want to reference each child object in the Patrol_Route parent and store them in a list. We'll spend the next section implementing that technique in our code.

Referencing the patrol locations

Now that we understand the basics of procedural programming, it's time to get a reference to our patrol locations and assign them to a usable list:

1. Add the following code to EnemyBehavior:

    ```
    public class EnemyBehavior : MonoBehaviour
    {
        // 1
        public Transform PatrolRoute;
    ```

```
    // 2
    public List<Transform> Locations;
    void Start()
    {
        // 3
        InitializePatrolRoute();
    }

    // 4
    void InitializePatrolRoute()
    {
        // 5
        foreach(Transform child in PatrolRoute)
        {
            // 6
            Locations.Add(child);
        }
    }
    void OnTriggerEnter(Collider other)
    {
        // ... No changes needed ...
    }
    void OnTriggerExit(Collider other)
    {
        // ... No changes needed ...
    }
}
```

2. Select **Enemy** in the **Hierarchy** window and drag the **Patrol Route** object from the **Hierarchy** window onto the **Patrol Route** variable in **EnemyBehavior**:

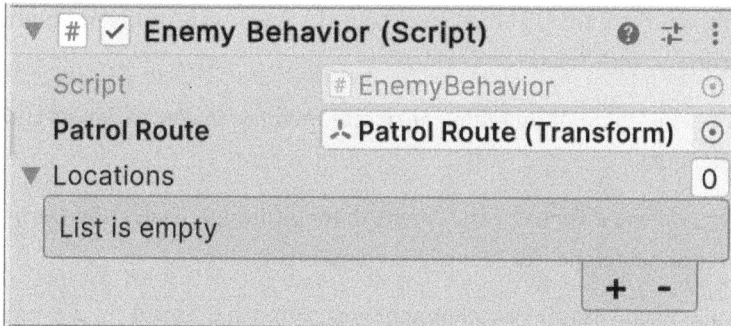

Figure 9.11: Dragging Patrol_Route to the Enemy script

3. Run the game and hit the arrow icon next to the **Locations** variable in the **Inspector** window to see the list populate:

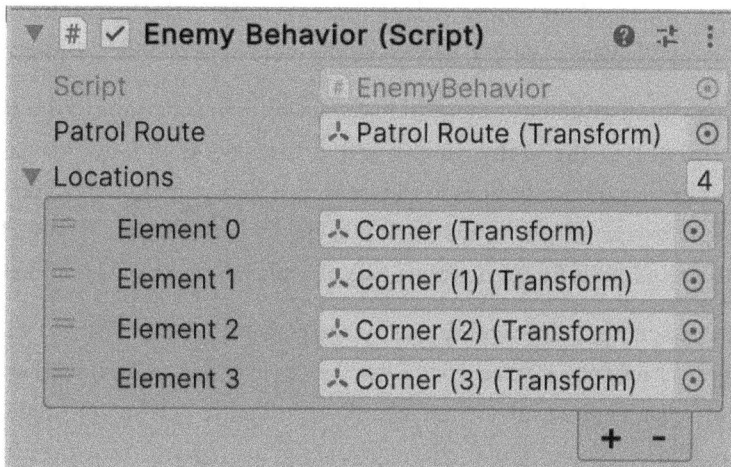

Figure 9.12: Testing procedural programming

Let's break down the code:

1. First, we declare a variable for storing the Patrol Route empty parent GameObject.

2. Then, we declare a List variable to hold all the child Transform components in Patrol Route.

3. After that, we use Start() to call the InitializePatrolRoute() method when the game begins.

4.   Next, we create `InitializePatrolRoute()` as a private utility method to procedurally fill **Locations** with `Transform` values:

Remember that not including an access modifier makes variables and methods private by default.

5.   Then, we use a `foreach` statement to loop through each child GameObject in `Patrol Route` and reference its `Transform` component:

   a.   Each `Transform` component is captured in the local child variable declared in the `foreach` loop.

6.   Finally, we add each sequential child `Transform` component to the list of locations using the `Add()` method as we loop through the child objects in `Patrol Route`:

   a.   This way, no matter what changes we make in the **Hierarchy** window, **Locations** will always be filled in with all the child objects under the `Patrol Route` parent.

While we could have assigned each location GameObject to **Locations** by dragging and dropping them directly from the **Hierarchy** window into the **Inspector** window, it's easy to lose or break these connections; making changes to the location object names, object additions or deletions, or project updates can all throw a wrench in a class's initialization. It's much safer, and more readable, to procedurally fill GameObject lists or arrays in the `Start()` method.

Due to that reasoning, I also tend to use `GetComponent()` in the `Start()` method to find and store component references attached to a given class instead of assigning them in the **Inspector** window. However, in situations where components you're looking for might be in other child objects or nested in complex prefabs, it may be easier to drag-and-drop the components directly in the **Inspector** window.

Now, we need the enemy object to follow the patrol route we laid out, which is your next task.

Moving the enemy

With a list of patrol locations initialized on `Start()`, we can grab the Enemy `NavMeshAgent` component and set its first destination.

Update `EnemyBehavior` with the following code and hit **Play**:

```
// 1
using UnityEngine.AI;
```

```
public class EnemyBehavior : MonoBehaviour
{
    public Transform PatrolRoute;
    public List<Transform> Locations;
    // 2
    private int _locationIndex = 0;
    // 3
    private NavMeshAgent _agent;
    void Start()
    {
        // 4
        _agent = GetComponent<NavMeshAgent>();

        InitializePatrolRoute();

        // 5
        MoveToNextPatrolLocation();
    }

    void InitializePatrolRoute()
    {
        // ... No changes needed ...
    }

    // 6
    void MoveToNextPatrolLocation()
    {
        _agent.destination = Locations[_locationIndex].position;
    }

    void OnTriggerEnter(Collider other)
    {
        // ... No changes needed ...
    }
```

```
    void OnTriggerExit(Collider other)
    {
        // ... No changes needed ...
    }
}
```

Let's break down the code:

1.   First, we add the UnityEngine.AI using directive so that EnemyBehavior has access to Unity's navigation classes, in this case, NavMeshAgent.

2.   Then, we declare a variable to keep track of which patrol location the enemy is currently walking toward. Since List items are zero-indexed, we can have the Enemy prefab move between patrol points in the order they are stored in **Locations**.

3.   Next, we declare a variable to store the NavMeshAgent component attached to the Enemy GameObject. This is private because no other classes should be able to access or modify it.

4.   After that, we use GetComponent() to find and return the attached NavMeshAgent component to the agent.

5.   Then, we call the MoveToNextPatrolLocation() method on Start().

6.   Finally, we declare MoveToNextPatrolLocation() as a private method and set _agent. destination:

     •   destination is a Vector3 position in 3D space.

     •   Locations[_locationIndex] grabs the Transform item in **Locations** at a given index.

     •   Adding .position references the Transform component's Vector3 position.

Now, when our scene starts, locations are filled with patrol points and MoveToNextPatrolLocation() is called to set the destination position of the NavMeshAgent component to the first item at _ locationIndex 0 in the list of locations. The next step is to have the enemy object move from the first patrol location to all the other locations in sequence.

Our enemy moves to the first patrol point just fine, but then it stops. What we want is for it to continually move between each sequential location, which will require additional logic in Update() and MoveToNextPatrolLocation(). Let's create this behavior.

Add the following code to `EnemyBehavior` and hit **Play**:

```
public class EnemyBehavior : MonoBehaviour
{
    // ... No changes needed ...
    void Update()
    {
        // 1
        if(_agent.remainingDistance < 0.2f && !_agent.pathPending)
        {
            // 2
            MoveToNextPatrolLocation();
        }
    }
    void MoveToNextPatrolLocation()
    {
        // 3
        if (Locations.Count == 0)
            return;

        _agent.destination = Locations[_locationIndex].position;
        // 4
        _locationIndex = (_locationIndex + 1) % Locations.Count;
    }
    // ... No other changes needed ...
}
```

Let's break down the code:

1. First, we declare the `Update()` method and add an `if` statement to check whether two different conditions are true:

    - `remainingDistance` returns how far the `NavMeshAgent` component currently is from its set destination, so we're checking that it is less than `0.2`

    - `pathPending` returns a `true` or `false` Boolean, depending on whether Unity is computing a path for the `NavMeshAgent` component

2. If _agent is very close to its destination, and no other path is being computed, the `if` statement returns `true` and calls `MoveToNextPatrolLocation()`.

3. Here, we added an `if` statement to make sure that **Locations** isn't empty before the rest of the code in `MoveToNextPatrolLocation()` is executed:

    *   If **Locations** is empty, we use the `return` keyword to exit the method without continuing.

    *   `if` statements that only have one line of code can be written without any brackets, which can make them easier to write and read (but this is entirely a personal preference).

    *   This is referred to as **defensive programming**, and, coupled with refactoring, it is an essential skill to have in your arsenal as you move toward more intermediate C# topics. We will consider refactoring at the end of the chapter.

4. Then, we set `_locationIndex` to its current value, +1, followed by the modulo (%) of `Locations.Count`:

    *   This will increase the index from 0 to 4 and then restart it at 0 so that our Enemy prefab moves in a continuous path.

    *   The `modulo` operator returns the remainder of two values being divided: 2 divided by 4 has a remainder of 2 when the result is an integer, so `2 % 4 = 2`. Likewise, 4 divided by 4 has no remainder, so `4 % 4 = 0`.

Dividing an index by the maximum number of items in a collection is a quick way to always find the next item. If you're rusty on the `modulo` operator, revisit *Chapter 2*.

We now need to check that the enemy is moving toward its set patrol location every frame in `Update()`; when it gets close, `MoveToNextPatrolLocation()` is fired, which increments `_locationIndex` and sets the next patrol point as the destination.

If you drag the **Scene** view down next to the **Console** window, as shown in *Figure 9.13*, and hit **Play**, you can watch the Enemy prefab walk around the corners of the level in a continuous loop:

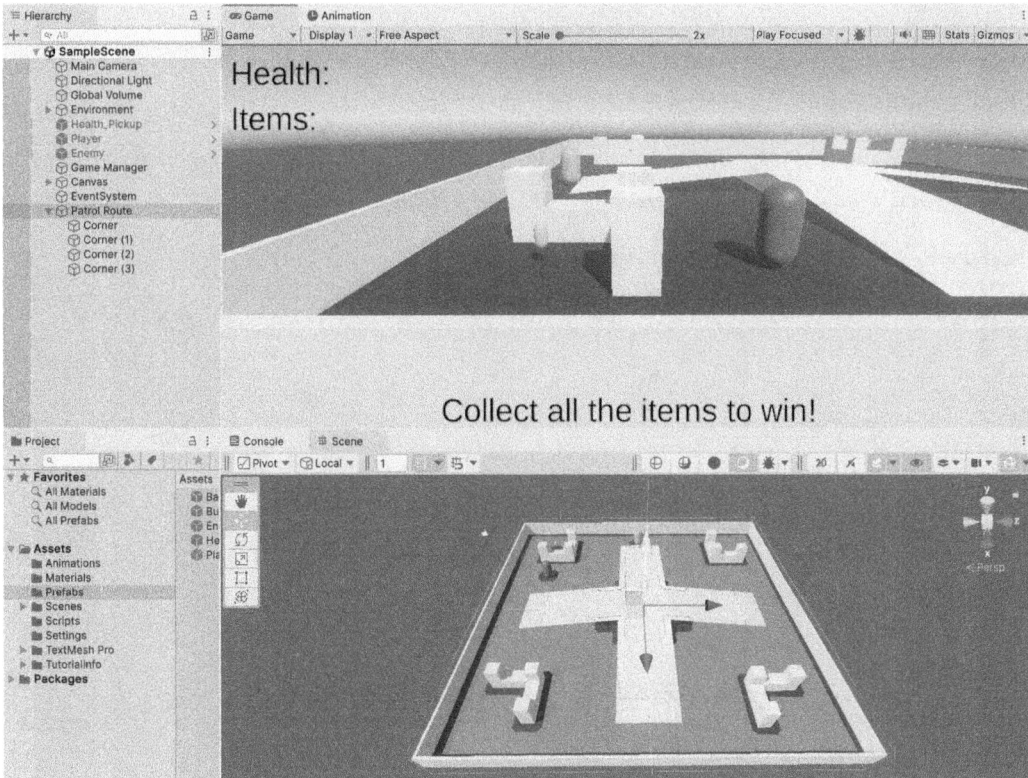

Figure 9.13: Testing the enemy patrol route

The enemy now follows the patrol route around the outside of the map, but it doesn't seek out the player and attack when it's within a preset range. We'll use the NavAgent component to do just that in the next section.

Enemy game mechanics

Now that our enemy is on a continuous patrol circuit, it's time to give it some interaction mechanics of its own; there wouldn't be much risk or reward if we left it walking around with no way to act against us.

Seek and destroy: Changing the agent's destination

In this section, we'll be focusing on switching the target of the enemies' NavMeshAgent component when the player gets too close and dealing damage if a collision occurs. When the enemy successfully lowers the player's health, it will return to its patrol route until its next run-in with the player.

However, we're not going to leave our player helpless; we'll also add code to track enemy health, detect when an enemy is successfully hit with one of the player's bullets, and when an enemy needs to be destroyed.

Now that the Enemy prefab is moving around on patrol, we need to get a reference to the player's position and change the destination of NavMeshAgent if it gets too close.

Add the following code to EnemyBehavior:

```
public class EnemyBehavior : MonoBehaviour
{
    // 1
    public Transform Player;

    // ... No other variable changes needed ...
    void Start()
    {
        _agent = GetComponent<NavMeshAgent>();
        // 2
        Player = GameObject.Find("Player").transform;
        // ... No other changes needed ...
    }
    /* ... No changes to Update,
            InitializePatrolRoute, or
            MoveToNextPatrolLocation ... */
    void OnTriggerEnter(Collider other)
    {
        if(other.name == "Player")
        {
            // 3
            _agent.destination = Player.position;
            Debug.Log("Enemy detected!");
        }
    }
    void OnTriggerExit(Collider other)
    {
        // .... No changes needed ...
    }
}
```

Let's break down the code:

1. First, we declare a public variable to hold the Player capsule's Transform value.

2. Then, we use GameObject.Find("Player") to return a reference to the Player object in the scene:

    a. Adding .transform directly references the object's Transform value in the same line.

3. Finally, we set _agent.destination to the player's Vector3 position in OnTriggerEnter() whenever the player enters the enemies' attack zone that we set up earlier with a Collider component.

If you play the game now and get too close to the patrolling enemy, you'll see that it breaks from its path and comes straight for you. Once it reaches the player, the code in the Update() method takes over again and the Enemy prefab resumes its patrol.

We still need the enemy to be able to hurt the player in some way, which we'll learn how to do in the next section.

Lowering player health

While our enemy mechanic has come a long way, it's still anti-climactic to have nothing happen when the Enemy prefab collides with the player prefab. To fix this, we'll tie in the new enemy mechanics with the game manager.

Update PlayerBehavior with the following code and hit **Play**:

```
public class PlayerBehavior : MonoBehaviour
{
    // ... No changes to public variables needed ...
    // 1
    private GameBehavior _gameManager;

    void Start()
    {
        _rb = GetComponent<Rigidbody>();
        _col = GetComponent<CapsuleCollider>();
        // 2
        _gameManager = GameObject.Find("Game Manager")
            .GetComponent<GameBehavior>();
```

```
    }
    /* ... No changes to Update,
           FixedUpdate, or
           IsGrounded ... */
    // 3
    void OnCollisionEnter(Collision collision)
    {
        // 4
        if(collision.gameObject.name == "Enemy")
        {
            // 5
            _gameManager.HP -= 1;
        }
    }
}
```

Let's break down the code:

1. First, we declare a private variable to hold the reference to the instance of GameBehavior we have in the scene.

2. This finds and returns the GameBehavior script that's attached to the Game Manager object in the scene:

    a. Using GetComponent() on the same line as GameObject.Find() is a common way to cut down on unnecessary lines of code.

3. Since our player is the object being collided with, it makes sense to declare OnCollisionEnter() in PlayerBehavior.

4. Next, we check for the name of the colliding object; if it's the Enemy Prefab, we execute the body of the if statement.

5. Finally, we subtract 1 from the public HP variable using the _gameManager instance to reduce the player's health each time they are hit.

Collisions between two objects work both ways, so you could also put this code in the EnemyBehavior script and look for a collision with the Player object. Remember, we're using our big Sphere Collider to detect when the player is in range, but here we're using Capsule Collider to detect collisions when the player gets hit (GameObjects can have multiple colliders).

Whenever the enemy now tracks and collides with the player, the game manager will fire the set property on HP. The UI will update with a new value for player health, which means we have an opportunity to put in some additional logic for the loss condition later on. For now, let's move on to detecting when bullets hit our enemies and potentially take them out of commission.

Detecting bullet collisions

Now that we have our loss condition, it's time to add a way for our player to fight back and survive enemy attacks.

Open up EnemyBehavior and modify it with the following code:

```
public class EnemyBehavior : MonoBehaviour
{
    //... No other variable changes needed ...
    // 1
    private int _lives = 3;
    public int EnemyLives
    {
        // 2
        get { return _lives; }
        // 3
        private set
        {
            _lives = value;
            // 4
            if (_lives <= 0)
            {
                Destroy(this.gameObject);
                Debug.Log("Enemy down.");
            }
        }
    }
    /* ... No changes to Start,
           Update,
           InitializePatrolRoute,
           MoveToNextPatrolLocation,
           OnTriggerEnter, or
           OnTriggerExit ... */
```

```
    // 5
    void OnCollisionEnter(Collision collision)
    {
        if(collision.gameObject.name == "Bullet(Clone)")
        {
            // 6
            EnemyLives -= 1;
            Debug.Log("Critical hit!");
        }
    }
}
```

Let's break down the code:

1. First, we declare a private int variable called _lives with a public backing variable called EnemyLives. This will let us control how EnemyLives is referenced and set, just like in GameBehavior.

2. Then, we set the get property to always return _lives.

3. Next, we use a private set to assign the new value of EnemyLives to _lives to keep them both in sync.

    We haven't seen private get or private set before, but they can have access modifiers just like any other executable code. Declaring get or set as private means that only the parent class has access to their functionality.

4. Then, we add an if statement to check whether _lives is less than or equal to 0, meaning that the enemy should be dead:

    a. When that's the case, we destroy the Enemy GameObject and print out a message to the console saying Enemy down.

5. Because Enemy is the object getting hit with bullets, it's sensible to include a check for those collisions in EnemyBehavior with OnCollisionEnter().

6. Finally, if the name of the colliding object matches a bullet clone object, we decrement EnemyLives by 1 and print out another message:

    a. Notice that the name we're checking for is Bullet(Clone), even though our bullet prefab is named Bullet. This is because Unity adds the (Clone) suffix to any object created with the Instantiate() method, which is how we made them in our shooting logic.

b. You can also check for the GameObject's tag, but since that's a Unity-specific feature, we're going to leave the code as is and do things with pure C#.

Now, the player can fight back when the enemy tries to take one of its lives by shooting it three times and destroying it. Again, our use of the get and set properties to handle additional logic proves to be a flexible and scalable solution. With that done, your final task is to update the game manager with a loss condition.

Updating the game manager

To fully implement the loss condition, we need to update the manager class:

1. Open up GameBehavior and add the following code:

```
public class GameBehavior : MonoBehaviour
{
    // ... No other variable changes...
    // 1
    public Button LossButton;

    private int _itemsCollected = 0;
    public int Items
    {
        // ... No changes needed ...
    }
    private int _playerHP = 10;
    public int HP
    {
        get { return _playerHP; }
        set {
            _playerHP = value;
                HealthText.text = "Health: " + HP;
            // 2
            if(_playerHP <= 0)
            {
                ProgressText.text= "You want another life
                    with that?";
                LossButton.gameObject.SetActive(true);
                Time.timeScale = 0;
```

```
        }
        else
        {
            ProgressText.text = "Ouch... that's got hurt.";
        }
    }
  }
}
```

💡 **Quick tip**: Enhance your coding experience with the **AI Code Explainer** and **Quick Copy** features. Open this book in the next-gen Packt Reader. Click the **Copy** button

(1) to quickly copy code into your coding environment, or click the **Explain** button

(2) to get the AI assistant to explain a block of code to you.

```
                                                        Copy    Explain
function calculate(a, b) {
    return {sum: a + b};                                  1        2
};
```

🔖 **The next-gen Packt Reader** is included for free with the purchase of this book. Scan the QR code OR go to https://packtpub.com/unlock, then use the search bar to find this book by name. Double-check the edition shown to make sure you get the right one.

2. In the **Hierarchy** window, right-click on **Win Condition**, choose **Duplicate**, and name it `Loss Condition`:

    a. Click the arrow to the left of **Loss Condition** to expand it, select the **Text** object, and change the text to `You lose....`

3. Select **Game Manager** in the **Hierarchy** window and drag **Loss Condition** into the **Loss Button** slot in the **Game Behavior (Script)** component:

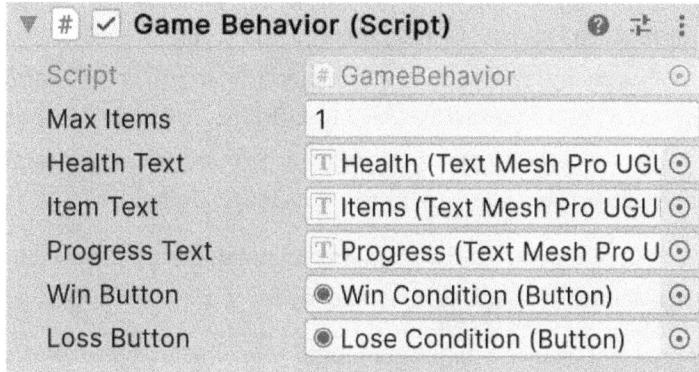

Figure 9.14: Game behavior script with text and button variables completed in the Inspector pane

Let's break down the code:

1. First, we declare a new button that we want to show when the player loses the game.
2. Then, we add an `if` statement to check when `_playerHP` drops below `0`:

    • If it's true, `ProgessText` and `Time.timeScale` are updated and the **Loss Condition** button is activated.

    • If the player is still alive following an enemy collision, `ProgessText` shows a different message: **Ouch... that's got to hurt.**

3. Now, change `_playerHP` to `1` in `GameBehavior.cs` and get the `Enemy` prefab to collide with you and observe what happens.

That's a wrap! You've successfully added a "smart" enemy that can damage the player and be damaged right back, as well as a loss screen through the game manager.

Before we finish this chapter, there's one more important topic that we need to discuss, and that's how to avoid repeating code.

Repeated code is the bane of all programmers, so it makes sense to learn how to keep it out of your projects early on!

Refactoring and keeping it DRY

The **Don't Repeat Yourself (DRY)** acronym is the software developer's conscience: it tells you when you're in danger of making a bad or questionable decision and gives you a feeling of satisfaction after a job well done.

In practice, repeated code is part of programming life. Trying to avoid it by constantly thinking ahead will put up so many roadblocks in your project that it won't seem worthwhile to carry on. A more efficient—and sane—approach to dealing with repeating code is to quickly identify it when and where it occurs and then look for the best way to remove it. This task is called **refactoring**, and our GameBehavior class could use a little of its magic right now.

You may have noticed that we set the progress text and timescale in two separate places, but we could easily make ourselves a utility method to do this for us in a single place.

As you get more comfortable with programming, you won't need to clean up after yourself as much—you'll naturally learn how to make things easier on yourself in advance and reduce the need for refactoring after every new addition. However, that doesn't mean refactoring should be ignored; it's always important to check your code for opportunities you may have missed to write cleaner, more efficient code.

To refactor the existing code, you'll need to update GameBehavior.cs as follows:

```
public class GameBehavior: MonoBehaviour
{
    // 1
    public void UpdateScene(string updatedText)
    {
        ProgressText.text = updatedText;
        Time.timeScale = 0f;
    }
    private int _itemsCollected = 0;
    public int Items
    {
        get { return _itemsCollected; }
        set
        {
```

```
            _itemsCollected = value;
            ItemText.text = "Items Collected: " + Items;
            if (_itemsCollected >= MaxItems)
            {
                WinButton.gameObject.SetActive(true);
                // 2
                UpdateScene("You've found all the items!");
            }
            else
            {
                ProgressText.text = "Item found, only " + (MaxItems - _
itemsCollected) + " more to go!";
            }
        }
    }
    private int _playerHP = 10;
    public int HP
    {
        get { return _playerHP; }
        set
        {
            _playerHP = value;
            HealthText.text = "Player Health: " + HP;
            if (_playerHP <= 0)
            {
                LossButton.gameObject.SetActive(true);
                // 3
                UpdateScene("You want another life with that?");
            }
            else
            {
                ProgressText.text = "Ouch... that's got hurt.";
            }
            Debug.LogFormat("Lives: {0}", _playerHP);
        }
    }
}
```

Let's break down the code:

1. We declared a new method called `UpdateScene()`, which takes in a string parameter that we want to assign to `ProgressText` and sets `Time.timeScale` to 0.

2. We deleted our first instance of duplicated code and used our new method to update our scene when the game is won.

3. We deleted our second instance of duplicated code and used our new method to update the scene when the game is lost.

There's always more to refactor if you look in the right places.

Summary

With that, our enemy and player interactions are complete. We can dish out damage as well as take it, lose lives, and fight back, all while updating the on-screen GUI. Our enemies use Unity's navigation system to walk around the arena and change to attack mode when within a specified range of the player. Each GameObject is responsible for its behavior, internal logic, and object collisions, while the game manager keeps track of the variables that govern the game's state. Lastly, we learned about simple procedural programming and how much cleaner code can be when repeated instructions are abstracted out into their methods.

You should feel a sense of accomplishment at this point, especially if you started this book as a total beginner. Getting up to speed with a new programming language while building a working game is no easy trick. In the next chapter, you'll be introduced to some intermediate topics in C#, including new type modifiers, method overloading, interfaces, and class extensions.

Pop quiz: AI and navigation

a. How is a `NavMeshSurface` component created in a Unity scene?

b. What component identifies a GameObject to a `NavMeshSurface`?

c. Executing the same logic on one or more sequential objects is an example of which programming technique?

d. What does the acronym DRY stand for?

Don't forget to check your answers against mine in the *Pop Quiz Answers* appendix to see how you did!

Subscribe to Game Dev Assembly Newsletter!

We are excited to introduce **Game Dev Assembly**, our brand-new newsletter dedicated to everything game development. Whether you're a programmer, designer, artist, animator, or studio lead, you'll get exclusive insights, industry trends, and expert tips to help you build better games and grow your skills. Sign up today and become part of a growing community of creators, innovators, and game changers: `https://packt.link/gamedev-newsletter`

Scan the QR code to join instantly!

Join our community on Discord

Join our community's Discord space for discussions with the authors and other readers: `https://packt.link/gamedevelopment`.

10

Revisiting Types, Methods, and Classes

Now that you've programmed the game's mechanics and interactions with Unity's built-in classes, it's time to expand your core C# knowledge and focus on the intermediate applications of the foundation we've laid. We'll revisit old friends—variables, types, methods, and classes—but we'll target their deeper applications and relevant use cases. Many of the topics we'll be covering don't apply to *Hero Born* in its current state, so some examples will be standalone rather than being applied directly to the game prototype.

I'll be throwing a lot of new information your way, so if you feel overwhelmed at any point, don't hesitate to revisit the first few chapters to remind yourself of the foundational concepts. We'll also be using this chapter to break away from gameplay mechanics and features specific to Unity by focusing on the following topics:

- Intermediate modifiers
- Method overloading
- Using the out and ref parameters
- Working with interfaces
- Abstract classes and overriding
- Extending class functionality
- Namespace conflicts
- Type aliasing

Access modifiers

While we've gotten into the habit of pairing the public and private access modifiers with our variable declarations, as we did with player health and items collected, there remains a laundry list of modifier keywords that we haven't seen. We can't go into detail about every one of them in this chapter, but the five that we'll focus on will further your understanding of the C# language and give your programming skills a boost.

This section will cover the first three modifiers in the following list, while the remaining two will be discussed later on in the *Intermediate OOP* section:

- `const`
- `readonly`
- `static`
- `abstract`
- `override`

You can find a full list of available modifiers at `https://docs.microsoft.com/en-us/dotnet/csharp/language-reference/keywords/modifiers`.

Let's start with the first three access modifiers provided in the preceding list.

Constant and read-only properties

There will be times when you need to create variables that store constant, unchanging values (which also happen to be efficient with how much memory they take up). Adding the `const` keyword after a variable's access modifier will do just that, but only for built-in C# types. For example, you couldn't mark an instance of our `Character` class as a constant. A good candidate for a constant value is `MaxItems` in the `GameBehavior` class:

```
public const int MaxItems = 4;
```

The preceding code would essentially lock the value of `MaxItems` at 4, making it unchangeable. The problem you'll run into with constant variables is that they can only be assigned a value in their declaration, meaning we can't leave `MaxItems` without an initial value. As an alternative, we can use `readonly`, which won't let us write to the variable, meaning it can't be changed:

```
public readonly int MaxItems;
```

Using the `readonly` keyword to declare a variable will give us the same unmodifiable value as a constant, while still letting us assign its initial value at any time. A good place for this would be the `Start()` or `Awake()` method in one of our scripts.

Using static classes

We've already gone over how objects, or instances, are created from a class blueprint and that all properties and methods belong to that particular instance, as we had with our very first `Character` class instance. While this is great for object-oriented functionality, not all classes need to be instantiated, and not all properties need to belong to a specific instance. However, static classes are sealed, meaning they cannot be used in class inheritance.

Utility methods are a good case for this situation, where we don't necessarily care about instantiating a particular Utility class instance since all its methods wouldn't be dependent on a particular object. Your task is to create such a utility method in a new script.

Let's create a new class to hold some of our future methods that deal with raw computations or repeated logic that doesn't depend on the gameplay:

1. Create a new C# script in the `Scripts` folder and name it `Utilities`.

2. Open it up and add the following code:

```
using System.Collections;
using System.Collections.Generic;
using UnityEngine;

// 1
using UnityEngine.SceneManagement;

// 2
public static class Utilities
{
    // 3
    public static int PlayerDeaths = 0;

    // 4
    public static void RestartLevel()
    {
```

```
            SceneManager.LoadScene(0);
            Time.timeScale = 1.0f;
        }
    }
```

3. In GameBehavior, delete the code inside RestartLevel() and instead call the new
    Utilities method with the following code:

```
public void RestartScene()
{
    Utilities.RestartLevel();
}
```

Let's break down the code:

1. First, we added the using SceneManagement directive so that we can access the LoadScene()
    method.

2. Then, we declared Utilities as a public static class that does not inherit from
    MonoBehaviour because we won't need it to be in the game scene.

3. Next, we created a public static variable to hold the number of times our player has died
    and restarted the game.

4. Thereafter, we declared a public static method to hold our level restart logic, which is
    currently hardcoded in GameBehavior.

5. Finally, our update to GameBehavior calls RestartLevel() from the static Utilities class
    when the win or the lose button is pressed. Notice that we didn't need an instance of the
    Utilities class to call the method because it's static—it's just *dot notation*.

We've now extracted the restart logic from GameBehavior and put it into its static class, which
makes it easier to reuse across our code base. Marking it as static will also ensure that we never
have to create or manage instances of the Utilities class before we use its class members.

Non-static classes can have properties and methods that are static and non-static. However, if
an entire class is marked as static, all properties and methods must follow suit.

That wraps up our second visit of variables and types, which will enable you to build out your
own set of utilities and tools when managing larger and more complex projects down the road.
Now it's time to move on to methods and their intermediate capabilities, which includes method
overloading and ref and out parameters.

Revisiting methods

Methods have been a big part of our code since we learned how to use them in *Chapter 3*, but there are two intermediate use cases we haven't covered yet: method overloading and using the ref and out parameter keywords.

Overloading methods

The term **method overloading** refers to creating multiple methods with the same name but with different signatures. A method's signature is made up of its name and parameters, which is how the C# compiler recognizes it. Take the following method as an example:

```
public bool AttackEnemy(int damage) {}
```

The method signature of AttackEnemy() is written as follows:

```
AttackEnemy(int)
```

Now that we know the signature of AttackEnemy(), it can be overloaded by changing the number of parameters or the parameter types themselves, while still keeping its name. This provides added flexibility when you need more than one option for a given operation.

The RestartLevel() method in Utilities is a great example of a situation where method overloading comes in handy. Right now, RestartLevel() only restarts the current level, but what happens if we expand the game so that it includes multiple scenes? We could refactor RestartLevel() to accept parameters, but that often leads to bloated and confusing code.

The RestartLevel() method is, once again, a good candidate for testing out our new knowledge. Your task is to overload it to take in different parameters.

Let's add an overloaded version of RestartLevel():

1. Open up Utilities and add the following code:

    ```
    public static class Utilities
    {
        public static int PlayerDeaths = 0;

        public static void RestartLevel()
        {
            SceneManager.LoadScene(0);
            Time.timeScale = 1.0f;
    ```

```
        }

        // 1
        public static bool RestartLevel(int sceneIndex)
        {
            // 2
            SceneManager.LoadScene(sceneIndex);
            Time.timeScale = 1.0f;
            // 3
            return true;
        }
    }
```

2. In `GameBehavior`, update the call to the `Utilities.RestartLevel()` method to the following:

```
public void RestartScene()
{
    Utilities.RestartLevel(0);
}
```

Let's break down the code:

1. First, we declared an overloaded version of the `RestartLevel()` method that takes in an `int` parameter and returns a `bool`.

2. Then, it calls `LoadScene()` and passes in the `sceneIndex` parameter instead of manually hardcoding that value.

3. Next, the method returns `true` after the new scene is loaded and the `timeScale` property has been reset.

4. Finally, our update to `GameBehavior` calls the overloaded `RestartLevel()` method and passes in 0 as the `sceneIndex`.

Overloaded methods are automatically detected by Visual Studio and are displayed by number, as shown here:

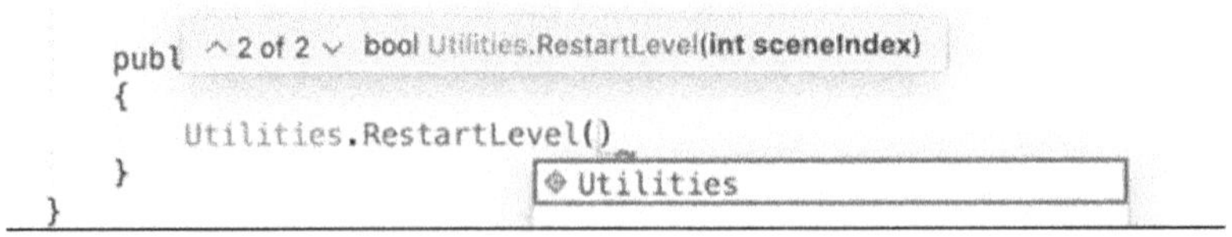

Figure 10.1: Multiple method overloads in Visual Studio

> **Note**
>
> To provide a complete view of the Unity Editor, all our screenshots are taken in full-screen mode. For color versions of all book images, use this link: `https://packt.link/gbp/9781805808718`.

The functionality in the `RestartLevel()` method is now much more customizable and can account for additional situations you may need later. In this case, it is restarting the game from any scene we choose.

Method overloading is not limited to static methods—this was just in line with the previous example. Any method can be overloaded as long as its signature differs from the original.

Next up, we're going to cover two additional topics that can take your method game to a whole new level—ref and out parameters.

ref parameters

When we talked about classes and structs back in *Chapter 5*, we discovered that not all objects are passed the same way: value types are passed by copy, while reference types are passed by reference. However, we didn't go over how objects, or values, are used when they're passed into methods as parameter arguments.

By default, all arguments are passed by value, meaning that a variable passed into a method will not be affected by any changes that are made to its value inside the method body. This protects us from making unwanted changes to existing variables when we use them as method parameters. While this works for most cases, there are situations where you'll want to pass in a method argument by reference so that it can be updated and have that change reflected in the original variable. Prefixing a parameter declaration with either the ref or out keyword will mark the argument as a reference.

Here are a few key points to keep in mind about using the ref keyword:

- Arguments have to be initialized before being passed into a method.
- You don't need to initialize or assign the reference parameter value before ending the method.
- Properties with get or set accessors can't be used as ref or out arguments.

Let's create a method to update PlayerDeaths to see the method arguments that are being passed by reference in action.

Open up Utilities and add the following code:

```
public static class Utilities
{
    public static int PlayerDeaths = 0;
    // 1
    public static string UpdateDeathCount(ref int countReference)
    {
        // 2
        countReference += 1;
        return "Next time you'll be at number " + countReference;
    }
    public static void RestartLevel()
    {
        // ... No changes needed ...
    }
    public static bool RestartLevel(int sceneIndex)
    {
        // 3
        Debug.Log("Player deaths: " + PlayerDeaths);
        string message = UpdateDeathCount(ref PlayerDeaths);
        Debug.Log("Player deaths: " + PlayerDeaths);
        Debug.Log(message);
        SceneManager.LoadScene(sceneIndex);
        Time.timeScale = 1.0f;
        return true;
    }
}
```

Let's break down the code:

1. First, we declare a new static method named `UpdateDeathCount()` that returns a string and takes in an `int` passed by reference.

2. Then, it updates the reference parameter directly, incrementing its value by 1 and returning a string that contains the new value.

3. Finally, it debugs the `PlayerDeaths` variable in `RestartLevel(int sceneIndex)` before and after it is passed by reference to `UpdateDeathCount()`. We also store a reference to the returned string value from `UpdateDeathCount()` in the `message` variable and print it out.

If you play the game and lose, the debug log will show that `PlayerDeaths` has increased by 1 inside `UpdateDeathCount()` because it was passed by reference and not by value:

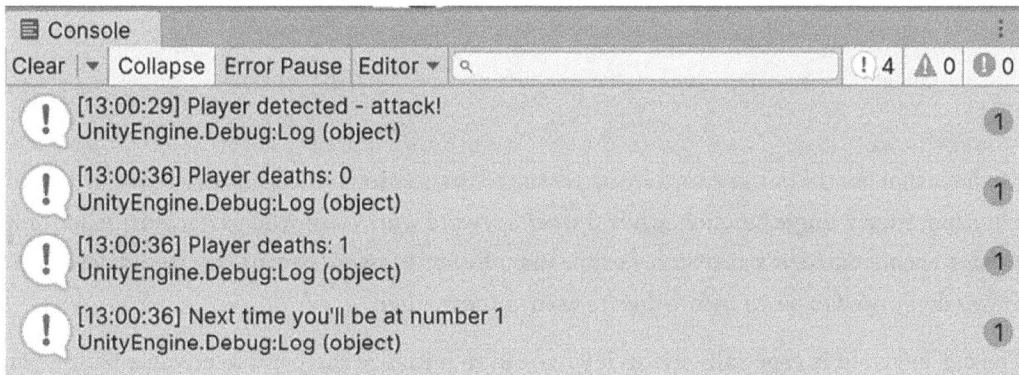

Figure 10.2: Example output from ref parameters

For clarity, we could have updated the player death count without a `ref` parameter because `UpdateDeathCount()` and `PlayerDeaths` are in the same script. However, if this wasn't the case and you wanted the same functionality, `ref` parameters are super useful.

We're using the `ref` keyword in this situation for the sake of our example, but we could have also updated `PlayerDeaths` directly inside `UpdateDeathCount()` or added logic inside `RestartLevel()` to only fire `UpdateDeathCount()` when the restart was due to a loss.

Now that we know how to use a `ref` parameter in our project, let's take a look at the out parameter and how it serves a slightly different purpose.

out parameters

The out keyword does the same job as ref but with different rules, which means they're similar tools but they're not interchangeable—each has its own use cases:

- Arguments do not need to be initialized before being passed into a method.

- The out parameter *must* be initialized or assigned in the calling method before it's returned.

For instance, we could have replaced the ref keyword with the out keyword in UpdateDeathCount() as long as we initialized or assigned the countReference parameter before returning from the method:

```
public static string UpdateDeathCount(out int countReference)
{
    countReference += 1;
    return "Next time you'll be at number " + countReference;
}
```

Methods that use the out keyword are better suited to situations where you need to return multiple values from a single function, while the ref keyword works best when a reference value only needs to be modified. It's also more flexible than the ref keyword because the initial parameter values don't need to be set before they're used in the method.

The out keyword is especially useful if you need to initialize the parameter value before you change it. Even though these keywords are a little more esoteric, it's important to have them in your C# toolkit for special use cases.

With these new method features under our belts, it's time to revisit the big one: **object-oriented programming (OOP)**. There's so much to this topic that it's impossible to cover everything in a chapter or two, but there are a few key tools that will come in handy early on in your development career. OOP is one of those topics that you're encouraged to follow up on after finishing this book.

Intermediate OOP

An object-oriented mindset is crucial to creating meaningful applications and understanding how the C# language works behind the scenes. The tricky part is that classes and structs by themselves aren't the end of the line when it comes to OOP and designing your objects. They'll always be the building blocks of your code, but classes are limited to single inheritance, meaning they can only ever have one parent or superclass, and structs can't inherit at all.

So, the question you should be asking yourself right about now is simple: *"How can I create objects from the same template and have them perform different actions based on a specific scenario?"*

To answer this question, we'll be learning about interfaces, abstract classes, and class extensions.

Interfaces

One of the ways to gather groups of functionality together is through interfaces. Like classes, interfaces are blueprints for data and behaviors, but with one important difference: they can't have any actual implementation logic or stored values.

Instead, they contain the implementation blueprint, and it's up to the adopting class or struct to fill in the public values and methods outlined in the interface. Any adopting classes *must* implement the interface or the compiler will complain, which forces consistency across any classes that use the interface.

You can use interfaces with both classes and structs, and there's no upper limit to how many interfaces a single class or struct can adopt.

Remember, a single class can only have one parent class, and structs can't subclass at all. Breaking out functionality into interfaces lets you build up classes like building blocks, picking and choosing how you want them to behave like food from a menu. This would be a huge efficiency boost to your code base, breaking away from long, messy subclassing hierarchies.

For example, what if we wanted our enemies to be able to shoot back at our player when they're in close range? We could create a parent class that both the player and enemy could derive from, which would base them both on the same blueprint. The problem with that approach, however, is that enemies and players won't necessarily share the same behaviors and data.

The more efficient way to handle this would be to define an interface with a blueprint for what shootable objects need to do, and then have both the enemy and player adopt it. That way, they have the freedom to be separate and exhibit different behaviors while still sharing common functionality.

Refactoring the shooting mechanic into an interface is a challenge I'll leave to you, but we still need to know how to create and adopt interfaces in code. For this example, we'll create an interface that all manager scripts might need to implement to share a common structure.

Create a new C# script in the `Scripts` folder, name it `IManager`, and update its code as follows:

```
using System.Collections;
using System.Collections.Generic;
using UnityEngine;
// 1
public interface IManager
{
    // 2
    string State { get; set; }
    // 3
    void Initialize();
}
```

Let's break down the code:

1. First, we declare a public interface called `IManager` using the `interface` keyword.

2. Then, we add a string variable to `IManager` named `State` with `get` and `set` accessors to hold the current state of the adopting class.

    All interface properties need at least a get accessor to compile but can have both get and set accessors if necessary.

3. Finally, we define a method named `Initialize()` with no return type for the adopting class to implement. However, you could absolutely have a return type for a method inside an interface; there's no rule against it.

You've now created a blueprint for all manager scripts, meaning that each manager script adopting this interface needs to have a `State` property and an `Initialize()`method. Your next task is to use the `IManager` interface, which means it needs to be adopted by another class.

To keep things simple, let's have the game manager adopt our new interface and implement its blueprint.

Update `GameBehavior` with the following code:

```
// 1
public class GameBehavior : MonoBehaviour, IManager
{
    // 2
    private string _state;
```

```
    // 3
    public string State
    {
        get { return _state; }
        set { _state = value; }
    }
    // ... No other changes needed ...
    void Start()
    {
        ItemText.text += _itemsCollected;
        HealthText.text += _playerHP;
        // 4
        Initialize();
    }
    // 5
    public void Initialize()
    {
        _state = "Game Manager initialized..";
        Debug.Log(_state);
    }
}
```

Let's break down the code:

1.   First, we declare that GameBehavior adopts the IManager interface using a comma and
     its name, just like with subclassing.

2.   Then, we add a private variable that we'll use to back the public State value we have to
     implement from IManager.

3.   Next, we add the public State variable declared in IManager and use _state as its private
     backing variable.

4.   After that, we call the Initialize() method inside the Start() method.

5.   Finally, we declare the Initialize() method declared in IManager with an implemen-
     tation that sets and prints out the public State variable.

With this, we specified that `GameBehavior` adopts the `IManager` interface and implemented its `State` and `Initialize()` members, as shown here:

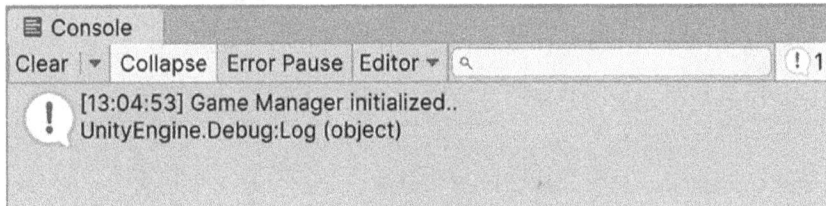

Figure 10.3: Example output from an interface

🔍 **Quick tip**: Need to see a high-resolution version of this image? Open this book in the next-gen Packt Reader or view it in the PDF/ePub copy.

📖 **The next-gen Packt Reader** and a **free PDF/ePub copy** of this book are included with your purchase. Scan the QR code OR visit `https://packtpub.com/unlock`, then use the search bar to find this book by name. Double-check the edition shown to make sure you get the right one.

The great thing about this is that the implementation is specific to `GameBehavior`; if we had another manager class, we could do the same thing but with different logic. Just for fun, let's set up a new manager script to test this out:

1. In the `Scripts` folder, create a new C# script and name it `DataManager`.

2. Update the new script with the following code and adopt the `IManager` interface:

```
using System.Collections;
using System.Collections.Generic;
using UnityEngine;
public class DataManager : MonoBehaviour, IManage
```

```
    {
        private string _state;
        public string State
        {
            get { return _state; }
            set { _state = value; }
        }
        void Start()
        {
            Initialize();
        }
        public void Initialize()
        {
            _state = "Data Manager initialized..";
            Debug.Log(_state);
        }
    }
```

3. Drag and drop the new script onto the Game_Manager object in the **Hierarchy** panel.

4. Click **Play** and scroll to the beginning of the console logs, as these should be the first messages you see:

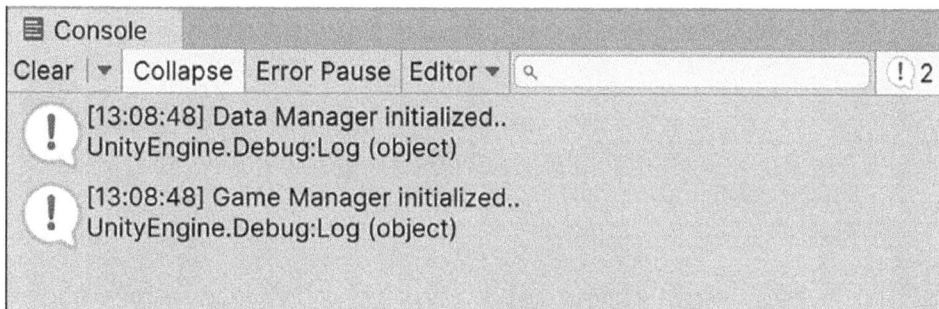

Figure 10.4: Output from Data Manager initialization

While we could have done all of this with subclassing, we'd be limited to one parent class for all our managers. Instead, we have the option of adding new interfaces if we choose. We'll revisit this new manager script in *Chapter 12*. This opens up a whole world of possibilities for building classes, one of which is a new OOP concept called abstract classes.

Abstract classes

Another approach to separating common blueprints and sharing them between objects is the **abstract class**. Like interfaces, abstract classes cannot include any implementation logic for their methods; they can, however, store variable values. This is one of the key differences from interfaces—in situations where you might need to set initial values, an abstract class would be the way to go.

Any class that subclasses from an abstract class must fully implement all variables and methods marked with the abstract keyword. They can be particularly useful in situations where you want to use class inheritance without having to write out a base class's default implementation.

For example, let's take the IManager interface functionality we just wrote and see what it would look like as an abstract base class. *Don't change any of the actual code in our project*, as we still want to keep things working as they are:

```
// 1
public abstract class BaseManager
{
    // 2
    protected string _state = "Manager is not initialized...";
    public abstract string State { get; set; }
    // 3
    public abstract void Initialize();
}
```

Let's break down the code:

1. First, we declare a new class named BaseManager using the abstract keyword.

2. Then, we create two variables:

    •   A protected string named _state that can only be accessed by classes that inherit from BaseManager. We've also set an initial value for _state, something we couldn't do in our interface.

    •   We also have an abstract string named State with get and set accessors to be implemented by the subclass.

3. Finally, we add Initialize() as an abstract method, also to be implemented in the subclass.

In doing so, we have created an abstract class that does the same thing as an interface. In this setup, BaseManager has the same blueprint as IManager, allowing any subclasses to define their implementations of state and Initialize() using the override keyword:

```
// 1
public class CombatManager: BaseManager
{
    // 2
    public override string State
    {
        get { return _state; }
        set { _state = value; }
    }
    // 3
    public override void Initialize()
    {
        _state = "Combat Manager initialized..";
        Debug.Log(_state);
    }
}
```

If we break down the preceding code, we can see the following:

1. First, we declare a new class called CombatManager that inherits from the BaseManager abstract class.
2. Then, we add the State variable implementation from BaseManager using the override keyword.
3. Finally, we add the Initialize() method implementation from BaseManager using the override keyword again and set the protected _state variable.

Even though this is only the tip of the iceberg of interfaces and abstract classes, their possibilities should be jumping around in your programming brain. Interfaces will allow you to spread and share pieces of functionality between unrelated objects, leading to a building block-like assembly when it comes to your code.

Abstract classes, on the other hand, will let you keep the single-inheritance structure of OOP while separating a class's implementation from its blueprint. These approaches can even be mixed and matched, as abstract classes can adopt interfaces just like non-abstract ones.

As always with complicated topics, your first stop should be the documentation. Check it out at `https://docs.microsoft.com/en-us/dotnet/csharp/language-reference/keywords/abstract` and `https://docs.microsoft.com/en-us/dotnet/csharp/language-reference/keywords/interface`.

You won't always need to build a new class from scratch. Sometimes, it's enough to add the feature or logic you want to an existing class, which is called a class extension.

Class extensions

Let's step away from custom objects and talk about how we can extend existing classes so that they fit our own needs. The idea behind class extensions is simple: take an existing built-in C# class and add on any functionality that you need it to have. Since we don't have access to the underlying code that C# is built on, this is the only way to get custom behavior out of objects the language already has.

Classes can only be modified with methods—no variables or other entities are allowed. However limiting this might be, it makes the syntax consistent:

```
public static returnType MethodName(this ExtendingClass localVal) {}
```

Extension methods are declared using the same syntax as normal methods, but with a few caveats:

- All extension methods need to be marked as static.
- The first parameter needs to be the `this` keyword, followed by the name of the class we want to extend and a local variable name:
    - This special parameter lets the compiler identify the method as an extension, and gives us a local reference for the existing class.
    - Any class methods and properties can then be accessed through the local variable.
- It's mandatory to store extension methods inside a static class, which, in turn, is stored inside its namespace. This allows you to control what other scripts have access to your custom functionality.

Your next task is to put class extensions into practice by adding a new method to the built-in C# `String` class. Let's take a look at extensions in practice by adding a custom method to the `String` class.

Create a new C# script in the Scripts folder, name it CustomExtensions, and add the following code:

```
using System.Collections;
using System.Collections.Generic;
using UnityEngine;
// 1
namespace CustomExtensions
{
    // 2
    public static class StringExtensions
    {
        // 3
        public static void FancyDebug(this string str)
        {
            // 4
            Debug.LogFormat("This string contains {0} characters.",
                str.Length);
        }
    }
}
```

Let's break down the code:

1. First, we declare a namespace named CustomExtensions to hold all the extension classes and methods.

2. Then, we declare a static class named StringExtensions for organizational purposes; each group of class extensions should follow this setup.

3. Next, we add a static method named FancyDebug() to the StringExtensions class:

    a. The first parameter, this string str, marks the method as an extension.

    b. The str parameter will hold a reference to the actual text value that FancyDebug() is called from; we can operate on str inside the method body as a stand-in for all string literals.

4. Finally, a debug message is printed out whenever FancyDebug() is executed, using str. Length to reference the string variable that the method is called on.

In practice, this will let you add any of your own custom functionality to existing C# classes or even your own custom ones. Now that the extension is part of the String class, let's test it out. To use our new custom string method, we'll need to include it in whatever class we want to have access to it.

Open up GameBehavior and update its contents to match the following code:

```
using System.Collections;
using System.Collections.Generic;
using UnityEngine;
// 1
using CustomExtensions;

public class GameBehavior : MonoBehaviour, IManager
{
    // ... No variable changes needed ...
    void Start()
    {
        // ... No changes needed ...
    }
    public void Initialize()
    {
        _state = "Game Manager initialized..";

        // 2
        _state.FancyDebug();
        Debug.Log(_state);
    }
}
```

Let's break down the code:

1. First, we add the CustomExtensions namespace with a using directive at the top of the file.
2. Then, we call FancyDebug() on the _state string variable with dot notation inside Initialize() to print out the number of individual characters its value has.

Extending the entire string class with FancyDebug() means that any string variable has access to it. Since the first extension method parameter has a reference to whatever string value FancyDebug() is called on, its length will be printed out properly, as shown here:

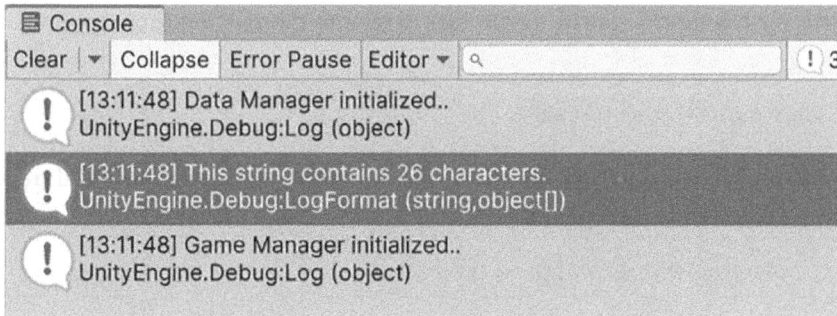

Figure 10.5: Example output from a custom extension

A custom class can also be extended using the same syntax, but it's more common to just add extra functionality directly into the class if it's one you control.

The last topic we'll explore in this chapter is *namespaces*, which we briefly learned about earlier in the book. In the next section, you'll learn about the larger role that namespaces play in C# and how to create a type alias.

Namespace conflicts and type aliasing

As your applications get more complicated, you'll start to section off your code into **namespaces**, ensuring that you have control over where and when it's accessed. You'll also use third-party software tools and plugins to save on time implementing a feature from the ground up that someone else has already made available. Both of these scenarios show that you're progressing with your programming knowledge, but they can also cause namespace conflicts.

Namespace conflicts happen when there are two or more classes or types with the same name, which happens more often than you'd think.

Good naming habits tend to produce similar results, and before you know it, you're dealing with multiple classes named Error or Extension, and Visual Studio is throwing out errors. Luckily, C# has a simple solution to these situations: **type aliasing**.

Defining a **type alias** lets you explicitly choose which conflicting type you want to use in a given class, or create a more user-friendly name for a long-winded existing one. Type aliases are added at the top of the class file with a using directive, followed by the alias name and the assigned type:

```
using AliasName = type;
```

For instance, if we wanted to create a type alias to refer to the existing Int64 type, we could say the following:

```
using CustomInt = System.Int64;
```

Now that CustomInt is a type alias for the System.Int64 type, the compiler will treat it as an Int64, letting us use it like any other type:

```
public CustomInt PlayerHealth = 100;
```

You can use type aliasing with your custom types, or existing ones with the same syntax, as long as they're declared at the top of script files with the other using directives.

For more information on the using keyword and type aliasing, check out the C# documentation at https://docs.microsoft.com/en-us/dotnet/csharp/language-reference/keywords/using-directive.

Summary

With new modifiers, method overloading, class extensions, and object-oriented skills under our belts, we are only one step away from the end of our C# journey. Remember, these intermediate topics are intended to get you thinking about more complex applications of the knowledge you've been gathering throughout this book; don't think that what you've learned in this chapter is all that there is to know about these concepts. Take it as a starting point and continue from there.

In the next chapter, we'll discuss the basics of generic programming, get a little hands-on experience with delegates and events, and wrap up with an overview of exception handling.

Pop quiz: Leveling up

a.   Which keyword would mark a variable as unmodifiable but requires an initial value?

b.   How would you create an overloaded version of a base method?

c.   What is the main difference between classes and interfaces?

d.   How would you solve a namespace conflict in one of your classes?

Don't forget to check your answers against mine in the *Pop Quiz Answers* appendix to see how you did!

Subscribe to Game Dev Assembly Newsletter!

We are excited to introduce **Game Dev Assembly**, our brand-new newsletter dedicated to everything game development. Whether you're a programmer, designer, artist, animator, or studio lead, you'll get exclusive insights, industry trends, and expert tips to help you build better games and grow your skills. Sign up today and become part of a growing community of creators, innovators, and game changers: `https://packt.link/gamedev-newsletter`

Scan the QR code to join instantly!

Unlock this book's exclusive benefits now

UNLOCK NOW

Scan this QR code or go to `https://packtpub.com/unlock`, then search this book by name.

Note: Keep your purchase invoice ready before you start.

11

Specialized Collection Types and LINQ

In *Chapter 10*, we revisited variables, types, and classes to see what they had to offer beyond the basic features introduced at the beginning of the book. In this chapter, we'll take a closer look at new collection types and learn about their intermediate-level capabilities and how to filter, order, and transform data with LINQ queries.

Remember, being a good programmer isn't about memorizing code; it's about choosing the right tool for the right job. Each of the new collection types in this chapter has a specific purpose. For most scenarios where you need a collection of data, a list or array works just fine. However, when you need temporary storage or control over the order of collection elements, or more specifically, the order in which they are accessed, look to stacks and queues. When you need to perform operations that depend on every element in a collection to be unique, meaning not duplicated, look to HashSets. Before you get started with the code, let's lay out the topics you'll be learning:

- Introducing stacks
- Peeking and popping elements
- Working with queues
- Adding, removing, and peeking elements
- Using HashSets
- Performing operations
- Filtering data with LINQ queries

Introducing stacks

At its most basic level, a **stack** is a collection of elements of the same specified type (or a special-ized array if that helps you visualize them better). The length of a stack is variable, meaning it can change depending on how many elements it's holding. The important difference between a stack and a list or array is how the elements are stored. While lists or arrays store elements by index, stacks follow the **last-in-first-out** (**LIFO**) model, meaning the last element in the stack is the first accessible element.

This is useful when you want to access elements in reverse order. You should note that stacks can store null and duplicate values. A helpful analogy is a stack of plates—the last plate you put on the stack is the first one you can easily get to (or a plastic cup dispenser you fill from the top and take a cup from the bottom). Once it's removed, the next-to-last plate you stacked is accessible, and so on.

All the collection types in this chapter are a part of the System.Collections.Generic namespace, meaning you need to add the following code to the top of any file that you want to use them in:

```
using System.Collections.Generic;
```

Now that you know what you're about to work with, let's look at the basic syntax for declaring stacks.

A stack variable declaration needs to meet the following requirements:

- The Stack keyword, its element type between left and right arrow characters, and a unique name
- The new keyword to initialize the stack in memory, followed by the Stack keyword and element type between arrow characters
- A pair of parentheses capped off by a semicolon

In blueprint form, it looks like this:

```
Stack<elementType> name = new Stack<elementType>();
```

Unlike the other collection types you've worked with, stacks can't be initialized with elements when they're created. Instead, all elements must be added after the stack is created.

C# supports a non-generic version of the stack type that doesn't require you to define the type of element in the stack:

```
Stack myStack = new Stack();
```

However, this is less safe and more costly than using the preceding generic version, so the preceding generic version is recommended. You can read more about Microsoft's recommendation at https://github.com/dotnet/platform-compat/blob/master/docs/DE0006.md.

Your next task is to create a stack of your own and get hands-on experience working with its class methods. But before you do that, let's create a Loot struct to make things more interesting:

1. In the Scripts folder, create a new C# script named Loot.

2. Update Loot.cs to match the following code:

```
using System.Collections;
using System.Collections.Generic;
using UnityEngine;

// 1
public struct Loot
{
    // 2
    public string Name;
    public int Rarity;

    // 3
    public Loot(string name, int rarity)
    {
        this.Name = name;
        this.Rarity = rarity;
    }
}
```

Breaking the Loot struct down, it goes as follows:

1. First, we declare a public struct.

2. Then, we add two public variables, one for the name and one for the rarity of type string and int, respectively.

3. Finally, we add a constructor that takes in string and int and assigns those values to the struct properties.

To test this out, let's modify the existing item collection logic in *Hero Born* by using a stack to store possible loot that can be collected. A stack works nicely here because we won't have to worry about supplying indexes to get loot items; we can just get the last one added every time:

1. Open `GameBehavior.cs` and add in a new namespace (so we can access the `Stack` type) and a stack variable named `LootStack`:

```
// 1
using System.Collections.Generic;
// 2
public Stack<Loot> LootStack = new Stack<Loot>();
```

2. Update the `Initialize()` method with the following code to add new items to the stack:

```
public void Initialize()
{
    _state = "Game Manager initialized..";
    _state.FancyDebug();
    Debug.Log(_state);
    // 3
    LootStack.Push(new Loot("Sword of Doom", 5));
    LootStack.Push(new Loot("HP Boost", 1));
    LootStack.Push(new Loot("Golden Key", 3));
    LootStack.Push(new Loot("Pair of Winged Boots", 2));
    LootStack.Push(new Loot("Mythril Bracer", 4));
}
```

3. Add a new method to the bottom of the script to print out the stack information:

```
// 4
public void PrintLootReport()
{
    Debug.LogFormat("There are {0} random loot items waiting
        for you!", LootStack.Count);
}
```

4. Open `ItemBehavior.cs` and call `PrintLootReport()` from the `GameManager` instance:

```
void OnCollisionEnter(Collision collision)
{
    if(collision.gameObject.name == "Player")
```

```
        {
                Destroy(this.transform.parent.gameObject);
                Debug.Log("Item collected!");
                GameManager.Items += 1;

                // 4
                GameManager.PrintLootReport();
        }
}
```

Breaking this down, it does the following:

1. We create an empty stack with elements of type string to hold the loot items we'll add next.
2. We use the Push() method to add Loot objects to the stack (which are initialized with item names and rarities), increasing its size each time.
3. Next, we print out the stack count whenever the PrintLootReport() method is called.
4. Finally, we call PrintLootReport() inside OnCollisionEnter every time an item is collected by the player.

Now, hit **Play** in Unity, collect an item prefab, and look at the new Loot report that's printed out:

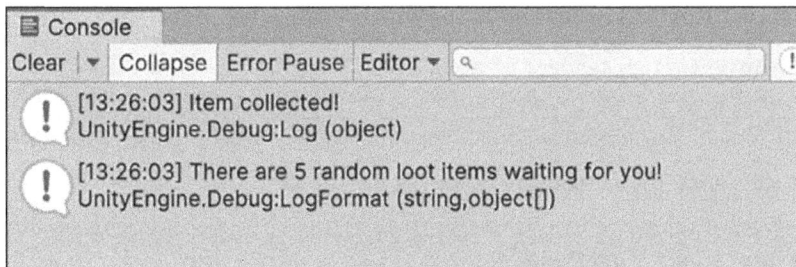

Figure 11.1: Output from using stacks

> **Note**
>
> To provide a complete view of the Unity editor, all our screenshots are taken in full-screen mode. For color versions of all the images in the book, use this link: https://packt.link/gbp/9781805808718.

Since we haven't actually subtracted the item from the stack when we collect the in-game item, the count will always be 5. But our next task will do just that with the Pop() and Peek() methods that already exist in the Stack class.

Popping and peeking

We've already talked about how stacks store elements using the LIFO method. Now, we need to look at how elements are accessed in a familiar but different collection type—by peeking and popping:

- The Peek() method returns the next item on the stack without removing it, letting you "peek" at it without changing anything
- The Pop() method returns and removes the next item on the stack, essentially "popping" it off and handing it to you

Both methods can be used by themselves or together, depending on what you need. You'll get hands-on experience with both methods in the following section.

Your next task is to grab the last item added to LootStack. In our example, the last element is determined programmatically in the Initialize() method, but you could always programmatically randomize the order in which the loot items were added to the stack in Initialize(). Either way, update PrintLootReport() in GameBehavior with the following code:

```
public void PrintLootReport()
{
    // 1
    var currentItem = LootStack.Pop();
    // 2
    var nextItem = LootStack.Peek();
    // 3
    Debug.LogFormat("You got a {0}! You've got a good chance of finding
        a {1} next!", currentItem.Name, nextItem.Name);
    Debug.LogFormat("There are {0} random loot items waiting for you!",
        LootStack.Count);
}
```

Here's what's going on:

1. We call Pop() on LootStack, remove the next item on the stack and store it. Remember, stack elements are ordered by the LIFO model.

2. Then, we call Peek() on LootStack and store the next item on the stack without removing it.

3. Finally, we add a new debug log to print out the item that was popped off and the next item on the stack.

You can see from the console that a *Mythril Bracer*, the last item added to the stack, was popped off first, followed by a *Pair of Winged Boots*, which was peeked at but not removed. You can also see that LootStack has four remaining elements that can be accessed:

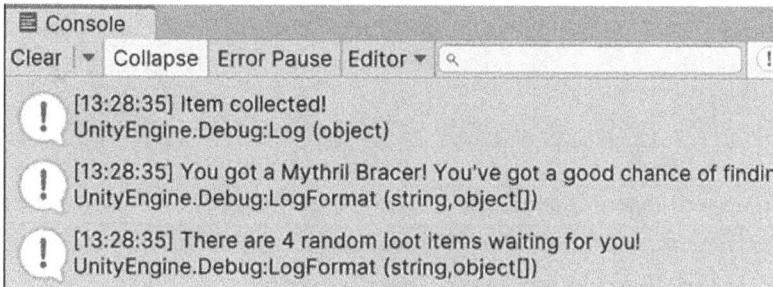

Figure 11.2: Output from popping and peeking on a stack

Our player can now pick up loot items in the reverse order that they were added to the stack. For instance, the first item picked up will always be a *Mythril Bracer*, followed by a *Pair of Winged Boots*, then a *Golden Key*, and so on.

Now that you know how to create, add, and query elements from a stack, we can move on to some common methods that you have access to through the stack class.

Common methods in a stack class

Each of the methods in this section is for example purposes only; they are not included in our game as we don't need the functionality:

1. First, you can use the Clear() method to empty out or delete the entire contents of a stack:

```
// Empty the stack and reverting the count to 0
LootStack.Clear();
```

2. If you want to know whether an element exists in your stack, use the Contains() method and specify the element you're looking for:

```
// Returns true for "Golden Key" item
var item = new Loot("Golden Key", 3);
var itemFound = LootStack.Contains(item);
```

3. If you need to copy the elements of a stack to an array, the CopyTo( ) method will let you specify the destination and the starting index for the copy operation. This feature is helpful when you need to insert stack elements at a specific place in an array. Note that the array you want to copy the stack elements to must already exist:

```
// Creates a new array of the same length as LootStack
Loot[] CopiedLoot = new Loot[5];
/*
Copies the LootStack elements into the new CopiedLoot array at index
0. The index parameter can be set to any index where you want the
copied elements to be stored
*/
LootStack.CopyTo(CopiedLoot, 0);
```

4. If you need to convert a stack into an array, simply use the ToArray( ) method. This conversion creates a new array out of your stack, which is different than the CopyTo( ) method, which copies the stack elements to an existing array:

```
// Copies an existing stack to a new array
LootStack.ToArray();
```

You can find the entire list of stack methods in the C# documentation at https://docs.microsoft.com/dotnet/api/system.collections.generic.stack-1?view=netcore-3.1.

That wraps up our introduction to stacks, but we're going to talk about its cousin, the queue, in the following section.

Working with queues

Like stacks, queues are collections of elements or objects of the same type. The length of any queue is variable, just like a stack, meaning its size changes as elements are added or removed.

However, queues follow the **first-in-first-out (FIFO)** model, meaning the first element in the queue is the first accessible element. You should note that queues can store null and duplicate values but can't be initialized with elements when they're created. The code in this section is for example purposes only and is not included in our game.

A queue variable declaration needs to have the following:

*   The Queue keyword, its element type between left and right arrow characters, and a unique name

- The new keyword to initialize the queue in memory, followed by the Queue keyword and element type between arrow characters

- A pair of parentheses capped off by a semicolon

In blueprint form, a queue looks as follows:

```
Queue<elementType> name = new Queue<elementType>();
```

C# supports a non-generic version of the queue type that doesn't require you to define the type of element it stores:

```
Queue myQueue = new Queue();
```

However, this is less safe and more costly than using the preceding generic version. You can read more about Microsoft's recommendation at https://github.com/dotnet/platform-compat/blob/master/docs/DE0006.md.

An empty queue all by itself isn't all that useful; you want to be able to add, remove, and peek at its elements whenever you need, which is the topic of the following section.

Adding, removing, and peeking

Since the LootStack variable in the previous sections could easily be a queue, we'll keep the following code out of our game scripts for efficiency. However, feel free to explore the differences, or similarities, between these classes in your own code:

- To create a queue of string elements, use the following:

```
// Creates a new Queue of string values.
Queue<string> activePlayers = new Queue<string>();
```

- To add elements to the queue, call the Enqueue() method with the element you want to add:

```
// Adds string values to the end of the Queue.
activePlayers.Enqueue("Harrison");
activePlayers.Enqueue("Alex");
activePlayers.Enqueue("Haley");
```

- To see the first element in the queue without removing it, use the Peek() method:

```
// Returns the first element in the Queue without removing it.
var firstPlayer = activePlayers.Peek();
```

- To return and remove the first element in the queue, use the Dequeue() method:

```
// Returns and removes the first element in the Queue.
var firstPlayer = activePlayers.Dequeue();
```

Now that you know how to work with the basic features of a queue, feel free to explore the more intermediate and advanced methods that the queue class offers.

Queues and stacks share almost the exact same features, so we won't go over them a second time. You can find a complete list of methods and properties in the C# documentation at https:// docs.microsoft.com/dotnet/api/system.collections.generic.queue-1?view=netcore-3.1.

Before closing out the chapter, let's look at the **HashSet** collection type and the mathematical operations it's uniquely suited for.

Using HashSets

The last collection type we'll get our hands on in this chapter is the HashSet. This collection is very different from any other collection type that we've come across: it cannot store duplicate values and is not sorted, meaning its elements are not ordered in any way. Think of HashSets as dictionaries with just keys, instead of key-value pairs.

They can perform set operations and element lookups extremely fast, which we'll explore at the end of this section, and are best suited to situations where the element order and uniqueness are a top priority.

A HashSet variable declaration needs to meet the following requirements:

- The HashSet keyword, its element type between left and right arrow characters, and a unique name
- The new keyword to initialize the HashSet in memory, followed by the HashSet keyword and element type between arrow characters
- A pair of parentheses capped off by a semicolon

In blueprint form, it looks as follows:

```
HashSet<elementType> name = new HashSet<elementType>();
```

Unlike stacks and queues, you can initialize a HashSet with default values when declaring the variable:

```
HashSet<string> people = new HashSet<string>();
// OR
HashSet<string> people = new HashSet<string>() { "Joe", "Joan", "Hank"};
```

To add elements, you can use the Add() method and specify the new element:

```
people.Add("Walter");
people.Add("Evelyn");
```

To remove an element, you can call Remove() and specify the element you want to delete from the HashSet:

```
people.Remove("Joe");
```

That's it for the easy stuff! This should start to feel pretty familiar at this point in your programming journey. set operations are where the HashSet collection really shines, which is the topic of the following section.

Performing set operations

set operations need two things: a calling collection object and a passed-in collection object.

The calling collection object is the HashSet you want to modify based on which operation is used, while the passed-in collection object is used for comparison by the set operation. We'll get into this in more detail in the following code, but first, let's go over the three main set operations that crop up in programming scenarios the most often.

In the following definitions, currentSet refers to the HashSet calling an operation method and specifiedSet refers to the passed-in HashSet method parameter. The modified HashSet is always the current set:

```
currentSet.Operation(specifiedSet);
```

There are three main operations that we'll be working with in the rest of this section:

- UnionWith adds the elements of the current and specified sets together.
- IntersectWith stores only the elements that are in both the current and specified sets.
- ExceptWith subtracts the elements of the specified set from the current set.

There are two more groups of set operations that deal with subset and superset computations, but these are targeted at specific use cases that are beyond the scope of this chapter. You can find all the relevant information for these methods at `https://docs.microsoft.com/dotnet/api/ system.collections.generic.hashset-1?view=netcore-3.1`.

Let's say we have two sets of player names—one for active players and one for inactive players:

```
HashSet<string> activePlayers = new HashSet<string>() {
    "Harrison", "Alex", "Haley"};
HashSet<string> inactivePlayers = new HashSet<string>() {
    "Kelsey", "Walter"};
```

We would use the `UnionWith()` operation to modify a set to include all the elements in both sets:

```
activePlayers.UnionWith(inactivePlayers);
/* activePlayers now stores "Harrison", "Alex", "Haley",
    "Kelsey", "Walter"*/
```

Now, let's say we have two different sets—one for active players and one for premium players:

```
HashSet<string> activePlayers = new HashSet<string>() {
    "Harrison", "Alex", "Haley"};
HashSet<string> premiumPlayers = new HashSet<string>() {
    "Haley", "Walter"};
```

We would use the `IntersectWith()` operation to find any active players that are also premium members:

```
activePlayers.IntersectWith(premiumPlayers);
// activePlayers now stores only "Haley"
```

What if we wanted to find all active players who are not premium members? We would do the opposite of what we did with the `IntersectWith()` operation by calling `ExceptWith`:

```
HashSet<string> activePlayers = new HashSet<string>() {
    "Harrison", "Alex", "Haley"};
HashSet<string> premiumPlayers = new HashSet<string>() { "Haley",
    "Walter"};
activePlayers.ExceptWith(premiumPlayers);
// activePlayers now stores "Harrison" and "Alex" but removed "Haley"
```

Notice that I'm using brand-new instances of the two example sets for each operation because the current set is modified after each operation is executed. If you keep using the same sets throughout, you will get different results.

Now that you've learned how to perform fast mathematical operations with HashSets, it's time to drive home what we've learned.

Intermediate collections roundup

Before you move on, let's drive home some key points from what we've just learned. Topics that don't always have a one-to-one relationship with the actual game prototype we're building need a little extra love sometimes. The one question I'm sure you're asking yourself at this point is: *why use any of these other collection types when I could just use lists for everything?* That's a perfectly valid question. The easy answer is that stacks, queues, and HashSets offer better performance than lists when applied in the correct circumstances. For example, when you need to store items in a specific order, and access them in a specific order, a stack would be more efficient than a list.

The more complicated answer is that using different collection types enforces how your code is allowed to interact with them and their elements. This is a mark of good code design, as it removes any ambiguity on how you're planning to use a collection. With lists everywhere, things get confusing when you don't remember what functions you're asking them to perform.

As with everything we've learned in this book, it's always best to use the right tool for the job at hand. More importantly, you need to have different tools available for that to be an option.

Querying data with LINQ

We've covered a few different ways to store elements, or sequences of values, in this chapter—the one thing we haven't talked about is how to get specific subsets of data back out. So far, our game's loot is stored in a Stack variable, and we can always pop off the next loot element in the order they are stored, but that doesn't help us when we want to filter down the stack (or any other collection type we've discussed in this book) to specific elements that fit predefined criteria.

For example, say we wanted to get a list of all the elements in the Loot stack with a rarity value of 3 or more. We could absolutely use a looping statement, but that leads to a lot of code and manual checks if we wanted to add more parameters to our filter.

Instead, C# has a specific set of features for querying data called **LINQ**, which stands for **Language Integrated Query**. LINQ is fast, efficient, and, most importantly, customizable for complex data filtering, which is what we'll explore throughout the rest of this chapter.

LINQ basics

The best way I've found to approach LINQ features is to think of what a query really is: a question. When you have a set of data you want to narrow down or filter, you're essentially asking the data a question like: *which elements meet criteria A and B while excluding criterion C?* One of the great things about LINQ is that the questions already exist in the form of extension methods, which can be chained together to form even more complex queries.

LINQ extension methods work on any collection type that implements IEnumerable<T>, which includes **lists**, **dictionaries**, **queues**, **stacks**, and **arrays**. You can find a complete list of extension methods at https://learn.microsoft.com/dotnet/api/system.linq.enumerable.

This might sound confusing without concrete examples, so let's take a look at the three-step process behind LINQ queries:

1. **First, you need a data source**—the collection type holding all the data elements you're trying to filter, order, or group.

2. **Second, you create a query**—the rules you want to apply to the data source you're working with. Continuing with our scores example, we'll use the Where extension method to filter our scores values by setting a predicate. A predicate is a rule or criterion that evaluates a certain condition.

3. **Third, you run the query**—the data source needs to be iterated over with a looping statement for the query commands to execute. This is called **deferred execution.**

Since we already have a stack of loot in our game, let's write a query that filters out the loot items based on their rarity level:

1. Open GameBehavior.cs and add a new using directive to the top of the script so we can access the LINQ extension methods:

   ```
   using System.Linq;
   ```

2. Add a new method after PrintLootReport and create a new query variable using the Where() extension method:

   ```
   public void FilterLoot()
   {
   ```

```
            var rareLoot = LootStack.Where();
    }
```

3. When adding the first parentheses after the Where() method, Visual Studio will let you
    know that the extension method is expecting a predicate argument in the form of a del-
    egate with a specific method signature (in this case, Func<Loot, bool>, as shown in
    Figure 11.3).

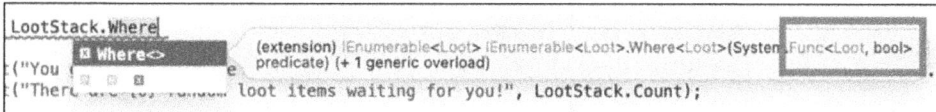

Figure 11.3: Predicate signature for the Where() extension method

> **Delegates**
>
> A delegate is a C# type that holds references to methods—just like integers
> hold numbers and strings hold text characters. Methods stored in a delegate
> have input parameters and return types just like the regular methods we've
> seen so far. The real magic of delegates is that they can be used as arguments
> in other methods, which is the case with LINQ queries. We'll talk about dele-
> gates in *Chapter 13*, but for now, just think of them as containers for methods.
>
> If you want to get a jump on delegates, you can find the documentation at
> https://learn.microsoft.com/dotnet/csharp/programming-guide/
> delegates.

4. Since we need a delegate, or method, that matches the predicate argument for the Where()
    extension method, let's create a new method underneath FilterLoot() that checks
    whether a loot item's rarity is greater than or equal to 3.

    The predicate method signature we need to match is Func<Loot, bool>, which means
    we need a method that takes in a Loot item as an argument and returns a Boolean. Each
    time the Where query iterates over a loot item, it'll evaluate the predicate condition and
    return true or false:

```
    public bool LootPredicate(Loot loot)
    {
        return loot.Rarity >= 3;
    }
```

5. Now that we have a method with the proper matching signature, we can pass `LootPredicate` into the `Where()` method and loop through each item with a debug log. Remember, the query won't take effect until you iterate through the data source:

```
public void FilterLoot()
{
    var rareLoot = LootStack.Where(LootPredicate);

    foreach (var item in rareLoot)
    {
        Debug.LogFormat("Rare item: {0}!", item.Name);
    }
}
```

6. Finally, call `FilterLoot()` at the bottom of the `Initialize` method and hit **Play**:

```
public void Initialize()
{
// ... No other changes needed ...
    FilterLoot();
}
```

Let's summarize what we've just put together:

1. We added the `System.Linq` namespace to access LINQ extension methods.
2. We created a method to hold our LINQ query and used the `Where()` extension method to filter out loot items that don't meet our criteria.
3. We created a delegate method that takes in a `Loot` item and checks whether its rarity level is greater than or equal to 3.
4. We used the delegate method as our LINQ predicate and looped through the loot stack to execute the query.

When you run the game, you'll see three items print out to the console instead of all five of our Loot items, because only three have a rarity value of 3 or higher. Notice the order of the items matches the order they were added to the stack:

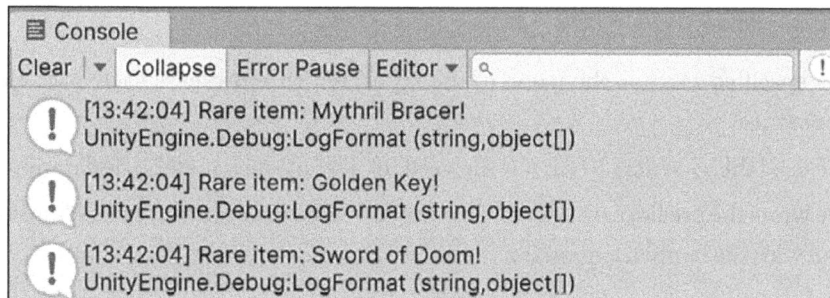

Figure 11.4: Console output of the LINQ filter query

That was a lot of new information and techniques to digest all at once, but there's a light at the end of the tunnel. While you could create delegates for each criterion, C# has a handy syntax to make the entire process easier to manage and read—**lambda expressions**.

Lambda expressions

Lambda expressions are anonymous functions, meaning they don't have or need a name but still have method arguments (inputs) and return types, which makes them perfect for LINQ queries.

Lambda expression syntax can be broken down into the following template:

```
input => expression
```

Like a local variable, the input name is up to you, and C# will infer the correct type from the LINQ extension method.

The => symbols in the preceding template are shorthand for *"go to the method expression."*

For our example, we can translate the entire LootPredicate() method into one line of code by using a lambda expression. The Where() method is looking for a Loot input type and a bool return type, so replace the predicate in FilterLoot() with a lambda:

```
public void FilterLoot()
{
    var rareLoot = LootStack.Where(item => item.Rarity >= 3);

    foreach (var item in rareLoot)
    {
        Debug.LogFormat("Rare item: {0}!", item.Name);
    }
}
```

Let's break this down:

1. We specified `item` as the name of the input, which represents each `Loot` element in `LootStack`.

2. We used the `=>` syntax to cut out the need for a whole new method declaration.

3. We wrote the predicate the exact same way as we did in `LootPredicate`; it's just all in one line with the lambda expression.

When you run the game again, you'll see the exact same output in the console, but the code is much cleaner, making it easier to chain multiple LINQ operations together, which we'll talk about next.

Chaining queries

In our game, filtering loot items using a single query is cool, but the real power of LINQ is in creating customized, complex queries by chaining extension methods together. Chaining queries is similar to writing a paragraph: each thought is separated by a period, but they are read in sequence.

Our next task is to add a second query onto our loot stack, this time specifying the order the rare items are in when they come out the other end of the LINQ statement. Update the `rareLoot` query inside the `FilterLoot()` method as follows:

```
public void FilterLoot()
    {
        // 1
        var rareLoot = LootStack
            .Where(item => item.Rarity >= 3)
            .OrderBy(item => item.Rarity);

        foreach (var item in rareLoot)
        {
                Debug.LogFormat("Rare item: {0}!", item.Name);
        }
    }
```

This is what we did for our first query:

1. We added a LINQ extension method to `LootStack`, this time using `OrderBy`.

2. We used a lambda expression to order the items by their rarity levels from lowest to highest.

    For clarity, it's best practice to move each LINQ query onto its own line, starting with the period character. This makes it much easier to read and understand what's going on with more complex queries.

3. Run the game again and you'll see that the order of our rare items has changed, now showing the *Golden Key* first because it has the lowest rarity we allowed in our filter, and moving up from there:

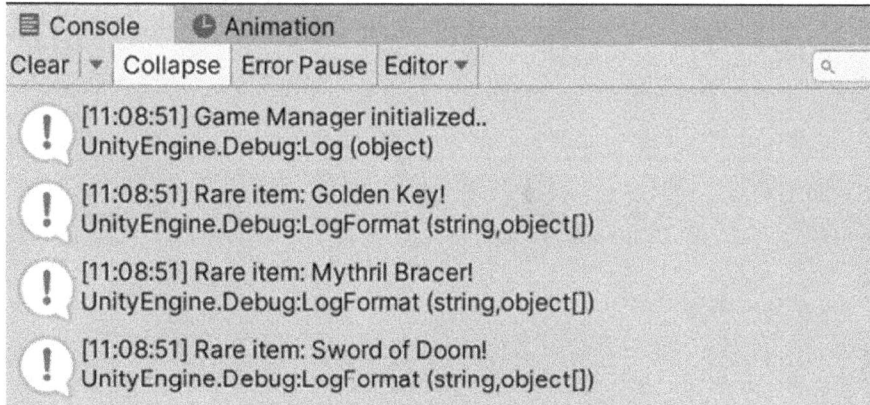

Figure 11.5: Console output of the LINQ order query

C# provides a huge variety of LINQ extension methods, so even though we're sticking to a relatively simple example for our loot items, this is the tip of the data management iceberg. There's no limit to how many queries you can chain together, so these can be as complicated as you want!

In the next section, we'll talk about one of the most powerful filtering options you have in your arsenal – transforming filtered data into new types right from LINQ queries.

Transforming data into new types

When your data gets more complicated, as it tends to do, there are scenarios where you may have a huge amount of information in each element that you're trying to query. Let's say you had a player database with player information stored in a list; you might not need every player property all the time, especially when the queried items have a massive amount of information in them. For example, after filtering out the players you don't want, you may only need each player's name, level, and high score, but not their email address or location. This is where the Select extension method comes in.

The Select method lets you transform the data from a LINQ query into a new type without stepping out of the LINQ query itself. You can not only execute your filtering and ordering criteria, but you can also specify exactly how the information comes out the other end.

In our example, each Loot item only has two properties—a name and a rarity. Let's update the current LINQ query to leave out the rarity value once we've established which items are rare and which are not.

In GameBehavior.cs, update the rareLoot query inside the FilterLoot() method by adding the Select extension method to create a new anonymous type:

```
var rareLoot = LootStack
.Where(item => item.Rarity >= 3)
.OrderBy(item => item.Rarity)
.Select(item => new
{
        item.Name
});
```

Anonymous types let you encapsulate properties into an object without having to explicitly define the object type, like a shortcut to creating a new object without the added declaration syntax. This is perfect for LINQ queries, since we don't need the extra headache of creating a new object class just to project our filtered data into a new containing type.

Let's break this new code down:

1. We added the Select LINQ extension method, which lets us specify which Loot properties we want to carry over into a new type.

2. We named the input item and used the => syntax again, but for the expression, we used the same syntax for creating an object with the new keyword and two curly brackets, { }.

3. Inside the expression brackets, we added the property we want to keep, item.name, which will leave out the rarity property in this new anonymous type we created.

4. The resulting anonymous type from our LINQ query will be Loot items that only have their name property.

When you run the game again, you won't see any difference in the console output, but if you try and access the rarity property on any of the items in the debug log, you'll get an error because the new anonymous type doesn't contain that property.

Again, transforming your queried elements into new, pared-down anonymous types makes dealing with large amounts of data much easier, less cumbersome, and, most importantly, faster, especially when your scenario doesn't need all the items' data.

Now, before we end the chapter, there's one more piece of LINQ that comes in handy depending on your preference for clean code—LINQ query comprehension syntax.

Simplifying with optional syntax

The C# language is always trying to make things more efficient and readable for its developers, and LINQ is no different. The LINQ query comprehension syntax was available back in C# 3.0, so it's been around for a while, but it's completely optional. Essentially, it's an even more shorthand option for writing LINQ queries without the need for lambda expressions. In my experience, this is the easiest to write and read when it comes to LINQ queries.

Our next task is to translate our rare loot query from the method and lambda code we wrote into the query comprehension syntax. In `GameBehavior.cs`, update the `rareLoot` query as follows:

```
// 1
var rareLoot = from item in LootStack
               // 2
               where item.Rarity >= 3
               // 3
               orderby item.Rarity
               // 4
               select item;
```

The query flow should look familiar, but let's break down the syntax differences:

1. First, we grabbed each input item from the `LootStack` data source. This syntax means we don't need to expressly write out an input in subsequent queries as we did with lambda expressions.

2. Second, we used the `where` query (lowercase) without the dot notation and just went straight for the expression predicate.

3. Third, we added another `orderby` query (lowercase again) without the dot notation and used the same expression from the previous example.

4. Finally, the `select` query (lowercase) must be added, followed by the resulting input at the end of all queries when you're using the LINQ query comprehension syntax.

If you're wondering how to mimic the transformation into an anonymous type on the last line, you can still do that with the following code update:

```
select new { item.name };
```

But there's a catch with this optional shorthand—only the most commonly used extension methods have counterparts in query comprehension syntax. However, you can use the optional shorthand and the lambda expression method together; they just require a little added syntax.

For example, if we wanted to skip the first rare item in our query (which doesn't have a comprehension syntax equivalent), we would add parentheses around our optional syntax and then continue as normal by adding dot notation extension methods:

```
var rareLoot = (from item in LootStack
                where item.Rarity >= 3
                orderby item.Rarity
                select new { item.Name })
                  .Skip(1);
```

Play the game one last time and you'll see that *Golden Key* was removed from our filtered rare loot, while everything still works the same:

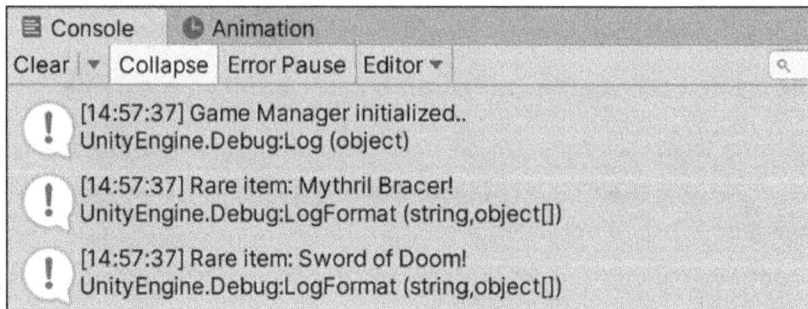

Figure 11.6: Console output from optional syntax query

LINQ is a powerful tool when you're managing information in games and applications, but it's a big area of possibility. Don't stop here in your exploration of data queries—take these basics and expand them to get the most out of your data!

Summary

Congratulations, you're almost at the finish line! In this chapter, you learned about three new collection types and how they can be used in different situations.

Stacks are great if you want to access your collection elements in the reverse order that they were added, queues are your ticket if you want to access your elements in sequential order, and both are ideal for temporary storage. The important difference between these collection types and lists or arrays is how they can be accessed with popping and peeking operations. Lastly, you learned about the almighty HashSet, its performance-based mathematical set operations, and LINQ queries for data manipulation. In situations where you need to work with unique values and perform additions, comparisons, or subtractions on large collections, these are key.

In the next chapter, you'll be taken a little deeper into the intermediate world of C# with delegates, generics, and more as you approach the end of this book. Even after all you've learned, the last page is still just the beginning of another journey.

Pop quiz: Intermediate collections

a. Which collection type stores its elements using the LIFO model?

b. Which method lets you query the next element in a stack without removing it?

c. Can stacks and queues store null values?

d. How would you subtract one HashSet from another?

Don't forget to check your answers against mine in the *Pop Quiz Answers* appendix to see how you did!

Subscribe to Game Dev Assembly Newsletter!

We are excited to introduce **Game Dev Assembly,** our brand-new newsletter dedicated to everything game development. Whether you're a programmer, designer, artist, animator, or studio lead, you'll get exclusive insights, industry trends, and expert tips to help you build better games and grow your skills. Sign up today and become part of a growing community of creators, innovators, and game changers: https://packt.link/gamedev-newsletter

Scan the QR code to join instantly!

Join our community on Discord

Join our community's Discord space for discussions with the authors and other readers: `https://`
`packt.link/gamedevelopment`.

12

Saving, Loading, and Serializing Data

Every game you've ever played works with data, whether it's your player stats, game progress, or online multiplayer scoreboards. Your favorite game also manages internal data, meaning the programmers used hardcoded information to build levels, keep track of enemy stats, and write helpful utilities. In other words, data is everywhere.

In this chapter, we're going to start with how both C# and Unity handle the filesystem on your computer, and move on to reading, writing, and serializing our game data. Our focus is on working with the three most common data formats you'll likely come across: text files, XML, and JSON.

By the end of this chapter, you'll have a foundational understanding of your computer's filesystem, data formats, and basic read-write functionality. This will be the foundation you build your game data on, creating a more enriching and engaging experience for your players. You'll also be in a good position to start thinking about what game data is important enough to save, and how your C# classes and objects will look in different data formats.

Along the way, we will cover the following topics:

- Introducing text, XML, and JSON formats
- Understanding the filesystem
- Working with different stream types
- Reading and writing game data
- Serializing objects

Introducing data formats

Data can take different forms in programming, but the three formats you should be familiar with at the beginning of your data journey are as follows:

- **Text**, which is what you're reading right now.
- **XML (Extensible Markup Language)**, which is a way of encoding document information so it's readable for you and a computer.
- **JSON (JavaScript Object Notation)**, which is a human-readable text format made up of attribute-value pairs and arrays.

Each of these data formats has its own strengths and drawbacks, as well as applications in programming. For instance, text is generally used to store simpler, non-hierarchical, or nested information. XML is better at storing information in a document format, while JSON has a more diverse range of capabilities, specifically with database information and server communication with applications.

You can find more information about XML at `https://www.xml.com` and JSON at `https://www.json.org`.

Data is a big topic in any programming language, so let's start off by breaking down what XML and JSON formats actually look like in the next two sections.

Breaking down XML

A typical XML file has a standardized format. Each element of the XML document has the following:

- An opening tag (`<element_name>`)
- A closing tag (`</element_name>`)
- Support for tag attributes (`<element_name attribute= "attribute_name"></element_name>`)

A basic file will start with the version and encoding being used, then the starting or root element, followed by a list of element items, and finally, the closing element. As a blueprint, it would look like this:

```
<?xml version="1.0" encoding="utf-8"?>
<root_element>
    <element_item>[Information goes here]</element_item>
    <element_item>[Information goes here]</element_item>
```

```
    <element_item>[Information goes here]</element_item>
</root_element>
```

> 💡 **Quick tip**: Enhance your coding experience with the **AI Code Explainer** and **Quick Copy** features. Open this book in the next-gen Packt Reader. Click the **Copy** button (**1**) to quickly copy code into your coding environment, or click the **Explain** button (**2**) to get the AI assistant to explain a block of code to you.

```
                                            Copy    Explain
function calculate(a, b) {
    return {sum: a + b};                     1        2
};
```

> 🔒 **The next-gen Packt Reader** is included for free with the purchase of this book. Scan the QR code OR go to `https://packtpub.com/unlock`, then use the search bar to find this book by name. Double-check the edition shown to make sure you get the right one.

XML data can also store more complex objects using child elements. For example, we'll be turning a list of weapons into XML using the Weapon class. Since each weapon has properties for its name and damage value, that will look like this:

```
// 1
<?xml version="1.0"?>
// 2
<ArrayOfWeapon>
    // 3
    <Weapon>
    // 4
```

```
        <name>Sword of Doom</name>
        <damage>100</damage>
    // 5
    </Weapon>
    <Weapon>
        <name>Butterfly knives</name>
        <damage>25</damage>
    </Weapon>
    <Weapon>
        <name>Brass Knuckles</name>
        <damage>15</damage>
    </Weapon>
// 6
</ArrayOfWeapon>
```

Let's break down the preceding example to make sure we've got it right:

1. The XML document starts with the version being used.

2. The root element is declared with an opening tag named ArrayOfWeapon, which will hold all our element items.

3. A Weapon item is created with an opening tag named Weapon.

4. Its child properties are added with opening and closing tags on a single line for name and damage.

5. The weapon item is closed, and two more weapon items are added.

6. The array is closed, marking the end of the document.

The good news is our application doesn't have to manually write our data in this format. C# has an entire library of classes and methods to help us translate simple text and class objects directly into XML.

We'll dive into practical code examples, but first, we need to understand how JSON works.

Breaking down JSON

The JSON data format is similar to XML, but without the tags. Instead, everything is based on attribute-value pairs, like the **Dictionary** collection type we worked with back in *Chapter 4*. Each JSON document starts with a parent dictionary that holds as many attribute-value pairs as you need.

Dictionaries use open and closed curly braces ({ }), a colon separates each attribute and value, and each attribute-value pair is separated by a comma:

```
// Parent dictionary for the entire file
{
    // List of attribute-value pairs to store your data
    "attribute_name": value,
    "attribute_name": value
}
```

JSON can also have child or nested structures by setting the value of an attribute-value pair to an array of attribute-value pairs. For instance, if we want to store a weapon, it would look like this:

```
// Parent dictionary
{
    // Weapon attribute with value set to a child dictionary
    "weapon": {
        // Attribute-value pairs with weapon data
        "name": "Sword of Doom",
        "damage": 100
    }
}
```

Finally, JSON data is often made up of lists, arrays, or objects. Continuing our example, if we wanted to store a list of all the weapons our player could choose, we would use a pair of square brackets to denote an array:

```
// Parent dictionary
{
    // List of weapon attributes as an array of weapons
    "weapons": [
        // Each weapon object stored as its own dictionary
        {
            "name": "Sword of Doom",
            "damage": 100
        },
        {
            "name": "Butterfly knives",
            "damage": 25
        },
```

```
        {
            "name": "Brass Knuckles",
            "damage": 15
        }
    ]
}
```

You can mix and match any of these techniques to store any kind of complex data you need, which is one of JSON's main strengths. But just like with XML, don't be overtaken by the new syntax – C# and Unity both have helper classes and methods to translate text and class objects into JSON without us having to do any heavy lifting. Reading XML and JSON is sort of like learning a new language – the more you use it, the more familiar it becomes. Soon it'll be second nature!

Now that we've dipped our toes into data formatting basics, we can start talking about how the filesystem on your computer works and what properties we can access from our C# code.

Understanding the filesystem

When we say **filesystem**, we're talking about something you're already familiar with – how files and folders are created, organized, and stored on your computer. When you create a new folder on your computer, you can name it and put files or other folders inside it.

It's also represented by an icon, which is both a visual cue and a way to drag, drop, and move it anywhere you like.

Everything you can do on your desktop, you can do in code. All you need is the name of the folder, or directory as it's called, and a location to store it. Anytime you want to add a file or subfolder, you reference the parent directory and add your new content.

To drive the filesystem home, let's start building out the DataManager class we created and attached to the Game Manager object in the **Hierarchy** in *Chapter 10*:

Open the DataManager script and update it with the following code to print out a few filesystem properties:

```
using System.Collections;
using System.Collections.Generic;
using UnityEngine;

// 1
using System.IO;
```

```
public class DataManager : MonoBehaviour, IManager
{
    // ... No variable changes needed ...

    public void Initialize()
    {
        _state = "Data Manager initialized..";
        Debug.Log(_state);

        // 2
        FilesystemInfo();
    }
    public void FilesystemInfo()
    {
        // 3
        Debug.LogFormat("Path separator character:
            {0}",Path.PathSeparator);
        Debug.LogFormat("Directory separator character: {0}",
            Path.DirectorySeparatorChar);
        Debug.LogFormat("Current directory: {0}",
            Directory.GetCurrentDirectory());
        Debug.LogFormat("Temporary path: {0}", Path.GetTempPath());
    }
}
```

Let's break down the code:

1. First, we add the System.IO namespace, which has all the classes and methods we need to work with the filesystem.

2. We call the FilesystemInfo() method we create in the next step.

3. We create the FilesystemInfo() method to print out a few filesystem properties. Every operating system handles its filesystem paths differently – a path is the location of a directory or file written in a string. On macOS, the following applies:

    •   Paths are separated by a colon (:).

    •   Directories are separated by a forward slash (/).

    •   The current directory path is where the *Hero Born* project is stored.

    •   The temporary path is the location of your filesystem's temporary folder.

If you're on other platforms and operating systems, make sure to check the Path() and Directory() methods for yourself before working with the filesystem.

Run the game and take a look at the output:

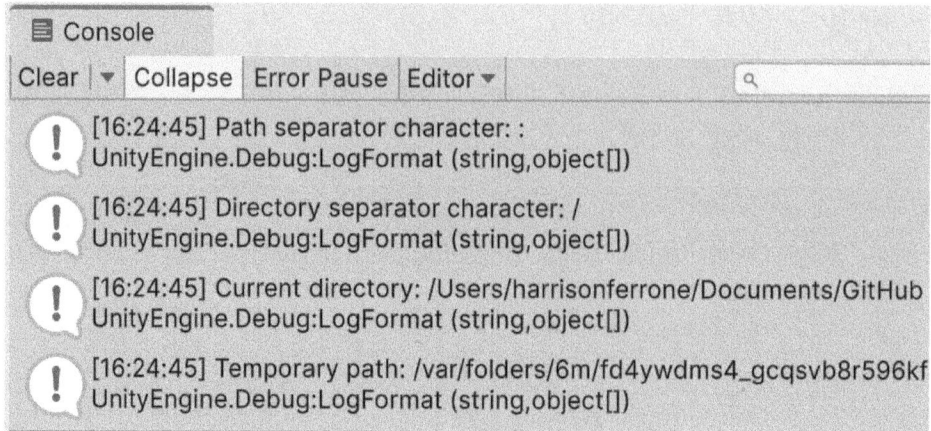

Figure 12.1: Console messages from Data Manager

> **Note**
>
> To provide a complete view of the Unity editor, all our screenshots are taken in full-screen mode. For color versions of all book images, use the following link: https://packt.link/gbp/9781805808718.

The Path and Directory classes are the foundation we're going to be building on to store our data in the following sections. However, they're both large classes, so I encourage you to look into their documentation as you continue your data journey.

You can find more documentation for the Path class at: https://docs.microsoft.com/en-us/dotnet/api/system.io.path and the Directory class at: https://docs.microsoft.com/en-us/dotnet/api/system.io.directory.

Now that we have a simple example of filesystem properties printed out in our DataManager script, we can create a filesystem path to the location where we want to save our data.

Working with asset paths

In a purely C# application, you would have to choose what folder to save your files in and write out the folder path in a string. However, Unity provides a handy pre-configured path as part of the Application class where you can store persistent game data. Persistent data means the information is saved and kept each time the program runs, which makes it ideal for this kind of player information.

It's important to know that the path to Unity's persistent data directory is cross-platform, meaning that it's different according to whether you're building a game for iOS, Android, Windows, or another platform. You can find out more information in the Unity documentation at https://docs.unity3d.com/ScriptReference/Application-persistentDataPath.html.

The only update we need to make to DataManager is to create a private variable to hold our path string. We're making this private because we don't want any other script to be able to access or change the value. That way, DataManager is responsible for all data-related logic and nothing else.

Add the following variable to DataManager.cs:

```
public class DataManager : MonoBehaviour, IManager
{
    // ... No other variable changes needed ...

    // 1
    private string _dataPath;
    // 2
    void Awake()
    {
        _dataPath = Application.persistentDataPath + "/Player_Data/";

        Debug.Log(_dataPath);
    }

    // ... No other changes needed ...
}
```

Let's break down our code update:

1. We created a private variable to hold the data path string.
2. We set the data path string to the application's `persistentDataPath` value, added a new folder name called `Player_Data` using open and closed forward slashes, and printed out the complete path.

> **Important note**
>
> It's important to note that `Application.persistentDataPath` can only be used in a `MonoBehaviour` method such as `Awake()`, `Start()`, `Update()`, and so on, and the game needs to be running for Unity to return a valid path.

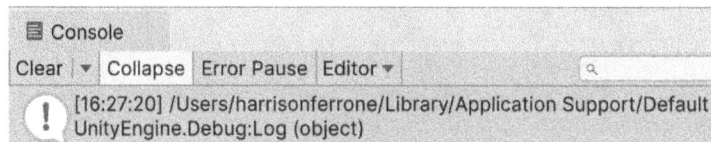

```
Console
Clear  ▼  Collapse  Error Pause  Editor ▼                                    Q
   [16:27:20] /Users/harrisonferrone/Library/Application Support/Default
   UnityEngine.Debug:Log (object)
```

Figure 12.2: File path for Unity persistent data files

🔍 **Quick tip**: Need to see a high-resolution version of this image? Open this book in the next-gen Packt Reader or view it in the PDF/ePub copy.

📖 **The next-gen Packt Reader** and a **free PDF/ePub copy** of this book are included with your purchase. Scan the QR code OR visit `https://packtpub.com/unlock`, then use the search bar to find this book by name. Double-check the edition shown to make sure you get the right one.

Since I'm using a Mac, my persistent data folder is nested inside my /Users folder. Remember to check out https://docs.unity3d.com/ScriptReference/Application-persistentDataPath.html to find out where your data is stored if you're using a different device.

When you're not working with a predefined asset path like Unity's persistent data directory, C# has a handy method called Combine() in the Path class for automatically configuring path variables.

The Combine() method can take up to four strings as input parameters or an array of strings representing the path components. For example, a path to your User directory might look like this:

```
var path = Path.Combine("/Users", "hferrone", "Chapter_12");
```

This takes care of any potential cross-platform issues with separating characters and back or forward slashes in paths and directories.

Now that we have a path to store our data, let's create a new directory, or folder, in the filesystem. This will let us store our data securely and between game runs, as opposed to temporary storage, where it would be deleted or overwritten.

Creating and deleting directories

Creating a new directory folder is straightforward – we check to see if one already exists with the same name on the same path, and if not, we tell C# to create it for us. Everyone has their own ways of dealing with duplicates in their files and folders, so we'll be repeating a fair bit of duplicate-checking code in the rest of the chapter.

I'd still recommend following the **Don't Repeat Yourself** (**DRY**) principle in real-world applications; the duplicate checking code is only repeated here to make the examples complete and easy to understand:

1. Add the following method to DataManager:

```
public void NewDirectory()
{
    // 1
    if(Directory.Exists(_dataPath))
    {
        // 2
        Debug.Log("Directory already exists...");
        return;
    }
    // 3
```

```
        Directory.CreateDirectory(_dataPath);
        Debug.Log("New directory created!");
    }
```

2. Call the new method inside `Initialize()`:

```
    public void Initialize()
    {
        _state = "Data Manager initialized..";
        Debug.Log(_state);
        NewDirectory();
    }
```

Let's break down what we did:

1. First, we check whether the directory folder already exists using the path we created in the last step.
2. If it's already been created, we send ourselves a message in the console and use the `return` keyword to exit the method without going any further.
3. If the directory folder doesn't exist, we pass the `CreateDirectory()` method our data path and log that it's been created.

Run the game and make sure that you see the right debug logs in the console, as well as the new directory folder in your persistent data folder.

If you can't find it, use the `_dataPath` value we printed out in the previous step.

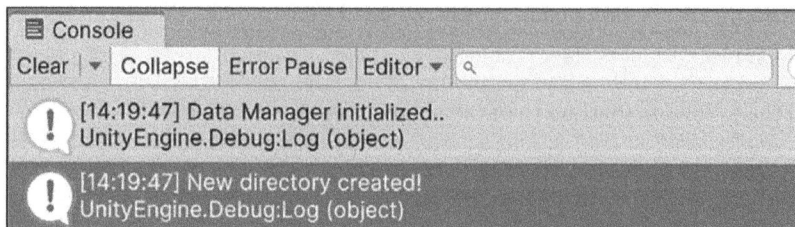

Figure 12.3: Console message for new directory creation

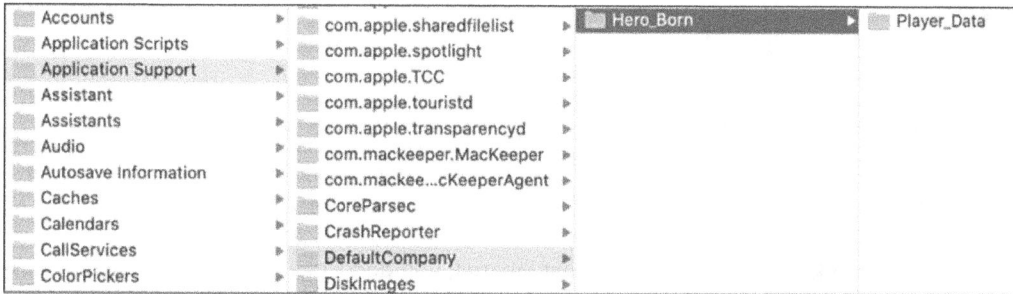

Figure 12.4: New directory created on the desktop

If you run the game a second time, no duplicate directory folder will be created, which is exactly the kind of safe code we want.

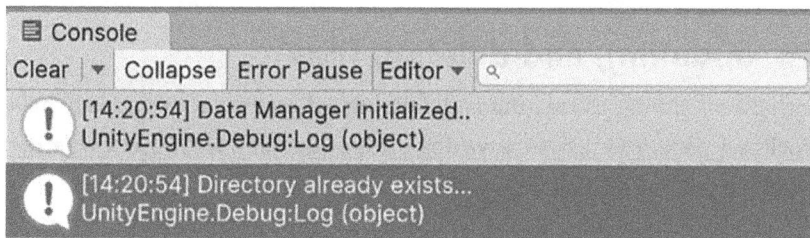

Figure 12.5: Console message for duplicate directory folders

Deleting a directory is very similar to how we created it – we check whether it exists, then we use the Directory class to delete whatever folder is at the path we pass in.

Add the following method to DataManager:

```
public void DeleteDirectory()
{
    // 1
    if(!Directory.Exists(_dataPath))
    {
        // 2
        Debug.Log("Directory doesn't exist or has already been
            deleted...");
```

```
        return;
    }
    // 3
    Directory.Delete(_dataPath, true);
    Debug.Log("Directory successfully deleted!");
}
```

Since we want to keep the directory we just created, you don't have to call this function right now. However, if you want to try it out, all you need to do is replace `NewDirectory()` with `DeleteDirectory()` in the `Initialize()` function.

An empty directory folder isn't super useful, so let's create our first text file and save it in our new location.

Creating, updating, and deleting files

Working with files is similar to creating and deleting a directory, so we already have the basic building blocks we need. To make sure we don't duplicate data, we'll check whether the file already exists, and if not, we'll create a new one in our new directory folder.

We'll be working with the `File` class for this section, which has a ton of helpful methods to help us implement our features. You can find the entire list at `https://docs.microsoft.com/en-us/dotnet/api/system.io.file`.

An important point to drive home about files before we start is that they need to be opened before you can add text, and they need to be closed after you're finished. If you don't close the file you're programmatically working with, it will stay open in the program's memory. This both uses computation power for something you're not actively editing and can create potential memory leaks.

We're going to be writing individual methods for each action we want to perform (create, update, and delete). We're also going to check whether the files we're working with exist or not in each case, which is repetitive. I've structured this part of the book so you can get a solid grasp of each of the procedures. However, you can absolutely combine them into more economical methods after you've learned the basics.

Take the following steps to create a new text file:

1. Add a new private string path for the new text file and set its value in `Awake()`:

    ```
    private string _textFile;
    void Awake()
    {
    ```

```
        _textFile = _dataPath + "Save_Data.txt";
        // ... No other changes needed ...
    }
```

2. Add a new method to `DataManager`:

```
public void NewTextFile()
{
    // 1
    if (File.Exists(_textFile))
    {
        Debug.Log("File already exists...");
        return;
    }
    // 2
    File.WriteAllText(_textFile, "<SAVE DATA>\n");
    // 3
    Debug.Log("New file created!");
}
```

3. Call the new method in `Initialize()`:

```
public void Initialize()
{
    _state = "Data Manager initialized..";
    Debug.Log(_state);
    NewTextFile();
}
```

Let's break down our new code:

1. We check whether the file already exists, and if it does, we return out of the method to avoid duplicates:

   It's worth noting that this approach works well for new files that aren't going to be changed. We'll cover updating and overwriting data to files in the next exercise.

2. We use the `WriteAllText()` method because it does everything we need all in one:

   - A new file is created using our `_textFile` path.
   - We add a title string that says `<SAVE DATA>` and add two new lines with the `\n` characters.
   - Then the file is closed for us automatically.

3. We print out a log message to let us know everything went smoothly.

When you play the game now, you'll see the debug log in the console and the new text file in your persistent data folder location:

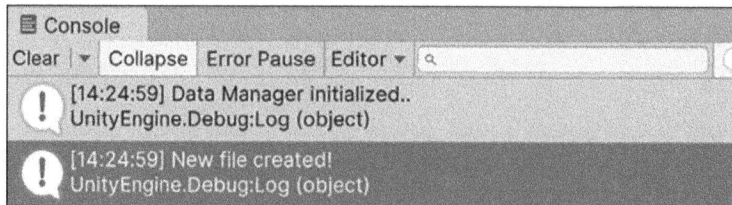

Figure 12.6: Console messages for new file creation

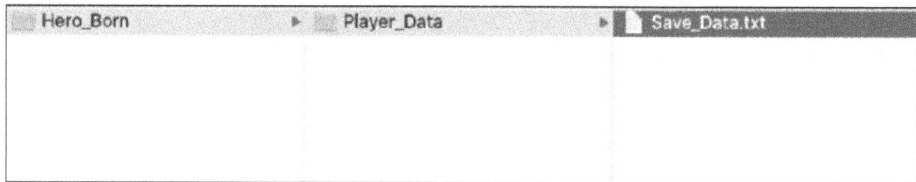

Figure 12.7: New file created on desktop

To update our new text file, we'll do a similar set of operations. It's always nice to know when a new game is started, so your next task is to add a method to write that information to our data file:

1. Add a new using directive to the top of `DataManager`:

   ```
   using System;
   ```

2. Add a new method to `DataManager`:

   ```
   public void UpdateTextFile()
   {
       // 1
       if (!File.Exists(_textFile))
       {
           Debug.Log("File doesn't exist...");
           return;
   ```

```
        }

        // 2
        File.AppendAllText(_textFile, $"Game started:{DateTime.Now}\n");
        // 3
        Debug.Log("File updated successfully!");
    }
```

3. Call the new method in `Initialize()`:

```
    public void Initialize()
    {
        _state = "Data Manager initialized..";
        Debug.Log(_state);

        UpdateTextFile();
    }
```

Let's break down the preceding code:

1. If the file exists, we don't want to duplicate it, so we just exit out of the method without any further action.

2. If the file does exist, we use another all-in-one method called `AppendAllText()` to add the game's start time:

    - This method opens the file.
    - It adds a new line of text that's passed in as a method parameter.
    - It closes the file.

3. Print out a log message to let us know everything went smoothly.

Play the game again and you'll see our console message and a new line in our text file with the new game's date and time:

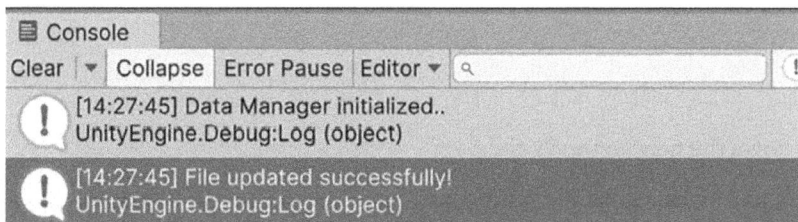

Figure 12.8: Console messages for updating the text file

| Hero_Born | ▶ | Player_Data | ▶ | Save_Data.txt |

Figure 12.9: Text file data updated

In order to read our new file data, we need a method to grab all the file's text and hand it back to us in a string. Luckily, the File class has methods to do just that:

1. Add a new method to DataManager:

```
// 1
public void ReadFromFile(string filename)
{
    // 2
    if (!File.Exists(filename))
    {
        Debug.Log("File doesn't exist...");
        return;
    }

    // 3
    Debug.Log(File.ReadAllText(filename));
}
```

2. Call the new method in Initialize() and pass in _textFile as a parameter:

```
public void Initialize()
{
    _state = "Data Manager initialized..";
    Debug.Log(_state);

    ReadFromFile(_textFile);
}
```

Let's break down the new method's code:

1. We create a new method that takes in a string parameter for the file we want to read.
2. If the file doesn't exist, there's no action needed, so we exit out of the method.

3. We use the ReadAllText() method to get all the file's text data as a string and print it out to the console.

Play the game and you'll see a console message with our previous save and a new one!

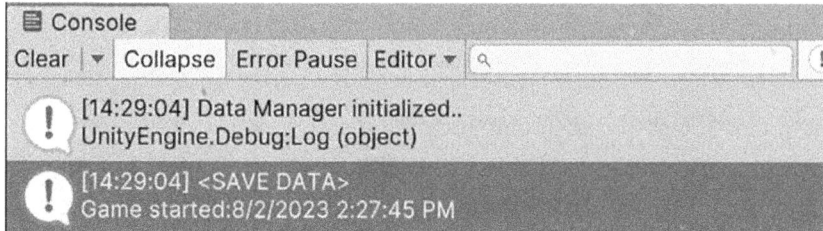

Figure 12.10: Console message with saved text data read from file

Lastly, let's add a method to delete our text file if we want. We're not actually going to use this method, as we want to keep our text file as is, but you can always try it out for yourself:

```
public void DeleteFile(string filename)
{
    if (!File.Exists(filename))
    {
        Debug.Log("File doesn't exist or has already been deleted...");

        return;
    }

    File.Delete(_textFile);
    Debug.Log("File successfully deleted!");
}
```

Now that we've dipped our toes a little deeper into the filesystem waters, it's time to talk about a slightly upgraded way of working with information – data streams!

Working with streams

So far, we've been letting the File class do all of the heavy lifting with our data. What we haven't talked about is how the File class, or any other class that deals with reading and writing data, does that work under the hood.

For computers, data is made up of bytes. Think of bytes as the computer's atoms; they make up everything – there's even a C# byte type. When we read, write, or update a file, our data is converted into an array of bytes, which are then streamed to or from the file using a `Stream` object. The data stream is responsible for carrying the data as a sequence of bytes to or from a file, acting as a translator or intermediary for us between our game application and the data files themselves.

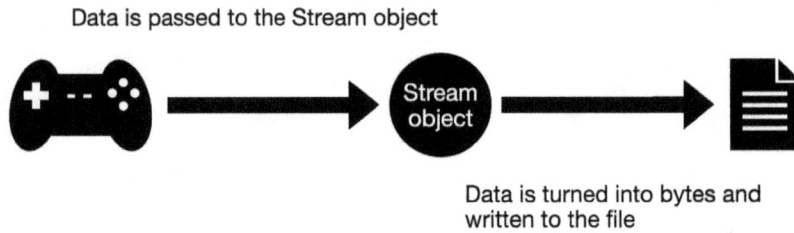

Figure 12.11: Diagram of streaming data to a file

The `File` class uses `Stream` objects for us automatically, and there are different `Stream` subclasses for different functionality:

- Use `FileStream` to read and write data to your files
- Use `MemoryStream` to read and write data to memory
- Use `NetworkStream` to read and write data to other networked computers
- Use `GZipStream` to compress data for easier storage and downloading

In the coming sections, we'll get into managing stream resources, using helper classes called `StreamReader` and `StreamWriter` to create, read, update, and delete files. You'll also learn how to format XML more easily using the `XmlWriter` class.

Managing your stream resources

One important topic we haven't talked about yet is resource allocation. What that means is some processes in your code will put computing power and memory on a sort of layaway plan where you can't touch it. These processes will wait until you explicitly tell your program or game to close and return the layaway resources to you, so you're back to full power. Streams are one such process, and they need to be closed after you're done using them. If you don't properly close your streams, your program will keep using those resources even though you're not.

Luckily, C# has a handy interface called `IDisposable` that all `Stream` classes implement. This interface only has one method, `Dispose()`, which tells the stream when to give you back the resources it's been using.

You don't have to worry too much about this, as we'll cover an automatic way to make sure your streams are always closed correctly. Resource management is just a good programming concept to understand.

We'll be using FileStream for the rest of the chapter, but we'll be doing so with convenience classes called StreamWriter and StreamReader. These classes leave out the manual conversion of data to bytes, but still use FileStream objects themselves.

Using StreamWriter and StreamReader

Both the StreamWriter and StreamReader classes serve as helpers for using objects belonging to FileStream to write and read text data to a specific file. These classes are a big help because they create, open, and return a stream you can use with minimal boilerplate code. The example code we've covered so far is fine for small data files, but streams are the way to go if you're dealing with large and complex data objects.

All we need is the name of the file we want to write to or read from, and we're all set. Your next task is to use a stream to write text to a new file:

1. Add a new private string path for the new streaming text file and set its value in Awake():

```
private string _streamingTextFile;


void Awake()
{
    _streamingTextFile = _dataPath + "Streaming_Save_Data.txt";
    // ... No other changes needed ...
}
```

2. Add a new method to DataManager:

```
public void WriteToStream(string filename)
{
    // 1
    if (!File.Exists(filename))
    {
        // 2
        StreamWriter newStream = File.CreateText(filename);

        // 3
        newStream.WriteLine("<Save Data> for HERO BORN \n");
```

```
            newStream.Close();
            Debug.Log("New file created with StreamWriter!");
        }


        // 4
        StreamWriter streamWriter = File.AppendText(filename);


        // 5
        streamWriter.WriteLine("Game ended: " + DateTime.Now);
        streamWriter.Close();
        Debug.Log("File contents updated with StreamWriter!");
    }
```

3. Delete or comment out the methods in `Initialize()` that we used in the previous section and add in our new code:

    ```
    public void Initialize()
    {
        _state = "Data Manager initialized..";
        Debug.Log(_state);

        WriteToStream(_streamingTextFile);
    }
    ```

Let's break down the new method in the preceding code:

1. First, we check that the file doesn't exist using its name.

2. If the file hasn't been created yet, we add a new `StreamWriter` instance called `newStream`, which uses the `CreateText()` method to create and open the new file.

3. Once the file is open, we use the `WriteLine()` method to add a header, close the stream, and print out a debug message.

4. If the file already exists and we just want to update it, we grab our file through a new `StreamWriter` instance using the `AppendText()` method, so our existing data doesn't get overwritten.

5. Finally, we write a new line with our game data, close the stream, and print out a debug message:

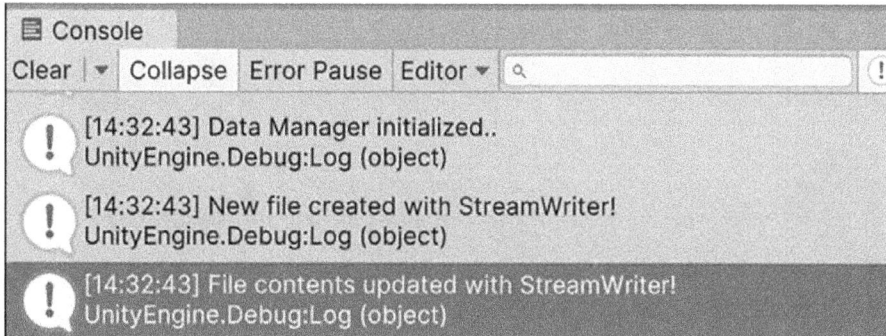

Figure 12.12: Console messages for writing and updating text with a stream

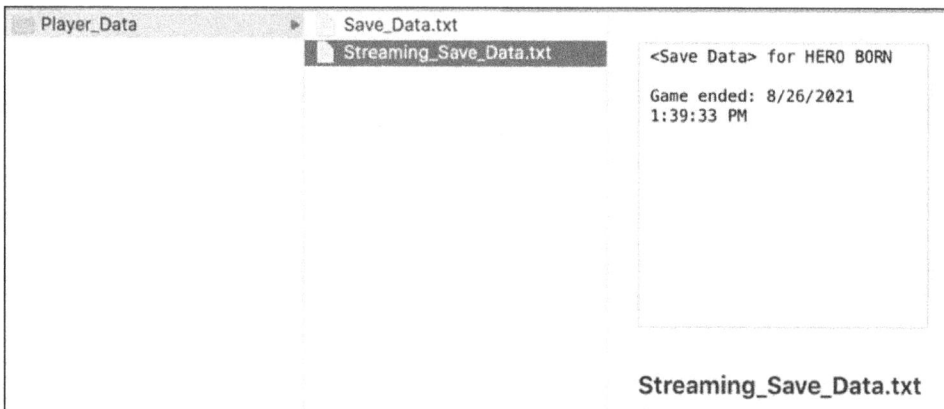

Figure 12.13: New file created and updated with a stream

Reading from a stream is almost exactly like the ReadFromFile() method we created in the last section. The only difference is that we'll use a StreamReader instance to open and read the information. Again, you want to use streams when you're dealing with big data files or complex objects instead of manually creating and writing to files with the File class:

1. Add a new method to DataManager:

```
public void ReadFromStream(string filename)
{
    // 1
    if (!File.Exists(filename))
    {
```

```
        Debug.Log("File doesn't exist...");
        return;
    }
    // 2
    StreamReader streamReader = new StreamReader(filename);
    Debug.Log(streamReader.ReadToEnd());
}
```

2. Call the new method in `Initialize()` and pass in `_streamingTextFile` as a parameter:

```
public void Initialize()
{
    _state = "Data Manager initialized..";
    Debug.Log(_state);

    ReadFromStream(_streamingTextFile);
}
```

Let's break down our new code:

1. First, we check that the file doesn't exist, and if it doesn't, then we print out a console message and exit the method.

2. If the file does exist, we create a new `StreamReader` instance with the name of the file we want to access and print out the entire contents using the `ReadToEnd` method:

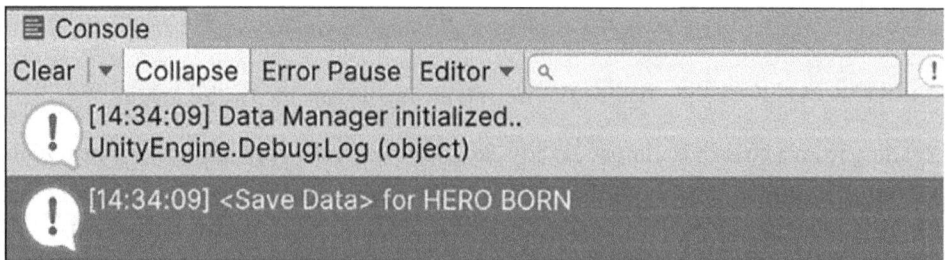

Figure 12.14: Console printing out saved data read from a stream

As you'll start to notice, a lot of our code is starting to look the same. The only difference is our use of stream classes to do the actual reading-writing work. However, it's important to keep in mind how different use cases will determine which route you take. Refer back to the beginning of this section to review how each stream type is different.

So far, we've covered the basic features of a **Creating, Reading, Updating, and Deleting (CRUD)** application using text files. But text files aren't the only data format you'll be using in C# games and applications. You're likely to see lots of XML and JSON in the wild once you start working with databases and your own complex data structures, which text can't compare to in efficiency or storage.

In the next section, we'll work with some basic XML data, then talk about an easier way to manage streams.

Creating an XMLWriter

Sometimes, you won't just have plain old text to write and read from a file. Your project might require XML-formatted documents, in which case, you'll need to know how to use a regular `FileStream` to save and load XML data.

Writing XML data to a file isn't all that different from what we've been doing with text and streams. The only difference is we'll explicitly create a `FileStream` and use it to create an instance of an `XmlWriter`. Think of the `XmlWriter` class as a wrapper that takes our data stream, applies XML formatting, and spits out our information as an XML file. Once we have that, we can structure the document in the proper XML format using methods from the `XmlWriter` class and close the file.

Your next task is to create a file path for a new XML document and add the ability to write XML data to that file using the `DataManager` class:

1. Add the new XML using directive to the top of the `DataManager` class:

    ```
    using System.Xml;
    ```

2. Add a new `private string` path for the new XML file and set its value in `Awake()`:

    ```
    private string _xmlLevelProgress;
    void Awake()
    {
        _xmlLevelProgress = _dataPath + "Progress_Data.xml";
        // ... No other changes needed ...
    }
    ```

3. Add a new method at the bottom of the `DataManager` class:

    ```
    public void WriteToXML(string filename)
    {
        // 1
    ```

```
    if (!File.Exists(filename))
    {
        // 2
        FileStream xmlStream = File.Create(filename);

        // 3
        XmlWriter xmlWriter = XmlWriter.Create(xmlStream);

        // 4
        xmlWriter.WriteStartDocument();
        // 5
        xmlWriter.WriteStartElement("level_progress");

        // 6
        for (int i = 1; i < 5; i++)
        {
            xmlWriter.WriteElementString("level", "Level-" + i);
        }

        // 7
        xmlWriter.WriteEndElement();

        // 8
        xmlWriter.Close();
        xmlStream.Close();
    }
}
```

4. Call the new method in `Initialize()` and pass in `_xmlLevelProgress` as a parameter:

```
public void Initialize()
{
    _state = "Data Manager initialized..";
    Debug.Log(_state);

    WriteToXML(_xmlLevelProgress);
}
```

Let's break down our XML writing method:

1. First, we check whether the file already exists.

2. If the file doesn't exist, we create a new `FileStream` using the new path variable we created.

3. We then create a new `XmlWriter` instance and pass it our new `FileStream`.

4. Next, we use the `WriteStartDocument` method to specify XML version 1.0.

5. Then we call the `WriteStartElement` method to add the opening root element tag named `level_progress`.

6. Now, we can add individual elements to our document using the `WriteElementString` method, passing in `level` as the element tag and the level number using a `for` loop and its index value of `i`.

7. To close the document, we use the `WriteEndElement` method to add a closing `level` tag.

8. Finally, we close the writer and stream to release the stream resources we've been using.

If you run the game now, you'll see a new `.xml` file in our `Player_Data` folder with the level progress information:

Figure 12.15: New XML file created with document data

You'll notice that there is no indenting or formatting, which is expected because we didn't specify any output formatting. We're not going to use any of them in this example because we'll be talking about a more efficient way of writing XML data in the next section on serialization.

You can find the list of output formatting properties at `https://docs.microsoft.com/dotnet/api/system.xml.xmlwriter#specifying-the-output-format`.

The good news is that reading an XML file is no different than reading any other file. You can call either the Readfromfile() or Readfromstream() method inside Initialize() and get the same console output:

```
public void Initialize()
{
    _state = "Data Manager initialized..";
    Debug.Log(_state);
    ReadFromStream(_xmlLevelProgress);
}
```

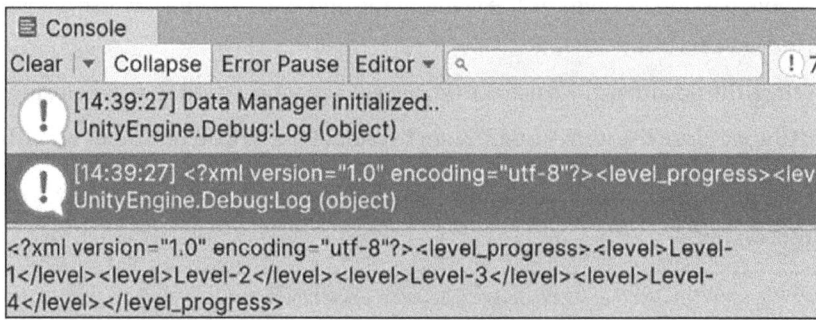

Figure 12.16: Console output from reading the XML file data

Now that we've written a few methods using streams, let's take a look at how to efficiently, and more importantly, automatically, close any stream.

Automatically closing streams

When you're working with streams, wrapping them in a using statement automatically closes the stream for you by calling the Dispose() method from the IDisposable interface we mentioned earlier. This way, you never have to worry about unused allocated resources your program might be keeping open for no reason.

The syntax is almost exactly the same as what we've already done, except we use the using keyword at the beginning of the line, then reference a new stream inside a pair of parentheses, followed by a set of curly braces. Anything we want the stream to do, such as read or write data, is done inside the curly braces block of code. For example, creating a new text file as we did in the WriteToStream() method would look like this:

```
// The new stream is wrapped in a using statement
using(StreamWriter newStream = File.CreateText(filename))
```

```
{
    // Any text goes inside the curly braces
    newStream.WriteLine("<Save Data> for HERO BORN \n");
}
```

As soon as the stream logic is inside the code block, the outer using statement automatically closes the stream and returns the allocated resources to your program. From here on out, I'd recommend always using this syntax to write your streaming code. It's more efficient, much safer, and will demonstrate your understanding of basic resource management!

With our text and XML stream code working, it's time to move on. If you're wondering why we didn't stream any JSON data, it's because we need to add one more tool to our data toolbox – serialization!

Serializing data

When we talk about serializing and deserializing data, what we're really talking about is translation. While we've been translating our text and XML piecemeal in previous sections, being able to take an entire object and translate it in one shot is a great tool to have.

By definition:

- The act of **serializing** an object translates the object's entire state into another format.
- The act of **deserializing** is the reverse, taking the data from a file and restoring it to its former object state.

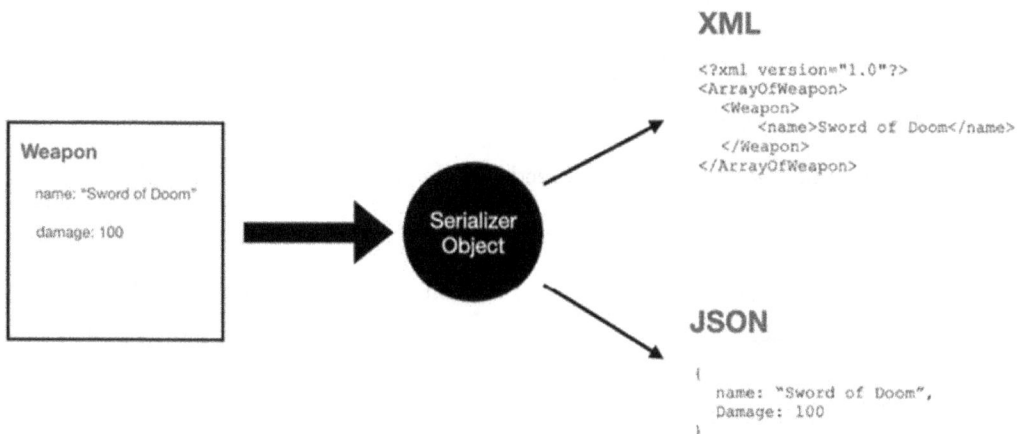

Figure 12.17: Example of serializing an object into XML and JSON

Let's take a practical example from the preceding image – an instance of our Weapon class. Each weapon has its own name and damage properties and associated values, which are called its **state**. The state of an object is unique, which allows the program to tell them apart.

An object's state also includes properties or fields that are reference types. For instance, if we had a Character class that had a Weapon property, C# would still recognize the weapon's name and damage properties when serializing and deserializing. You might hear objects with reference properties referred to as object graphs out in the programming world.

Before we jump in, it's worth noting that serializing objects can be tricky if you're not keeping a close eye on making sure the object properties match the data from a file, and vice versa. For example, if there's a mismatch between your class object properties and the data being deserialized, the serializer will return an empty object.

To really get the hang of this, let's take our Weapon example and turn it into working code.

Serializing and deserializing XML

Your task for the rest of this chapter is to serialize and deserialize a list of weapons into XML and JSON, with XML going first!

1. Open the Weapon.cs file and add the using System namespace and a serializable attribute so Unity and C# know the object can be serialized:

```
using System;
[Serializable]
public struct Weapon
{
    // ... No other changes needed ...
}
```

2. Add a new Serialization using directive to the top of the DataManager class:

```
using System.Xml.Serialization;
```

3. In the DataManager class, add two new variables, one for the XML file path and one for the list of weapons:

```
// ... No other variable changes needed ...
private string _xmlWeapons;
private List<Weapon> weaponInventory = new List<Weapon>
{
```

```
            new Weapon("Sword of Doom", 100),
            new Weapon("Butterfly knives", 25),
            new Weapon("Brass Knuckles", 15),
    };
```

4. Set the XML file path value in `Awake()`:

```
void Awake()
{
    // ... No other changes needed ...
    _xmlWeapons = _dataPath + "WeaponInventory.xml";
}
```

5. Add a new method at the bottom of the `DataManager` class:

```
public void SerializeXML()
{
    // 1
    var xmlSerializer = new XmlSerializer(typeof(List<Weapon>));

    // 2
    using(FileStream stream = File.Create(_xmlWeapons))
    {
        // 3
        xmlSerializer.Serialize(stream, weaponInventory);
    }
}
```

6. Call the new method in `Initialize()`:

```
public void Initialize()
{
    _state = "Data Manager initialized..";
    Debug.Log(_state);

    SerializeXML();
}
```

Let's break down our new method:

1. First, we create an XmlSerializer instance and pass in the type of data we're going to be translating. In this case, _weaponInventory is of type List<Weapon>, which is what we use in the typeof operator:

    The XmlSerializer class is another helpful formatting wrapper, just like the XmlWriter class we used earlier.

2. Then, we create a FileStream using the _xmlWeapons file path and wrapped in a using code block to make sure it's closed properly.

3. Finally, we call the Serialize() method and pass in the stream and the data we want to translate.

Run the game again to see the new XML document we created with our Weapon data without having to specify any additional formatting!

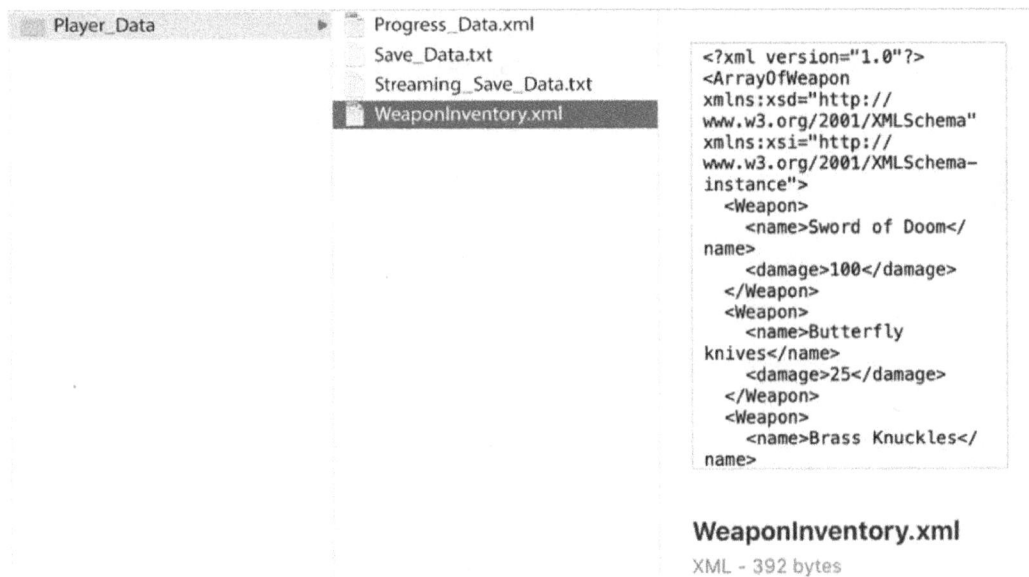

```xml
<?xml version="1.0"?>
<ArrayOfWeapon
xmlns:xsd="http://
www.w3.org/2001/XMLSchema"
xmlns:xsi="http://
www.w3.org/2001/XMLSchema-
instance">
  <Weapon>
    <name>Sword of Doom</
name>
    <damage>100</damage>
  </Weapon>
  <Weapon>
    <name>Butterfly
knives</name>
    <damage>25</damage>
  </Weapon>
  <Weapon>
    <name>Brass Knuckles</
name>
```

WeaponInventory.xml

XML - 392 bytes

Figure 12.18: XML output in the weapon inventory file

To read back our XML into a list of weapons, we set up everything almost exactly the same, except we use the Deserialize() method from the XmlSerializer class instead:

1. Add the following method to the bottom of the `DataManager` class:

```
public void DeserializeXML()
{
    // 1
    if (File.Exists(_xmlWeapons))
    {
        // 2
        var xmlSerializer = new XmlSerializer(typeof(List<Weapon>));

        // 3
        using (FileStream stream = File.OpenRead(_xmlWeapons))
        {
            // 4
            var weapons =
                (List<Weapon>)xmlSerializer.Deserialize(stream);

            // 5
            foreach (var weapon in weapons)
            {
                Debug.LogFormat("Weapon: {0} - Damage: {1}",
                    weapon.Name, weapon.Damage);
            }
        }
    }
}
```

2. Call the new method in `Initialize()` and pass in _xmlWeapons as a parameter:

```
public void Initialize()
{
    _state = "Data Manager initialized..";
    Debug.Log(_state);

    DeserializeXML();
}
```

Let's break down the `DeserializeXML()` method:

1. First, we check whether the file exists.

2. If the file exists, we create an `XmlSerializer` object and specify that we're going to put the XML data back into a `List<Weapon>` object.

3. Then, we open up a `FileStream` with the `_xmlWeapons` filename:

    We're using `File.OpenRead()` to specify that we want to open the file for reading, not writing.

4. Next, we create a variable to hold our deserialized list of weapons:

    We put the explicit `List<Weapon>` cast in front of the call to `Deserialize()` so that we get the correct type back from the serializer.

5. Finally, we use a `foreach` loop to print out each weapon's name and damage values in the console.

When you run the game once again, you'll see that we get a console message for each weapon we deserialized from the XML list:

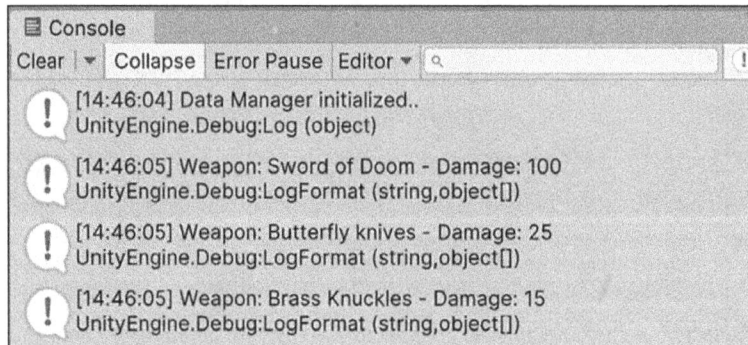

Figure 12.19: Console output from deserializing XML

That's all we need to do for XML data, but before we finish the chapter, we still need to learn how to work with JSON!

Serializing and deserializing JSON

When it comes to serializing and deserializing JSON, Unity and C# aren't completely in sync. Essentially, C# has its own `JsonSerializer` class that works the exact same way as the `XmlSerializer` class we used in the previous examples.

In order to access the JSON serializer, you need the `System.Text.Json` using directive. Here's the rub – Unity doesn't support that namespace. Instead, Unity uses the `System.Text` namespace, and implements its own JSON serializer class called `JsonUtility`.

Because our project is in Unity, we're going to work with Unity's supported serialization class. However, if you're working with a non-Unity C# project, the concepts are the same as the XML code we just wrote.

You can find a complete how-to that includes code from Microsoft at `https://docs.microsoft.com/en-us/dotnet/standard/serialization/system-text-json-how-to#how-to-write-net-objects-as-json-serialize`.

Your next task is to serialize a single weapon to get the hang of the `JsonUtility` class:

1. Add a new `Text` using directive to the top of the `DataManager` class:

    ```
    using System.Text;
    ```

2. Add a new `private` string path for the new XML file and set its value in `Awake()`:

    ```
    private string _jsonWeapons;
    void Awake()
    {
        _jsonWeapons = _dataPath + "WeaponJSON.json";
    }
    ```

3. Add a new method at the bottom of the `DataManager` class:

    ```
    public void SerializeJSON()
    {
        // 1
        Weapon sword = new Weapon("Sword of Doom", 100);
        // 2
        string jsonString = JsonUtility.ToJson(sword, true);

        // 3
        using(StreamWriter stream = File.CreateText(_jsonWeapons))
        {
            // 4
            stream.WriteLine(jsonString);
        }
    }
    ```

4. Call the new method in Initialize() and pass in _jsonWeapons as a parameter:

```
public void Initialize()
{
    _state = "Data Manager initialized..";
    Debug.Log(_state);

    SerializeJSON();
}
```

Here's the breakdown of the serialization:

1. First, we need a weapon to work with, so we create one with our class initializer.

2. Then, we declare a variable to hold the translated JSON data when it's formatted as a string and call the ToJson() method:

    The ToJson() method we're using takes in the sword object we want to serialize and a Boolean value of true, so the string is pretty printed with proper indenting. If we didn't specify a true value, the JSON would still print out; it would just be a regular string, which isn't easily readable.

3. Now that we have a text string to write to a file, we create a StreamWriter stream and pass in the _jsonWeapons filename.

4. Finally, we use the WriteLine() method and pass it the jsonString value to write to the file.

Run the program and look at the new JSON file we created and wrote data into!

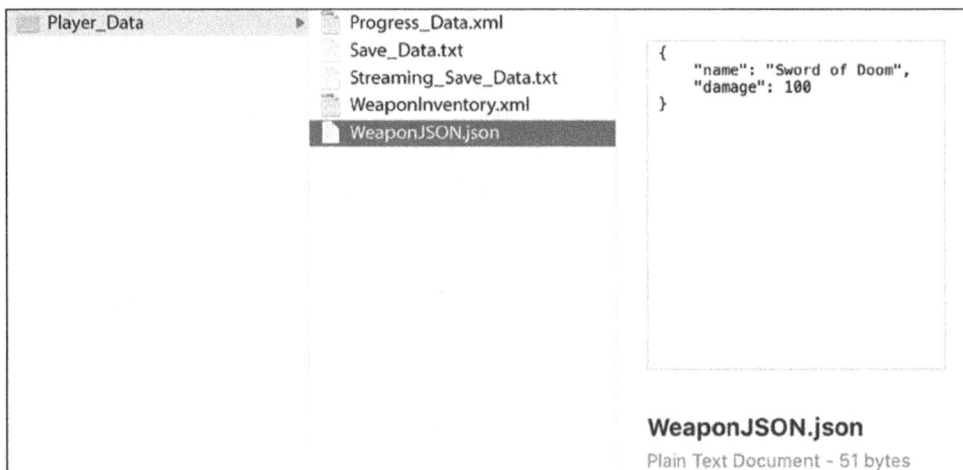

WeaponJSON.json

Plain Text Document - 51 bytes

Figure 12.20: JSON file with weapon properties serialized

Now let's try and serialize the list of weapons we used in the XML examples and see what happens.

Update the `SerializeJSON()` method to use the existing list of weapons instead of the single sword instance:

```
public void SerializeJSON()
{
    string jsonString = JsonUtility.ToJson(weaponInventory, true);

    using(StreamWriter stream =
      File.CreateText(_jsonWeapons))
    {
        stream.WriteLine(jsonString);
    }
}
```

When you run the game again, you'll see that the JSON file data was overwritten, and all we ended up with is an empty array:

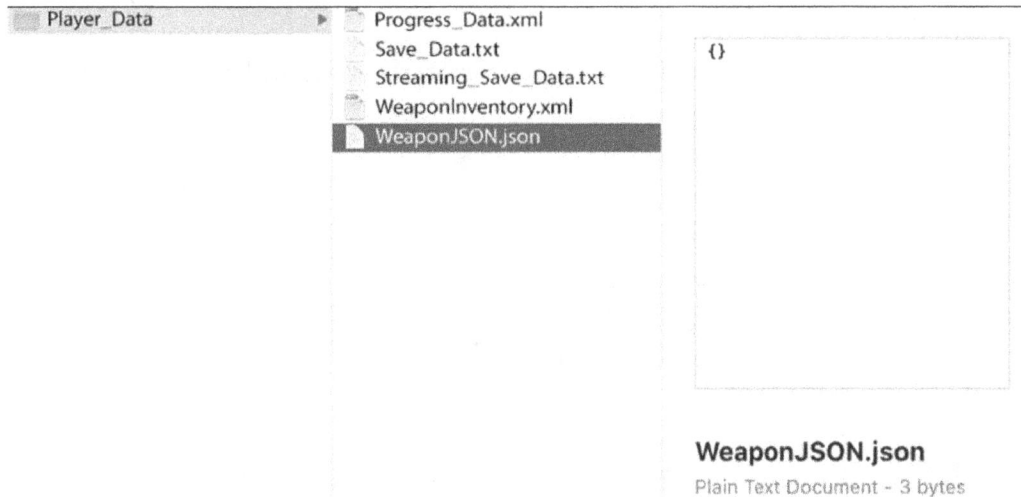

WeaponJSON.json
Plain Text Document - 3 bytes

Figure 12.21: JSON file with an empty object after serialization

Again, this is because the way Unity handles JSON serialization doesn't support lists or arrays by themselves. Any list or array needs to be part of a class object for Unity's `JsonUtility` class to recognize and handle it correctly. In addition, the `JsonUtility` class doesn't support `Dictionary` or complex types out of the box.

However, Unity supports alternatives such as **Newtonsoft** (`https://www.newtonsoft.com/json`), which you can find at `https://docs.unity3d.com/Packages/com.unity.nuget.newtonsoft-json@3.0/manual/index.html`.

Don't panic; if we think about this, it's a fairly intuitive fix – we just need to create a class that has a list or weapons property and use that when we serialize our data into JSON!

1. In the `Scripts` folder, create a new C# script named `WeaponShop` and update its contents to match the following code:

    ```csharp
    using UnityEngine;
    using System;
    using System.Collections.Generic;

    [Serializable]
    public class WeaponShop
    {
        public List<Weapon> inventory;
    }
    ```

2. Back in the `DataManager` class, update the `SerializeJSON()` method with the following code:

    ```csharp
    public void SerializeJSON()
    {
        // 1
        WeaponShop shop = new WeaponShop();
        // 2
        shop.inventory = weaponInventory;

        // 3
        string jsonString = JsonUtility.ToJson(shop, true);

        using(StreamWriter stream = File.CreateText(_jsonWeapons))
        {
            stream.WriteLine(jsonString);
        }
    }
    ```

Let's break down the changes we just made:

1. First, we create a new variable called shop, which is an instance of the WeaponShop class.

2. Then we set the inventory property to the weaponInventory list of weapons we already declared.

3. Finally, we pass the shop object to the ToJson() method and write the new string data to the JSON file.

Run the game again and look at the pretty printed list of weapons we've created:

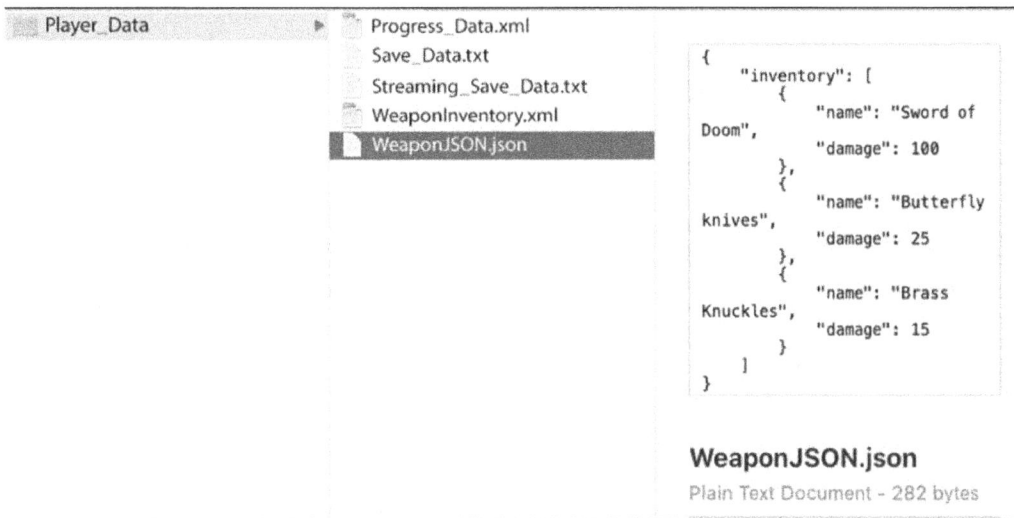

```
Player_Data        ▶    Progress_Data.xml
                        Save_Data.txt
                        Streaming_Save_Data.txt
                        WeaponInventory.xml
                        WeaponJSON.json
```

```
{
    "inventory": [
        {
            "name": "Sword of
Doom",
            "damage": 100
        },
        {
            "name": "Butterfly
knives",
            "damage": 25
        },
        {
            "name": "Brass
Knuckles",
            "damage": 15
        }
    ]
}
```

WeaponJSON.json

Plain Text Document - 282 bytes

Figure 12.22: List object properly serialized into JSON

Deserializing JSON text back into an object is the reverse process of what we just did:

1. Add a new method at the bottom of the DataManager class:

```
public void DeserializeJSON()
{
    // 1
    if(File.Exists(_jsonWeapons))
    {
        // 2
        using (StreamReader stream = new StreamReader(_jsonWeapons))
        {
            // 3
            var jsonString = stream.ReadToEnd();
```

```
        // 4
        var weaponData = JsonUtility.FromJson<WeaponShop>
            (jsonString);

        // 5
        foreach (var weapon in weaponData.inventory)
        {
            Debug.LogFormat("Weapon: {0} - Damage: {1}",
                weapon.Name, weapon.Damage);

        }
    }
}
```

2. Call the new method in `Initialize()` and pass `_jsonWeapons` in as a parameter:

```
public void Initialize()
{
    _state = "Data Manager initialized..";
    Debug.Log(_state);

    DeserializeJSON();
}
```

Let's break down the `DeserializeJSON()` method:

1. First, we check whether the file exists.

2. If it does exist, we create a stream with the `_jsonWeapons` file path wrapped in a `using` code block.

3. Then, we use the stream's `ReadToEnd()` method to grab the entire JSON text from the file.

4. Next, we create a variable to hold our deserialized list of weapons and call the `FromJson()` method:

    Notice that we specify that we want to turn our JSON into a `WeaponShop` object with the `<WeaponShop>` syntax before passing in the JSON string variable.

5. Finally, we loop through the weapon shop's inventory list property and print out each weapon's name and damage values in the console.

Run the game one last time and you'll see a console message printed out for each weapon in our JSON data:

[15:10:51] Directory already exists...
UnityEngine.Debug:Log (object)

[15:10:51] Weapon: Sword of Doom - Damage: 100
UnityEngine.Debug:LogFormat (string,object[])

[15:10:51] Weapon: Butterfly knives - Damage: 25
UnityEngine.Debug:LogFormat (string,object[])

[15:10:51] Weapon: Brass Knuckles - Damage: 15
UnityEngine.Debug:LogFormat (string,object[])

Directory already exists...
UnityEngine.Debug:Log (object)
DataManager:NewDirectory () (at Assets/Scripts/DataManager.cs:73)
DataManager:Initialize () (at Assets/Scripts/DataManager.cs:56)
DataManager:Start () (at Assets/Scripts/DataManager.cs:47)

Figure 12.23: Console output from deserializing a list of JSON objects

Data roundup

Every individual module and topic we've covered in this chapter can be used by itself or combined to suit your project's needs. For example, you could use text files to store character dialog and only load it when you need to. This would be more efficient than having the game keep track of it every time it runs, even when the information isn't being used.

You could also put character data or enemy statistics into either an XML or JSON file and read from the file anytime you need to level up a character or spawn a new monster. Finally, you could fetch data from a third-party database and serialize it into your own custom classes. This is a super common scenario with storing player accounts and external game data.

You can find a list of data types that can be serialized in C# at https://docs.microsoft.com/en-us/dotnet/framework/wcf/feature-details/types-supported-by-the-data-contract-serializer. Unity handles serialization a little differently, so make sure you check the available types at https://docs.unity3d.com/ScriptReference/SerializeField.html.

The point I'm trying to make is that data is everywhere, and it's your job to create a system that handles it the way your game needs, brick by brick.

Summary

And that's a wrap on the basics of working with data! Congratulations on making it through this monster chapter intact. Data in any programming context is a big topic, so take everything you've learned in this chapter as a jumping-off point.

You already know how to navigate the filesystem and create, read, update, and delete files. You also learned how to effectively work with text, XML, and JSON data formats, as well as data streams. You also know how to take an entire object's state and serialize or deserialize it into both XML and JSON. All in all, learning these skills was no small feat. Don't forget to review and revisit this chapter more than once; there's a lot here that might not become second nature on the first run-through.

In the next chapter, we'll get our hands on live web requests for data that lives online and how to get that information directly into our game!

Pop quiz: Data management

a.   Which namespace gives you access to the Path and Directory classes?

b.   In Unity, what folder path do you use to save data between runs of your game?

c.   What data type do Stream objects use to read and write information to files?

d.   What happens when you serialize an object into JSON?

Don't forget to check your answers against mine in the *Pop Quiz Answers* appendix to see how you did!

Unlock this book's exclusive benefits now

UNLOCK NOW

Scan this QR code or go to https://packtpub.com/unlock, then search this book by name.

Note: Keep your purchase invoice ready before you start.

13

Connecting to the World Wide Web

One of the greatest advantages a programmer has when it comes to data is knowing how (and where) to get it. As you saw from the last chapter, it's entirely possible to create, save, delete, and update data you create yourself; it's also possible and highly useful to access data that has already been compiled for you by someone else!

In this chapter, we're going to explore how to get our hands on live weather data from the internet, download it into our projects, and update the light source of our arena accordingly. This process is generally called **networking** in programming terminology, but since networking in game-related scenarios already describes multiplayer or networked play (a close cousin topic), we'll refer to our work in this chapter as **web requests.**

Along the way, we will cover the following topics:

- Introducing `UnityWebRequest` objects
- Coroutines and `yield` statements
- Receiving and deserializing responses
- Additional web request formats

Our main focus is to build strong foundational skills you can apply to *any* networking scenario, from understanding the basics of web requests and URL structure to data formats and error handling. Web requests are a big topic, so we won't be able to cover everything here – but rest assured, I'll always leave you resources you can explore to move your journey forward!

By the end of the chapter, you'll have the theory and hands-on skills to pursue this topic on your own (complete with a working web request manager for your troubles).

The web request blueprint

Before we get into any new code, let's lay a theoretical foundation for our work in this chapter. I like to think of web requests as a call-and-response workflow; we send out a request for information stored in a certain location (the **call**), and the requested information is sent back to us in one format or another (the **response**). And yes, there's a lot more to it than that, but keep this simple model in your head throughout the chapter, and everything will fall into place.

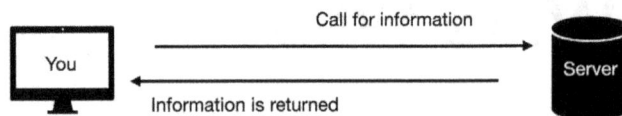

Figure 13.1: Web request call and response flow

All information on the internet is transmitted using the **Hypertext Transfer Protocol (HTTP)** (and nowadays, **Hypertext Transfer Protocol Secure** or **HTTPS**). You use this every time you open Google or Chrome and type in a website address or when your phone downloads images or game updates. We use a **Uniform Resource Locator (URL)** to specify the location of the resource we're looking for on the internet. For example, typing in `https://www.google.com/maps` in your browser sends a request to Google Maps for its web page information, which is then displayed on your screen.

You can find more information on HTTP and URLs at `https://en.wikipedia.org/wiki/HTTP` and `https://en.wikipedia.org/wiki/URL`, respectively.

Normally, all this work is hidden from us, but every piece of the puzzle is carefully handled in code to make it seem like magic. In our case, we're responsible for creating the web request itself, providing the correct address for the information we want using a URL, and processing the data we receive, as shown in *Figure 13.2*.

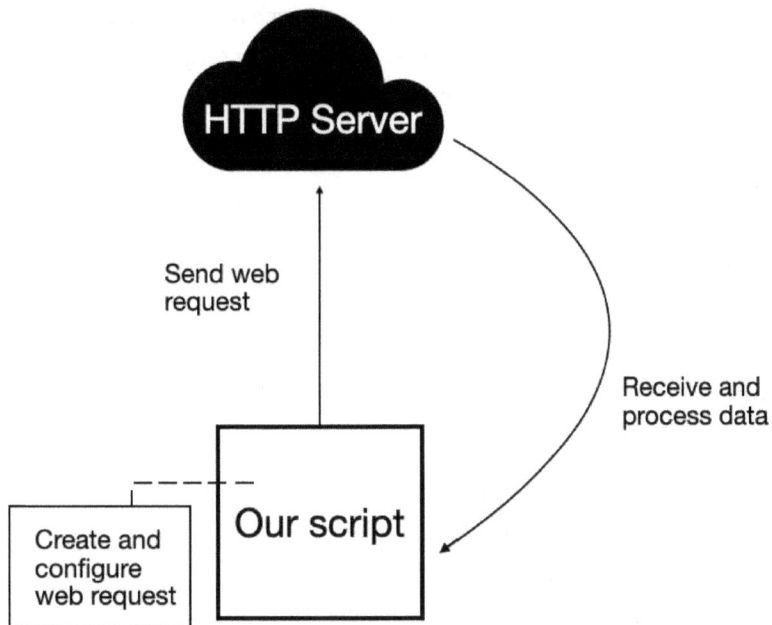

Figure 13.2: Web request blueprint diagram

Before we move on, we should take note of an important point with web requests – they come in multiple flavors. The request type we've been talking about up until now is called a GET request (because we're *getting* information), but there are also PUT, POST, and DELETE operations we can use.

We're only going to work with GET requests in *Hero Born*, but we'll talk more about these other request types in the *Additional web request formats* section at the end of the chapter.

Creating the request manager

Unity has its own handy class for web requests called UnityWebRequest, which provides everything we need to communicate with servers on the web and handle the flow of communication and information. We will be creating a UnityWebRequest instance just like we've done with other classes we've used up to this point, configure it how we want, and then send it off into the ether to bring us back our data.

You can find the documentation for the UnityWebRequest class at https://docs.unity3d.com/ScriptReference/Networking.UnityWebRequest.html.

Our first task is to add a manager script to handle all our web request features, so let's create that script now. In the `Scripts` folder, create a new MonoBehaviour script named `WebRequestManager` and update its contents to match the following code:

```
using UnityEngine;

// 1
public class WebRequestManager : MonoBehaviour, IManager
{
    // 2
    private string _state;
    public string State
    {
        get { return _state; }
        set { _state = value; }
    }

    // 3
    public void Initialize()
    {
        _state = "Web Request Manager initialized..";
        Debug.Log(_state);
    }

    // 4
    void Start()
    {
        Initialize();
    }
}
```

Let's break down our manager setup:

1. We update `WebRequestManager` to inherit from both `MonoBehaviour` and `IManager`.
2. We add a `State` variable with a private backing field required by the `IManager` interface.
3. We then declare the required `Initialize()` method from the `IManager` interface to set and debug a state value.
4. Finally, we call `Initialize()` in `Start()`.

Drag the new `WebRequestManager` script onto **Game Manager** in the **Hierarchy** and make sure everything is working and matches *Figure 13.3* (this is our third manager script, so there shouldn't be any surprises here):

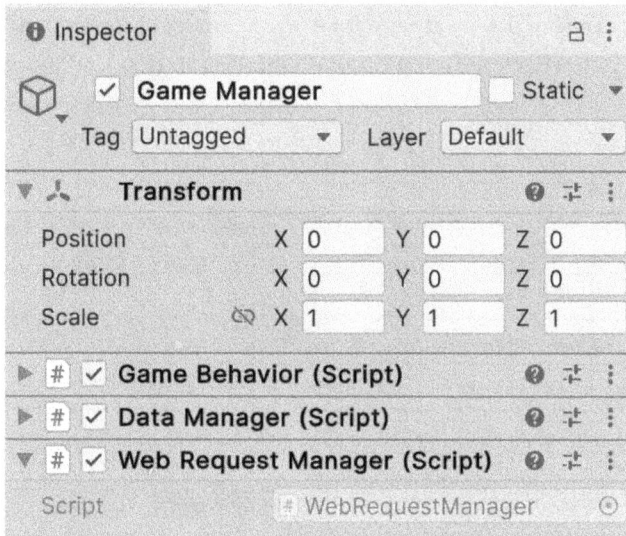

Figure 13.3: WebRequestManager script attached to Game Manager

Now, we can start fleshing out our web request logic, starting with a URL (the location of our data).

Formatting a URL

A typical URL consists of several components, which we'll break down in the following table using the `https://www.google.com/maps` example again:

Structure	Description	Example
Scheme	The protocol used to access the information (usually HTTP or HTTPS)	`https`
Host	The domain or IP address of the server hosting the information	`www.google.com`
Path	The specific location of the resource on the server	`/maps`
Query string	Optional request data we're passing to the server to dynamically filter for the exact content we want	N/A

Table 13.1: URL structure formatting and descriptions

URL formatting and encoding are bigger topics than we can comfortably cover here, but you can find more detailed information at https://en.wikipedia.org/wiki/URL#Syntax.

We're going to use a server called **Open-Meteo** for this chapter, which lets us make free web requests for a wide range of live weather data without any permission or access codes. It has a great user-friendly page that spits out a URL for whatever data selections you make (https://open-meteo.com/en/docs?hourly=#current_weather), but I've also prepared the following URL for this example:

Structure	URL
Scheme	https
Host	api.open-meteo.com
Path	v1/forecast
Query string	?latitude=40.71&longitude=-74.01&current_weather=true

Table 13.2: URL example breakdown with structure and values

You can find Open-Meteo online at https://open-meteo.com/.

The entire URL (https://api.open-meteo.com/v1/forecast?latitude=40.71&longitude=-74.01&current_weather=true) finds the current weather data for New York City, which is what we'll use for the rest of the chapter.

Configuring the web request

Unity has made creating and sending a basic GET request extremely simple for us (wonderful, since this topic can be hard to understand at first). Let's put together the pieces of our request by updating WebRequestManager.cs to match the following code, which adds our URL as a string variable, instantiates a UnityWebRequest instance, and sends it on its way to bring us back our weather data:

```
using UnityEngine;

// 1
using UnityEngine.Networking;
using System.Collections;

public class WebRequestManager : MonoBehaviour, IManager
{
    // 2
```

```csharp
    private string _url = "https://api.open-meteo.com/v1/forecast
        ?latitude=40.71&longitude=-74.01&current_weather=true";

    private string _state;
    public string State { //... No changes needed...   }

    public void Initialize()
    {
        _state = "Web Request Manager initialized..";
        Debug.Log(_state);

        //3
        FetchData();
    }

    void Start()
    {
        Initialize();
    }

    // 4
    private void FetchData()
    {

        // 5
        UnityWebRequest request = UnityWebRequest.Get(_url);

        // 6
        request.SendWebRequest();

        // 7
        Debug.Log(request.result);
    }
}
```

Let's break down our new code:

1. We include the necessary namespaces for accessing the `UnityWebRequest` class and collection types.

2. Then, we add a new variable to store the URL string.

3. We call `FetchData()` at the end of the `Initialize()` method.

4. Next, we create `FetchData()` with no return type.

5. We create a new `UnityWebRequest` instance using the static preconfigured `.Get` function.

6. We then pass in `_url` as a required method parameter.

7. We call `SendWebRequest()` to fire off the call to the URL address.

8. Finally, we debug the request result sent back.

Remember the lifecycle in *Figure 13.2*? That's what we've just created in code—we took our formatted URL, used it to configure the web request, sent the request to the server, and logged the response. Your game is now connected to (and interacting with) the outside world!

Run the game and take a look at the console to see the result, as shown in Figure 13.4:

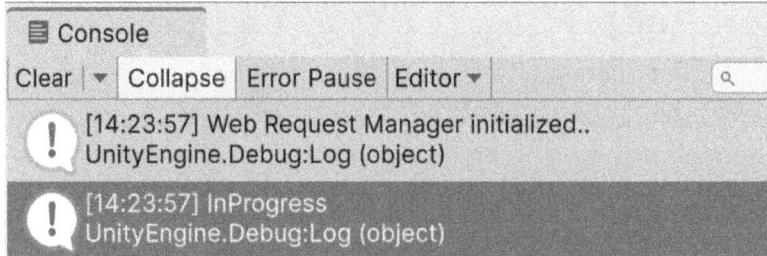

Figure 13.4: UnityWebRequest result when running

You might notice that while the code does run with no errors, the request result says **InProgress**, but how can the request be in progress if the code has finished running? To answer that question, we need to talk about how to give certain blocks of code enough time to finish doing their work before we return a result, and to do that, we need to understand a little about asynchronous programming.

Synchronous versus asynchronous code

There are two main paradigms when it comes to how code executes—synchronous and asynchronous:

*   **Synchronous** code runs line by line until the code block (or task) is finished, which stops the application from doing anything else.

Using a driving analogy, synchronous code is a single-lane, one-way street—only one direction to go, with no room to pass other cars or parking spots for stopping.

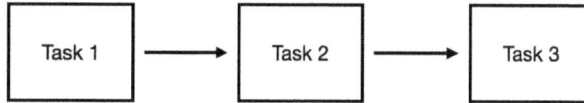

Figure 13.5: Synchronous code tasks running in sequence

- **Asynchronous** code starts a task but lets the application keep running while the task is waiting to finish its work.

  This is like switching from that one-way street to a four-lane roadway with parking on the side, room to pass, and start and stop traffic in both directions.

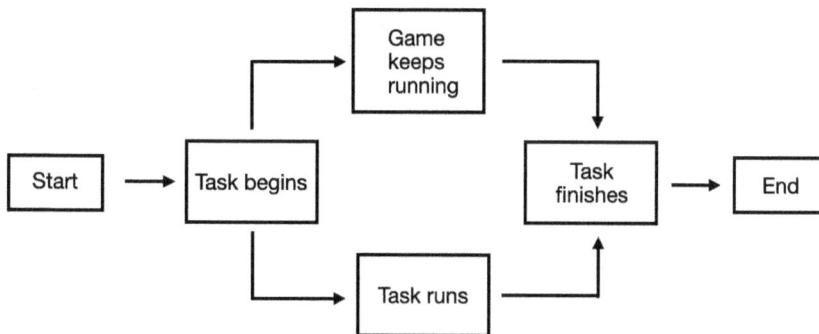

Figure 13.6: Asynchronous code tasks running in parallel

In Unity and C# projects, all code runs on something called the **main thread** by default. The main thread controls the primary path of execution for all your code (like a street does for cars), which means we're responsible for not blocking traffic. When synchronous code runs, it blocks the main thread; each task runs in sequence and politely waits for the task in front to finish its work before starting the next task.

Threading is another advanced topic that we can't cover here, but you can find more information at https://learn.microsoft.com/en-us/dotnet/standard/threading/using-threads-and-threading.

While this is how the main thread is supposed to work (and every line of code we've written so far has been synchronous and works just fine), we shouldn't use synchronous code to send a web request because we'd be knowingly setting up a traffic jam in our code for an unknown amount of time. This is where asynchronous code comes in!

Using Unity coroutines

Unity has its own way of handling asynchronous code using **coroutines**. Coroutines are methods that can suspend and resume code execution under your control, essentially firing off a task in one frame and resuming running in another frame. Sounds like a perfect fit for our web request, right?

All coroutine methods need to have an `IEnumerator` return type and a `yield return` statement somewhere in the method body. The `IEnumerator` return type lets Unity give us the pause and resume functionality we're looking for in our asynchronous code, and the `yield return` statement is the point where the code is suspended (like yielding at a stop sign, then continuing once the coast is clear).

You can find more information on coroutines at `https://docs.unity3d.com/Manual/Coroutines.html`.

Since our web request would work better as an asynchronous operation, let's update `WebRequestManager.cs` to match the following code, which changes `FetchData()` into a coroutine and calls it using the `StartCoroutine()` method to let Unity know we're using asynchronous code:

```
public class WebRequestManager : MonoBehaviour, IManager
{
    private string _url = "https://api.open-meteo.com/v1/forecast
        ?latitude=40.71&longitude=-74.01&current_weather=true";

    private string _state;
    public string State { //… No changes needed…  }

    void Start()  { //… No changes needed…  }

    public void Initialize()
    {
        _state = "Web Request Manager initialized..";
        Debug.Log(_state);

        // 1
```

```
        StartCoroutine(FetchData());
    }


    // 2
    private IEnumerator FetchData()
    {
        UnityWebRequest request = UnityWebRequest.Get(_url);


        // 3
        yield return request.SendWebRequest();


        Debug.Log(request.result);
    }
}
```

Let's break down our changes:

1. We call FetchData() using the StartCoroutine() method.

2. Then, we update the return type of FetchData() to IEnumerator.

3. Finally, we add a yield return statement when SendWebRequest() is called.

    This pauses FetchData() until the request is finished fetching the data, without blocking the main thread or freezing the game while we wait.

Run the game again, wait a few seconds, and you'll see a **Success** response in the console when the request comes back to us!

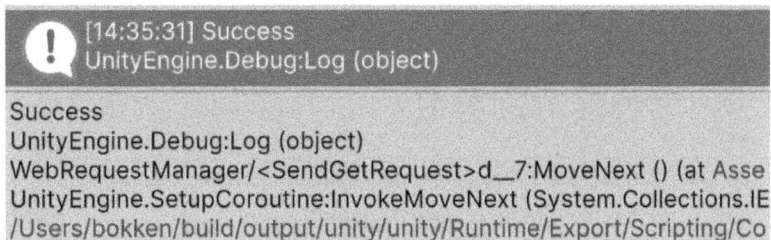

Figure 13.7: UnityWebRequest result using coroutines

With our asynchronous code pausing and resuming correctly, we can move on to dealing with the actual contents of the request response from Open-Meteo.

Managing request responses

UnityWebRequest can have a variety of results when it comes back to us, including **Success**, **In-Progress**, and **ConnectionError**, among others. We already have access to the request result, so let's check whether it's a success or not, and then either unpack the returned weather data or print out a request error.

You can find more information on request result options at `https://docs.unity3d.com/ ScriptReference/Networking.UnityWebRequest.Result.html`.

Update `WebRequestManager.cs` to match the following code, which uses the built-in `downloadHandler` property of `UnityWebRequest` to access the data returned by the web request. `downloadHandler` is a Unity class that automatically handles the response information sent back from the server and has a useful text property we can use to easily get the data.

You can find full documentation on the `DownloadHandler` class at `https://docs.unity3d.com/ ScriptReference/Networking.DownloadHandler.html`:

```
public class WebRequestManager : MonoBehaviour, IManager
{
    private string _url = "https://api.open-meteo.com/v1/forecast
        ?latitude=40.71&longitude=-74.01&current_weather=true";

    private string _state;
    public string State { //… No changes needed…   }

    public void Initialize() { //… No changes needed…   }
    void Start() { //… No changes needed…   }

    private IEnumerator FetchData()
    {
        UnityWebRequest request = UnityWebRequest.Get(_url);
        yield return request.SendWebRequest();

        // 1
        if (request.result == UnityWebRequest.Result.Success)
        {
            // 2
            Debug.Log(request.downloadHandler.text);
```

```
            }
        // 3
        else
        {
            Debug.Log(request.error);
        }
    }
}
```

Let's break down our response-handling code:

1. We check whether the request result is a success.

2. If successful, we debug the entire data response as a text string.

3. If not successful, we debug the request error.

Run the game again, wait the required seconds for the request to go and come back, and you'll see a really big text string of JSON data, as shown in *Figure 13.8*:

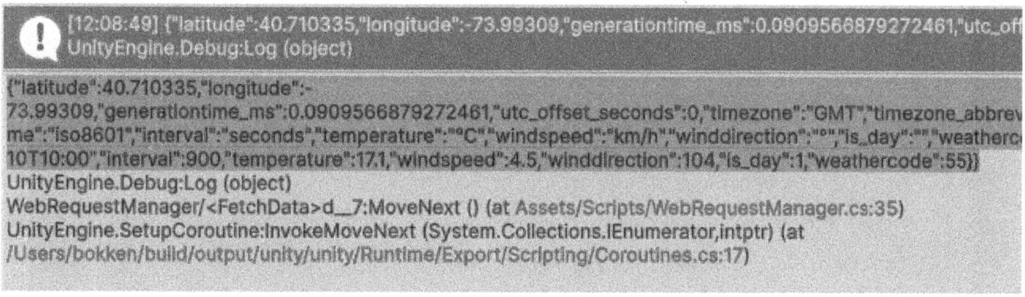

Figure 13.8: UnityWebRequest JSON result data

Now that we have data to work with, it's time to put the data formatting skills we are learning in the last chapter to use again in the next section.

Do it yourself

You can change the latitude and longitude values in _url variable to anything you want—try getting the weather in London (51.51, -0.13) or Tokyo (35.68, 139.65) for fun!

Deserializing request data

The first thing I generally do after getting data back from a web request is make it readable for humans. Copy all the data between the curly brackets in our debug log (in the console) and paste it into https://jsonparser.org/ or take a look at *Figure 13.9* to see the data in a more accessible format.

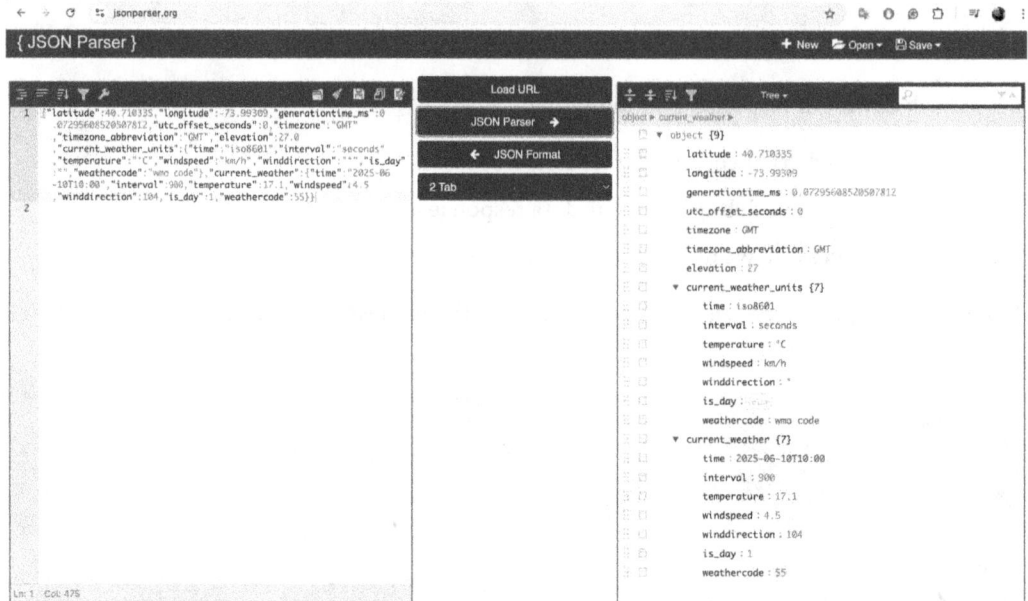

Figure 13.9: JSON result data in online parser

Just like we did in *Chapter 12*, we need to create a class that mirrors the JSON structure we got from the web request in order for Unity to serialize that data into an object we can use in our game. The nice part is that we get to pick and choose which data properties we want (we're not stuck with an all-or-nothing approach to the request data).

Take a look at *Figure 13.10*, and you'll see the data we want (temperature and is_day) is in the child object named current_weather:

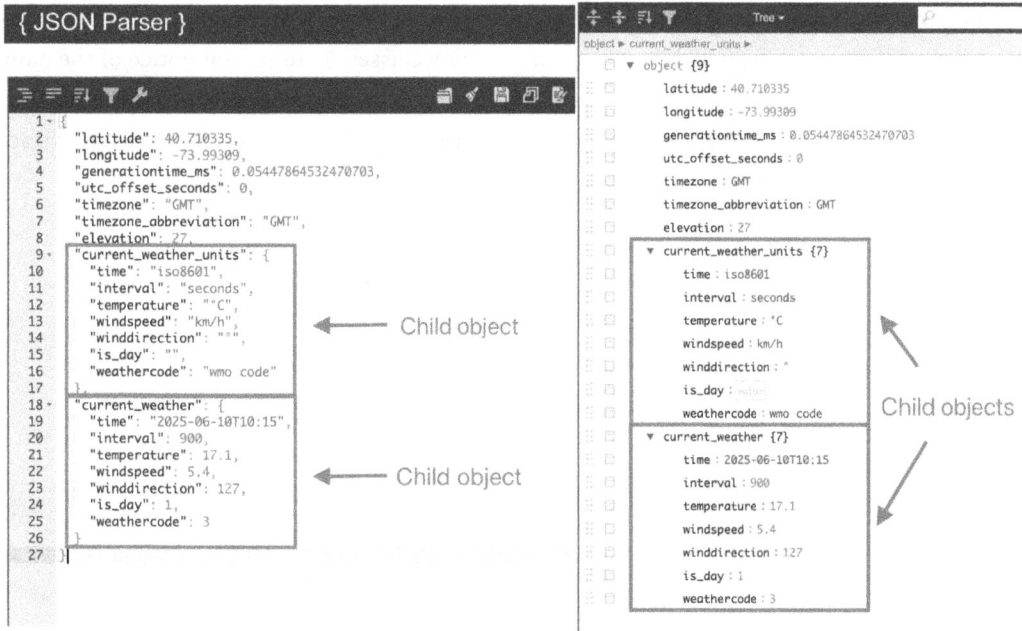

Figure 13.10: JSON result data with child objects highlighted

What we need is a nested class structure mirroring the JSON data schema and the properties we want to extract:

- Response data (parent object class)
  - current_weather (child object class)
    - temperature (property)
    - is_day (property)

In our case, we only want the temperature and is_day properties to adjust our game lighting accordingly, which means we need two new classes – a weather data parent class (to hold the entire JSON response) and a CurrentWeather class (to hold the current_weather JSON child object data).

In the `Scripts` folder, create a new C# script named `WeatherJSON` and update its contents to match the following code, which lays out our two new classes. Take special notice of the naming conventions and types we're using for each property (current_weather, temperature, and is_day)—these need to *exactly* match the JSON property names for Unity to automatically extract and correctly assign the data:

```
// 1
using UnityEngine;
using System;

// 2
[Serializable]
public class WeatherData
{
    // 3
    public CurrentWeather current_weather;
}

// 4
[Serializable]
public class CurrentWeather
{
    // 5
    public float temperature;
    public int is_day;
}
```

Let's break down our new data classes:

1. We add the necessary using statements.

2. We declare a new serializable `WeatherData` class.

3. We add a `CurrentWeather` property matching the JSON format.

4. We declare a new serializable `CurrentWeather` class.

5. We add `temperature` and `is_day` properties to match the JSON format.

Now, update WebRequestManager.cs once again to match the following code, which uses the JsonUtility class to neatly deserialize the response JSON data using the new WeatherData and CurrentWeather classes:

```
private IEnumerator FetchData()
    {
        UnityWebRequest request = UnityWebRequest.Get(_url);
        yield return request.SendWebRequest();

        if (request.result == UnityWebRequest.Result.Success)
        {
            // 1
            string jsonResponse = request.downloadHandler.text;

            // 2
            WeatherData weather =
                JsonUtility.FromJson<WeatherData>(jsonResponse);

            // 3
            Debug.Log($"Temp: {weather.current_weather.temperature},
                Daytime: {weather.current_weather.is_day}");
        }
        else
        {
            Debug.Log(request.error);
        }
    }
```

Let's break down the new code:

1. We store the JSON response data from request.downloadHandler.text.
2. We deserialize the JSON data using the JsonUtility.FromJson() method, using WeatherData as the parent (container) class.
3. We debug the temperature and is_day properties in the console.

Run the game again, wait a few seconds for the web request to return, and your console should be showing values for temperature and is_day!

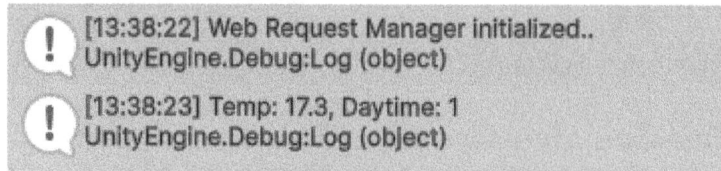

[13:38:22] Web Request Manager initialized..
UnityEngine.Debug:Log (object)

[13:38:23] Temp: 17.3, Daytime: 1
UnityEngine.Debug:Log (object)

Figure 13.11: JSON data deserialized into a custom class

Now the question is – what do we do with this new information we've gathered from the ether? Anything we want! But more specifically, we're going to use it to set the lighting in our game to day or night in the next section.

Adjusting the game lighting

Update WebRequestManager.cs one last time to match the following code, which adds a DirectionalLight property and updates the intensity value according to whether it's day or night in New York City right now:

```
public class WebRequestManager : MonoBehaviour, IManager
{
    // 1
    public Light DirectionalLight;

    //… No other variable changes …

    public void Initialize() { //… No changes needed…  }
    void Start() { //… No changes needed…  }

    private IEnumerator FetchData()
    {
        UnityWebRequest request = UnityWebRequest.Get(_url);
        yield return request.SendWebRequest();

        if (request.result == UnityWebRequest.Result.Success)
        {
            string jsonResponse = request.downloadHandler.text;
            WeatherData weather =
                JsonUtility.FromJson<WeatherData>(jsonResponse);
```

```
            Debug.Log($"Temp: {weather.current_weather.temperature},
                Daytime: {weather.current_weather.is_day}");


            // 2
            UpdateLighting(weather);
        }
        else
        {
            Debug.Log(request.error);
        }
    }


    // 3
    private void UpdateLighting(WeatherData weather)
    {
        // 4
        if (weather.current_weather.is_day == 1)
        {
            DirectionalLight.intensity =
                weather.current_weather.temperature / 4;
        }
        else
        {
            DirectionalLight.intensity = 0.0f;
        }
    }
}
```

Let's break down our lighting code:

1. We add a public DirectionalLight property for assignment in **Inspector**.

2. We call UpdateLighting() after the web request returns with weather data.

3. We then declare the UpdateLighting() method with a WeatherData parameter.

4. We set the DirectionalLight intensity to daytime or night accordingly.

Drag the `Directional Light` object from the **Hierarchy** pane onto the **Directional Light** property of **Web Request Manager** in the **Inspector** pane and hit **Play**!

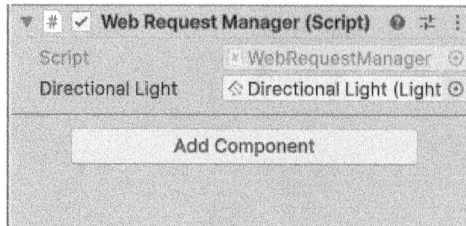

Figure 13.12: Directional Light set in the Web Request Manager component

Depending on what time of day it is in New York when you run the game, you'll see the intensity of the `Light` component change once the response data is received, as shown in *Figure 13.13*:

Figure 13.13: Directional Light intensity changed based on response data

That's a wrap on our introductory tour of web requests, but before we go, I'm going to point you in the direction of further study and intermediate topics to take your games to the next level.

Additional web request formats

As I mentioned in the *The web request blueprint* section at the beginning of the chapter, you have a menu of choices when it comes to what kind of web request operation you want to run.

Let's break down the most common request types in the following table:

Request type	Definition
GET	Requests data from a specific address (read-only, no effect on the data itself)
POST	Sends data to a server (creates a new data resource or updates an existing one)

| PUT | Replaces data with new data (completely overwrites the existing data resource) |
| DELETE | Removes a specific resource (no data left behind) |

Table 13.3: HTTP request types and definitions

Each of these request types has its own requirements, which would take another book to discuss fully. However, you can find more information on all HTTPS request types at `https://developer.mozilla.org/en-US/docs/Web/HTTP/Reference/Methods`, and how these can be used with `UnityWebRequest` instances at `https://docs.unity3d.com/ScriptReference/Networking.UnityWebRequest.html`.

A word on authentication

Not all servers are free or open to the public, which is where the question of authentication comes in. Think of authentication like sending along an invitation or secret handshake with your web request so the server knows you're allowed to be at the party (and access its data).

Again, this topic is a little too broad to cover here, but you can find good starting points at `https://developer.mozilla.org/en-US/docs/Web/HTTP/Guides/Authentication` and `https://learn.microsoft.com/en-us/dotnet/framework/wcf/feature-details/understanding-http-authentication`. There are also tons of YouTube tutorials that cover Unity-specific implementations (so a quick search may be in order).

Summary

And that's a wrap on our dive into web requests and pulling live data into our games! We've covered everything from web request lifecycles and configuring `UnityWebRequest` instances to handling status codes and unpacking JSON data. While the GET request example we built is only a small example of web request functionality, you have a strong foundation to move into more complex data needs in your own projects.

In the next chapter, we'll discuss the basics of generic programming, get a little hands-on experience with delegates and events, and wrap up with an overview of exception handling.

Pop quiz: Requesting data

a.　What protocol is used to transmit data on the internet?

b.　In Unity, what class handles web requests?

c.　What coding paradigm is best for pausing and resuming code tasks?

d.　What needs to match when deserializing JSON into custom classes?

Don't forget to check your answers against mine in the *Pop Quiz Answers* appendix to see how you did!

Subscribe to Game Dev Assembly Newsletter!

We are excited to introduce **Game Dev Assembly**, our brand-new newsletter dedicated to everything game development. Whether you're a programmer, designer, artist, animator, or studio lead, you'll get exclusive insights, industry trends, and expert tips to help you build better games and grow your skills. Sign up today and become part of a growing community of creators, innovators, and game changers: https://packt.link/gamedev-newsletter

Scan the QR code to join instantly!

Join our community on Discord

Join our community's Discord space for discussions with the authors and other readers: https://packt.link/gamedevelopment

14

Exploring Generics, Delegates, and Beyond

The more time you spend programming, the more you start thinking about systems. Structuring how classes and objects interact, communicate, and exchange data are all examples of systems we've worked with so far; the question now is how to make them safer and more efficient.

Since this will be the last practical chapter of the book, we'll be going over examples of generic programming concepts, delegation, event creation, and error handling. Each of these topics is a large area of study, so take what you learn here and expand on it in your projects. After we complete our practical coding, we'll finish up with a brief overview of design patterns and how they'll play a part in your programming journey going forward.

We'll cover the following topics in this chapter:

- Generic programming
- Using delegates
- Creating events and subscriptions
- Throwing and handling errors
- Understanding design patterns

Introducing generics

All of our code so far has been very specific in terms of defining and using types. However, there will be cases where you need a class or method to treat its entities in the same way, regardless of their type, while still being type-safe.

Generic programming allows us to create reusable classes, methods, and variables using a placeholder, rather than a concrete type.

When a generic class instance is created at compile time or a method is used, a concrete type will be assigned, but the code itself treats it as a generic type. Being able to write generic code is a huge benefit when you need to work with different object types in the same way, for example, custom collection types that need to be able to perform the same operations on elements regardless of type, or classes that need the same underlying functionality.

We've already seen this in action with the List type, which is a generic type. We can access all its addition, removal, and modification functions regardless of whether it's storing integers, strings, or individual characters.

While you might be asking yourself why we don't just subclass or use interfaces, you'll see in our examples that generics help us in a different way.

Generic classes

Creating a **generic class** works the same as creating a non-generic class, but with one important difference: its generic type parameter. Let's take a look at an example of a generic collection class we might want to create to get a clearer picture of how this works:

```
public class SomeGenericCollection<T> {}
```

We've declared a generic collection class named SomeGenericCollection and specified that its type parameter will be named T. Now, T will stand in for the element type that the generic list will store and can be used inside the generic class just like any other type.

Whenever we create an instance of SomeGenericCollection, we need to specify the type of values it can store:

```
SomeGenericCollection<int> highScores = new SomeGenericCollection<int>();
```

In this case, highScores stores integer values and T stands in for the int type, but the SomeGenericCollection class will treat any element type the same.

You have complete control over naming a generic type parameter, but the industry standard in many programming languages is a capital T. If you are going to name your type parameters differently, consider starting the name with a capital T for consistency and readability.

Let's create a more game-focused example next with a generic Shop class to store some fictional inventory items with the following steps:

1. Create a new C# script in the Scripts folder, name it Shop, and update its code to the following:

```csharp
using System.Collections.Generic;

// 1
public class Shop<T>
{
    // 2
    public List<T> inventory = new List<T>();
}
```

2. Create a new instance of Shop in GameBehavior:

```csharp
public class GameBehavior : MonoBehaviour, IManager
{
    // ... No other changes needed ...

    public void Initialize()
    {
        // 3
        var itemShop = new Shop<string>();
        // 4
        Debug.Log("Items for sale: " + itemShop.inventory.Count);
    }
}
```

Let's break down the code:

1. We declare a new generic class named IShop with a T type parameter.
2. We add a List<T> inventory of the T type to store whatever item types we initialize the generic class with.
3. We then create a new instance of Shop<string> in GameBehavior and specify string values as the generic type.

4. Finally, we print out a debug message with the inventory count:

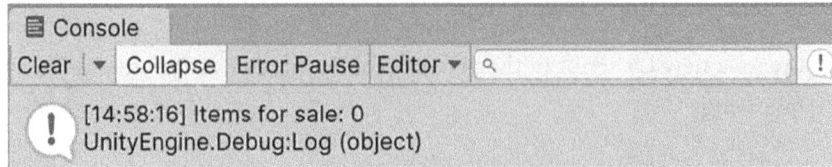

Figure 14.1: Console output from a generic class

> **Note**
>
> To provide a complete view of the Unity Editor, all our screenshots are taken in full-screen mode. For color versions of all book images, use this link: `https://packt.link/gbp/9781805808718`.

Nothing new has happened here yet in terms of functionality, but Visual Studio now recognizes Shop as a generic class because of its generic type parameter, T. This sets us up to include additional generic operations, such as adding inventory items or finding how many of each item is available.

It's worth noting here that generics aren't supported by the Unity serializer by default. If you want to serialize generic classes, as we did with custom classes in the last chapter, you need to add the Serializable attribute to the top of the class, as we did with our Weapon class. You can find more information at `https://docs.unity3d.com/ScriptReference/SerializeReference.html`.

Generic methods

A standalone **generic method** can have a placeholder type parameter, just like a generic class, which allows it to be included inside either a generic or non-generic class as needed:

```
public void GenericMethod<T>(T genericParameter) {}
```

The T type can be used inside the method body and defined when the method is called:

```
GenericMethod<string>("Hello World!");
```

If you want to declare a generic method inside a generic class, you don't need to specify a new T type:

```
public class SomeGenericCollection<T>
{
    public void NonGenericMethod(T genericParameter) {}
}
```

When you call a non-generic method that uses a generic type parameter, there's no issue because the generic class has already taken care of assigning a concrete type:

```
SomeGenericCollection<int> HighScores = new SomeGenericCollection
    <int> ();
highScores.NonGenericMethod(35);
```

Generic methods can be overloaded and marked as static, just like non-generic methods. If you want the specific syntax for those situations, check out the following link: https://docs.microsoft.com/en-us/dotnet/csharp/programming-guide/generics/generic-methods.

Your next task is to create a method that adds new generic items to the inventory and use it in the GameBehavior script.

Since we already have a generic class with a defined type parameter, let's add a non-generic method to see them working together:

1. Open up Shop.cs and update the code as follows:

```
public class Shop<T>
{
    public List<T> inventory = new List<T>();
    // 1
    public void AddItem(T newItem)
    {
        inventory.Add(newItem);
    }
}
```

2. Now, open GameBehavior.cs and add an item to itemShop:

```
public class GameBehavior : MonoBehaviour, IManager
{
    // ... No other changes needed ...

    public void Initialize()
    {
        var itemShop = new Shop<string>();

        // 2
        itemShop.AddItem("Potion");
```

```
            itemShop.AddItem("Antidote");
            Debug.Log("Items for sale: " + itemShop.inventory.Count);
        }
    }
```

Let's break down the code:

1. We declare a method for adding `newItems` of the `T` type to the inventory.

2. This adds two string items to `itemShop` using `AddItem()` and prints out a debug log:

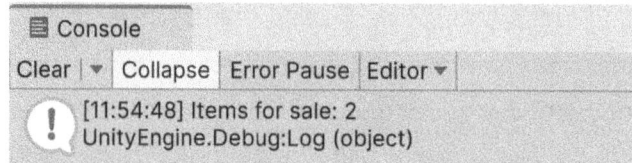

Figure 14.2: Console output after adding an item to a generic class

> ⚲ **Quick tip**: Need to see a high-resolution version of this image? Open this book in the next-gen Packt Reader or view it in the PDF/ePub copy.
>
> ⬛ **The next-gen Packt Reader** and a **free PDF/ePub copy** of this book are included with your purchase. Scan the QR code OR visit `https://packtpub.com/unlock`, then use the search bar to find this book by name. Double-check the edition shown to make sure you get the right one.

We wrote `AddItem()` to take in a parameter of the same type as our generic `Shop` instance. Since `itemShop` was created to hold string values, we can add the `Potion` and `Antidote` string values without any issues.

However, if you try and add an integer, for example, you'll get an error saying that the generic type of itemShop doesn't match, as shown in *Figure 14.3*:

```
var itemShop = new Shop<string>();
itemShop.AddItem(35);
```

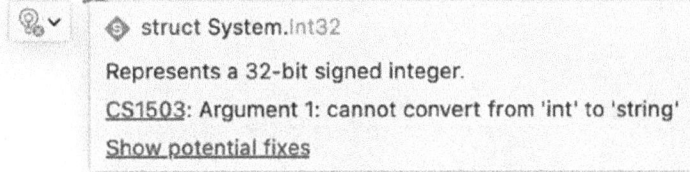

struct System.Int32

Represents a 32-bit signed integer.

CS1503: Argument 1: cannot convert from 'int' to 'string'

Show potential fixes

Figure 14.3: Conversion error in a generic class

Now that you've written a generic method, you need to know how to use multiple generic types in a single class. For example, what if we wanted to add a method to the Shop class that finds out how much of a given item is in stock? We can't use the T type again because it's already been defined in the class definition, just like we couldn't declare multiple variables with the same name in the same class. So what do we do?

Add the following method to the bottom of the Shop class:

```
// 1
public int GetStockCount<U>()
{
    // 2
    var stock = 0;
    // 3
    foreach (var item in inventory)
    {
        if (item is U)
        {
            stock++;
        }
    }
    // 4
    return stock;
}
```

Let's break down our new method:

1. We declare a method that returns an int value for how many matching items of the U type we find in the inventory.

> **Note**
>
> Generic type parameter naming is completely up to you, just like naming variables. Conventionally, they start at T and continue in alphabetical order from there.

2. Then, we create a variable to hold the number of matching stock items we find and eventually return from the inventory.
3. Next, we use a foreach loop to go through the inventory list and increase the stock value every time a match is found.
4. Finally, this would return the number of matching stock items.

The problem here is that we're storing string values in our shop, so if we try and look up how many string items we have, we'll get the full inventory:

```
Debug.Log("Items for sale: " + itemShop.GetStockCount<string>());
```

This would print a message to the console as shown in *Figure 14.4*:

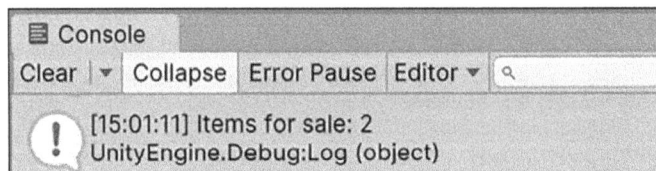

Figure 14.4: Console output from using multiple generic string types

On the other hand, if we tried to look up integer types in our inventory, we'd get no results because we're only storing strings:

```
Debug.Log("Items for sale: " + itemShop.GetStockCount<int>());
```

This would print a message to the console as shown in *Figure 14.5*:

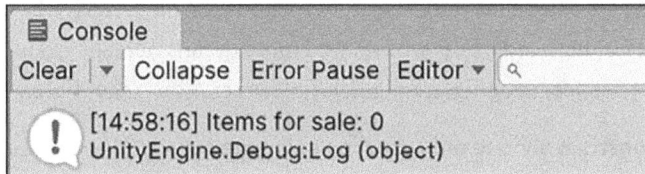

Figure 14.5: Console output using multiple non-matching generic types

Neither of these scenarios is ideal since we can't make sure our shop inventory is storing and can be searched for the same item type. But here's where generics really shine—we can add rules for our generic classes and methods to enforce the behavior we want, which we'll cover in the next section.

Constraint type parameters

One of the great things about generics is that their type parameters can be limited. This might contradict what we've learned about generics so far, but just because a class *can* contain any type doesn't mean it should be allowed to. For example, think of a game where you need to store a list of characters, but you want the character list to be limited to enemy types. You could check each character before adding it to the list, but that wouldn't be efficient. Instead, we can just say that the list only accepts enemy types and leave it at that.

To constrain a generic type parameter, we need a new keyword and a syntax we haven't seen before:

```
public class SomeGenericCollection<T> where T: ConstraintType {}
```

The where keyword defines the rules that T must pass before it can be used as a generic type parameter. It essentially says SomeGenericClass can take in any T type as long as it conforms to the constraining type. The constraining rules aren't anything mystical or scary; they're concepts we've already covered:

- Adding the class keyword would constrain T to types that are classes.
- Adding the struct keyword would constrain T to types that are structs.
- Adding an interface, such as IManager, as the type would limit T to types that adopt the interface.
- Adding a custom class, such as Character, would constrain T to only that class type.

If you need a more flexible approach to account for classes that have subclasses, you can use where T : U, which specifies that the generic T type must be of, or derive from, the U type. This is a little advanced for our needs, but you can find more details here: https://docs.microsoft. com/en-us/dotnet/csharp/programming-guide/generics/constraints-on-type-parameters.

Just for fun, let's constrain Shop to only accept a new type called Collectable:

1. Create a new script in the Scripts folder, name it Collectable, and add the following code:

```
using System.Collections;
using System.Collections.Generic;
using UnityEngine;

public class Collectable
{
    public string name;
}

public class Potion : Collectable
{
    public Potion()
    {
        this.name = "Potion";
    }
}

public class Antidote : Collectable
{
    public Antidote()
    {
        this.name = "Antidote";
    }
}
```

All we've done here is declare a new class called Collectable with a name property, and created subclasses for potions and antidotes. With this structure, we can enforce Shop to only accept Collectable types, and our stock-finding method to only accept Collectable types as well, so we can compare them and find matches.

2. Open up Shop and update the class declaration:

```
public class Shop<T> where T : Collectable
```

3. Update the GetStockCount() method to constrain U to equal whatever the initial generic T type is:

```
public int GetStockCount<U>() where U : T
{
    var stock = 0;
    foreach (var item in inventory)
    {
        if (item is U)
        {
            stock++;
        }
    }
    return stock;
}
```

4. In GameBehavior, update the itemShop instance to the following code:

```
var itemShop = new Shop<Collectable>();
itemShop.AddItem(new Potion());
itemShop.AddItem(new Antidote());
Debug.Log("Items for sale: " + itemShop.GetStockCount<Potion>());
```

5. This will result in a debug log showing only one potion for sale because that's the Collectable type we specified:

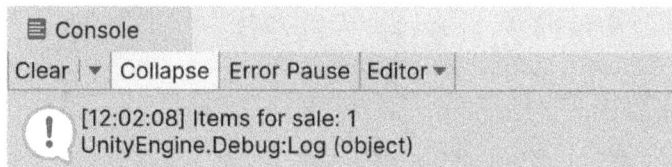

Figure 14.6: Output from updated GameBehavior script

In our example, we can ensure that only Collectable types are allowed in our shops. If we accidentally try and add non-Collectable types in our code, Visual Studio will alert us about trying to break our own rules, as shown in *Figure 14.7*:

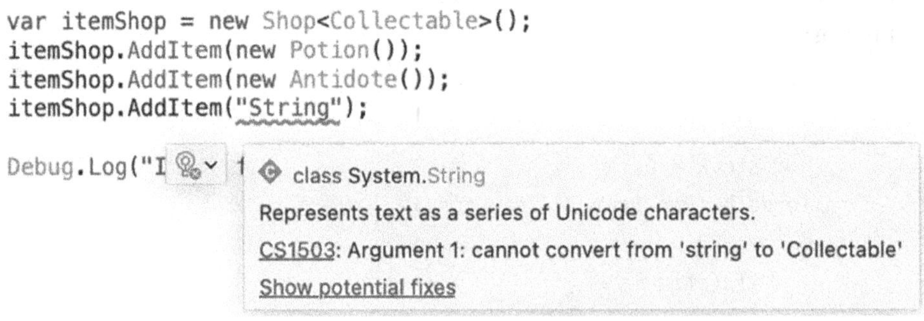

```
var itemShop = new Shop<Collectable>();
itemShop.AddItem(new Potion());
itemShop.AddItem(new Antidote());
itemShop.AddItem("String");
```

```
Debug.Log("I  ⟋ˇ  1  ◉  class System.String
                       Represents text as a series of Unicode characters.
                       CS1503: Argument 1: cannot convert from 'string' to 'Collectable'
                       Show potential fixes
```

Figure 14.7: Error with incorrect generic type

Adding generics to Unity objects

Generics also work with Unity scripts and GameObjects. For example, we can easily create a generic destroyable class to use on any MonoBehaviour or object component we want to delete from the scene. If this sounds familiar, it's what BulletBehavior does for us, but it's not applicable to anything other than that script. To make this more scalable, let's make any script that inherits from MonoBehaviour destroyable:

1. Create a new script in the Scripts folder, name it Destroyable, and add the following code:

```
using UnityEngine;

public class Destroyable<T> : MonoBehaviour where T : MonoBehaviour
{
    public float OnscreenDelay = 3f;

    void Start()
    {
        Destroy(this.gameObject, OnscreenDelay);
    }
}
```

2. Delete all the code inside BulletBehavior and inherit from the new generic class:

```
public class BulletBehavior : Destroyable<BulletBehavior>
{

}
```

We've now turned our BulletBehavior script into a generic destroyable object. Nothing changes in the Bullet Prefab, but we can make any other object destroyable by inheriting from the generic Destroyable class. In our example, this would boost code efficiency and reusability if we created multiple projectile Prefabs and wanted them all to be destroyable, but at different times.

Generic programming is a powerful tool in our toolbox, but with the basics covered, it's time to talk about an equally important topic as you progress in your programming journey—delegation!

Delegating actions

There will be times when you need to pass off, or delegate, the execution of a method from one file to another. In C#, this can be accomplished through delegate types, which store references to methods and can be treated like any other variable. The only caveat is that the delegate itself and any assigned method need to have the same signature, just like integer variables can only hold whole numbers and strings can only hold text.

Creating a delegate is a mix between writing a function and declaring a variable:

```
public delegate returnType DelegateName(int param1, string param2);
```

You start with an access modifier followed by the delegate keyword, which identifies it to the compiler as a delegate type. A delegate type can have a return type and name as a regular function, as well as parameters if needed. However, this syntax only declares the delegate type itself; to use it, you need to create an instance as we do with classes:

```
public DelegateName someDelegate;
```

With a delegate type variable declared, it's easy to assign a method that matches the delegate signature:

```
public DelegateName someDelegate = MatchingMethod;
public void MatchingMethod(int param1, string param2)
{
    // ... Executing code here ...
}
```

Notice that you don't include the parentheses when assigning MatchingMethod to the someDelegate variable, as it's not calling the method at this point. What it's doing is delegating the calling responsibility of MatchingMethod to someDelegate, which means we can call the function as follows:

```
someDelegate();
```

This might seem cumbersome at this point in your C# skill development, but I promise you that being able to store and execute methods like variables will come in handy down the road.

Creating a debug delegate

Let's create a simple delegate type to define a method that takes in a string and eventually prints it out using an assigned method. Open up GameBehavior and add the following code:

```
public class GameBehavior : MonoBehaviour, IManager
{
    // ... No other changes needed ...

    // 1
    public delegate void DebugDelegate(string newText);

    // 2
    public DebugDelegate debug = Print;

    public void Initialize()
    {
        _state = "Game Manager initialized..";
        _state.FancyDebug();

        // 3
        debug(_state);

        // ... No changes needed ...
    }

    // 4
    public static void Print(string newText)
    {
        Debug.Log(newText);
```

```
    }
}
```

Let's break down the code:

1. We declare a public `delegate` type named `DebugDelegate` to hold a method that takes in a string parameter and returns `void`.

2. Then, we create a new `DebugDelegate` instance named debug and assign it a method with a matching signature named `Print()`.

3. Next, we replace the `Debug.Log(_state)` code inside `Initialize()` with a call to the debug delegate instance instead.

4. Finally, we declare `Print()` as a static method that takes in a string parameter and logs it to the console:

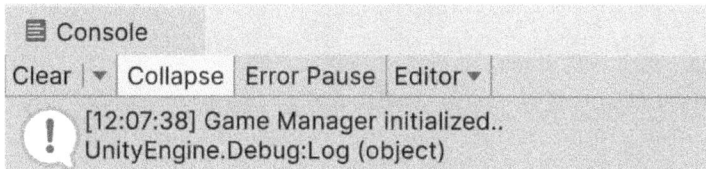

Figure 14.8: Console output from a delegate action

Nothing in the console has changed, but instead of directly calling `Debug.Log()` inside `Initialize()`, that operation has been delegated to the debug delegate instance. While this is a simplistic example, delegation is a powerful tool when you need to store, pass, and execute methods as their types.

In Unity, we've already worked with examples of delegation by using the `OnCollisionEnter()` and `OnCollisionExit()` methods, which are methods that are called through delegation. In the real world, custom delegates are most useful when paired with events, which we'll see in a later section of this chapter.

Delegates as parameter types

Since we've seen how to create `delegate` types for storing methods, it makes sense that a `delegate` type could also be used as a method parameter itself. This isn't that far removed from what we've already done, but it's a good idea to cover our bases.

Let's see how a `delegate` type can be used as a method parameter.

Update GameBehavior with the following code:

```
public class GameBehavior : MonoBehaviour, IManager
{
    // ... No changes needed ...
    public void Initialize()
    {
        _state = "Game Manager initialized..";
        _state.FancyDebug();
        debug(_state);

        // 1
        LogWithDelegate(debug);
    }

    // 2
    public void LogWithDelegate(DebugDelegate del)
    {
        // 3
        del("Delegating the debug task...");
    }
}
```

Let's break down the code:

1. We call LogWithDelegate() and pass in our debug variable as its type parameter.

2. We declare a new method that takes in a parameter of the DebugDelegate type.

3. We call the delegate parameter's function and pass in a string literal to be printed out:

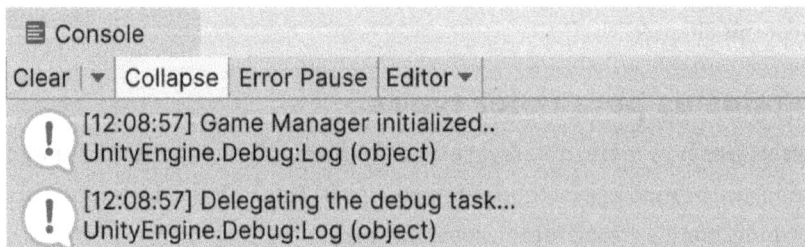

Figure 14.9: Console output of a delegate as a parameter type

We've created a method that takes in a parameter of the DebugDelegate type, which means that the actual argument passed in will represent a method and can be treated as one. Think of this example as a delegation chain, where LogWithDelegate() is two steps removed from the actual method doing the debugging, which is Print(). Creating a delegation chain like this isn't always a common solution in a game or application scenario, but when you need to control levels of delegation, it's important to understand the syntax involved. This is especially true in scenarios where your delegation chain is spread across multiple scripts or classes.

It's easy to get lost with delegation if you miss an important mental connection, so go back and review the code from the beginning of the section and check the docs at https://docs.microsoft.com/en-us/dotnet/csharp/programming-guide/delegates/.

Now that you know how to work with basic delegates, it's time to talk about how events can be used to efficiently communicate information between multiple scripts. Honestly, the best use case for a delegate is being paired with events, which we'll dive into next.

Firing events

C# events allow you to essentially create a subscription system based on actions in your games or apps. For instance, if you wanted to send out an event whenever an item is collected or when a player presses the spacebar, you could do that. However, when an event fires, it doesn't automatically have a subscriber or receiver to handle any code that needs to execute after the event action.

Any class can subscribe or unsubscribe to an event through the calling class the event is fired from; just like signing up to receive notifications on your phone when a new post is shared on Facebook, events form a kind of distributed-information superhighway for sharing actions and data across your application.

Declaring events is similar to declaring delegates in that an event has a specific method signature. We'll use a delegate to specify the method signature we want the event to have, then create the event using the delegate type and the event keyword:

```
public delegate void EventDelegate(int param1, string param2);
public event EventDelegate eventInstance;
```

This setup allows us to treat eventInstance as a method because it's a delegate type, which means we can send it out at any time by calling it:

```
eventInstance(35, "John Doe");
```

Unity also has its own built-in event type called `UnityAction` that can be customized however you need (but is less optimized for performance than C# events). Check out the following link for more information and code: `https://docs.unity3d.com/2023.2/Documentation/ScriptReference/Events.UnityAction.html`.

Your next task is to create an event of your own and fire it off in the appropriate place inside `PlayerBehavior`.

Creating and invoking events

Let's create an event to fire off any time our player jumps. Open up `PlayerBehavior` and add the following changes:

```
public class PlayerBehavior : MonoBehaviour
{
    // ... No other variable changes needed ...

    // 1
    public delegate void JumpingEvent();

    // 2
    public static event JumpingEvent playerJump;

    void Start()
    {
        // ... No changes needed ...
    }

    void Update()
    {
        // ... No changes needed ...
    }

    void FixedUpdate()
    {
        if(_isJumping && IsGrounded())
        {
            _rb.AddForce(Vector3.up * jumpVelocity,
                ForceMode.Impulse);
```

```
            // 3
            playerJump();
        }
    }


    // ... No changes needed in IsGrounded or OnCollisionEnter
}
```

Let's break down the code:

1. We declare a new `delegate` type that returns `void` and takes in no parameters.

2. Create an event of the `JumpingEvent` type, named `playerJump`, that can be treated as a method that matches the preceding delegate's `void` return and no parameter signature.

   We made this event static so it can be accessed without needing to find the specific instance of `PlayerBehavior` in the scene (which is something you'll frequently see with events and actions).

3. This calls `playerJump` after the force is applied in `Update()`.

We have successfully created a simple `delegate` type that takes in no parameters and returns nothing, as well as an event of that type to execute whenever the player jumps. Each time the player jumps, the `playerJump` event is sent out to all of its subscribers to notify them of the action.

After the event fires, it's up to its subscribers to process it and do any additional operations, which we'll see in the *Handling event subscriptions* section next.

Handling event subscriptions

Right now, our `playerJump` event has no subscribers, but changing that is simple and very similar to how we assigned method references to `delegate` types in the last section:

```
someClass.eventInstance += EventHandler;
```

Since events are variables that belong to the class they're declared in, and subscribers will be other classes, a reference to the event-containing class is necessary for subscriptions. The `+=` operator is used to assign a method that will fire when an event executes, just like setting up an out-of-office email.

Like assigning delegates, the method signature of the event handler method must match the event's type. In our previous syntax example, that means EventHandler needs to be the following:

```
public void EventHandler(int param1, string param2) {}
```

In cases where you need to unsubscribe from an event, you simply do the reverse of the assignment by using the -= operator:

```
someClass.eventInstance -= EventHandler;
```

Event subscriptions are generally handled when a class is initialized or destroyed, making it easy to manage multiple events without messy code implementations.

Now that you know the syntax for subscribing and unsubscribing to events, it's your turn to put this into practice in the GameBehavior script.

Now that our event is firing every time the player jumps, go back and update GameBehavior.cs with the following code to capture the action:

```
public class GameBehavior : MonoBehaviour, IManager
{
    // 1
    void OnEnable()
    {
        // 2
        PlayerBehavior.playerJump += HandlePlayerJump;
        debug("Jump event subscribed...");
    }

    // 3
    public void HandlePlayerJump()
    {
        debug("Player has jumped...");
    }

    // ... No other changes ...
}
```

Let's break down the code:

1. We declare the OnEnable() method, which is called whenever the object the script is attached to becomes active in the scene.

2. OnEnable is a method in the MonoBehaviour class, so all Unity scripts have access to it. This is a great place to put event subscriptions instead of Awake() because it only executes when the object is active, not just in the process of loading.

3. This subscribes to the playerJump event declared in PlayerBehavior with a method named HandlePlayerJump() using the += operator.

4. This declares the HandlePlayerJump() method with a signature that matches the event's type and logs a success message using the debug delegate each time the event is received.

Now, each time you jump, you'll see a debug message with the event message shown in *Figure 14.10*:

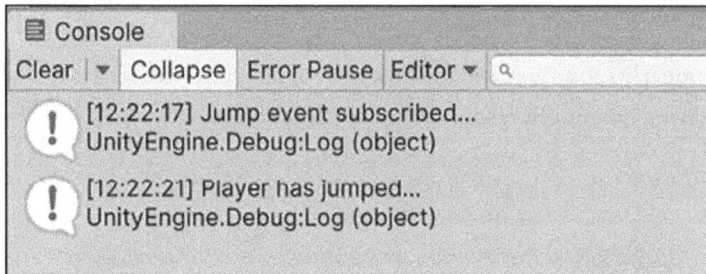

Figure 14.10: Console output from a delegate event firing

Since event subscriptions are configured in scripts, and scripts are attached to Unity objects, our job isn't done yet. We still need to handle how we clean up subscriptions when the object is destroyed or removed from the scene, which we'll cover in the next section.

Cleaning up event subscriptions

Even though our player is never destroyed in our prototype, that's a common feature in games when you lose. It's always important to clean up event subscriptions because they take up allocated resources, as we discussed with streams in *Chapter 12*.

We don't want any subscriptions hanging around after the subscribed object has been destroyed, so let's clean up our jumping event. Add the following code to GameBehavior after the OnEnable() method:

```
// 1
private void OnDisable()
```

```
{
    // 2
    PlayerBehavior.playerJump -= HandlePlayerJump;
    debug("Jump event unsubscribed...");
}
```

Let's break down our new code addition:

1. We declare the `OnDisable()` method, which belongs to the `MonoBehaviour` class and is the companion to the `OnEnable()` method we used earlier.

    Any cleanup code you need to write should generally go in this method, as it executes when the object the script is attached to is inactive.

2. We then unsubscribe the `playerJump` event from `HandlePlayerJump` using the `-=` operator and print out a console message.

Now our script properly subscribes and unsubscribes to an event when the GameObject is enabled and disabled, leaving no unused resources in our game scene.

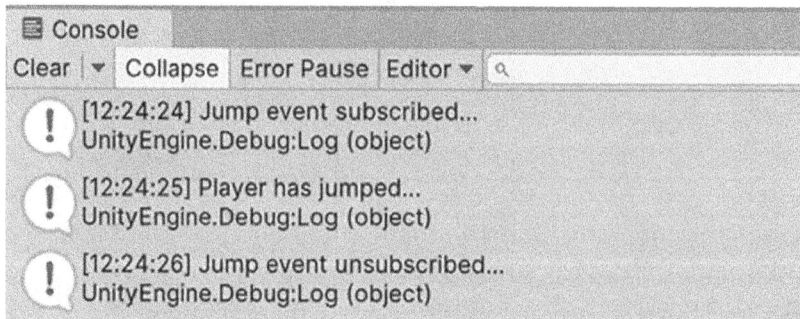

Figure 14.11: Console output from a delegate event firing

That wraps up our discussion on events. Now, you can broadcast them to every corner of your game from a single script and react to scenarios such as a player losing life, collecting items, or updating the UI. However, we still have to discuss a very important topic that no program can succeed without, and that's **error handling**.

Handling exceptions

Efficiently incorporating errors and exceptions into your code is both a professional and personal benchmark in your programming journey. Before you start yelling, *"Why would I add errors when I've spent all this time trying to avoid them?!"*, you should know that I don't mean adding errors to break your existing code.

It's quite the opposite—including errors or exceptions and handling them appropriately when pieces of functionality are used incorrectly makes your code base stronger and less prone to crashes, not weaker.

Throwing exceptions

When we talk about adding errors, we refer to the process as **exception throwing**, which is an apt visual analogy. Throwing exceptions is part of something called **defensive programming**, which essentially means that you actively and consciously guard against improper or unplanned operations in your code. To mark those situations, you throw out an exception from a method that is then handled by the calling code.

Let's take an example: say we have an if statement that checks whether a player's email address is valid before letting them sign up. If the email address entered is not valid, we want our code to throw an exception:

```
public void ValidateEmail(string email)
{
    if(!email.Contains("@"))
    {
        throw new System.ArgumentException("Email is invalid");
    }
}
```

We use the throw keyword to send out the exception, which is created with the new keyword followed by the exception we specify. System.ArgumentException() will log the information about where and when the exception was executed by default, but can also accept a custom string if you want to be more specific.

ArgumentException is a subclass of the Exception class and is accessed through the System class shown previously. C# comes with many built-in exception types, including subclasses for checking for null values, out-of-range collection values, and invalid operations. Exceptions are a prime example of using the right tool for the right job. Our example only needs the basic ArgumentException, but you can find the full descriptive list here: https://docs.microsoft.com/en-us/dotnet/api/system.exception#Standard.

Let's keep things simple on our first foray into exceptions and make sure that our level only re-starts if we provide a positive scene index number:

1. Open up `Utilities` and add the following code to the overloaded version of `RestartLevel(int)`:

```
public static bool RestartLevel(int sceneIndex)
{
    // 1
    if(sceneIndex < 0)
    {
        // 2
        throw new System.ArgumentException("Scene index cannot be
            negative");
    }

    Debug.Log("Player deaths: " + PlayerDeaths);
    string message = UpdateDeathCount(ref PlayerDeaths);
    Debug.Log("Player deaths: " + PlayerDeaths);
    Debug.Log(message);

    SceneManager.LoadScene(sceneIndex);
    Time.timeScale = 1.0f;

    return true;
}
```

2. Change `RestartLevel()` in `GameBehavior` to take in a negative scene index and lose the game:

```
// 3
public void RestartScene()
{
    Utilities.RestartLevel(-1);
}
```

Let's break down the code:

1. We declare an if statement to check that sceneIndex is not less than 0 or a negative number.

2. Then, we throw ArgumentException with a custom message if a negative scene index is passed in as an argument.

3. Finally, we call RestartLevel() with a scene index of -1:

> [14:44:50] ArgumentException: Scene index cannot be negative
> Utilities.RestartLevel (System.Int32 sceneIndex) (at Assets/Scripts/Utilities.cs:37)

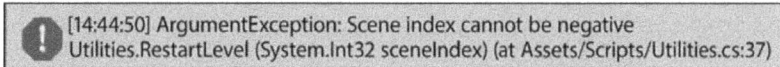

Figure 14.12: Console output when an exception is thrown

When we lose the game now, RestartLevel() is called, but since we're using -1 as the scene index argument, our exception is fired before any of the scene manager logic is executed. We don't have any other scenes configured in our game at the moment, but this defensive code acts as a safeguard and doesn't let us take an action that might crash the game (Unity doesn't support negative indexes when loading scenes).

Now that you've successfully thrown an error, you need to know how to handle the fallout from the error, which leads us to our next section and the try-catch statement.

Using try-catch

Now that we've thrown an error, it's our job to safely handle the possible outcomes that calling RestartLevel() might have, because, at this point, this is not addressed properly. The way to do this is with a new kind of statement, called try-catch:

```
try
{
    // Call a method that might throw an exception
}
catch (ExceptionType localVariable)
{
    // Catch all exception cases individually
}
```

The try-catch statement is made up of consecutive code blocks that are executed on different conditions; it's like a specialized if/else statement. We call any methods that potentially throw exceptions in the try block—if no exceptions are thrown, the code keeps executing without interruption.

If an exception is thrown, the code jumps to the catch statement that matches the thrown exception, just like switch statements do with their cases. catch statements need to define what exception they are accounting for and specify a local variable name that will represent it inside the catch block.

You can chain as many catch statements after the try block as you need to handle multiple exceptions thrown from a single method, provided they are catching different exceptions. Here is an example:

```
try
{
    // Call a method that might throw an exception
}
catch (ArgumentException argException)
{
    // Catch argument exceptions here
}
catch (FileNotFoundException fileException)
{
    // Catch exceptions for files not found here
}
```

There's also an optional finally block that can be declared after any catch statements that will execute at the very end of the try-catch statement, regardless of whether an exception was thrown:

```
finally
{
    // Executes at the end of the try-catch no matter what
}
```

Your next task is to use a try-catch statement to handle any errors thrown from restarting the level unsuccessfully. Now that we have an exception that is thrown when we lose the game, let's handle it safely.

Update GameBehavior with the following code and lose the game again:

```
public class GameBehavior : MonoBehaviour, IManager
{
    // ... No variable changes needed ...
```

```
public void RestartScene()
{
    // 1
    try
    {
        Utilities.RestartLevel(-1);
        debug("Level successfully restarted...");
    }
    // 2
    catch (System.ArgumentException exception)
    {
        // 3
        Utilities.RestartLevel(0);
        debug("Reverting to scene 0: " + exception.ToString());
    }
    // 4
    finally
    {
        debug("Level restart has completed...");
    }
}
```

Let's break down the code:

1. We declare the try block and move the call to RestartLevel() inside with a debug command to print out if the restart is completed without any exceptions.

2. Then, we declare the catch block and define System.ArgumentException as the exception type it will handle, and exception as the local variable name.

3. We restart the game at the default scene index if the exception is thrown.

4. We use the debug delegate to print out a custom message, plus the exception information, which can be accessed from exception and converted into a string with the ToString() method.

   Since exception is of the ArgumentException type, there are several properties and methods associated with the Exception class that you can access. These are often useful when you need detailed information about a particular exception.

5. We add a `finally` block with a debug message to signal the end of the exception-handling code:

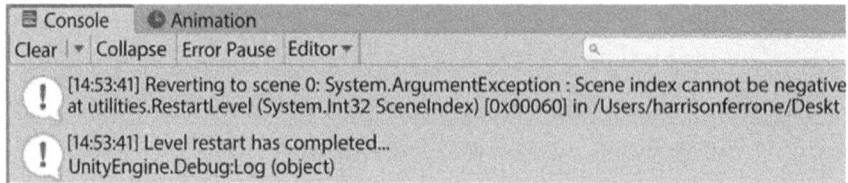

Figure 14.13: Console output of a complete try-catch statement

When `RestartLevel()` is called now, our `try` block safely allows it to execute, and if an error is thrown, it's caught inside the `catch` block. The `catch` block restarts the level at the default scene index, and the code proceeds to the `finally` block, which simply logs a message for us.

It's important to understand how to work with exceptions, but you shouldn't get into the habit of putting them everywhere in your code. This will lead to bloated classes and might affect the game's processing time. Instead, you want to use exceptions where they are most needed—in validation or data processing, rather than game mechanics.

C# allows you the freedom to create your exception types to suit any specific needs your code might have, but that's beyond the scope of this book. It's just a good thing to remember for the future: https://docs.microsoft.com/en-us/dotnet/standard/exceptions/how-to-create-user-defined-exceptions.

Summary

While this chapter brings us to the end of our practical adventure into C# and Unity 6, I hope that your journey into game programming and software development has just begun. You've learned everything from creating variables, methods, and class objects to writing your game mechanics, enemy behavior, and more.

The topics we've covered in this chapter have been a level above what we dealt with for the majority of this book, and with good reason. You already know your programming brain is a muscle that you need to exercise before you can advance to the next plateau. That's all generics, events, and design patterns are: just the next rung up the programming ladder.

In the next chapter, I will leave you with resources, further reading, and lots of other helpful (and, dare I say, cool) opportunities and information about the Unity community and the software development industry at large.

Happy coding!

Pop quiz: Intermediate C#

a. What is the difference between a generic and a non-generic class?

b. What needs to match when assigning a value to a `delegate` type?

c. How would you unsubscribe from an event?

d. Which C# keyword would you use to send out an exception in your code?

Don't forget to check your answers against mine in the *Pop Quiz Answers* appendix to see how you did!

Subscribe to Game Dev Assembly Newsletter!

We are excited to introduce **Game Dev Assembly**, our brand-new newsletter dedicated to everything game development. Whether you're a programmer, designer, artist, animator, or studio lead, you'll get exclusive insights, industry trends, and expert tips to help you build better games and grow your skills. Sign up today and become part of a growing community of creators, innovators, and game changers: `https://packt.link/gamedev-newsletter`

Scan the QR code to join instantly!

15

The Journey Continues

If you started this book as a complete newcomer to the world of programming, you will have come a long way; congratulations on your achievement! If you started the book knowing a bit about Unity or another scripting language, guess what? Congratulations to you as well. If you began with all the topics and concepts we covered already firmly solidified in your head, you guessed it: congratulations! There is no such thing as an insignificant learning experience, no matter how much or how little you may think you came away with. Revel in the time you spent learning something new, even if it only turned out to be a new keyword.

As you reach the end of this journey, it's important to look back at the skills you've acquired along the way. As with all instructional content, there's always more to learn and explore, so this chapter will focus on cementing the following topics and giving you resources for your next adventure:

- Diving deeper
- Object-oriented programming and beyond
- Design patterns
- Approaching Unity projects
- C# and Unity resources
- Unity certifications
- Next steps and future learning

Diving deeper

While we've done a good amount of work with variables, types, methods, and classes throughout this book, there are still areas of C# that were left unexplored.

Learning a new skill shouldn't be a simple bombardment of information without context; it should be a careful stack of bricks, one on top of the other, each building on the foundational knowledge already acquired.

Here are some of the concepts you'll want to look into as you progress in your programming journey, regardless of whether it's with Unity or diving into .NET with C#:

- Optional and dynamic variables
- Debugging approaches
- Concurrent programming
- Networking and RESTful APIs
- Recursion and reflection
- Design patterns
- Functional programming

As you revisit the code we've written throughout this book, think not just about what we have accomplished but also about how the different parts of our project work together. Our code is modular, meaning actions and logic are self-contained. Our code is flexible because we've used **object-oriented programming** (**OOP**) techniques, which makes it easy to improve and update. Our code is clean and doesn't repeat, making it readable to anyone who looks at it down the line, even if that's us.

The takeaway here is that digesting basic concepts takes time. Things don't always sink in on the first try, and the "Aha!" moments don't always come when you expect. The key is to keep learning new things, but always with one eye on your foundation.

Let's take our own advice and revisit the tenets of OOP in the next section.

Remembering your object-oriented programming

OOP is a vast field of expertise, and its mastery requires not only study but also time spent applying its principles to real-life software development.

With all the foundational information you have learned in this book, it might seem like a mountain you're just better off not even attempting to climb. However, when you feel that way, take a step back and revisit these key concepts from *Chapter 5*:

- Classes are blueprints for objects you want to create in code.
- They can contain properties, methods, and events.

- They use constructors to define how they are instantiated.

- Instantiating objects from a class blueprint creates a unique instance of that class.

- Classes are reference types, meaning when the reference is copied, it's not a new instance.

- Structs are value types, meaning when a struct is copied, a brand-new instance is created.

- Classes can use inheritance to share common behavior and data with subclasses.

- Classes use access modifiers to encapsulate their data and behaviors.

- Classes can be composed of other classes or struct types.

- Polymorphism allows subclasses to be treated the same as their parent class.

- Polymorphism also allows subclass behaviors to be changed without affecting the parent class.

Once you've mastered OOP, there are other programming paradigms to explore, such as functional and reactive programming. A simple online search will get you going in the right direction.

Design patterns primer

Before we wrap up the book, I want to talk about a concept that will play a huge part in your programming career: **design patterns**. Googling design patterns or software programming patterns will give you a host of definitions and examples, which can be overwhelming if you've never encountered them before. Let's simplify the term and define a design pattern that meets the following requirement: A template for solving programming problems or situations that you'll run into on a regular basis during any kind of application development. These are not hardcoded solutions—they're more like tested guidelines and best practices that can be adapted to fit a specific situation.

There's a lot of history behind how design patterns became an integral part of the programming lexicon, but that excavation is up to you.

If this concept strikes a chord with your programming brain, start with the book *Design Patterns: Elements of Reusable Object-Oriented Software* and its authors, the *Gang of Four*: Erich Gamma, Richard Helm, Ralph Johnson, and John Vlissides.

This barely scratches the surface of what design patterns can do in real-world programming situations. I highly encourage you to dig into their history and application—they'll be one of your best resources going forward.

Next, even though the goal of this book has been to teach you C#, we can't forget about everything we've learned about Unity.

Approaching Unity projects

Even though Unity is a 3D game engine, it still has to follow the principles set down by the code it's built on. When you think of your game, remember that the GameObjects, components, and systems you see on screen are just visual representations of classes and data; they're not magical or unknown—they're the result of taking the programming foundations you've learned in this book to their advanced conclusion.

Everything in Unity is an object, but that doesn't mean all C# classes have to work within the engine's MonoBehaviour framework. Don't be limited to thinking only about in-game mechanics; branch out and define your data or behavior the way your project needs.

Lastly, always ask yourself how you can best separate code out into pieces of functionality instead of creating huge, bloated, thousand-line classes. Related code should be responsible for its behavior and stored together. That means creating separate MonoBehaviour classes and attaching them to the GameObjects they affect. I said it at the beginning of this book and I'll say it again: programming is more a mindset and contextual framework than syntax memorization. Keep training your brain to think like a programmer and eventually, you won't be able to see the world any differently.

Unity features we didn't cover

We managed to briefly cover many of Unity's core features in *Chapter 6*, but there is still so much more that the engine has to offer. These topics aren't in any particular order of importance, but if you're going forward with Unity development, you'll want to have at least a passing familiarity with the following:

- Shaders and effects
- Scriptable objects
- Editor extension scripting
- Non-programmatic UI
- ProBuilder and Terrain tools
- PlayerPrefs and saving data
- Model rigging
- Animator states and transitions

You should also go back and dive into lighting, navigation, particle effects, and animation features in the editor.

Next steps

Now that you have a basic level of literacy in the C# language, you're ready to seek out additional skills and syntax. This most commonly takes the form of online communities, tutorial sites, and YouTube videos, but it can also include textbooks such as this one. Transitioning from being a reader to an active member of the software development community can be tough, especially with the abundance of options out there, so I've laid out some of my favorite C# and Unity resources to get you started.

C# resources

When I'm developing games or applications in C#, I always have the Microsoft documentation open in a window I can get to easily. If I can't find an answer to a specific question or problem, I'll start checking out the community sites I use most often:

- **C# Corner**: https://www.c-sharpcorner.com
- **Dot Net Perls**: http://www.dotnetperls.com
- **Stack Overflow**: https://stackoverflow.com

Since most of my C# questions relate to Unity, I tend to gravitate toward those kinds of resources, which I've laid out in the next section.

Unity resources

The best Unity learning resources can be found at the source; video tutorials, articles, free assets, and documentation are all available from https://unity3d.com.

However, if you're looking for community answers or a specific solution to a programming problem, give the following sites a visit:

- **Unity Forum**: https://forum.unity.com
- **Unity Learn**: https://learn.unity.com
- **Unity Answers**: https://answers.unity.com
- **Unity Discord channel**: https://discord.com/invite/unity
- **Stack Overflow**: https://stackoverflow.com

There is also a huge video tutorial community on YouTube if that's more your speed; here are my top four:

- **Brackeys**: `https://www.youtube.com/user/Brackeys`
- **Sykoo**: `https://www.youtube.com/user/SykooTV/videos`
- **Renaissance Coders**: `https://www.youtube.com/channel/UCkUIs-k38aDaImZq2Fgsyjw`
- **BurgZerg Arcade**: `https://www.youtube.com/user/BurgZergArcade`

The Packt library also has a wide variety of books and videos on Unity, game development, and C#, available at `https://www.packtpub.com/all-products`.

Unity certifications

Unity now offers various levels of certification for programmers and artists that will lend a certain amount of credibility and empirical skill ranking to your resume. These are great if you're trying to break into the game industry as a self-taught or non-computer science major, and they come in the following flavors:

- Certified User:
    - Programmer
    - Artist
    - VR Developer
- Certified Associate:
    - Game Developer
    - Programmer
    - Artist
- Certified Professional:
    - Programmer
    - Artist
- Certified Expert:
    - Programmer

Unity also provides preparatory courses in-house and through third-party providers to help you get ready for the various certifications. You can find all the information at `https://certification.unity.com`.

Never let a certification, or the lack of one, define your work or what you put out into the world. Your last hero's trial is to join the development community and start making your mark.

Hero's trial: Putting something out into the world

The last task I'll offer you in this book is probably the hardest, but also the most rewarding. Your assignment is to take your C# and Unity knowledge and create something to put out into the software or game development communities. Whether it's a small game prototype or a full-scale mobile game, get your code out there in the following ways:

- Join GitHub (`https://github.com`)
- Get active on Stack Overflow, Unity Answers, and Unity Forums
- Sign up to publish custom assets on the Unity Asset Store (`https://assetstore.unity.com`)

Whatever your passion project is, put it out into the world.

Summary

You might be tempted to think that this marks the end of your programming journey, but you couldn't be more wrong. There is no end to learning, only a beginning. We set out to understand the building blocks of programming, the basics of the C# language, and how to transfer that knowledge into meaningful behaviors in Unity. If you've gotten to this last page, I'm confident you've achieved those goals, and you should be too.

One last word of advice that I wish someone had told me when I first started: you're a programmer if you say you are. There will be plenty of people in the community who will tell you that you're an amateur, that you lack the experience necessary to be considered a "real" programmer, or, better yet, that you need some kind of intangible professional stamp of approval. That's false: you're a programmer if you practice thinking like one regularly, aim to solve problems with efficiency and clean code, and love the act of learning new things. Own that identity; it'll make your journey one hell of a ride.

Subscribe to Game Dev Assembly!

We are excited to introduce **Game Dev Assembly**, our brand-new newsletter dedicated to everything game development. Whether you're coding, designing, animating, or managing a studio, we've got insights, trends, and expert advice to help you create, innovate, and thrive. Sign up now and get exciting benefits:

`https://packt.link/gamedev-newsletter`

Join our community on Discord

Join our community's Discord space for discussions with the authors and other readers: `https://packt.link/gamedevelopment`

16

Unlock Your Book's Exclusive Benefits

Your copy of this book comes with the following exclusive benefits:

- ☁ Next-gen Packt Reader
- ✦ AI assistant (beta)
- 🖥 DRM-free PDF/ePub downloads

Use the following guide to unlock them if you haven't already. The process takes just a few minutes and needs to be done only once.

How to unlock these benefits in three easy steps

Step 1

Have your purchase invoice for this book ready, as you'll need it in *Step 3*. If you received a physical invoice, scan it on your phone and have it ready as either a PDF, JPG, or PNG.

For more help on finding your invoice, visit `https://www.packtpub.com/unlock-benefits/help`.

> **Note:** Did you buy this book directly from Packt? You don't need an invoice. After completing Step 2, you can jump straight to your exclusive content.

Step 2

Scan this QR code or go to `https://packtpub.com/unlock`.

On the page that opens (which will look similar to Figure 16.1 if you're on desktop), search for this book by name. Make sure you select the correct edition.

<packt>   Q Search...   Subscription 🛒 👤

Explore Products   Best Sellers   New Releases   Books   Videos   Audiobooks   Learning Hub   Newsletter Hub   Free Learning

Discover and unlock your book's exclusive benefits

Bought a Packt book? Your purchase may come with free bonus benefits designed to maximise your learning. Discover and unlock them here

●────────────────○────────────────○
Discover Benefits   Sign Up/In   Upload Invoice

Need Help?

✦ **1. Discover your book's exclusive benefits**   ∧

    Q Search by title or ISBN

    CONTINUE TO STEP 2

👥 **2. Login or sign up for free**   ∨

☁ **3. Upload your invoice and unlock**   ∨

Figure 16.1: Packt unlock landing page on desktop

Step 3

Once you've selected your book, sign in to your Packt account or create a new one for free. Once you're logged in, upload your invoice. It can be in PDF, PNG, or JPG format and must be no larger than 10 MB. Follow the rest of the instructions on the screen to complete the process.

Need help?

If you get stuck and need help, visit `https://www.packtpub.com/unlock-benefits/help` for a detailed FAQ on how to find your invoices and more. The following QR code will take you to the help page directly:

Note: If you are still facing issues, reach out to `customercare@packt.com`.

Pop Quiz Answers

Chapter 1: Getting to Know Your Environment

Pop quiz: Dealing with scripts

a	Unity and Visual Studio have a symbiotic relationship
b2	The Reference Manual
c3	None, as it is a reference document, not a test
d4	When the new file appears in the **Project** tab with the filename in edit mode, which will make the class name the same as the filename and prevent naming conflicts

Chapter 2: The Building Blocks of Programming

Pop quiz: C# building blocks

a	Storing a specific type of data for use elsewhere in a C# file
b2	Methods store executable lines of code for fast and efficient reuse
c3	By adopting MonoBehaviour as its parent class and attaching it to a GameObject
d	To access variables and methods of components or files attached to different GameObjects

Chapter 3: Diving into Variables, Types, and Methods

Pop quiz: Variables and methods

a	Using camelCase
b	Declare the variable as public
c	public, private, protected, and internal
d	When an implicit conversion doesn't already exist
e	The type of data returned from the method, the name of the method with parentheses, and a pair of curly brackets for the code block
f	To allow parameter data to be passed into the code block
g	The method will not return any data
h	The Update() method is called every frame

Chapter 4: Control Flow and Collection Types

Pop quiz 1: if, and, or but

a	True or false
b	The NOT operator, written with the exclamation mark symbol (!)
c	The AND operator, written with double ampersand symbols (&&)
d	The OR operator, written with double bars (||)

Pop quiz 2: All about collections

a	The location where data is stored
b	The first element in an array or list is 0, as they are both zero-indexed
c	No—when an array or a list is declared, the type of data it stores is defined, making it impossible for elements to be of different types
d	An array cannot be dynamically expanded once it is initialized, which is why lists are a more flexible choice as they can be dynamically modified

Chapter 5: Working with Classes, Structs, and OOP

Pop quiz: All things OOP

a	The constructor
b	By copy, rather than by reference like classes
c	Encapsulation, inheritance, composition, and polymorphism
d	GetComponent

Chapter 6: Getting Your Hands Dirty with Unity

Pop quiz: Basic Unity features

a	Primitives
b	The z-axis
c	Drag the GameObject into the Prefabs folder
d	Keyframes

Chapter 7: Movement, Camera Controls, and Collisions

Pop quiz: Player controls and physics

a	`Vector3`
b	`InputManager`
c	A **Rigidbody** component
d	`FixedUpdate`

Chapter 8: Scripting Game Mechanics

Pop quiz: Working with mechanics

a	A set or collection of named constants that belong to the same variable
b	Using the `Instantiate()` method with an existing Prefab
C	The get and set accessors
d	`OnGUI()`

Chapter 9: Basic AI and Enemy Behavior

Pop quiz: AI and navigation

a	It's generated automatically from the level geometry
b	`NavMeshAgent`
c	Procedural programming
d	Don't repeat yourself

Chapter 10: Revisiting Types, Methods, and Classes

Pop quiz: Leveling up

a	`Readonly`
b	Change the number of method parameters or their parameter types
c	Interfaces cannot have method implementations or stored variables
d	Create a type alias to differentiate conflicting namespaces

Chapter 11: Specialized Collection Types and LINQ

Pop quiz: Intermediate collections

a	Stacks
b	Peek
c	Yes
d	ExceptWith

Chapter 12: Saving, Loading, and Serializing Data

Pop quiz: Data management

a	The System.IO namespace
b	Application.persistentDataPath
c	Streams read and write data as bytes
d	The entire C# class object is converted into JSON format

Chapter 13: Connecting to the World Wide Web

Pop quiz: Requesting data

a	HTTPS (Hypertext Transfer Protocol Secure)
b	UnityWebRequest
c	Asynchronous
d	Class property names and types

Chapter 14: Exploring Generics, Delegates, and Beyond

Pop quiz: Intermediate C#

a	Generic classes need to have a defined type parameter
b	The values() method and the delegates() method signature
c	The -= operator
d	The throw keyword

Subscribe to Game Dev Assembly Newsletter!

We are excited to introduce **Game Dev Assembly**, our brand-new newsletter dedicated to everything game development. Whether you're a programmer, designer, artist, animator, or studio lead, you'll get exclusive insights, industry trends, and expert tips to help you build better games and grow your skills. Sign up today and become part of a growing community of creators, innovators, and game changers: `https://packt.link/gamedev-newsletter`.

Scan the QR code to join instantly!

Join our community on Discord

Join our community's Discord space for discussions with the authors and other readers: `https://packt.link/gamedevelopment`

‹packt›

packtpub.com

Subscribe to our online digital library for full access to over 7,000 books and videos, as well as industry leading tools to help you plan your personal development and advance your career. For more information, please visit our website.

Why subscribe?

- Spend less time learning and more time coding with practical eBooks and Videos from over 4,000 industry professionals
- Improve your learning with Skill Plans built especially for you
- Get a free eBook or video every month
- Fully searchable for easy access to vital information
- Copy and paste, print, and bookmark content

At www.packtpub.com, you can also read a collection of free technical articles, sign up for a range of free newsletters, and receive exclusive discounts and offers on Packt books and eBooks.

Other Books You May Enjoy

If you enjoyed this book, you may be interested in these other books by Packt:

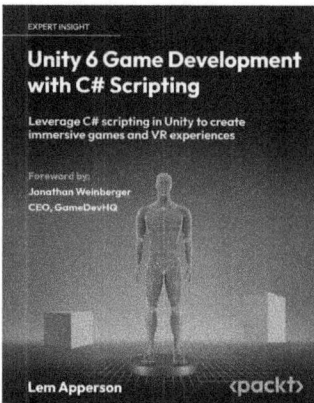

Unity 6 Game Development with C# Scripting

Lem Apperson

ISBN: 978-1-83588-040-1

- Create, modify, and interact with game objects in the Unity scene
- Explore techniques to implement game logic and mechanics using C#
- Manage game assets efficiently using asset bundles
- Create engaging and intuitive user interfaces to enhance user experience in games
- Explore strategies for developing both 2D and 3D games in Unity
- Build techniques for debugging C# scripts and optimize game performance
- Implement multiplayer features using Unity's networking capabilities

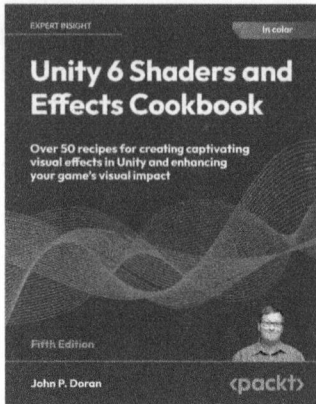

Unity 6 Shaders and Effects Cookbook

John P. Doran

ISBN: 978-1-83546-857-9

- Understand the principles of shaders, along with how to work in Shader Graph
- Harness URP and HDRP packages for efficient shader creation
- Enhance game visuals with modern shader techniques
- Optimize shaders for performance and aesthetics
- Master the math and algorithms behind the commonly used lighting models
- Transform your game's atmosphere with the Post Processing Stack
- Develop sophisticated shader effects by leveraging fragment shaders and grab-pass techniques

Packt is searching for authors like you

If you're interested in becoming an author for Packt, please visit authors.packt.com and apply today. We have worked with thousands of developers and tech professionals, just like you, to help them share their insight with the global tech community. You can make a general application, apply for a specific hot topic that we are recruiting an author for, or submit your own idea.

Share your thoughts

Now you've finished *Learning C# by Developing Games with Unity 6, Eighth Edition*, we'd love to hear your thoughts! Scan the QR code below to go straight to the Amazon review page for this book and share your feedback or leave a review on the site that you purchased it from.

https://packt.link/r/1805808710

Your review is important to us and the tech community and will help us make sure we're delivering excellent quality content.

Index

Symbols

3D space 164, 165

3D space, in Unity
enemy agents, moving 281
enemy agents, setting up 279-281
navigating 274
navigation components 274, 275
NavMeshSurface, adding 275-279

A

abstract class 318, 319

abstracting 135

access modifiers 58, 304
constant 304
internal 58
protected 58
read-only properties 304
static classes, using 305, 306
using 58, 59

actions
delegating 427-430

animations
creating, in code 184-187
creating, in Unity Animation
window 187-190
curves 193

tangents 193, 194

Animation window 184

Animator window 184
reference link 184

application lifecycle 48

area lights 182

arrays 103-106
index 104
multidimensional arrays 105
range exceptions 106
subscripts 104

art style 160

asynchronous code
versus synchronous code 401

B

backing variable 247

baking 274

base constructors 145, 147

Blender
reference link 162

C

C# 445
concepts 446

camel casing 66

camera behavior
  scripting 207-210

classes 40, 41, 128
  blueprints 41, 42
  communication 42
  constructors, using 132-134
  creating 128, 129
  fields, adding 130-132
  methods, declaring 134-136
  objects, instantiating 129, 130
  reference link 41

class extensions 320-323

class scope 67

clips 184

code debugging 54, 56

collection types 103
  arrays 103
  dictionary 111
  lists 107

Collider component 211, 212, 217, 218

comments 43
  adding 44, 45
  multi-line comments 44
  single-line comments 43

Common Type System (CTS) 60

Component Design Pattern 224

composition 147

compound collider 212

concept 160

constraint type parameters 423-426

constructor overloading 133

constructors
  using 132-134

control flow 85

control schemes 160

core mechanics 160

Creating, Reading, Updating, and Deleting
    (CRUD) 375

C# resources 449
  locating 24, 25

C# scripts 15
  GameObject, handling 45-47
  working with 15-17

C# statement
  writing 52, 53

C# with Unity 13
  C# scripts, working with 15-17
  Visual Studio Code editor 17
  Visual Studio Code, setting up 14, 15

D

data formats 352
  Extensible Markup Language (XML) 352
  JavaScript Object Notation (JSON) 352
  text 352

data roundup 391

data streams
  closing, automatically 378, 379
  resources, managing 370
  StreamReader, using 371-375
  StreamWriter, using 371-374
  working with 369
  XMLWriter, creating 375-378

data, with LINQ
  lambda expressions 343, 344
  queries, chaining 344, 345
  querying 339
  simplifying, with optional syntax 347, 348
  transforming, into new types 345-347

debug delegate
  creating 428, 429

defensive programming 437

delegates
  using, as parameter types 429, 430

deserializing 379
  in JSON 384-390
  in XML 380-384

design patterns 447

dictionary 111
  creating 112
  key-value pairs, working with 113

directional lights 182

directives 265
  game, pausing 266-269
  game, restarting 266-269

Directory class
  reference link 358

documentation
  accessing 22-24
  exploring 22

Don't Repeat Yourself (DRY) 38, 134
  refactoring and keeping it 298, 300

dot notation 42, 43, 56

drywall
  putting up 171, 172

E

Editor tools 170, 171

elements 103

encapsulation 143, 144

enemy agents
  moving 281
  setting up 279-281

enemy game mechanics 289
  bullet collisions, detecting 293-295
  game manager, updating 295-298

  player health, lowering 291, 292
  seek and destroy 289, 291

enumerations 228
  underlying types 229-232

environments
  reference link 163

error handling 436

events
  creating 432, 433
  firing 431

event subscriptions
  cleaning up 435, 436
  handling 433-435

exceptions
  handling 436
  handling, with try-catch 439-442
  throwing 437-439

exception throwing 437

Extensible Markup Language (XML) 352-354
  reference link 352

F

fall-through 100

fall-through cases 100-102

filesystem 356-358
  asset paths, working with 359, 361
  directory, creating 361-364
  directory, deleting 361-364
  files, creating 364-368
  files, deleting 364-368
  files, updating 364-368

first-in-first-out (FIFO) model 334

fly-through mode 171

foreach loop 118-120

for loop 114-118

frame rate 81

G

game design document (GDD) 160

game design primer 160

game levels

building 162

game manager

creating 245

GameObjects 81

reference link 170

generic class 416, 417

generic method 418-422

generic programming 415

generics 415, 416

adding, to Unity objects 426, 427

get properties 247-249

global scope 67

Grand Theft Auto

reference link 161

GUI

creating 251

player stats, displaying 251-261

win and loss conditions 261-265

H

HashSets

set operations, performing 337-339

using 336, 337

health pickup

creating 180

Hero Born game 161

Hero Born one-pager

art style 161

concept 161

control schemes 161

core mechanics 161

story 161

win/lose conditions 161

Hierarchy panel 173

Hypertext Transfer Protocol (HTTP) 394

**Hypertext Transfer Protocol
    Secure (HTTPS)** 394

I

if-else statement 86-90

implementing 95, 96

multiple conditions, evaluating 94

nesting statement 93

NOT operator, using 91-93

inferred declarations 65

infinite loops 124

inheritance 144, 145

instantiation 129

item collection

updating 250, 251

iteration 114

iteration statement 114

foreach loop 118-120

for loop 114-118

infinite loops 124

key-value pairs, looping 120

while loop 121-124

J

JavaScript Object Notation (JSON) 354-356

reference link 352

K

keyframes

recording 190-192

key-value pairs
  looping 120

keywords 56

kinematic movement 212

L

lambda expressions 343, 344

Language Integrated Query (LINQ) 340
  basics 340-343

last-in-first-out (LIFO) model 328

layer masks 232
  working with 232-238

Light component
  properties 183, 184

lighting 181
  precomputed lighting 181
  real-time lighting 181

lightmap 181

light probe groups
  reference link 182

lights
  area lights 182
  creating 181
  directional lights 182
  point lights 182
  spotlights 182

lists 107
  accessing 109-111
  modifying 109, 110
  setting up 108, 109

local scope 67

local space 174

LookAt() method 210

LTS (Long Term Support) version 6

M

macOS
  Unity 6, setting up 9, 10

main thread 401

match expression 98

materials
  applying 166-168

member scope 67

memory address 30

method overloading 307

methods 36, 71, 72, 307
  actions 37
  as arguments 80
  as logic detours 74, 75
  common Unity methods, dissecting 81
  declaring 72-74
  naming 74
  overloading methods 307-309
  parameters, specifying 76, 78
  placeholders 37-40
  reference link 37
  ref parameters 309-311
  return values, specifying 78
  return values, using 79, 80

method signature 73

MonoBehaviour 48

MonoBehaviour script 15

multidimensional arrays 105, 106

multi-line comments 44

multiple conditions
  evaluating 94

N

namespace conflicts 323

namespaces 265, 266, 323
  game, pausing 266-269
  game, restarting 266-269

NavMeshAgent 274

NavMeshObstacle 274

NavMeshSurface 274
  adding 275-279

nesting statement 93

Newtonsoft
  reference link 387

non-kinematic movement 212

NOT operator
  using 91-93

O

object build-up
  managing 243, 244

object-oriented programming
    (OOP) 128, 312, 446, 447
  abstract class 318, 319
  applying, in Unity 149
  class extensions 320-323
  interfaces 313-317
  namespace conflicts 323, 324
  type aliasing 323, 324

objects
  instantiating 239, 240

one-page document 161

OOP, in Unity
  components, accessing 151
  components, accessing in code 151-154
  drag and drop 155
  objects, are class act 150, 151

OOP, mindset
  base constructors 145, 147
  composition 147
  encapsulation 143, 144
  inheritance 144, 145
  integrating 143
  polymorphism 148, 149

Open-Meteo 398

operators 68-70

out parameters 312

P

parent object 173

Pascal case 66

Path class
  reference link 358

patrol locations
  referencing 281-284

pattern matching 98-100

Physics roundup 225

player movement
  managing 198
  with Transform component 199, 201

player properties
  tracking 245, 246

point lights 182

polymorphism 148, 149

precomputed lighting 181

Precomputed Realtime Global
    Illumination 181
  reference link 181

Prefabs
  working with 174-179

primitives
  creating 162-164

ProBuilder tool
reference link 162

procedural programming 281
enemy, moving 284-289
patrol locations, referencing 28-284

Q

queues
adding 335, 336
peeking 335, 336
removing 335
working with 334, 335

R

range exceptions 106

real-time lighting 181

refactoring 298

reference types 140, 141

reflection probes
reference link 182

ref parameters 309-311

RestartLevel() method 309

Rigidbody component 211, 213-216, 228

S

scene navigation features
reference link 171

Scripting Reference 24

selection statements 85

serializing 379
in JSON 384-390
in XML 380-384

serializing data 379, 380

set operations
performing 337-339

set properties 247-249

shooting mechanic
adding 240-243

shooting projectiles 239

single-line comments 43

spaghetti code 38

spotlights 182

stack class
methods 333, 334

stacks 328-332
popping and peeking 332, 333

Start() method 81

state 380

static classes
using 305, 306

story 160

string data type 62

string interpolation 62

structs
declaring 136-139

subscript operator 104

switch statement 97
fall-through cases 100-102
pattern matching 98-100

synchronous code
versus asynchronous code 400

T

technical design document (TDD) 160

TextMeshPro 253
reference link 253

threading 401

Transform component

player input 203, 204

player movement 199-207

vectors 201, 202

try-catch

used, for handling exceptions 439-442

type aliasing 323

type conversions 63

explicit conversions 64

implicit conversions 63, 64

U

UI Documents (UXML) 252

UI Toolkit documentation

reference link 252

Uniform Resource Locator (URL) 394

Unity

OOP, applying 149

Unity 6 4

editor, navigating 12, 13

environment, setting up 4-9

project, creating 10-12

setting up, on macOS 9, 10

Unity certifications 450

Unity class 41

Unity coroutines

using 402, 403

Unity features 448

Unity Hub 6

Unity methods

dissecting 81

Start() method 81

Update() method 81, 82

Unity objects

generics, adding to 426, 427

Unity physics system

Collider component 211, 212, 217, 218

Collider triggers, using 221

enemy, creating 221-224

Health_Pickup object 218-221

Rigidbody component 211

Rigidbody component movement 213-216

working with 211

Unity projects 448

Unity resources 449

Update() method 81, 82

utility function 228

V

value types 141, 142

variable declarations 56

type declaration 57

type-only declarations 57

value declaration 57

variables 56

access modifiers, using 58, 59

as placeholders 31-36

defining 30, 31

names 31

reference link 30

variable scope 67, 68

class scope 67

global scope 67

local scope 67

member scope 67

variable types

common built-in types 60-63

conversions 63, 64

custom types 65

inferred declarations 65

naming conventions 66

working with 59

variable visibility 68

vectors 201, 202

Visual Studio Code 13, 17

C# file, opening 17

C# files, syncing 20, 21

pitfall 19

setting up, in Unity 6 14, 15

W

web request

additional formats 412, 413

configuring 398-400

data, deserializing 406-410

game lighting, adjusting 410, 412

responses, managing 404, 405

synchronous code, versus
asynchronous code 400-402

Unity coroutines, using 402, 403

web request blueprint 394, 395

request manager, creating 395-397

URL, formatting 397, 398

while loop 121-124

white-boxing 169

win/lose conditions 160

world space 174

X

XMLWriter

creating 375-378